*THE INVESTOR'S
INFORMATION
SOURCEBOOK*

BY THE SAME AUTHOR
Getting Yours
Information USA
Lesko's New Tech Sourcebook

THE INVESTOR'S INFORMATION SOURCEBOOK

MATTHEW LESKO

SHARON ZAROZNY, *Research Director*

PERENNIAL LIBRARY

HARPER & ROW, PUBLISHERS, New York
Cambridge, Philadelphia, San Francisco, Washington
London, Mexico City, São Paulo, Singapore, Sydney

THE INVESTOR'S INFORMATION SOURCEBOOK. Copyright © 1988 by Matthew Lesko. All rights reserved. Printed in the United States of America. No part of this book may be used or reproduced in any manner whatsoever without written permission except in the case of brief quotations embodied in critical articles and reviews. For information address Harper & Row, Publishers, Inc., 10 East 53rd Street, New York, N.Y. 10022. Published simultaneously in Canada by Fitzhenry & Whiteside Limited, Toronto.

FIRST EDITION

Designed by Helen Barrow

Library of Congress Cataloging-in-Publication Data

Lesko, Matthew.
  The investor's information sourcebook.

  Includes index.
  1. Investments—United States—Handbooks, manuals, etc.   I. Title.
HG4921.L45   1988   332.6'78   87-45636
ISBN 0-06-055110-0   88 89 90 91 92 RRD 10 9 8 7 6 5 4 3 2 1
ISBN 0-06-096237-2 (pbk.) 88 89 90 91 92 RRD 10 9 8 7 6 5 4 3 2 1

Contents

Acknowledgments

I would like to thank Sharon Zarozny for her special dedication and thoroughness in ensuring that this book is complete and useful to all kinds of investors. Debra Samson, Cheryl Woodruff, Judy Marcus, and Clare Grosgebaur were especially helpful in designing and researching individual chapters of the book. And thanks also to Bonnie Montgomery, Lorraine Hartline, Toni Murray, Natalie Hartman, and Julie Dillon for their research and editorial efforts. And finally, I would like to express my appreciation to each of the experts who agreed to be listed as a resource in this book.

Introduction

The key to successful investing is information. And the key to information is knowing where to find it. Did you know, for example, that you can:

- tap a hundred industry experts who will tell you free of charge what is likely to happen to a stock long before anyone on Wall Street knows
- call a free recorded message that will give you a private lesson on Treasury bills or how to make investments, without charging a brokerage commission
- subscribe to free monthly economic newsletters written by some of the best economists in the country
- make one phone call and get a free listing of five financial planners in your zip code area
- get free books on topics like what you really have to know when reading a financial statement and how to take the mystery out of buying and selling options on cocoa futures

Investment information is truly the country's biggest "buyer beware" market. What one person on one side of the street is selling for $1,000, another person across the street is giving away for nothing. The problem is that the one offering it for free is not likely to have advertising money to promote his wares, while many aggressive brokers will spend millions banging you on the head trying to convince you that they have unique information that can make you rich.

If you want to understand how consumers have become conditioned about investment information, go and spend some time standing in front of a large stock brokerage office. You will notice a strange phenomenon. Millionaires arrive at the brokerage office in their chauffeur-driven limousines and give their money to some broker who probably commuted to work in a bus. Why do the affluent trust the judgment of such advisers? Perhaps because they believe that their broker is very knowledgeable about stocks and companies in which they have investments. But this cannot be; after all, how can a broker be that well informed about any company when he dedicates his time chiefly to looking for potential clients and making trades to earn commissions. And even if brokers have some hot tip about the potential of a company, they are sharing that information with 20,000 "special" clients. The real investment opportunities reside in having information others don't have.

The Investor's Information Sourcebook shows how you can obtain information other investors don't have and how you can get it without acting like Ivan Boesky. There is no magic to it. The trick is knowing where to look.

The next time a broker calls you about an exciting investment possibility, perhaps a computer graphics company, you can turn to the special feature Uncle Sam's Industry Experts and phone a government specialist who has probably devoted the last fifteen years of his or her life studying the computer graphics industry. This expert can share with you, for free, special analyses that forecast the industry into the next five years. These analysts can tell you where to get free, little-known market studies that cost the government millions to produce. If a private brokerage firm does such a study, it can spend only a fraction of what the U.S. government spends. Next you can consult the chapter How to Find Information on a Company and contact the various federal and state agencies where computer graphics companies must file public financial information. These corporate profiles often take months to get into reports published by investment advisers, even if they know all the offices keeping such records.

If you doubt that these free experts and information sources will talk to you, you're wrong. They are dying to talk to someone. Nobody knows such bureaucrats exist. When you call, you'll hear them saying, under their breath, "Finally someone called who wants to know what I have been spending a lifetime studying." And if you need more encouragement about how best to cultivate these experts, refer to the special feature Lesko's Lessons for Finding Information.

Learn the Best Investments for Tomorrow . . .
Not Yesterday

In the fast-changing world of investments, what is a likely good investment today was probably a bad investment yesterday and is likely to be an unwise investment in the future. New discoveries like superconductors can create new markets overnight. New legislation, such as tax reform, can slash the value of investments with the stroke of a pen. And world events like a crisis in the Middle East can cause prices of certain investments to go haywire. It has become virtually impossible to publish books or even magazine articles that contain timely investment recommendations. The publishing process takes too long and the answers change too quickly. What is published today is essentially yesterday's advice about investments. If you know the source of information, you can learn what the experts are recommending today and what will be in the bookstores and periodicals six months or a year into the future.

Although the answers keep changing, the sources don't. The same organizations and individuals specializing in particular investment topics today are likely still to be experts in those topics tomorrow. A book of answers can only provide good answers for the day it was written. A book of sources can give you the answers for any day in the future. Information is power, and knowing the source of information in a volatile society can make you even more powerful.

The Investor's Information Sourcebook goes right to the heart of this dilemma of the information age. It provides readers with over 3,000 resources for identifying the future investment opportunities.

Cut Through the "Investment-Info" Explosion

The recent information explosion has created more problems for investors than it has solved. If you are interested in learning about an investment such as money market funds, consider falling back on old homework skills and visit your public library. Expect to be surprised. In all likelihood, computer terminals have replaced musty old card catalogs. And these computers are probably hooked up to databases that can identify all books and articles written on the subject. Typing in a key phrase like "money market funds" can generate a few thousand citations, which, of course, creates a bigger problem. Now you are faced with the task of selecting the useful references from the bad ones. You also have to figure out how to get those articles of interest not available from the library. What becomes obvious is that anyone with access to a photocopier can be a publisher nowadays, and even though computers are great for handling quantity they do a lousy job evaluating quality.

However, I have attempted to cope with the information explosion problem by interviewing dozens of experts in each of the investment fields covered; as a result, this sourcebook represents a consensus of the best sources of information that have stood the test of time. Each category could have contained thousands of information leads but the value of a good sourcebook is in its ability to eliminate information overload and identify *only those sources that are worth investigating.*

3,000 Organizations, Government Offices, Experts, etc.

Organizations, publications, individuals, and even on-line computer databases that provide the latest information on a given investment are identified for each investment category. Examples include:

- nonprofit groups like the American Association of Individual Investors, which provides low-cost home study courses on investing in stocks
- government offices such as the U.S. Bureau of Mines that will send you free monthly newsletters to keep ahead of the commodities market
- experts like William Droms, a Georgetown University professor and noted bond expert, who has consented to share advice with our readers

- traditional publishers like Dow Jones, *Money* magazine, *Business Week,* and *Forbes* that offer special features covering various types of investment opportunities

The name, address, and telephone number is included for each organization so that you can easily contact them by phone or mail. A complete description of their services, publications, and other products is also provided to allow an informed buying decision before contacting the organization.

Over 100 Free Recorded Messages

Using your telephone is one of the best techniques to stay abreast of any investment. Why wait for a weekly, monthly, or even a daily publication to come out to know the status of your investment. These recorded messages can also keep you ahead of other investors by giving you immediate information about changes in the investment environment. For example, you can call:

- the Federal National Mortagage Association, which offers a recording giving the latest rates and yields for adjustable rate mortgages
- the Federal Reserve Board, which announces the latest interest rates on government securities
- the U.S. Department of Commerce, which releases the latest economic indicators a whole day before the news shows up on the front page of the *Wall Street Journal*

460 Free Publications

It seems organizations and government offices give away many books covering all aspects of investments, even some that may rival this sourcebook. If you are a novice investor and just getting your feet wet, you will want to get copies of:

- *Before You Say Yes, 15 Questions to Ask About Investments*
- *Insider's Guide to the* Wall Street Journal
- *How the Securities Investor Protection Corporation Protects You*
- *A Guide to Personal Financial Planning*
- *You and Your Money*
- *How the Bond Market Works*
- *Understanding Wall Street*
- *The Catalog of Investments*
- *The ABC's of Figuring Interest*
- *What Every Investor Should Know*
- *How to Estimate Your Retirement Income Needs*

If you are a seasoned professional, you will be interested in obtaining copies of:

- *Executive Financial Planning*
- *Questions to Ask at Stockholder Meetings*
- *Overseeing and Transferring Wealth: A Guide to Estate Planning*
- *Investing in Stocks for Capital Appreciation, Income and Total Return*
- *Standard and Poor's Outlook: Annual Forecast*
- *Characteristics and Risks of Standardized Options*
- *A Spotter's Guide to Commodities Fraud*
- *Economic Index Futures: An Introduction to the Concept of Shifting*
- *Essays on Inflation*
- the weekly newsletter "Foreign Exchange Rates"

Sources and Topics Never Covered Elsewhere

Not only is the concept of this book different from other investment manuals, many of the sources and topics covered here will never be included in any kind of book. With over fourteen years of business-information-gathering experience, I wanted to make sure that *the average investor had access to the same information as my Fortune 500 clients.* For example, I show how to get:

- 5,000 free market-studies from government offices
- free newsletters that monitor the economy
- information on which companies allow you to reinvest in their stock with no brokerage commissions
- free information on computer investing
- free three-month subscriptions to investment newsletters costing up to $300 annually
- the names of over 200 investment experts you can call for free advice
- free help and money to invest in your own business or nonprofit organization
- information on sixty government programs that provide money for investments in real estate
- free help when your broker screws up or goes bankrupt
- free speakers on investments for your club or group

What's Wrong with This Book

After reading this introduction you may believe that this is an ideal book; I certainly tried to make that the case. Well, it's not. The main problem with this book, as with all investment guides, is timeliness. However, the problem with this book is nowhere as serious. Unlike out-of-date investment manuals that offer advice that can cost you your life savings, an old sourcebook will only cost you a few extra phone calls or postage stamps. We have included current names, addresses, and telephone numbers for each source, but, like the yellow pages, anything can be out-of-date as soon as it is published. If an old telephone number does not lead you to the new one, call the information operator in the city where the organization is listed. Most likely the organization is still in the same area and the recorded telephone trace has lapsed with time. If all this fails, call me at 301-657-1200. I will be happy to try to help.

Good luck investigating your future investments.

Matthew Lesko
Chevy Chase, MD

Part One

STARTING POINTS

■ ■ ■ ■ ■ ■ ■ ■ ■ ■ ■ ■ ■ ■ ■ ■ ■ ■

This book is a directory of information resources.
The author and publisher make no claims
about the validity of the information or advice
made available by any of the resources.

■ ■ ■ ■ ■ ■ ■ ■ ■ ■ ■ ■ ■ ■ ■ ■ ■ ■

The First Step for Beginners and Experienced Investors

Are you ready to take the plunge and start investing? The word from the pros is investigate and do your homework *before* you put any money down. Take a hard look at both the people you plan to do business with and the company or product you plan to invest in. And be on your guard when the returns promised or implied seem bigger than reality. Fraudulent schemes abound, so beware.

Investing can be exciting—and confusing. So where do you begin to get to know the field? Many experts we spoke with said you do not need to spend lots of money buying books and services geared toward teaching you to invest. Instead, the most frequent advice we got is that you should immerse yourself in the library, the *Wall Street Journal, Barron's, Changing Times, Forbes,* TV and radio financial talk or news shows, and take a course or two offered by community colleges and brokerage firms. Do this for six months and you'll be ready to start investing. The biggest hurdle for new investors is learning the jargon of the field. Once you have that down the mysteries disappear and you'll be ready to join the league. A few experts told us that if you can't stand this learning process the next best method is to put a few of your dollars into a *small* investment. If you value your money, you'll suddenly find yourself enthralled with how the financial market works.

Another excellent way to learn about investing is to join—or start—an investment club. These are small groups of people who meet regularly to share the research they've done on various stocks and other investment vehicles. The members then pool their experience and money, investing in an agreed on mutual fund, stock, or other financial opportunity. The American Association of Individual Investors, described in this chapter, is an umbrella organization for many of these clubs; they will gladly send you information about starting or joining a group.

There are literally thousands of investing publications and services out there. We approached this chapter keeping your budget in mind, and asking the experts: "If someone were given a choice between simply spending money or using that money to invest, what would you recommend?" That weeded out a lot. Furthermore, the library—public, business, or brokerage house—kept getting great reviews. You can get access at libraries to most of the resources in this section, even expensive services such as Value Line. Just call around to find which library has what you need.

A controversial resource for investment tracking is the investment advisory service or newsletter. At last count we were told there are more than 1,300

■ ■

Stockbrokers Rated Average in Honesty and Ethics

In 1985, before Ivan Boesky became a household name, most Americans rated stockbrokers as no more and no less honest and ethical than the rest of us. Only 10 percent of those surveyed by the Gallup Organization considered stockbrokers to be less honest and ethical than the population as a whole. Opinions may have changed since then.

■ ■

of them! *Hulbert's Financial Digest* is considered a good resource for its tracking and rating of about seventy-five of the best. But before you rush to subscribe to one, ask yourself if you really need this service. Several financial analysts we spoke with said no, you really don't. To begin with, these letters are costly though tax deductible—annual subscriptions range from $100 to $900, with the average around $150.

Beginning investors may find the information in these newsletters too technical or their charts and jargon too sophisticated. But some experienced investors may find them useful tools for predicting which stock groups may perform best or when to buy and sell. To judge this service for yourself, simply check the newsletter ads in the *Wall Street Journal.* Select a few newsletters that sound interesting and contact the publisher requesting free samples for two or three months. If a publisher won't comply, a broker told us, you should not even consider subscribing to the service. After you've received some samples compare them and make your own decision.

Lastly, there's the issue of brokers. Do you really need one? It usually depends entirely on you and the time and energy you want to devote to tracking the financial market. Even if you decide to use a broker, you should become as knowledgeable as possible about your investment.

If you plan to become serious about the world of investing, you'll need to monitor the economy, follow financial news, know what's happening with inflation and interest rates, understand—and stay ahead of—the crowd, and know how to research financial services you plan to use as well as companies and products you might want to invest in. This chapter and several others throughout the book are meant to help you do just that.

AGENCIES, INSTITUTES, AND ORGANIZATIONS

American Association of Individual Investors
612 North Michigan Avenue
Chicago, IL 60611   312-280-0170

This national, nonprofit association, with 95,000 members nationwide and chapters in thirty-six cities, provides a solid education in investing for all levels of experience, from the novice to the more sophisticated investor. The organization sponsors seminars and provides speakers on investment techniques. It also offers the following publications:

- *The AAII Journal*—a forty-page magazine, published ten times a year, featuring interviews with investment professionals, news about various financial products, evaluations of stocks, and stock screening. A subscription is included in the annual membership fee of $48 a year or is available to nonmembers for $45 a year.
- *The Individual Investor's Guide to No-Load Mutual Funds*—a book-length annual report, approximately 300 pages, containing information (not rankings) of no-load mutual funds. Cost is $19.95 for nonmembers.
- *The Individual Investor's Microcomputer Resource Guide*—this book provides basic information on selecting investment hardware and software, as well as book reviews and a discussion of on-line financial systems. In addition, the *Resource Guide* has hundreds of service listings for investment software programs and financial information systems. Cost is $9 to members and $11 to nonmembers.
- *Computerized Investing*—published every two months, this newsletter provides information on how to use your microcomputer for investing. Regular features include: how-to articles, reviews of investment software, a directory of public domain programs, book reviews, and evaluations of financial data systems. Annual subscription is $24 for members and $48 for nonmembers.

Brokerage Houses

Many brokerage firms offer free services and publications to help you learn about financial opportunities and how to invest wisely. Look in your phone book under "Stockbrokers" or "Securities Brokers and Dealers."

Large, full-service firms such as Merrill Lynch, Shearson Lehman Brothers, Paine Webber, E. F. Hutton, Prudential Bache, and Dean Witter Reynolds have offices nationwide. These firms have a lot of capital at their disposal and they use it to structure new products to meet clients' (and potential clients') needs. Generally, their brokers are knowledgeable about all types of investment opportunities, from stocks and bonds to mutual funds, commodities, and international investments. Often these firms provide free seminars, personal counsel-

Most Americans Don't Own Stock

If you are actively involved in investments, you may be surprised to know that fewer than one in three participants in a *Business Week* survey have owned stock in the last three years.

ing, literature, and investment services. These houses do not charge any fee for advice or counseling sessions. A fee is charged only when the broker is purchasing or selling a stock for you. His/her commission is based on the total price of the shares sold.

Most full-service brokerage houses offer free reports, compiled by their team of research analysts, on the various stocks, commodities, and other investments the brokerage house is involved in. Before selecting a firm to do business with, you should compare reports from various companies, using the accuracy and style of the report as a criterion for selecting a brokerage house. Another fact to consider is your rapport with the individual broker—the experts say you should select someone you trust and can relate to easily. Experts also recommend that when you deal initially with a brokerage house you should contact the manager, explain your needs, and ask him/her to select a possible broker for you. The manager will know which member of his/her staff has the experience and background most advantageous to your particular situation.

Many of the major brokerage houses have excellent libraries you can take advantage of. Their collections often include resources for doing company research, access to on-line services such as Value Line, and the important directories of the trade.

Smaller firms (either local or regional) generally specialize in a few types

Reasons Noninvestors Choose to Sit on the Sidelines

Lack of spare cash is the most often cited reason noninvestors give when asked why they don't invest in the stock market. Fewer than 10 percent of the people surveyed by Louis Harris and Associates stay out of the market for fear of losing money.

of investments, such as stocks and bonds. They may or may not provide financial planning services.

Discount brokers mainly take orders to buy and sell stocks, bonds, and other securities. They don't generally offer advice or financial planning services—but they do offer commission fees up to one third less than those charged by full-service brokers. Experts recommend that novice investors should first work with a full-service broker to learn the field and after perhaps a year or so move on to a discount brokerage service.

If you're in doubt as to what firm to use, or who's a reputable broker, check with the senior (not junior) officers of your bank, as they usually are quite knowledgeable about financial services in the community.

Courses

Adult and continuing education programs in counties throughout the United States frequently sponsor seminars or classes on investing. The courses are usually quite inexpensive, and most cover the general terms of investing. Classes usually meet one night a week for five to eight weeks. To locate a class, check with your local community college, high school, or university.

Brokerage houses offer free seminars on all types of investment vehicles. You can often find a listing of these in the business calendar section of your newspaper. You could also call the managers of the brokerage houses in your area to learn about seminars.

Dow Jones & Company, Inc
The Educational Service Bureau
PO Box 300
Princeton, NJ 08540   609-452-2000

If you are a student or a professor, you may be able to take advantage of this company's program, which offers discounts on *Wall Street Journal* subscriptions. Groups of seven or more students are eligible; have your professor call the Educational Service Bureau to arrange it. Your professor will get a complimentary subscription. Dow Jones offers a variety of well-respected

---

Inny, Meeny, Minny, Mo?

Accountants, bankers, and relatives provide most relied-on investment advice and information, a *Money* magazine survey showed. The top two choices of household decision makers were bankers and accountants, but one in four respondents relied on a relative for advice.

publications, described in the What To Read category of this chapter. Free publications you may want to ask for include:

- *The Wall Street Journal Educational Edition*—a special, two-section edition of the *Wall Street Journal* and the complete guide not only to what's in the Journal, but how it's created. There is plenty of background material on the features, columns, and statistical information that appear every day. In addition, there's information about other publications and services of Dow Jones. Free. Your order is limited to no more than fifty copies.

- *The ABCs of Option Trading*—a booklet explaining the vocabulary of the fast-growing options market. The objectives and strategies of options traders are explained. This booklet is designed to be used with *Barron's National Business and Financial Weekly*. Free.

- *Barron's Educational Edition*—this forty-four-page, special edition of *Barron's* provides a complete introduction and overview for readers. *Barron's* editors and writers explain their weekly columns, and selected *Barron's* feature articles are reprinted. In addition, Dr. Martin E. Zweig, a professor of finance at Iona College, explains how to make technical stock-market forecasts with the data from *Barron's* Market Laboratory pages. Free.

- *The ABCs of Market Forecasting*—by Martin Zweig, this booklet guides you through a typical edition of the Market Laboratory pages of *Barron's National Business and Financial Weekly*. He demonstrates what the various market indicators are and how investors may want to use them. This is ideal for students who have not been exposed to the indicators that gauge the movement of the financial markets. This booklet is designed to be used with *Barron's* each week. Free.

Investor Relations Departments

If you want to know exactly how your investment is being used, public companies have stockholders' representatives whose job it is to answer that

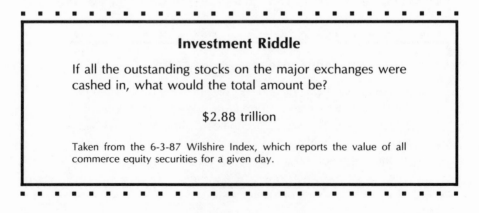

Investment Riddle

If all the outstanding stocks on the major exchanges were cashed in, what would the total amount be?

$2.88 trillion

Taken from the 6-3-87 Wilshire Index, which reports the value of all commerce equity securities for a given day.

kind of question. Call the company's headquarters and ask for the Investor Relations Department. The annual report for each company will name the contact, or you could consult one or more at the various publications which are published by Moody's Investor Services and can be found at your local library.

Securities and Exchange Commission

450 5th Street, NW   202-272-7440—Office of Consumer Affairs
Washington, DC 20549   202-272-7460—publications

Created in 1934 by an act of Congress, the SEC administers laws that relate to the field of securities and finance and seeks to provide protection for investors and the public in their securities transactions. A company offering securities for public sale must register with the SEC an accurate disclosure of the material facts concerning the company and the securities for sale so investors may make a realistic appraisal. The SEC does not give advice as to the merits of securities; that responsibility rests with the investor.

And by the way, if you are an investor who acquires 5 percent or more of a company's shares, you must report that to the SEC within ten days on a form called 13D. The SEC publishes a daily summary of these 13D filings in the *SEC News Digest,* which you can look at in the SEC's public libraries in Chicago, Los Angeles, New York, and Washington, D.C.

The SEC publishes a seven-page free booklet, *Investigate Before You Invest.* It explains how to shop for securities and how to protect yourself against fraudulent securities.

The Securities Investor Protection Corporation (SIPC)

900 17th Street, NW
Washington, DC 20006   202-223-8400

Suppose you invest in a company through a reputable broker-dealer or brokerage firm which goes under. What happens to your money? The SIPC is a federal corporation which insures the accounts of securities customers of member broker-dealers in case the brokerage firm fails. Customers are insured up to $500,000, of which no more than $100,000 can be for cash. Reimbursement to investors may take up to three months after SIPC processes the claims. For more information on the services of the SIPC, write for a free eleven-page brochure, *How SIPC Protects You,* which may reassure you about the protection of your stocks, bonds, CDs (Certificates of Deposit). However, the SIPC doesn't insure commodities or interests in gold and silver.

Investment Counsel Association of America, Inc.

50 Broad Street
New York, NY 10004   212-344-0999

Although most member firms of the Investment Counsel Association of America deal with corporate or institutional accounts, some may be of service

■ ■

LESKO'S LESSONS FOR FINDING INFORMATION

Some of the best information for your investments will be coming from nontraditional sources like experts in the federal government and professional associations. Learning to use these kinds of sources is much different from what you have learned in using more traditional sources. There is an art to using people to obtain information. It is not complicated, but very few people realize its potential value. Remember that any of these experts you contact for information, unlike a biased broker who wants your business, will not be paid by you. They will get the same paycheck whether they help you or not. Also remember that it is human nature for people to want to help you, but you have to give them a chance. Here are Lesko's ten lessons for using people information sources:

1. *Introduce yourself cheerfully.* The way you open the conversation will set the tone for the entire interview. Your greeting and initial comment should be cordial and cheery. They should give the feeling that this is not going to be just another telephone call but a pleasant interlude in his or her day.

2. *Be open and candid.* You should be as candid as possible with your source since you are asking the same of him. If you are evasive or deceitful in explaining your needs or motives, your source will be reluctant to provide you with information. If there are certain facts you cannot reveal, for reasons such as client confidentiality, explain just that. Most people will understand.

3. *Be optimistic.* Throughout the entire conversation, you should exude a sense of confidence. If you call and say "You probably aren't the right person" or "You don't have any information, do you?" it makes it easy for the person to say "You're right, I cannot help you." A positive attitude will encourage your source to stretch his mind to see how he might be able to help you.

4. *Be humble and courteous.* You can be optimistic and still be humble. Remember the adage that you can catch more flies with honey than you can with vinegar. People in general and experts in particular love to tell others what they know, as long as their positions of authority are not questioned or threatened.

5. *Be concise.* State your problem simply. A long-winded explanation may bore your contact and reduce your chances for getting a thorough reponse.

6. *Don't be a "gimme."* A "gimme" is someone who says "give me this" or "give me that" and has little consideration for the other person's time or feelings.

7. *Be complimentary.* This goes hand in hand with being humble. A well-placed compliment about your source's expertise or insight into a particular topic will serve you well. In searching for information in large organizations, you are apt to talk to many colleagues of your source, so it wouldn't hurt to convey the respect that your "Charlie Porter" commands, for example, "Everyone I spoke with said you are the person I must talk to." It is reassuring to know you have the respect of your peers.

8. *Be conversational.* Avoid spending the entire time talking about the information you need. Briefly mention a few irrelevant topics such as the weather, the

Washington Redskins, or the latest political campaign. The more social you are without being too chatty, the more likely that your source will open up.

9. Return the favor. You might share with your source information or even gossip you have picked up elsewhere. However, be certain not to betray the trust of your client or another source. If you do not have any pertinent information to share at the moment, it would still be a good idea to call back when you are further along in your research.

10. Send thank-you notes. A short note, typed or handwritten, will help insure that your source will be just as cooperative in the future.

■ ■

to the beginning investor. Member firms have experience in planning diversified securities portfolios, and fees are usually based on the market value of the portfolio being managed. More than a hundred firms belong to the association. If you are looking for an investment counselor/brokerage firm, call or write the association for a copy of its free membership directory. It provides the following information on the firms listed: person to contact, year firm was founded, number of clients, assets under supervision (in dollars), number of professional staff members, minimum account accepted (in dollars), minimum annual fee (if any), and types of accounts supervised (equities, fixed income, options, international securities, and so on). The directory will help you locate firms in your area—but you'll still have to do some checking to evaluate them.

The Microcomputer Investors Association
902 Anderson Drive
Fredericksburg, VA 22405   703-371-5474

Founded in 1976, this organization welcomes members who use microcomputers to assist in making and managing investments. Two types of membership are available. Participating members pay dues of $50 a year, and accept an obligation to furnish one article per year for the journal. Libraries or educational institutions may join for $40 per year.

> ■ *The Microcomputer Investor*—a monthly journal, published by the association, contains between sixteen and twenty articles on topics appealing to investors experienced and knowledgeable in the stock market, commodities, and computer technology. Journal, available to members only, is included in membership fee.

WHAT TO READ

The Complete Guide to Investment Opportunities
Free Press
866 Third Avenue   800-257-5755—order department
New York, NY 10022   609-461-6500—order department

Edited by Marshall E. Blume and Jack P. Friedman, here is a reference *Business Week* has called "one of the more valuable investment books of the year." A resource for the more sophisticated investor, its sixty chapters cover subjects from arbitrage to U.S. Treasury bills, with each area explained by a distinguished authority. Investors can quickly weigh the risks and rewards of stocks, bonds, commodities, real estate, futures, and mutual funds; they can also explore the enticing world of collectibles, whether they are interested in rare stamps, old masters, or comic books.

For each investment, the contributors discuss what factors determine its value, which investor it is suited for, where to find professional advice about it, how to buy and sell it, its tax implications, and relevant custodial concerns.

The 1,100-page book is available in bookstores and libraries, particularly college and university libraries. It costs $19.95.

Consumer Information Center
PO Box 100
Pueblo, CO 81002   Written requests only
A variety of good, free, or inexpensive publications are available from this federal center.

> ■ *Before You Say Yes: Fifteen Questions to Ask About Investments*— these questions will help you invest wisely, particularly when you buy commodities, and will help protect you against fraud and swindlers. Up to two copies are free, otherwise please enclose $1 when ordering more than two free booklets. Order #512P.

> ■ *What Every Investor Should Know (A Handbook from the US Securities and Exchange Commission)*—a forty-three-page booklet explaining the investments known as securities. Intended for the beginner, it covers the basics of stocks and bonds, investment companies, investment pools, tax shelters, real estate investment trusts (REITs), and U.S. government securities. It tells you how to choose an investment and how to protect yourself in case a brokerage firm you have invested with goes out of business. A glossary of investment terms is included, as well as phone numbers and addresses of regional and national offices of the U.S. Securities and Exchange Commission. Cost is $1. Order #113P.

Dow Jones-Irwin, Inc.
1824 Ridge Road   800-323-4450
Homewood, IL 60430   312-798-6000
Dow Jones-Irwin publishes many books on investing and learning about the stock market. Ask to be on their mailing list for their free catalog. A few books, recommended for the novice investor, are listed here:

> ■ *Life Cycle Investing: Investing for the Times of Your Life*—by Donald Nichols, this book identifies several stages in an investor's life. It is written for those who are just out of school, starting a family, or in their retirement

■ ■

TYPICAL "BOILER ROOM" INVESTMENT CONS—
AND WHAT TO LOOK OUT FOR

The Federal Trade Commission, with the help of state attorney generals' offices, is trying to put an end to "boiler room" investment operations. There is no typical type of fraud because many of these operations rely on current subjects which are hot in the news. In the past such cons have centered on diamonds, gem stones, oil leases, oil drilling ventures, rare coins, strategic metals, and licenses to operate cellular telephones. However, all these operations do have many aspects in common, and consumers can protect themselves by following a few simple rules:

- Don't invest in a deal with people you do not know anything about. And don't bother calling the Better Business Bureau or other organizations to see if there have been complaints because most of these companies are not in business long enough to establish a record.
- Don't invest in a product or commodity before you do some research.
- Ask for references in your local area.
- Ask the caller for a telephone number to call them back.

- Use common sense. There are no investments where you can "make a lot of money; make it quick, at no risk." It there were, there would be long lines at the bank to borrow money to make these investments.
- If you get taken by one of these scams, start screaming as loud as you can to the company. Many times they will pay you off just to keep you quiet.

■ ■

years. Various investment options are given and an explanation is given on how they can be applied. The book is geared toward the new investor and can be found in bookstores and libraries. It contains 321 pages and costs $15.95.

- *Starting Small: Investing Smart*—written by Donald Nichols, this book is designed for the new investor. It starts with basics, describing what stocks and bonds are and how you can use them in your investment program. This is an objective book which does not promote any particular investment philosophy and should be available in bookstores and libraries. The 192-page book costs $14.95.

- *The Dow Jones-Irwin Guide to On-Line Investing: Sources, Services, and Strategies*—written by Thomas A. Meyers, this comprehensive book pulls together the features and operating characteristics of the key on-line investor services. It shows you what is available from the different databases and how to use that information for your personal computer. The 208-page book costs $25.

Fidelity Investments

820 Devonshire Street   800-544-6666—sales department
Boston, MA 02101   617-523-1919

Fidelity Investments, an established and privately held investment management organization, offers literature for the beginning investor. Contact them for a publications listing and to get the following:

> ■ *The Fidelity-Guide to Investor Information*—this booklet offers basic information on various types of investments, investment objectives, the advantages of each type of investment, and how each may serve your needs. Covered are savings accounts and time deposits, government obligations, common stocks, bonds, unit investment trusts, mutual funds, asset management accounts, tax shelters, and retirement plans. The thirty-page booklet is for someone just getting started in investing. Free.

Gaining on the Market
by Charles J. Rolo
Little, Brown and Co.
34 Beacon Street
Boston, MA 02106   617-227-0730

This book, by the Wall Street columnist for *Money* magazine, describes investment strategy for stocks, bonds, options, mutual funds, and gold. Highly recommended for beginners. A 299-page hardcover, it costs $14.95.

Handbook of Investment Terminology
Investment Information Services Press
205 West Wacker Drive
Chicago, IL 60606   312-750-9300

Better than an alphabetical dictionary, this handbook by James B. Cloonan explains terms in a brief, concise way, grouping together other related terms and concepts in the same section. According to the publishers, "this book is to investing what Strunk and White has been to writing." Cost is $14.95.

An Insiders Guide to the Wall Street Journal
Wall Street Journal
200 Liberty Street
World Financial Center
New York, NY 10281   212-416-2000

Helpful hints on how to read the *Wall Street Journal* are provided in this booklet. In addition to an overview of the newspaper, there is a special section on understanding financial data in the *Journal.* Call or write the above address and it will be sent to you free.

Investing by Phone
Bureau of Consumer Protection
Federal Trade Commission
Washington, DC 20580   202-523-3575
   Watch out for so-called "boiler-room" investment operations. These are phone solicitations for your investment dollar, and are characterized by claims of "guaranteed profits" with almost "no risk." At the end of the call the salesperson will try to convince you to send him between $1,000 and $10,000. For more information on illegal "boiler-room" investment scams and how to protect yourself against unscrupulous phone solicitors, call or write for this free, one-page guide from the Federal Trade Commission.

John Wiley and Sons
605 Third Avenue   212-850-6000
New York, NY 10158   201-469-4400—order department
   John Wiley and Sons publishes a number of financial books. They put out a free catalog which may be ordered from the Product Information Department at the above address.

> ■ *Money Talks: Bob Rosefsky's Complete Program for Financial Success*—an almanac of advice for the novice and the experienced investor. The second edition, published in 1985, gives an overview of all types of financial instruments including wills, real estate, credit, stocks, money market funds, life and health insurance, financial planning for retirement, income taxes, and buying a home. There is a discussion of goal setting, budgeting, habits, and avoiding fraud. Bob Rosefsky is the host of the PBS TV program Personal Finance and has a radio program on KCBS in California entitled Money Talks. The paperback book is 687 pages long and costs $14.95.

Kiplinger's Changing Times Financial Services Directory
Editors Park
Hyattsville, MD 20782   202-887-6400
   How do you find qualified money management and investment experts? What resources are available to you if you choose to chart your own path in saving, spending, and investing? *Kiplinger's Changing Times Financial Services Directory* is packed with lists, tables, and easy-to-read text especially prepared to help you select the financial services you need. You'll find information to use in evaluating a broker or a bank, credit cards, financial planners, insurance coverage, and more. There is an excellent section on investment managers and investment advisory services and newsletters, plus information on databases and other financial products and services. This special directory was first offered in 1986 and is expected to be updated for publication again in spring 1987. For current availability, price (the 1986 edition costs $3.50) and ordering information, call or write *Changing Times*.

Marshall Loeb's Money Guide
34 Beacon Street
Little, Brown and Co.
Boston, MA 02106   617-227-0730

Loeb, managing editor of *Money* magazine, has compiled this 600-page guide from articles and columns by *Money* writers, editors, and reporters. It includes some 400 articles reduced and edited to teach you how to manage, invest, and spend your money.

One of the largest sections is on investments, including such topics as: scams, annual reports, interest rates, investment clubs, stock market, venture-capital shares, bonds, mutual funds, brokers, commodities, and gold. There is also a very interesting section on investing in art, collectibles, and memorabilia. Real estate investments, buying a home, tax shelters, IRAs, and savings accounts are also covered. This 1986 book can be bought in bookstores for $12.95.

Money Angles
Avon Books
1790 Broadway
New York, NY 10019   212-399-4500

Written by Andrew Tobias and published in 1984, this book presents the view that you are the best judge of the risks you want to take. Tobias gives you an insider's look at the financial world in order to help you make the right choices. He shows you *how* to think—instead of *what* to think—about money matters. The book covers mutual funds, municipal bonds, corporate reports and business news, borrowing, brokerage houses, and more. This is a readable book presented with a touch of humor.

Look for the book in your local library or bookstore. It is 232 pages long and costs $3.95 in paperback.

Money Dynamics Letter
Van Caspel and Company, Inc.
1300 Post Oak Boulevard, 22nd Floor
Houston, TX 77056   713-621-9733

This eight-page monthly newsletter by Venita Van Caspel, a respected financial planner and best-selling author (*The Power of Money Dynamics, Money Dynamics for the 80's, Money Dynamics for the New Economy*—all published by Simon and Schuster), offers sound financial planning and investment strategies, with information on specific mutual funds (analyzed in detail in terms of benefits and drawbacks) and a question-and-answer column for readers' concerns. Annual subscription is $75.

Newspapers and Magazines

Reading publications such as the *Wall Street Journal, Forbes, Barron's,* and *Changing Times* will educate you in investment jargon and keep you abreast of stock market trends and financial news in general. Refer to the chapter on magazines and newspapers.

The Only Investment Guide You'll Ever Need

Bantam Books
666 Fifth Avenue　　　　　　　　　　　　　　　800-223-6834
New York, NY 10103　　　　　　　　　　　　　212-765-3535

This book, by Andrew Tobias, covers many forms of investment. Today, more than ever, making your money work for you is of urgent importance. This best-selling guide, updated and revised in 1983, is said to help you come out hundreds or thousands of dollars ahead each year. Subjects covered are: defining your tax bracket; how much you should be paying for life insurance and how much you really need; why college students should try to set up an IRA or Keogh plan; how to earn 30 to 40 percent on everything; and how to save up to 75 percent on brokerage fees. The 179-page paperback costs $3.95.

Personal Investor

4300 Campus Drive
Newport Beach, CA 92660　　　　　　　　　　　714-756-8777

Subscription Inquiries:
PO Box 2816
Boulder, CO 80322　　　　　　　　　　　　　Written requests only

Billed as the "How-To Magazine for Investors," this slick, full-color bi-monthly magazine is packed with helpful information for the novice and the experienced investor. There is a section on computer databases and software and a "Personal Advisor" column that offers tips from market watchers on everything from penny stocks to mutual funds to T-bills and bonds. Annual subscription is $11.97 and single copies are $2.50.

Security Analysis

McGraw-Hill Book Company
Princeton Road
Hightstown, NJ 08520　　　　　　　　　　　　609-426-5254

Considered the bible of the industry, this textbook by Graham and Dodd is used by colleges and universities nationwide and has been read, and reread, by professionals in the field. The basics of investing in common stocks, bonds, and other securities are covered. Information about the fundamental structure of companies and what to look for when analyzing companies for investment purposes is discussed. Although the current edition was last updated in 1962 the book is still valuable. It can be found in most libraries or purchased for $41.95.

Simon and Schuster, Inc.
1230 Avenue of the Americas
New York, NY 10020   212-698-7000
Simon and Schuster offers several accurate and practical books for investors and investors-to-be:

■ *Successful Investing: A Complete Guide to Your Financial Future*—by the staff of United Business Service, this choice 412-page paperback, published in 1979 and updated every few years, is one of the most comprehensive yet easy-to-read guidebooks we've found on the topic of diversified investments. It is highly recommended for the beginner. It contains helpful charts and graphs, plus a twenty-page glossary of financial terms. The book covers investment strategies, stocks, bonds, government notes and bonds, tax-exempt bonds, mutual funds, specialized investment funds, options, commodities, real estate, and more. It provides the beginner with a basic education in reading financial data and analyzing specific industries. It tells you where to go for advice and how to choose a broker. It explains employee benefit plans, IRAs, and Keogh plans. It aids in retirement and estate planning. The book is available from the publisher or at bookstores and libraries. Cost is $12.95.

■ *The Power of Money Dynamics*—a best-selling, easy-to-read "textbook" for the novice investor. Its author, Venita Van Caspel, is a respected certified financial planner with more than twenty years' experience. She has hosted the television series *The Moneymakers,* and she has conducted numerous seminars on financial planning and investing for maximum gains. In *The Power of Money Dynamics,* Van Caspel shares her commonsense approach to putting your money to work for a secure and rewarding future. She discusses psychological aspects of financial planning and how to develop a winning attitute. She explains how to choose a financial planner and how to plan your investment strategy. She covers the stock market, real estate, commodities, turning tax liabilities into assets, life insurance, planning for college costs, and planning for retirement. The book contains 557 pages plus a glossary of investment terms and an appendix that includes numerous charts and graphs, tax-rate schedules, and a list of financial planning/investment companies and organizations. Cost is $21.95.

Sylvia Porter's New Money Book for the 80's
Doubleday and Co., Inc.
245 Park Avenue
New York, NY 10167   212-953-4561
Best-selling financial writer Sylvia Porter has put together a mammoth (1,272-page) reference book for families to use in their financial planning,

budgeting, bargain-hunting, and investing. Over 150 pages are devoted to investment information and strategy. "Your Guide to the Stock Markets" covers stock market terminology, how to read an annual report, how to start an investment club, and more. There are also sections on mutual funds, bonds, commodity markets, and real estate. *Sylvia Porter's New Money Book for the 80's* contains an extensive section on your rights as a consumer, with detailed listings of places you can write or call for help. Cost is $9.95 in paperback.

What to Do With What You've Got

American Association of Retired Persons (AARP)
c/o Scott, Foresman and Company
Department CATB
400 South Edward Street   800-554-4411
Mount Prospect, IL 60056   312-273-5900

By Peter Weaver and Annette Buchanan, this book gives information on how to identify, protect, and increase your assets no matter how large or small. Learn how to turn your investments into income producers. Figure your net worth. Cut down on expenses (without cutting back). Squeeze income out of your major assets. Step-by-step, easy-to-understand information helps you to develop a financial game plan for the 80s. The book includes a glossary, checklists, and work sheets.

The books contains 214 pages and costs $7.95. AARP members get a discount—for them the book costs $5.80.

Your Wealth-Building Years

Newmarket Press
18 East 48th Street
New York, NY 10017   212-832-3575

By Adriane G. Berg, this book shows how to capitalize on the money earned during your twenties and thirties. It describes such concepts as the money value of time, how to focus what you are working for as well as what you are working at, the chemistry of investments, and why debt can ge good. The cost is $8.95 in paperback.

Your Savings and Investment Dollar

Money Management Institute
Household International
2700 Sanders Road
Prospect Heights, IL 60070   312-564-5000

Here's everything the novice needs to know about the basics of personal/family financial planning (with worksheet for net worth included), choosing financial advisers, financial products and services, types of investments, investing in your own higher education or your own business, retirement planning, and estate planning. There is also a glossary of savings and investment terms, plus a list of organizations, books, pamphlets, and other resources. This easy-to-read, thirty-four-page illustrated booklet will cost you only seventy-five cents.

PEOPLE TO TALK TO

Larry Adam
Senior Vice President, Investments
Dean Witter Reynolds, Inc.
100 South Charles Street
Baltimore, MD 21202   301-539-0210
Host of *Money Matters,* an award-winning educational television program dedicated to consumer issues and the world of finance, Mr. Adam is a highly qualified investment professional available to answer your questions and make appropriate referrals.

Venita Van Caspel, CFP
President, Van Caspel and Company, Inc.
Financial Planners, Stockbrokers
Member NASD
1300 Post Oak Boulevard, 22nd Floor
Houston, TX 77056   713-621-9733
"We are spending millions of dollars teaching young people how to earn a dollar and not a penny teaching them what to do with it, and that is a miserable mistake. . . ." says Venita Van Caspel, one of America's most distinguished financial planners and registered investment advisers. She is the author of five best sellers on financial planning, including *The Power of Money Dynamics* and *Money Dynamics for the New Economy* (Simon and Schuster). She publishes a monthly newsletter and hosts a nationally televised PBS program called *The Moneymakers.*

Ralph R. Goldman
c/o Shearson/American Express, Inc.
Paragon Center   800-327-3130
2400 East Commercial Boulevard, Suite 102   800-327-5588
Fort Lauderdale, FL 33308   800-331-9757
Mr. Goldman, senior vice president of Shearson/American Express, is a talent scout for investors seeking money management services. Mr. Goldman has been in the securities industry since 1969. He serves clients in twenty-five states and seven foreign countries. He tracks the performance of 400 managers with assets of under $200 million and recommends to his clients those who meet his performance criteria. Goldman usually gets a broker's fee for his services. Selected as one of the top twenty investment executives in the coun-

try, Mr. Goldman frequently addresses investment conferences and business and charitable organizations. Mr. Goldman also publishes a free quarterly report listing the top five money managers (firms) in America.

Melvin O. Wright
Senior Vice President
Dean Witter Reynolds, Inc.
Sears House
633 Pennsylvania Avenue, NW
Washington, DC 20004   202-626-1708
     Drawing on his thirty-plus years' experience in the world of finance, Mr. Wright has been instrumental in setting up educational programs to help the general public understand investing and other money matters. He has taught, worked with community colleges, and currently is chairman of the advisory board for the *Money Matters* TV show. Mr. Wright is also a trustee of the Securities Industry Institute at the Wharton Business School of the University of Pennsylvania.

Newspapers and Magazines for Tracking News and Trends, and for Managing Your Money

Where can you find the most concise, up-to-date information on financial topics? In magazines and newspapers. Experts say the best way to learn about money is to immerse yourself in information. A good way to start and continue your investigation is by reading newspapers and magazines that specialize in financial matters.

Elsewhere in this book, you'll find references to innumerable books, organizations, experts, and other resources for in-depth information. This section describes publications that regularly give you condensed information on every imaginable money topic.

We have listed the major periodicals, which have varying degrees of sophistication. Read the descriptions and choose some that seem to be on your level. It's also a good idea to browse through some of them at the library to find out which ones focus on your areas of interest. If you're a beginner, start with *Changing Times* or *Sylvia Porter's Personal Finance* magazines with emphasis on personal finance. If you're more interested in stocks or business topics, the *Wall Street Journal* or *Forbes* may be on your level.

Whatever your level of knowledge, you should choose one or two periodicals from the following list. Either subscribe to them or read them often in the library. If you do, you can't avoid picking up the knowledge to stay up-to-date on your financial matters.

WHAT TO READ

Barron's: National Business and Financial Weekly
Subscriber Services
200 Burnett Road
Chicopee, MA 01021-9988

800-345-8505, ext. 326
800-662-5180, ext. 326—PA

Published by Dow Jones and Company, Inc., *Barron's* is a weekly newspaper especially for investors. Published only hours after the markets close, it contains up-to-date investment information. Stocks, bonds, options, real estate, commodities, and more are covered. It has profiles of new and promising companies and provides detailed analyses of thousands of stocks and bonds in dozens of markets worldwide.

A special offer to new subscribers was being offered when we called. A free copy of Dow Jones-Irwin's *Word on Wall Street,* an informative portfolio of definitions and examples of 2,000 terms from the investment world was being sent to each new subscriber. A one-year subscription to *Barron's* costs $82 and a single newsstand copy is $1.75.

Business Week
1221 Avenue of the Americas
New York, NY 10020   800-635-1200
This upscale weekly magazine, founded in 1929, offers a broad coverage of financial matters directed to upper and mid-level businesses and business professionals. It covers everything from personal finance and travel to stocks and bonds. A regular section on personal business covers such topics as investments, mortgages, taxes, and entertainment. Other sections include People, Science and Technology, Economic Analysis, and Business Outlook. An annual subscription costs $39.95 and a single newsstand copy is $2.

Changing Times
Editorial Offices:
1729 H Street, NW
Washington, DC 20006   202-887-6400

Subscription Information:
Editors Park
Hyattsville, MD 20782
Published monthly by the Kiplinger Washington Editors, Inc., this is a real "diamond in the rough" among the many slick, full-color consumer magazines available on the newsstands today. (In fact, you may not have seen it on your newsstand, but you can usually find it in the library.) It is packed with up-to-date, easy-to-read advice and information on all aspects of savings, financial planning, investing, protection from consumer ripoffs, and where to find bar-

---

Sources Investors Turn to
for Most of Their Financial Information

Newspapers are investors' biggest source of information according to a *Money* magazine survey. Nearly 40 percent of household decision makers relied on newspapers for financial information and advice; one in four respondents relied on magazines. Only 5 percent relied on courses and seminars.

gains in everything from travel to a college education to retail goods. There is a question-and-answer column in each issue. A special issue is released every January focusing exclusively on financial planning for the coming year. It contains features on savings, investments, taxes, insurance, retirement and estate planning, cash flow/family budgeting charts, and more. *Changing Times* costs $15 a year or $1.75 for a single issue.

Fact: The Money Management Magazine
305 East 46th Street
New York, NY 10017   212-319-6868—editorial offices

Subscription Information:
711 Third Avenue
New York, NY 10017   212-687-3965

Fact is a slick, sixty-two-page, full-color, consumer-oriented magazine especially for investors and those who want to learn more practical, sound ways to increase their gains. Each issue contains a ranking of the best performing mutual funds in six categories; an analysis of the performance of twenty-three different investments over six months, one year, three years, and five years; information on new companies and new ways to invest; a capsule summary of what investment advisers are saying; and news and updates on Wall Street (the month's best and worst stock performers) and Washington (government activities affecting your finances). *Fact* is published eleven times a year (monthly, except for a combined July/August issue). An annual subscription is $24 and a single copy is $2.50.

Financial World: The Magazine for Investors
Editorial Offices:
1450 Broadway
New York, NY 10018   212-869-1616

Subscription Inquiries:
PO Box 10750
Des Moines, IA 50340   800-247-5470

This biweekly magazine has everything for the beginning investor, as well as for more seasoned Wall Street strategists. Regular columns focusing on Wall Street action and trends, profiles of corporate leaders in new and promising companies, plus features on bonds, commodities, and stocks, as well as many helpful charts and graphs, appear in the magazine. There is an annual issue in January which offers experts' analyses of the economy and their choices for the best investments in the coming year. A one-year subscription to *Financial World* costs $44.95.

■ ■

INVESTMENT MAGAZINES

Listed below are the major investment- and business-oriented periodicals, along with frequency and circulation information.

Wall Street Journal; New York, NY; business days only; 1,952,283

Money; New York, NY; monthly; 1,862,-106

Changing Times; Washington, DC; monthly; 1,379,781

Business Week; New York, NY; weekly; 878,838

Nation's Business; Washington, DC; monthly; 862,410

Fortune; New York, NY; 27 times a year; 747,554

Forbes; New York, NY; biweekly; 733,-255

Inc. Magazine; Boston, MA; monthly; 606,577

Success; New York, NY; monthly; 407,-447

Savvy; New York, NY; monthly; 356,178

Sylvia Porter's Personal Finance Magazine; New York, NY; monthly; 350,-819

Venture; New York, NY; monthly; 330,-277

Industry Week; Cleveland, OH; every other Monday except in December; 328,637

Business Month; New York, NY; monthly; 301,505

The Economist; London, England; weekly; 300,885

Barron's National Business and Financial Weekly; New York, NY; weekly; 280,370

Harvard Business Review; Boston, MA; monthly; 207,037

Financial World; New York, NY; biweekly; 175,322

Entrepreneur; Los Angeles, CA; monthly; 132,872

Personal Investor; Irvine, CA; bimonthly; 106,398

Institutional Investor; New York, NY; monthly; 95,027

Investor's Daily; Los Angeles, CA; business days only; 56,428

Wall Street Transcript; New York, NY; weekly; 7,274

■ ■

Forbes
60 Fifth Avenue
New York, NY 10011   212-620-2200

Published biweekly, *Forbes* is a sophisticated magazine of interest to investors, business and industry executives, financial analysts, and entrepreneurs. It contains features, profiles of moguls, financial experts and investment professionals. An annual subscription is $42.

Forbes also offers its readers a home study program, *Forbes Stock Market Course.* This fifteen-lesson course comes in a 332-page loose-leaf binder, with many supplemental brochures and guides. The course covers how to pick the best stocks, how to negotiate the best price, how to get maximum return on your money. For many brokers, it's at the top of the list when clients ask for a guide to the stock market. You can receive the course for a ten-day inspection period. The program costs $76.50.

Fortune
1271 Avenue of the Americas
New York, NY 10020   212-586-1212
   Published bimonthly by Time, Inc., this magazine can be useful to investors even though its audience is primarily upper and middle management. It covers trends in the economy, government, and other areas that affect executives and how they manage their businesses. Subscription costs $44.55 per year.

Investor's Daily
1941 Armacost Avenue
PO Box 25970   800-831-2525
Los Angeles, CA 90025-9970   213-477-1453
   This impressive thirty-page daily financial newspaper is definitely not for mere dabblers or beginners learning about the stock market. Although there is some easy-to-read material featuring information about companies and their earnings, much of the paper is devoted to solid, sophisticated statistics, graphs, and charts which track daily changes in value for thirteen market sector indexes. A daily computer and technology section, a Friday real estate section, and economic news from Washington all appear. There is a daily price table of 196 stock groups which shows you how all the industry groups and sectors are performing so you can determine possible trends. Daily reporting of data on mutual funds, foreign markets, commodities futures, stock options, and more. A one-year subscription costs $84.

Money
Subscription Information:
PO Box 14429
Boulder, CO 80322-4429

"Money Helps" Column
Editorial Offices:
c/o Time-Life Building
Rockefeller Center
New York, NY 10020
   Published monthly by Time, Inc., this is perhaps the best-known consumer-oriented magazine for families and today's upwardly mobile career strategists who want to learn better ways to save, protect, manage, and invest their money. Each issue contains easy-to-read, practical information on Wall Street trends, mutual funds, savings rates, taxes, and tax writeoffs. It also features profiles of moneymakers and a question-and-answer column called "Money Helps" in which readers ask financial experts for advice. In addition to regular columns and features on travel, working parents, eduation costs, and money management/budgeting, *Money* sometimes offers new subscribers

special premiums, such as free "how-to" manuals on various topics. These manuals are also available on the newsstands twice a year. A one-year subscription to *Money* costs $29.95 and a single copy is $2.50.

The Moneypaper

2 Madison Avenue
Larchmont, NY 10538   914-833-0270

The Moneypaper has been ranked among the top financial publications in payoff of stock recommendations, and although it is promoted as a financial advisory newspaper for women, it contains information of interest to both men and women. Top money experts and nationally known professionals from business and legal fields, plus well-known authors and psychologists, contribute to this monthly newspaper, which features interviews, advice, and articles on investments, taxes, savings, financial planning, and much more. There is a capsule summary of important financial news culled from over seventy publications. *The Moneypaper* has been recommended by *Ms.* magazine as an excellent tool for "increasing your investment savvy" and for being tax-deductible when used for tax/investment information and advice. It is a consumer-oriented newspaper format, with illustrations and photographs. Cost is $39 a year. Reprints of articles are $3 each.

Sylvia Porter's Personal Finance Magazine

Editorial Offices:
380 Lexington Avenue
New York, NY 10017   212-557-9100

Subscription Inquiries:
PO Box 1928
Marion, OH 43305   614-383-3141

This new full-color consumer magazine, available at many newsstands, is similar to *Money* in content and style, but with more of a "how-to" focus. Published ten times a year by well-known financial advice columnist Sylvia Porter and her staff, this magazine provides regular sections on investing, mutual funds, taxes, and real estate, plus a "financial makeover" of a family or individual and a question-and-answer column of readers' concerns. It offers tips and common-sense strategies for the best use of your assets. A one-year subscription costs $19.97. A single copy is $2.50.

The Wall Street Journal

Subscriber Services
PO Box 30
Chicopee, MA 01021-9983   800-841-1600, ext. 508

The bible of financial/investment information newspapers, the *Wall Street Journal* is an issue-packed daily newspaper for investors and stock-market watchers worldwide. Published by Dow Jones, the *Journal* has more than 400 reporters around the world who cover stories and developments in politics, personal finance, labor and management, taxes, and technology. It helps you broaden your perspective on economic and business issues and gain practical insights into current investment strategies. Current subscription rate (September 1987) is $119 a year or call toll-free for update. Upon request the *Wall Street Journal* will send you a free copy of *An Insider's Guide to the Wall Street Journal.* This booklet gives helpful hints on how to read the newspaper. In addition to an overview, there is a special section on understanding financial data in the *Journal.*

Money Numbers

If you are an investor, an armchair economist, or a business executive who wants to monitor current business conditions the following recorded messages can keep you just as up to date as many of the commercial on-line databases that charge $70 per hour or more.

Commodities

CHICAGO BOARD OF TRADE

- Narrative and commentary about current market conditions and other news items: 312-922-7885
- Information on wheat, corn, oats, beans, oil, meal, plywood, crude oil, unleaded gas and heating oil: 312-922-9110
- Information on Treasury Bonds, CDR-GNMA, metals, gold, and silver: 312-922-9120

CHICAGO MERCANTILE EXCHANGE—312-930-8282: 120 recorded messages covering most commodities. After dialing the above number, key in the following on your touch-tone phone:

- Directory: ✳158
- Instructions: ✳136
- Special exchange number: ✳135
- Eligible options: ✳128
- Most active exchange contracts: ✳117
- Daily volume: ✳134
- Economic reports: ✳221
- Year-to-date volume: ✳434
- Monthly volume: ✳334
- Currency futures: ✳156
- Interest rates and precious metals: ✳155
- Agricultural contracts: ✳157
- Equity and lumber: ✳258
- Options on futures: ✳257

CLAYTON BROKERAGE FIRMS

- Continual update of market prices for commodities including grains, metals, stock indexes, livestock and currencies: 703-790-9121

COFFEE, SUGAR, AND COCOA EXCHANGE

- Updated price and volume information: 212-938-2847

KANSAS CITY BOARD OF TRADE

- Information on winter wheat and Value Line Stock Index futures: 816-753-1101

MIDAMERICA COMMODITY EXCHANGE

- Agricultural price update: 312-922-9110
- Financial update: 312-922-9120
- Financial and agricultural commentary: 312-922-7885

MINNEAPOLIS GRAIN EXCHANGE

- Information on wheat, germ, oats, barley, rye, soybeans, sunflower, and flax seed: 612-340-9438

NATIONAL GRAIN MARKET NEWS SUMMARY

- Price and other market news as well as commentary on grain: 816-842-5158

NEW YORK MERCANTILE EXCHANGE

- Price and volume information on crude oil: 212-938-8013
- Open interest for the day for crude oil: 212-938-8016
- Price and volume information on heating oil: 212-938-8011
- Price and volume information on gasoline: 212-938-8012
- Open interest for the day for heating oil and gasoline: 212-938-8017
- Price and volume information for platinum, palladium, and potatoes: 212-938-8014
- Open interest for the day for platinum, palladium, and potatoes: 212-938-8020

NEW YORK COMMODITY EXCHANGE

- Latest quote for gold and silver traded on the Exchange: 212-938-9020

U.S. DEPARTMENT OF AGRICULTURE

- Agriculture news features and highlights: 202-488-8358

Currency Exchange Rates

RUESCH INTERNATIONAL

- Current rate of exchange of all major currencies: 202-887-0980

DEAK PERERA

- Current exchange-rate information for major currencies: 800-368-5683

RIGGS NATIONAL BANK

- Foreign currency exchange rates for major currencies used by banks: 202-835-5324

Economic News

U.S. DEPARTMENT OF COMMERCE

- Economic news: 202-393-4100
- News highlights: 202-393-1847
- Weekend preview beginning Friday evening: 202-393-4102

U.S. DEPARTMENT OF LABOR

- Current labor statistics: 202-523-9658
- Labor-related press release information: 202-523-6899

CONGRESSIONAL RESEARCH SERVICE

- Latest economic indicators including price indexes, GNP, housing starts, international trade, etc.: 202-287-7034

FEDERAL RESERVE BOARD

- News highlights covering topics such as consumer installment debt, money supply, etc.: 202-452-3206

FEDERAL TRADE COMMISSION

- News from the Commission that can affect the economics of specific industries and companies: 202-326-2710

Energy News

U.S. DEPARTMENT OF ENERGY

- Energy conservation and renewable energy hotline: 800-523-2929

Gold Medallion Prices

U.S. MINT

- 800-368-5510 (in DC 202-783-3800, in AK, HI, PR, and VI 800-368-5500)

Income Tax Messages

INTERNAL REVENUE SERVICE

- Look in the back of your IRS tax package for your local telephone number to access 150 Tele-Tax messages, or call 800-424-1040. Once connected, key in the following numbers for investment-related tax issues (touch-tone phone required):

- Interest received: ∗132
- Dividend exclusion: ∗133
- Capital gains: ∗138
- Pensions and annuities: ∗139
- Rental income: ∗143
- Renting vacation property: ∗200
- Employee business expense: ∗214
- Tax shelters: ∗226
- Estate tax: ∗305
- Withholding on interest and dividends: ∗335
- Basis of assets: ∗401
- Depreciation: ∗402

Interest Rates

FEDERAL RESERVE BOARD BANKS

- Many of the regional banks provide recorded information on current interest rates based on government securities:

  New York: 212-720-6693
  Chicago: 312-786-1110
  Philadelphia: 215-574-6188
  Cleveland: 216-579-2001
  Richmond: 804-648-0880
  Atlanta: 404-521-8657
  Kansas City: 816-881-2364
  Dallas: 214-651-6177
  San Francisco: 415-974-2477

- Highlights of news including consumer debt, money supply, meetings, etc.: 202-452-3206

Options

CHICAGO BOARD OF OPTIONS

- Input and trade checking times: 312-786-7955
- New options listed: 312-786-7324
- Puts and call volume at end of the day: 312-786-7485
- Retail automatic execution services: 312-786-7500
- Debt closing prices: 312-786-7954
- Current prices for a seat on the Exchange: 312-786-7456

Stock Market News

FOLGER, NOLAN, FLEMING, DOUGLAS, INC.:

- Quotes during working hours and recording after 5 P.M.: 202-783-5252

Treasury Bills, Bonds, and Notes

U.S. DEPARTMENT OF TREASURY

- A lesson on how to buy government securities: 202-287-4217
- General information on Treasury Bills: 202-287-4091
- General information on Treasury Bonds and Notes: 202-287-4088
- Prices and yields on most recently sold US Savings Bonds, Retirement Plan Bonds and Individual Retirement Bonds (from 7:30 A.M. to 4:45 P.M.): 202-287-4100
- Telecommunication device for the deaf: 202-287-4097

Real Estate

FEDERAL NATIONAL MORTGAGE ASSOCIATION (FNMA)

- Rates and yields for lenders who sell adjustable-rate mortgages to FNMA: 202-537-6799
- Rates and yields for lenders who sell fixed-rate mortgages to FNMA: 202-537-7060

FEDERAL HOME LOAN MORTGAGE CORPORATION (FHLMC)

- Rates and yields for lenders who sell fixed-rate mortgages to FHLMC: 202-789-4500
- Rates and yields for lenders who sell adjustable-rate mortgages to FHLMC: 202-789-4488

Washington News

WHITE HOUSE

- News from the President: 800-424-9090 (in DC 202-456-7198)

HOUSE OF REPRESENTATIVES, U.S.

- Democrat version of what is happening on the floor of the House of Representatives: 202-225-7400
- Republican version of the above: 202-225-7430
- Democrats' legislation program: 202-225-1600
- Republicans' legislation program: 202-225-2020

SENATE, U.S.

- Democrat version of what is happening on the floor of the Senate: 202-224-8541
- Republican version of the above: 202-224-8601

FOR COMPUTER USERS

Electronic Bulletin Boards

U.S. DEPARTMENT OF COMMERCE

- The latest economic data from major government agencies: 202-377-3870 or 202-377-0433

SILICON VALLEY INFORMATION CENTER

- For information on high-tech industries and companies: 408-277-5758

BOSTON CITINET

- Lists all companies providing financial services in the Boston area as well as details on mortgage packages offered by Massachusetts banks and savings and loans: 617-247-3048

EXPORT IMPORT BANK

- For information on government financial assistance for selling overseas: 202-566-4602

MAX ULE & COMPANY

- Help for entrepreneurs looking for venture capital for computer-related firms: 212-986-1660

PEOPLE COMPUTER CONSULTANTS

- Keeps you up-to-date on inside gossip and growth patterns for companies in the computer-related industries: 408-923-7575

INVESTORS BBS

- A stockbroker in Boca Raton, FL, provides daily information on the most active stocks traded, as well as plenty of investment advice: 305-395-1267

LIBRARY RESEARCH

Many libraries around the country offer free research on any investment-related topic through their bulletin board systems. Here are a few to get you started:

- Louisville, KY, Free Public Library: 502-584-4162
- Chicago Public Library, North Pulaski Branch: 312-235-3200

- Liverpool, NY, Public Library: 315-457-3144
- Spokane, WA, Public Library: 509-838-4726

THE INVESTOR'S RESOURCE

- Help to get started in investing in real estate: 213-496-4538

PURDUE UNIVERSITY

- Newsletters and other types of news covering commodities: 317-494-6643

Definitions and Terminology

What, according to experts, is the biggest stumbling block for people when it comes to banking, investing, buying insurance or anything else concerning money matters? Jargon. Once you get that down, the experts claim, the mysteries of the world of finance disappear and you can start to gather the information you need, analyze it, and make wise choices.

To get yourself started you'll find an encyclopedia, dictionary, or glossary of terms indispensable. A reference work defining a broad spectrum of financial terms as well as individual glossaries for particular fields will be most helpful.

If you are new to the terminology, there are several ways you can pick up the jargon. First, read general financial news magazines and newspapers such as the *Wall Street Journal* or *Money* as well as the financial section of your local newspaper. Second, listen to financial news shows on radio and television. Again, when a term is foreign to you, look it up right away while the context and usage is fresh in your mind. Third, consider enrolling in an adult education class (usually free or low-cost) covering investments and financial planning. Often you will receive pamphlets, books, and other handouts defining investment terminology.

To select a dictionary that is right for your needs, you may want to browse in your local public library or bookstore. In the library, ask the reference librarian to tell you where the investment and financial-planning reference books are. If buying a dictionary, look for one that covers the fields that interest you, provides a clear and concise definition for each term, and uses the terms in a sentence or example.

You may also find short glossaries of terms in books on financial topics and in the many free handbooks published by associations listed throughout this sourcebook. If you are only interested in the language of a particular field, look up that topic in this book and call one of the major associations. Often it will be able to send you a free glossary of the terms most frequently used in the field.

More important, when dealing with financial experts, don't let them snow you. If you don't know the meaning of a term they are using, ask the dumbest question you can think of—"What does that mean?" As the so-called experts, they will be happy to explain, and if they can't, that's a clue to their expertise.

WHAT TO READ

Banking Language: A Running Press Glossary
by Laila Batz
Running Press
38 South 19th Street
Philadelphia, PA 19103   215-567-5080
Specialized banking terms and jargon used by banks are defined in this pocket-sized glossary. Clear, concise terms have been selected for business and professionals in the field of banking, as well as for consumers. The hundred-page book costs $3.70 prepaid.

Borrowers, Lenders, and Interest Rates
Federal Reserve Bank of Richmond
Public Services Department
PO Box 27622
Richmond, VA 23261   804-643-1250
This 1984 pamphlet describes the process of determining interest rates and provides definitions of credit terminology. Free.

Consumer Credit Terminology Handbook
Federal Reserve Bank of New York
Public Information Department
33 Liberty Street
New York, NY 10045   212-791-6134
Consumer credit terms used in everyday credit transactions are defined in this 1979 publication, also available in Spanish. This twenty-page booklet is free.

Dictionary of Banking and Finance
by Lewis E. Davids
Littlefield, Adams and Company
81 Adams Drive
Totowa, NJ 07512   201-256-8600
Terminology commonly found in banking and finance is defined in this 229-page dictionary. Particularly useful is an appendix containing a list of 131 sources for individual glossaries published by various associations, individuals, and agencies. Cost is $7.95.

■ ■

WHICH THIRTY STOCKS MAKE UP THE DOW JONES INDUSTRIAL AVERAGE?

Virtually all summaries of daily stock activity talk about "the Dow" being either up or down. In case you've ever wondered what stocks make up this exalted average, here they are:

Alcoa
Allied Signal, Inc.
American Express Co.
American Telephone and Telegraph
   (AT&T) Co.
Bethlehem Steel Corp.
Boeing
Chevron Corp.
Coca-Cola
E. I. du Pont de Nemours & Co.
Eastman Kodak Co.
Exxon Corp.
General Electric Co.
General Motors
Goodyear Tire & Rubber Co.
IBM Corp.

International Paper Co. Inc.
McDonald's Corp.
Merck & Co.
Minnesota Mining and Minerals
   (3M) Co.
Navistar International Corp.
Philip Morris Co.
Primerica
Procter and Gamble Co.
Sears, Roebuck & Co.
Texaco, Inc.
Union Carbide Corp.
USX Corp.
United Technologies Corp.
Westinghouse Corp.
F. W. Woolworth Co.

■ ■

Dictionary of Banking & Finance
John Wiley and Sons
Order Department
1 Wiley Drive
Somerset, NJ 08873   212-850-6418
     Recommended by experts in the field of banking, the 614-page dictionary covers a wealth of terms in finance, banking, and related fields such as computers. Included in the entries are quotations and listings of experts in the field. Cost is $14.95.

Dictionary of Business and Economics
Macmillan Publishing Company
Front and Brown streets
Riverside, NJ 08075   212-702-2000
     Useful for students, investors, business executives and financial specialists, this 507-page dictionary contains more than 3,000 entries. Fields covered include business, consumer economics, banking, finance, insurance, real estate, stocks, bonds, economic theory, and government monetary policies.

■ ■

THE ALPHABET SOUP OF INVESTMENT ADVISERS

Listed below are the major letters you may run into behind the name of an investment adviser and what they stand for. The M.S.F.S., J.D., and L.L.M. are degrees awarded from traditional universities and colleges. All the other letters are given by private associations or accrediting institutions.

C.F.P.	Certified Financial Planner
Ch.F.C.	Chartered Financial Consultant
C.L.U.	Chartered Life Underwriter
M.S.F.S.	Master of Science in Financial Services
C.P.A.	Certified Public Accountant
C.F.A.	Chartered Financial Analyst
R.I.A.	Registered Investment Adviser
C.P.C.U.	Chartered Property and Casualty Underwriter
R.H.U.	Registered Health Underwriter
J.D.	Juris Doctorate
L.L.M.	Master of Laws
M.I.A.	Member Appraisal Institute

■ ■

The entries provide definitions, explanations, diagrams, typical examples and samples of common forms and records. The cost of the dictionary is $28.

Dictionary of Economics and Business
Littlefield, Adams and Company
81 Adams Drive
Totowa, NJ 07512   201-256-8600
   For quick reference to over 5,000 terms, this 523-page dictionary is intended for the individual investor as well as the business professional. Entries cover commonly used terms in a broad range of fields from finance, business, economics, investments, labor, money, real estate, securities, and taxation. Cost is $7.95.

Dictionary of Finance and Investment Terms
Barron's Financial Guides
113 Crossways Park Drive
Woodbury, NY 11797   800-645-3476
   For the individual trying to understand anything from the language of money for personal financial planning to terms involved in corporate mergers, this provides definitions of over 2,500 terms in 352 pages. Fields covered

include stocks, bonds, banking, and corporate finance. It costs $6.95 plus $1.50 postage and handling.

Encyclopedia of Banking and Finance
Bankers Publishing Company
210 South Street
Boston, MA 02111   617-426-4495
Used extensively by bankers and financial professionals, this comprehensive encyclopedia of 1,024 pages can usually be found in your local public library. Over 4,000 in-depth entries provide historical background of terms used in banking, definitions, usage of terms with examples, recent trends, statistical data, citation of applicable laws, and, in many entries, sources for more information. Cost is $89.

Glossary of Federal Reserve Terms
Federal Reserve System
Board of Governors
Publications Service
Washington, DC 20551   202-452-3244
Definitions for many of the terms used in monetary policy and bank supervision and regulations are provided for the general public in this twenty-six-page glossary. Free.

Handbook of Investment Terminology
by James B. Cloonan, Ph.D.
Investment Information Services Press
205 West Wacker Drive
Chicago, IL 60606   312-750-9300
Better than an alphabetical dictionary, this *Handbook of Investment Terminology* explains boldface entry terms in a brief, concise way, grouping together related terms and concepts in one section. According to the publisher, "this book is to investing what Strunk and White has been to writing." Cost is $14.95.

Investors Information Kit
New York Stock Exchange, Inc.
Publications Division
11 Wall Street
New York, NY 10005   212-623-3000
Included in the *Investors Information Kit* is a twenty-one-page glossary defining common securities, options, and futures product terms. Entries are clear, concise and cross-referenced to similar terms. The glossary is especially useful to those just beginning to invest in stocks and bonds. Cost is $7 prepaid.

McGraw-Hill Dictionary of Modern Economics
McGraw-Hill Book Company
Princeton Road
Hightstown, NJ 08520   609-426-5254

The 1983 edition contains 1,400 definitions of economic terms and descriptions of important economic and research organizations throughout the world. This 632-page handbook provides for each term: a definition: a discussion of the subject, including a survey of opposing viewpoints; and a listing of bibliographic references for further inquiry. The handbook is available for $49.95.

Money A-Z: A Consumer's Guide to the Language of Personal Finance
Facts on File, Inc.
460 Park Avenue South
New York, NY 10016   212-683-2244

More than 1,400 terms are defined in this 256-page guide which addresses every level of understanding of economic terms. It is specifically geared toward terminology used by the individual investor. The dictionary is supplemented by a section on personal financial planning and costs $15.95.

The Money Encyclopedia
Harper & Row, Inc.
10 East 53rd Street
New York, NY 10022   800-233-4175

Hundreds of entries in this 669-page reference work explain almost every facet of the money system—from personal finance to corporate operations, from individual money-related matters such as insurance and wills to the worldwide economic system. Entries explain not only how the financial system works but also how you can apply this information to your financial circumstances. It is available for $26.50.

The VNR Dictionary of Business and Finance
Van Nostrand Reinhold Company, Inc.
Mail Order Service
7625 Empire Drive
Florence, KY 41042   606-525-6600

Geared to business professionals, this 500-page dictionary provides extensive coverage of business terms as well as terms used in real estate, securities, insurance, contracts, and the business-related aspects of government. Definitions are clarified with practical examples from current business usage. Cost is $18.95.

Words of Wall Street: 2000 Investment Terms Defined
by Allan Pessin and Joseph Ross
Dow Jones-Irwin
1818 Ridge Road
Homewood, IL 60430   312-798-6000
   Published in 1983, this is a handy dictionary of financial jargon and concepts explained in simple terms for the novice. This 297-page paperback glossary costs $9.95.

ADDITIONAL RESOURCES

   Many organizations have prepared glossaries, often available free of charge, explaining terms commonly used in their field of expertise. To find out about the availability of such publications, contact associations listed under subjects of interest to you in this sourcebook. Examples of offerings include:

Mutual Fund Fact Book
Investment Company Institute
11600 M Street, NW
Washington, DC 20036   202-293-7700
   Contained in the 104-page *Fact Book* is a glossary of thirty-nine terms useful for the beginner interested in understanding mutual funds. Entries provide definitions of terms and explanations of the types of funds described throughout the book. Cost is $4 prepaid.

How to Find Information on a Company

Traditional sources of information on companies can be found in the chapters THE FIRST STEP FOR BEGINNERS AND EXPERIENCED INVESTORS; NEWSPAPERS AND MAGAZINES FOR TRACKING NEWS AND TRENDS, AND FOR MANAGING YOUR MONEY; STOCKS; and BONDS. This section identifies those sources of company information which normally go unused by both the typical and the sophisticated investor. Real investment opportunities do not come about when you have the same information as everyone else in the market. To get ahead of the pack and be able to tap into sources others don't know about or are too lazy to investigate—that's what nontraditional information sources are all about.

When the staff of Information USA began doing company investigations in 1975, even the most sophisticated relied on only two major sources of information: 1) the Securities and Exchange Commission for companies that were traded on the major exchanges and 2) Dun & Bradstreet reports for all other companies.

In addition to the fact that they have become traditional sources which may not offer many information opportunities, these two resources have other limitations. The Securities and Exchange Commission only has information on approximately 10,000 publicly held companies in the United States. However, according to the IRS and the U.S. Bureau of the Census (each agency counts differently), there are between five and twelve million companies in the country. So where do you go if you want information on a division or a subsidiary of a publicly listed company which is not big enough to be identified in the company filings? Or if you want to buy a small company not listed on any of the major exchanges? Or if a company you are invested in is looking to purchase another smaller company? Or if you want information on a competitor of a company in which you are invested? These are all reasons why you need to know more than just the traditional information sources.

The problems with Dun & Bradstreet reports are more significant than the shortcomings of company filings at the SEC. The main drawback is that D & B reports have been established primarily for credit purposes and are supposed to indicate the company's ability to pay its bills. You will, therefore, find information from current creditors about whether a business is late in its payments, which may or may not be a useful indicator for evaluating the company.

If there is additional financial information in these reports you should also be aware of who in the company is providing D & B with information, and of their motives in doing so. The information contained in these reports does not carry the legal weight of the company information registered with the Securities and Exchange Commission. If a company lies about any of the information it turns over to the SEC, a corporate officer could wind up in jail. Dun & Bradstreet, however, collects its information by telephoning the company and asking it to provide certain information voluntarily. The company is under no obligation to comply and, equally important, is under no obligation to D & B to be honest. Unlike the government, Dun & Bradstreet cannot prosecute.

If the company you are interested in is like our company, Information USA, Inc., you will have problems using our Dun & Bradstreet report. We know our customers do not rely on these reports to do business with us and that anyone who wants this kind of information is likely to be either a competitor or simply just nosy. The information we supply to Dun & Bradstreet is a sanitized version, that which we want outsiders to see. Our only problem is in remembering what half-truths we told D & B last year so that our track record appears consistent. However, Information USA, Inc., would not and does not play such games with the financial information it files with the Maryland secretary of state.

This is why resourceful investors are starting to appreciate the value of the thousands of nontraditional sources such as public documents and industry experts that are available. We know that Dun & Bradstreet will not send you to jail if you lie to them, but the state of Maryland will.

AGENCIES, INSTITUTES, AND ORGANIZATIONS

Annual Reports Available from Companies

Generally free, annual reports can be obtained directly from a company's public relations department. Some firms will also send you copies of their reports filed with the Securities and Exchange Commission as well as transcripts of presentations made to brokerage societies.

Center for International Financial Analysis and Research, Inc.
601 Ewing Street, C-16
Princeton, NJ 08540   609-921-0910

This is an independent research group that collects annual reports for 5,000 foreign companies, in all different industries. You can buy a single report, partials by geographical area or industry, or a subscription to all reports. A single copy costs $25, an annual subscription costs $5,000, and a partial subscription varies.

Council on Economic Priorities
30 Irving Place
New York, NY 10003   212-420-1133

Reports prepared by the Council relate primarily to the social and political impact of American corporations in such areas as equal opportunity, environmental quality, and consumer practices. The cost of the studies varies (a full year's subscription fee is $100). The Council maintains a library, open to the public, which houses these reports, as well as other reference materials of use to company researchers. The Council's newsletters summarize its studies, and on request you can get a single issue free of charge. You can call the above number to find out what the Council has available on the company you're investigating.

County and Local Sources

County and local sources can prove to be the biggest bucket of worms as far as information sources are concerned. Unlike state government where there are a mere fifty varieties to choose from, there are over 5,000 different jurisdictions at the local level. Here are some basic checkpoints that can enhance your information-gathering efforts.

LOCAL NEWSPAPER

The local newspaper can provide the best leads for anything you are investigating at the local level. It is perhaps the best source mentioned in this book. A well-placed telephone call to the business editor or the managing editor, if there is not a business section, can prove most useful. In smaller towns, and even in suburbs of larger cities where there are suburban newspapers, a local business generates a good deal of news. A local reporter often knows the company like no one else in the country. The company executives are usually more open with the local media because they like to show off about how big they are, how much the company is growing, etc. A reporter is also likely to know company employees who can corroborate or refute the executive's remarks. Ask the local newspaper if you can get copies of all articles written about the company in question. After you review them, call the reporter to see what additional information may be stored in his or her head.

CHAMBER OF COMMERCE

Talking to the librarian, or to someone on the research staff, can help you identify sources of information about a company within the community. A friendly conversation with Chamber executives can also provide insight into a company's financial position and strategies.

LOCAL DEVELOPMENT AUTHORITY

Many local communities, counties, and regional areas have established development authorities to attract business and industry to their area. They operate in pretty much the same way as the state department of economic development described under State Regulators further in this section, and as a result collect a lot of data about the businesses in their area.

■ ■

UNCLE SAM'S INDUSTRY EXPERTS

One of the best places to begin to find out if your investment into a company or industry has potential value is to contact one of our country's free industry analysts located at the US Department of Commerce. These experts spend their careers concentrating on particular industrial sectors and can be contacted by mail (US Department of Commerce, Washington, DC 20230) or by phone, 202-377-1456.

This list is arranged according to the Standard Industrial Classification Code.

Construction	Area code for all phone numbers is 202	
Private residential construction	377-0132	Patrick MacAuley
Private nonresidential construction	377-0132	Patrick MacAuley
Publicly owned construction	377-0132	Patrick MacAuley
International construction	377-4002	Robert L. Lorensky
Construction Materials	377-0132	Charles B. Pitcher
Fabricated structural metal	377-0132	Franklin E. Williams
Cement	377-0132	Charles B. Pitcher
Concrete products	377-0132	Charles B. Pitcher
Prefabricated metal buildings	377-0132	Franklin E. Williams
Clay brick	377-0132	Charles B. Pitcher
Gypsum products	377-0132	Charles B. Pitcher
Electric Lighting and Wiring Equipment	377-4382	Richard A. Whitley
Wood Products	377-0382	Donald Butts
Logging operators	377-0378	Walter H. Fausel
Structural wood members	377-0377	Adair Mitchell
Millwork	377-0377	Adair Mitchell
Pallets and skids	377-0378	Walter H. Fausel
Wood preservation	377-0378	Walter H. Fausel
Wood panel products	377-0382	Donald W. Butts
Hardwood plywood and veneer	377-0382	Donald W. Butts
Softwood veneer and plywood	377-0382	Donald W. Butts
Particleboard	377-0382	Donald W. Butts
Pulp, Paper, and Board	377-0382	Donald W. Butts
Pulp mills	377-0375	Mary Anne Smith
Paper and board	377-0382	Donald W. Butts
Corrugated and solid fiber boxes	377-0376	Leonard S. Smith
Folding paperboard boxes	377-0376	Leonard S. Smith
Set-up paperboard boxes	377-0376	Leonard S. Smith
Sanitary food containers	377-0376	Leonard S. Smith
Bags, except textile bags	377-0376	Leonard S. Smith
Fiber cans, drums, and similar products	377-0376	Leonard S. Smith
Sanitary paper products	377-0376	Leonard S. Smith
Paper coating and glazing	377-0132	Iris A. Dean
Pressed and molded pulp goods	377-0132	Iris A. Dean
Other converted products	377-0132	Iris A. Dean

Metal Cans, Glass Containers, and Plastic Bottles	377-0613	Richard Blassey
Mining	634-1036	Barry Klein, Phillip Yasnowsky
Coal	377-1466	Erast N. Borissoff
Crude Petroleum and Natural Gas	252-1452	Gerard L. Lagace
Petroleum Refining	252-1347	Gregory P. Filas
Chemicals and Allied Products		
Ceramics	377-0128	Sobhag Narain
Regulations in the chemical industry	377-2565	J. B. Cox
Industrial Chemicals		
Alkalies and chlorine	377-0128	Sobhag Narain
Industrial gases	377-0128	Sobhag Narain
Industrial inorganic chemicals, NEC	377-0128	Sobhag Narain
Organic chemicals	377-0128	David H. Blank
Agricultural Chemicals	377-0128	Francis P. Maxey
Rubber and Plastics Materials	377-0128	David H. Blank
Coatings and Adhesives	377-0128	David G. Rosse
Cleaning Preparations and Cosmetics	377-0128	Leo McIntyre
Drugs	377-0128	Leo McIntyre
Rubber and Plastics Products	377-0128	David H. Blank
Ferrous Metals		
Steel mill products	377-0606	Ralph Thompson
Ferrous castings	377-0610	Robert A. Ricciuti
Nonferrous Metals		
Copper	377-0575	Robert C. Reiley
Lead	377-0575	David Stonfer
Zinc	377-0575	David Stonfer
Aluminum	377-0575	James S. Kennedy
Titanium	377-5157	James J. Manion, Jr.
Nickel	377-5158	Graylin W. Presbury
Platinum-group metals	377-5157	James J. Manion, Jr.
Tungsten	377-5125	Seward L. Jones
Nonferrous castings	377-0610	Robert A. Ricciuti
Metalworking Equipment		
Machine tools	377-0315	John A. Mearman
Flexible manufacturing systems	377-0315	John A. Mearman
Robotics	377-0315	John A. Mearman
Numerical controls	377-0315	John A. Mearman
Tools, dies, jigs, fixtures, and contract machining	377-0315	John A. Mearman
Metal-cutting tools	377-0316	Paul Sacharov
Power-driven hand tools	377-0312	Edward D. Abrahams
Foundry equipment	377-0316	Paul Sacharov

Industrial heating equipment	377-0316	Paul Sacharov
Welding apparatus	377-0316	Paul Sacharov
General Industrial Machinery	377-0305	Rolf F. Nordlie
Construction machinery	377-0679	John A. Lien
Pumps and compressors	377-0680	Edward J. McDonald
Miscellaneous internal combustion engines	377-0305	Rolf R. Nordlie
Blowers and fans	377-0312	Edward D. Abrahams
Air-conditioning, refrigeration, and heating equipment	377-4831	David L. Horridge
Special Industrial Machinery	377-0309	William E. Fletcher
Farm machinery	377-0679	John A. Lien
Mining machinery	377-0680	Edward J. McDonald
Oil field machinery	377-0680	Edward J. McDonald
Food products machinery	377-0310	Irvin Axelrod
Textile machinery	377-3509	Tyrena L. Holley
Paper industries machinery	377-0312	Edward D. Abrahams
Printing trades machinery	377-5956	Alexis Kemper
General Components	377-4810	William Fletcher
Power Equipment	377-4381	David S. Climer
Electrical Equipment	377-0682	Richard A. Whitley
Printing and Publishing	377-0379	William S. Lofquist
Newspapers	377-0379	William S. Lofquist
Periodicals	377-0380	Rose Marie Zummo Bratland
Book publishing	377-0379	William S. Lofquist
Book printing	377-0379	William S. Lofquist
Miscellaneous publishing	377-0379	William S. Lofquist
Commercial printing	377-0379	William S. Lofquist
Business forms	377-0380	Rose Marie Zummo Bratland
Greeting card publishing	377-0380	Rose Marie Zummo Bratland
Lithographic platemaking services	377-0380	Rose Marie Zummo Bratland
Computer Equipment and Software		
Computer equipment	377-0571	Raymond C. Ahlberg
Computer equipment	377-2053	Peggy Keshishian
Computer equipment	377-0574	Joyce Watson
Computer software	377-2990	Tim Miles
Radio and Television Communication Equipment	377-2872	Arthur Pleasants
Telephone and Telegraph Equipment and Services	377-4466 377-2006	Joseph F. Kellagher William J. Sullivan
Electronic Components	377-2957	Robert Eckelmann
Instruments for Measurement, Analysis, and Control	377-5466	Margaret T. Donnelly
Medical and Dental Instruments and Supplies	377-0550	Emily Arakaki
Photographic Equipment and Supplies	377-0574	Joyce Watson

Motor Vehicles

Passenger cars	377-0669	Robert V. Coleman
Trucks and buses	377-0675	John Hartmann
Motor vehicle parts and stampings	377-1419	Deborah A. Semb
Truck and bus bodies (including motor homes)	377-0675	John Hartmann
Truck trailers	377-0675	John Hartmann

Aerospace	377-0677	Randy Myers, Gene Kingsbury
Shipbuilding and Repair	426-5841	Thomas Vodicka, Edward Carlson
Railroad Freight Cars	377-0305	Rolf R. Nordlie

Basic Foods

Overview of food and beverage processing sector	377-2428	Cornelius F. Kenney
Meat and meat products	377-3346	Donald A. Hodgen
Processing fruits, vegetables, and specialities	377-3346	Donald A. Hodgen
Dairy products	377-2250	William V. Janis

Confectionary and Baked Goods

Confectionary products	377-2428	Cornelius F. Kenney
Bakery products	377-2250	William V. Janis
Cereal breakfast foods	377-2250	William V. Janis

Beverages

Alcoholic beverages	377-2428	Cornelius F. Kenney
Bottled and canned soft drinks	377-2428	Cornelius F. Kenney

Tobacco	377-2428	Cornelius F. Kenney
Textiles	377-4058	Kim Ilich
Apparel	377-4058	Giselle Jenkins-Picard

Leather and Leather Products	377-4034	James E. Byron
Leather tanning and finishing	377-4034	James E. Byron
Shoes and slippers	377-4034	James E. Byron
Luggage and personal leather goods	377-2132	Judith Corea

Household Consumer Durables	377-1178	John M. Harris
Household appliances	377-1178	John M. Harris
Household furniture	377-1140	Michael J. Maasen
Consumer electronics	377-0570	E. MacDonald Nyhen

Jewelry, Housewares, Kitchenware, and Tableware	377-1178	John M. Harris

Toys, Games, and Musical Instruments

Dolls, toys, games, and children's vehicles	377-1140	Michael Maasen
Musical instruments and parts	377-2132	Judith Corea

Bicycles, Motorcycles, Sporting and Athletic Goods, and Lawn and Garden Equipment	377-5127	Kevin Ellis

Information Services

Computer (data processing) services	377-4781	John E. Siegmund
Videotex and teletext	377-5820	Mary C. Inoussa
Electronic data base services	377-5820	Teri Flynn
Research and development	377-4781	Stephan Wasylko

Transportation Services

Airlines	377-5071	Frederick T. Elliott
Trucking	275-6854	E. Brinkley Garner
Railroads	426-7574	Joel P. Palley
Water transportation	426-4388	Frank Pentti

Wholesale Trade	377-4581	Theodore A. Nelson

Retail Trade

Food retailing	377-2428	Neil Kenney
Department, drug, apparel, furniture and eating places	377-3050	Marvin J. Margulies
Motor vehicle dealers	377-0342	Andrew Kostecka

Advertising	377-4581	Theodore A. Nelson
Hotels and Motels	377-4581	J. Richard Sousane
Travel Services	293-1040	Douglas C. Frechtling
Motion Pictures	377-4581	Theodore A. Nelson
Commercial Banking	377-0339	Wray O. Candilis
Savings Institutions	377-6763	Joseph A. McKenzie
Insurance	377-0347	Thomas R. Fenwick
Equipment Leasing	377-0346	M. Bruce McAdam
Franchising	377-0342	Andrew Kostecka
Health and Medical Services	377-0350	Simon Francis
Educational Services	377-0350	Simon Francis
Management, Consulting, and Public Relations Services	377-0346	M. Bruce McAdam
Operations and Maintenance Services	377-0345	J. Marc Chittum
Architectural and Engineering Services	377-5226	Jack Randolph

■ ■

LOCAL COURTS

Civil and criminal court actions can provide excellent source material for company investigations. Perdue, Inc., a private corporation in Maryland, revealed its annual sales figures while fighting Virginia sales tax in the courts. A recent search revealed four related financial suits filed against a large privately held campaign fund-raising firm in McLean, Virginia. If you are not near the court it may be worth hiring a local freelance reporter or researcher to help you. In most jurisdictions there are chronological indexes of both civil and criminal cases which are kept by the clerk of the court. These indexes record all charges or complaints made, the names of the defendants and plaintiffs in the event of civil cases, the date of the filing, the case number, and the disposition if one has been reached. Armed with the case number, you can request to see the case files from the clerk.

BETTER BUSINESS BUREAUS

In addition to the complaint history on a particular company, you can call your local Better Business Bureau to obtain some general business information, such as how long a company has been in business, if it has been incorporated and a description of its business principles.

Data Center
464 19th Street
Oakland, CA 94612   415-835-4692
The staff here offers a specialized research service on corporations charging a per hour and a per page fee. Such searches will be too costly for the average individual, but the center maintains a library of newspaper and periodical clippings on labor, corporate, and industry topics. It is open to the public Monday through Thursday from 1 P.M. to 5 P.M. and until 9 P.M. on Wednesday night. In the library you can find the Center's monthly *Corporate Responsibility Monitor,* a hundred-page collection of "the best of the press" on corporate responsibility for each previous month, including articles from the *New York Times, Washington Post, Los Angeles Times,* and other major publications. The cost of a year's subscription to the *Monitor* is $420.

Document Retrieval Services
The fastest way to get SEC documents may be through one of the many document retrieval companies which provide this service. Two of the major firms, described below, have toll-free numbers which you can call to find out if the company you are investigating has filed with the SEC. If it has, you can either purchase a copy from the retrieval firm or try your local library, where some SEC documents can be found on microfiche.

Before you order any of these SEC filings from a retrieval company, it is wise to ask for the total number of pages contained in each of the documents you want to obtain. Most of these firms charge by the page and you don't want to be surprised if a company's amendment to its 10-K (annual federal report) happens to run 500 pages in length.

Bechtel Information Services
1570 Shady Grove Road
Gaithersburg, MD 20877
301-258-4300
800-231-DATA

SEC has contracted Bechtel to film its documents and speed up their availability to the public. Bechtel can provide copies in microfiche, tape, diskette, and all forms of electronic transmission, as well as in hard copy at an average cost of between twenty and fifty-nine cents a page. You can get hard copy in about a week, but rush service is available at a higher cost.

Disclosure, Inc.
5161 River Road, Building 60
Bethesda, MD 20817
800-638-8241
301-951-1300

Copies of public corporation documents filed with the SEC and with the National Association of Securities Dealers are available from Disclosure, Inc. The company will send you hard copy in twenty-four hours, but if you are near one of Disclosure's demand centers in New York, Chicago, Los Angeles, or Washington, DC, you could receive it in as little as two hours. The prices are set according to document. For example, a 10-Q (quarterly federal report) is $5, a 10-K is $25, and an Annual Report to Shareholders is $15. Disclosure provides copies on tape, microfiche, compact disk, and on-line as well.

Other document retrieval companies include:

Cunningham & Hamlette
3815-B W Street, SE
Washington, DC 20020
202-789-2151

Federal Document Retrieval, Inc.
514 C Street
Washington, DC 20002
202-628-2229

Warren O. Flood Filing Service
82 T Street, NW
Washington, DC 20001
202-289-0239

Research Information Services
210 G Street, NE
Washington, DC 20002
202-737-7111

FACS, Inc.
73 Tremont Street #425
Boston, MA 02108
800-424-9428

Charles E. Simon & Company
1333 H Street, NW
Washington, DC 20005
202-289-5300

Washington Service Bureau
655 15th Street, NW
Washington, DC 20005
202-833-9200

Washington Document Service
450 5th Street, NW, Suite 1110
Washington, DC 20001
202-628-5200

Federal Regulators

The Securities and Exchange Commission is just one of the dozens of federal agencies that collect information on companies. However, with about 10,000 companies filing there it represents only a tip of the company information iceberg. The twenty-six agencies listed below collect information on over 100,000 companies. They are each involved in regulating specific industries and the companies within those industries. The information held at each office varies from agency to agency; however, most of the offices maintain financial or other information that most researchers would consider sensitive.

AIRLINES, AIR FREIGHT CARRIERS, AND AIR TAXIS

Office of Community and Consumer Affairs
US Department of Transportation
400 7th Street, SW, Room 10405
Washington, DC 20590
202-755-2220

AIRPORTS

Air Traffic Service Division
National Flight Data Center
Federal Aviation Administration
800 Independence Avenue, SW
Washington, DC 20591
202-426-3666

BANK HOLDING COMPANIES AND STATE MEMBERS
OF THE FEDERAL RESERVE SYSTEM

Freedom of Information Act Office
Board of Governors of the Federal Reserve System
20th Street and Constitution Avenue NW, Room B1122
Washington, DC 20551
202-452-3684

BANKS, NATIONAL

Communications Division, Public Affairs
Comptroller of the Currency
490 L'Enfant Plaza East, SW
Washington, DC 20219
202-447-1800

BARGE AND VESSEL OPERATORS

Financial Analysis, Tariffs
Federal Maritime Commission
1100 L Street, NW
Washington, DC 20573
202-523-5876

CABLE TELEVISION SYSTEM OPERATORS

Cable TV Bureau
Federal Communications Commission
1919 M, Street NW, Room 242
Washington, DC 20554
202-632-7480

COLLEGES, UNIVERSITIES, VOCATIONAL SCHOOLS, AND PUBLIC SCHOOLS

National Center for Educational Statistics
1200 19th Street, NW
Washington, DC 20208
202-254-6503

COMMODITY TRADING ADVISERS, COMMODITY POOL OPERATORS, AND FUTURES COMMISSION MERCHANTS

Commodity Futures Trading Commission
2033 K Street, NW
Washington, DC 20581
202-254-8630

CONSUMER PRODUCTS

Corrective Actions Division
US Consumer Product Safety Commission
5401 Westbard Avenue
Bethesda, MD 20816
301-492-6608

ELECTRIC AND GAS UTILITIES AND GAS PIPELINE COMPANIES

Federal Energy Regulatory Commission
US Department of Energy
825 North Capitol Street, NE
Washington, DC 20426
202-357-8370

EXPORTING COMPANIES

American International Traders Register
World Traders Data Reports Section
US Department of Commerce
Washington, DC 20230
202-377-4203

FEDERAL LAND BANK AND PRODUCTION CREDIT ASSOCIATIONS

Farm Credit Administration
1501 Farm Credit Drive
McLean, VA 22102
703-883-4000

FOREIGN CORPORATIONS

World Traders Data Report
US Department of Commerce
Washington, DC 20230
202-377-4203

GOVERNMENT CONTRACTORS

Federal Procurement Data Center
4040 North Fairfax Drive, Suite 900
Arlington, VA 22203
703-235-1634

HOSPITALS AND NURSING HOMES

National Center for Health Statistics
3700 East-West Highway
Hyattsville, MD 20782
301-436-8500

LAND DEVELOPERS

Office of Interstate Land Registration
US Department of Housing and Urban Development
451 7th Street, SW, Room 6262
Washington, DC 20410
202-755-7077

MINING COMPANIES

Mine Safety and Health
US Department of Labor
4015 Wilson Boulevard
Arlington, VA 22203
703-235-1452

NONPROFIT INSTITUTIONS

US Internal Revenue Service
Freedom of Information Reading Room
1111 Constitution Avenue, NW
Washington, DC 20224
202-566-3770

NUCLEAR POWER PLANTS

Nuclear Regulatory Commission
1717 H Street, NW
Washington, DC 20555
301-492-7715

PENSION PLANS

Division of Inquiries and Technical Assistance
Office of Pension and Welfare Benefits Programs
US Department of Labor
200 Constitution Avenue, NW
Washington, DC 20210
202-523-8776

PHARMACEUTICAL, COSMETIC AND FOOD COMPANIES

Associate Commissioner for Regulatory Affairs
US Food and Drug Administration
5600 Fishers Lane
Rockville, MD 20857
301-443-1594

PESTICIDE AND CHEMICAL MANUFACTURERS

US Environmental Protection Agency
Office of Pesticides and Toxic Substances
401 M Street, SW
Washington, DC 20460
202-382-2902

RADIO AND TELEVISION STATIONS

Broadcast Bureau
Federal Communications Commission
1919 M Street, NW
Washington, DC 20554
202-632-7136

RAILROADS, TRUCKING COMPANIES, BUS LINES, FREIGHT FORWARDERS, WATER CARRIERS, OIL PIPELINES, TRANSPORTATION BROKERS, EXPRESS AGENCIES

US Interstate Commerce Commission
12th Street and Constitution Avenue, NW, Room 3145
Washington, DC 20423
202-275-7524

SAVINGS AND LOAN ASSOCIATIONS

Federal Home Loan Bank Board
1700 G Street, NW
Washington, DC 20552
202-377-6000

TELEPHONE COMPANIES, OVERSEAS TELEGRAPH COMPANIES, MICROWAVE COMPANIES

Public Land and Mobile Service
Common Carrier Bureau
Federal Communications Commission
1919 M Street, NW
Washington, DC 20554
202-632-6910

Harvard Business School Case Services

Harvard Business School
Boston, MA 02163   617-495-6117

Case studies of major and minor companies, as well as subsidiaries of public companies, can provide valuable competitive intelligence. Thousands of such cases are identified in a publication titled "Directory of Harvard Business School Cases and Related Course Materials." The cost is $10. The book is indexed under 700 subject headings and the actual investigations are sold for $2 each.

U.S. Securities and Exchange Commission
450 5th Street, NW
Publications Section, Reference Branch
Washington, DC 20549   202-272-7450

Administering the federal laws relating to the field of securities and finance, the SEC is charged with protecting investors and the general public in their securities transactions. All companies selling securities to the public must register details about their company and its securities with the SEC so that investors have the information they need to make a realistic appraisal.

While the SEC does not give advice about securities investments, it does allow the public access to the documents it collects. These include quarterly (10-Q) and annual (10-K) reports, registration statements, proxy material, and other reports. You can examine these materials at the four major SEC Documents Rooms listed below. If the company you are researching has its headquarters or main office in the area served by the SEC's Atlanta, Boston, Denver, Fort Worth, or Seattle regional offices, you may also be able to look at documents in the appropriate regional office. Contact the SEC's Public Affairs Office in Washington, DC, for further details. If you can't get to an SEC office, you can order copies of corporate disclosure documents for a fee of ten cents a page. A four-to-six-week turnaround can be expected.

To help the public gain quick access to its materials, the SEC has contracted with two document retrieval companies (both described earlier in this chapter) to supply records to the public. Both charge a fee for their services and can get you materials within twenty-four hours. It should be noted that these two companies do not charge anyone for calling their 800 number and asking if any given company is required to file with the Securities and Exchange Commmission. Some local libraries and business school libraries also have copies of SEC documents.

Companies file dozens of documents with the SEC. At a minimum you should obtain a copy of the company's annual report, known as the 10-K. This disclosure form will give you the most current description of the company's activities, along with its annual financial statement. In addition to the 10-K you may also want to see the company's most recent financial statements by obtaining copies of all 10-Qs filed since their last 10-K. 10-Qs are basically quarterly financial statements which will bring you up-to-date since the last annual report.

The two other documents that may be of immediate interest are the 8-Ks and the Annual Report to Stockholders. An 8-K will show you any major developments that have occurred since the last annual report, such as information about a takeover or major lawsuit. The Annual Report to Stockholders, the glossy quasi-public relations tool that is sent to all those who own stock in the company, can provide another component in assembling a company's profile. The most interesting item in this report, which is not included in the regular annual report, is the message from the president. The message often provides insights into the company's future plans.

The SEC's Publications Office offers several free publications, including:

■ *Investigate Before You Invest*—of interest to potential investors, it explains how to shop for securities and protect yourself from con artists.

■ *Welcome to the SEC's Public Document Room*—describes sixty-six documents that companies file with the Securities and Exchange Commission.

SEC's main Documents Rooms are:

Corporate Headquarters
450 5th Street, NW
Washington, DC 20549

New York Regional Office
26 Federal Plaza
New York, NY 10278

Chicago Regional Office
Everett McKinley Dirksen Building
219 South Dearborn Street, Room 1204
Chicago, IL 60604

Los Angeles Regional Office
5757 Wilshire Boulevard, Suite 500 East
Los Angeles, CA 90036-3648

State Regulators

State regulatory offices are among the best for gathering information about any business activity: public or private companies or their divisions or subsidiaries. Anyone doing business within a state has to file information on their activities with various state regulatory offices. The amount of information they file and where they file varies from state to state. This means that you cannot just go to one magic place and obtain all the information you need.

The strategy in dealing with state offices is to get any information whatever, because each piece may contribute to your overall information mosaic. Although a full picture may be out of reach, the office of uniform commercial code can tell you to whom the company owes money and give you a description of the corporation's assets. The state office of corporations may not give you the total sales figure but if the company is headquartered out of state it may tell you the corporation's total sales in that state and what percentage this is of its total. With a little bit of multiplication you can estimate the total sales.

If you are going to do any digging at the state level, the following three offices are a must. They offer the biggest potential for the least amount of effort.

OFFICE OF CORPORATIONS—Every corporation, whether it is headquartered or has an office in a state, must file some information with a state agency. The corporations division or office of corporations is usually part of the office of the secretary of state. When a company incorporates or sets up an office in the state it must file incorporation papers, or something similar, that provide—at a minimum—the nature of the business, the names and addresses of its officers and agents, and the amount of capital stock in the company. In addition to this registration, every company must file some kind of annual report. These annual reports may or may not contain financial data. Some states require sales figures, others just ask for asset figures.

OFFICE OF UNIFORM COMMERCIAL CODE—Any organization, and for that matter, any individual, who borrows money and offers an asset as collateral, must file within the state at the office of uniform commercial code. A filing is made for each loan and each of the documents is available to the public. To obtain these documents is a two step process. The first step is to request a search to see if there are any filings for a certain company. The fee for a search is usually under $10.00. Such a search will identify the number of documents filed against the company. You will then have to request copies of each of these documents. The cost for each document averages only a few dollars. This office of uniform commercial code is usually located near or in the same office of corporations.

STATE SECURITIES OFFICE—The U.S. Securities and Exchange Commission in Washington, D.C., regulates only those companies that sell stock in their company across state lines. There is another universe of corporations that sell stock in their companies only within state lines. For such stock offerings, complete financial information is filed with the state securities regulator. These documents are similar to those filed at the U.S. Securities and Exchange Commission. But remember that the documents will vary from one state to the next and, equally important, the requirement of filing an annual report will differ from state to state. Usually a telephone call to the office in charge can tell you whether a particular company has ever offered stock intrastate. If so, you are in a position to get copies of these filings. Usually the secretary of state's office can refer you to the state's securities regulator. Because of differences between the fifty state governments, expect to make half a dozen calls before you locate the right office. Several starting places are described below with the simplest ones listed first.

STATE GOVERNMENT OPERATOR—The telephone information operator can give you the telephone number for the state government operator, and in turn you can ask for the phone number of the specific government office.

STATE DEPARTMENT OF COMMERCE—Now that every state is aggressively trying to get companies to expand or relocate to it, their state, these departments can serve as excellent starting points because they are familiar with the other government offices that regulate business. These departments have often established a "one-stop office" with a separate staff which is on call to help business find whatever information it needs.

STATE CAPITOL LIBRARY—Asking the state government operator to connect you to the state capitol library. A reference librarian can identify the state agency than can best answer to your queries.

DIRECTORIES—If you intend to dig around various state government offices frequently you might consider purchasing a state government directory. Usually the state office of administrative services will sell you a directory, or you might contact the state bookstore. If you want to purchase a directory that covers all fifty states consider:

> *Executive State Directory*—available from Carroll Publishing Company
> 1085 Thomas Jefferson Street, NW
> Washington, DC 20007
> 202-333-8620
> Cost is $125.

The three offices described above are only the starting places for information on companies. There are dozens of other state agencies that are brimming with valuable bits of data about individual corporations; these sources require a bit more care, however, because they can be used only under certain circumstances or require extra resourcefulness.

UTILITY AND CABLE TV REGULATORS—Utility companies are heavily regulated by state agencies, and as a result there is a lot of financial and operational information about them available. Most people know that gas and electric companies fall into this category, but you may not be aware that this also applies to water companies, bus companies, rail systems, telephone companies, telecommunications companies, and cable TV operators.

OTHER STATE REGULATORS—State government is very similar to the federal government in that its function is to regulate many of the activities of the business community. In those states where state laws and enforcement are very effective the federal government relies on the state to enforce the federal laws. For example, the U.S. Food and Drug Administration will use the records from the state of New Jersey for information on pharmaceutical manufacturers rather than sending out its own team of federal data collectors. The U.S. Environmental Protection Administration will use state records in those states that have strict environmental statutes rather than using its own resources.

FINANCIAL INSTITUTIONS—Banks, savings and loans, credit unions, and other financial institutions all file information with the state bank regulator. Many of these organizations are also regulated by federal agencies, so what you get from the state office often will be a copy of the form filed with the federal government.

ENVIRONMENT REGULATORS—Almost every state has an office that regulates pollutants in the air, water, and ground. Such departments are similar to the U.S. Environmental Protection Agency in Washington, D.C., and monitor new and old business for pollution of the environment. If the company you are investigating has plans to build a new plant in the state, get ready to collect some valuable information. Before construction can begin, the company must file information with the state environmental protection agency. These documents will detail the size of the plant, what kind of equipment it will use, and how much this equipment will be used. With such information, other manufacturers in the same business can tell exactly what the capacity and estimated volume of the plant will be. Sometimes there will be three separate offices with authority over air, water, or solid waste. Each will collect basically the same information, and they can be used, one against each other, to ensure that you get all the information you need.

ECONOMIC DEVELOPMENT—As mentioned earlier, every state is now trying actively to attract and develop business development within the state. The state's office of economic development or department of commerce is normally charged with this responsibility. To attract business to the state this agency has to know all about existing business throughout the state, which translates into who is doing what, how successful they are, and how large the company is. At a minimum, the economic development office can probably provide you with information on the number of employees of a given company. They will also be aware of records that other state government offices keep about the industry or company that interests you. The experts at this state agency are similar to the hundred industry analysts at the U.S. Department of Commerce, and can serve as excellent resources for collecting government information on an industry.

STATE GOVERNMENT CONTRACTORS—Although many states are not accustomed to sharing information with researchers, you should be able to obtain details about any purchase the state makes. If the company in question sells to the state, you should get copies of their contracts. Just like the federal government, which makes all this procurement information available, the public funds that the state spends guarantee that the public right to know how the money is being spent is upheld. You may have to enforce your rights under the state law, which is equivalent to the federal Freedom of Information Act.

MINORITY AND SMALL BUSINESS—Many states maintain special offices that track minority firms and other small companies. These offices can be helpful not only in identifying such businesses but may also be able to tell you the size or products of a given business. The small business office and possibly a separate minority business division normally fall under the state department of commerce.

ATTORNEY GENERAL—The state attorney general's office is the primary consumer advocate for the state against fraudulent practices by businesses operating within the state. So if the company you are investigating is selling consumer services or products it would be worth the effort to check with this office. In some states the attorney generals have begun to concentrate on certain areas. For example, the office in Denver specializes in gathering information on companies selling energy-saving devices, while that in New York investigates companies with computerized databases that provide scholarship information.

FOOD AND DRUG REGULATORS—Any company that produces, manufactures, or imports either food or drug products is likely to come under the jurisdiction of the state food and drug agency. This office makes routine inspection of facilities and the reports are generally accessible; however, a Freedom of Information Act request is sometimes necessary.

Suppliers, Observers, and Other Industry Sources

If these documentation sources fail to provide you with the information you need on a given company, your last resort is to go directly to the industry and try to pull the information out by talking with insiders.

Your first step is to begin casting around for someone in the industry who knows about the company in question. When hunting for an expert it is essential that you remain optimistic about finding one or several individuals who will have useful information.

People who know their industry will be able to give you the details you need about any company (i.e., its size, sales, profitability, market strategies). These sources will probably not be able to give you the precise figure on the balance sheet or profit-and-loss statement, but they will offer a very educated guess, likely to be within 10 to 20 percent of the exact figure. And usually this estimate is good enough for anyone to work with.

The real trick is finding the right people—the ones who know. Talk to them and get them to share their knowledge with you. How you treat them on the telephone will directly influence how much information they are willing to give you.

Industry experts are not concentrated in Washington, D.C., but are located all over the world, so you need to exercise some common sense to figure out where to find them. Here are some general guidelines:

The two reference sources—along with your telephone, an essential and perhaps the best research tool—that will help you track down industry specialists include:

■ *Encyclopedia of Associations*—this volume, published every August, provides the location, objectives, and other essential aspects of more than 17,700 trade associations, professional societies, labor unions, and similar groups that collect data and are therefore potential sources of information about the companies that are part of their association or industry. It is available at most libraries or can be purchased for $210 from Gale Research Company, Book Tower, Detroit, MI 48226, 313-961-2242.

■ 100 Industry Analysts at the US Department of Commerce—these analysts spend their careers studying the major industries in our country as well as the companies that comprise those industries. They can be contacted at: Industry Analysts, International Trade Administration, U.S. Department of Commerce, Room 442, Washington, DC 20230, 202-377-1461.

Other sources of experts who can provide you with company information are:

INDUSTRY OBSERVERS—These are specialists on staff at trade associations, think tanks, and at the U.S. Department of Commerce or the other government agencies. Anyone who concentrates on an industry has familiarity with the companies that comprise that industry.

TRADE MAGAZINES—You will find that there is at least one magazine that reports on every industry. The editors and reporters of these trade publications are also well acquainted with individual companies.

SUPPLIERS—Most industries have major suppliers, which must know about the industry they service and the companies within that industry. For example, the tire manufacturers anticipate every move among auto makers well before any other outsiders. Suppliers also have to know the volume of every manufacturer to whom they sell or intend to sell to, because of the obvious repercussions on the supplier's business. Every company is like this, even Information USA, Inc. We are basically a publisher, and if you talked to our printer you would get a pretty good picture of what we are doing.

WHAT TO READ

How to Read a Financial Report
Merrill Lynch, Pierce, Fenner & Smith, Inc.
111 19th Street, NW
Washington, DC 20036   202-659-7222
Designed to help you grasp the facts contained in corporate financial reports, this thirty-page booklet is available from your local Merrill Lynch

office. Using a mythical corporation as a model, the booklet explains step-by-step how to read a balance sheet. Free.

NASDAQ Company Directory

National Association of Securities Dealers
NASD Information Department
1735 K Street, NW
Washington, DC 20006   202-728-8000

Updated annually, this directory makes getting information on over-the-counter (OTC) stocks easier. It lists investor contacts, addresses, and phone numbers for around 3,600 actively traded OTC companies. The cost is $5.

1985 Shareholders Meetings

Ernst & Whinney
2000 National City Center
Cleveland, Ohio 44114   216-861-5000

Written for management but useful for investors as well, this twenty-two-page booklet lists sample queries that could come up in shareholder meetings. The questions pertain to areas such as overall operations, growth expectations, and the effect of recent tax legislation. Free.

Industry Information and Market Studies

The next time your broker calls and tells you that the industry of the future is something called biotechnology or your brother-in-law calls to borrow money from you to start his business developing educational software, you don't have to take their word for it that the industry they want you to put your money into is the wave of the future. You don't even have to rely on all the industry reports given to you by those who are biased in wanting to get your money. You can find independent data, market studies, reports, and professional expertise by contacting the sources in this chapter.

This section will show you how to identify existing commercial market studies, use computerized databases without owning a computer, and tap the world's largest source of free market studies—the United States government. The most important of all of these is likely to be government studies. Not only are they normally free or low-cost, they are also more valuable. Unlike market studies done by commercial organizations, which may invest between six and twelve months on a project, a government organization is likely to invest millions of dollars and several years. Also, most investors, and even analysts, are unaware of the availability of such information; this creates an even greater opportunity.

In this section you will also learn how to tap one of the most valuable of industry sources—free industry experts. Such experts can not only help you cut through all the published reports and data, they are likely to be able to give you the exact answer you need off the top of their heads or lead you to information sources, reports, or studies no one else knows about.

AGENCIES, INSTITUTES, AND ORGANIZATIONS

Existing Market Studies

In order to find relevant market studies that have already been published, there are several bases to check.

First: The databases described above are likely to cover the news of currently released market studies.

Second: Many industries have market research firms which specialize only in that industry. To identify these firms contact one or all of the following:

■ Industry Analyst—The best place to find a free industry analyst is at the International Trade Administration, US Department of Commerce, Room 442, Washington, DC 20230, 202-377-1461.

■ Trade Association Specialist—These specialists can be identified through the *Encyclopedia of Associations,* which is available in any library or from

Gale Research Company, Book Tower, Detroit, MI 48226, 313-961-2242. The cost is $210.
- Trade Magazine Editors—These can be found by contacting either one of the first two choices.

Third: Contact those organizations which publish market studies on many industries. The major ones are as follows:

Predicasts, Inc.
11001 Cedar Avenue
Cleveland, OH 44106
800-321-6388 or
216-795-3000

International Resources
    Development Inc.
6 Prowitt Street
Norwalk, CT 06855
203-866-7800

Frost and Sullivan, Inc.
106 Fulton Street
New York, NY 10038
212-233-1080

Creative Strategies International
5300 Stevens Creek Boulevard
San Jose, CA 95129
408-249-7550

Arthur D. Little, Inc.
Acorn Park
Cambridge, MA 02140
617-864-5770

Business Communications Co.
9 Viaduct Road
PO Box 2070C
Stamford, CT 06906
203-325-2208.

Fourth: Review the major databases and publications which index available market studies for sale. These include:
- *FIND/SVP Reports and Studies Index*—This is both a database and a book which identifies studies available from Wall Street investment firms and management consulting firms. For more information contact FIND/SVP, 500 Fifth Avenue, New York, NY 10110, 212-354-2424.
- *INVESTEXT*—This database provides full text of research reports produced by Wall Street and regional investment banking companies. Contact: Business Research Corp., 1660 Soldiers Field Road, Boston, MA 02135, 800-622-7878 or 617-787-2205.
- *ADL/On-Line*—This database gives abstracts and/or executive summaries of Arthur D. Little studies. On-line access is available on DIALOG. For more information contact Arthur D. Little, Inc., Acorn Park, Cambridge, MA 02140, 617-864-5770.

Trade Associations

Many trade associations conduct market studies of their members and/or industries. These reports may or may not be included in the sources described above. It is worth contacting relevant associations directly to ensure that you have not missed an important report. To identify a relevant association use the *Encyclopedia of Associations* (see reference above). This book is well indexed and available at most libraries. The proper association can normally be identified with a quick phone call or visit to a local library. If you cannot find what you need in this encyclopedia, the American Society of Association Executives may be of further help. Contact: Information Central, American Society of Association Executives, 1575 Eye Street, NW, Washington, DC 20005, 202-626-2723.

You should be aware that some associations will not sell their studies to nonmembers. However, there are some ways you can circumvent this problem.

- *Join the association*—Some memberships can be relatively inexpensive.
- *Use the antitrust laws*—The association may be violating antitrust laws if they do not make the study available to nonmembers. This does not mean the organization cannot charge you a whole lot more than they do for members. And you must keep in mind that the ultimate action in pursuing this it to take the association to court. But it is worth trying because many associations are very concerned about the antitrust laws, and by simply mentioning that you are going to check with your legal counsel about possible antitrust violations may be enough to shake free the report. If you want to investigate further about how an association may be violating antitrust laws, obtain a copy of the *Antitrust Guide For Association Executives*. It is available from the American Society of Association Executives (see address above). This book explores association executives' worries and ways to avoid possible antitrust problems. The cost is $30.

Government Libraries

Many business researchers are unaware of the fact that if a $1,500 market study, like a Frost and Sullivan or Predicasts study, carries a copyright, it may be available for free at the Library of Congress in Washington. The Library receives two copies of all copyrighted material and usually adds these reports to its collection. The problem is that these companies are aware that people use the Library of Congress to see these studies and, as a result, they often wait for the last possible legal moment before filing their copyright. This can be three months or more after the study is published, which means that it may take several more months before it gets into the collection.

When we were preparing material for this book our researchers found hundreds of current market studies on such topics as: Videotex and Teletex markets, advertising, equipment leasing in Europe, robot vision systems, speech recognition and voice systems, microcomputer educational software for the home, consumer telephone equipment, uninterruptible power systems and power line conditioning equipment, and high-tech drug delivery systems.

If you get to Washington it will certainly be worth your time to visit the Library and discover market studies in your area of interest.

The Library is basically set up for visiting researchers, so it may be a bit

■ ■

MOST OFTEN REQUESTED SEC DOCUMENTS

Listed below are short descriptions of those documents investors most frequently request to see from the Securities and Exchange Commission:

10K: This is an annual report which companies must file within ninety days after the end of the company's fiscal year. It includes a description of business, financial statements and supplementary data, management's discussion and analysis of financial conditions, and information on all legal proceedings.

10Q: This form is filed quarterly within forty-five days of the close of each quarter. It includes financial statements, management's discussions of operations, and information on legal proceedings.

8K: This current report is used to report any material events or corporate changes which are of importance to investors. It provides more current information on certain events than forms 10Q and 10K. It must be filed within fifteen days of the event.

Schedule 13D: This schedule discloses who owns more than 5 percent of stock in a given company. The information must be filed within ten days after ownership occurs.

Schedule 14D-1: This schedule is filed by those making a tender offer for certain stocks that would, if accepted, cause the person to own over 5 percent of the stock. The information is filed at the time of the offer.

■ ■

more difficult, but not impossible, to see these studies if you do not go to Washington. However, you can arrange to obtain these studies through an interlibrary loan. The best way to do this is by knowing the name of the study and telephoning the Reference Section at the Library of Congress to see if it is in their collection (telephone number noted below). If it is, then ask how to arrange an interlibrary loan. Any local library will also be happy to work with you on this matter.

If you do not know the title of a particular market study it will be a bit harder to work remotely. The Library is not set up to do this sort of general reference work over the telephone. You can try calling the telephone reference number below to see what kind of assistance you can get with such an inquiry.If you do not get the help you need contact the office of your United States representative or senator. You can call their local office in your area or contact their Washington office by calling the Capitol Hill switchboard at 202-224-3121. What you should request is a list of Library of Congress holdings covering a specific subject area of interest. Requesting the titles of all

■ ■

INVESTMENT RATING SERVICES

Have you ever heard that a bond is rated AAA? Well, below is a description of the major companies which provide such ratings.

■ *Moody's Investment Service:* A subsidiary of Dun & Bradstreet, Moody's rates most of the publicly held corporate and municipal bonds and many Treasury and government agency issues. It also rates commercial paper, preferred and common stocks, and municipal short-term issues. Moody's publishes eight bound manuals on an annual basis, as well as a weekly or semiweekly supplement providing detail on issuers and securities. Moody's is located in New York, New York.

■ *Dun & Bradstreet:* Owned by Dun & Bradstreet Corp., it publishes the Commercial Credit Report, which provides credit information and ratings for commercial firms. Dun & Bradstreet owns thirty-seven other companies and is located in New York, New York.

■ *Standard and Poor's:* Owned by McGraw-Hill, it publishes fifty different reports classifying stocks and bonds according to risk. They rate virtually every possible investment instrument, including 11,000 corporate bonds.

■ *A. M. Best Co.:* This privately owned company publishes books and reports on the financial soundness, management, and history of insurance companies (health, life, property, and casualty). It is located in Oldwick, New Jersey.

■ ■

Frost and Sullivan reports would not be of value because the publisher's name is not always an index term. How successful you are at getting the Library to help may depend a lot on when you call and on how good you are at working with people over the telephone. You can contact the the Library directly at:

> Telephone Reference Section
> Library of Congress
> 10 1st Street, SE
> Washington, DC 20540
> 202-287-5180

The Library of Congress is not the only collection that carries copies of expensive market studies which can be viewed on sight or through an interlibrary loan. Practically every major federal agency has a library that collects studies in those fields within their jurisdiction. The National Library of Medicine contains hundreds of market studies relating to health care; the Department of Energy has studies about the oil and gas industry; the Department of Defense maintains surveys of the aerospace industry, etc. If you cannot figure out which government agency is responsible for certain industries, either of the following books may help:

- *US Government Manual*—This is available from Government Printing Office, Superintendent of Documents, Washington, DC 20402, 202-783-3238. This cost is $12.
- *Information USA*—This book, by Matthew Lesko, is available at local bookstores and public libraries. The cost is $22.95. The publisher is Penguin Books in New York City.

If you don't have time to obtain either of these books, the following free resources are designed to help you learn how the government can help you:

- *The local or Washington office of your member of Congress.*
- *Your local federal information center*—Part of the General Services Administration, these offices are identified in your local telephone directory under U.S. Government.
- *Government operator*—The main switchboard for the federal government can be reached by calling 202-254-6000.

U.S. Congress

Each year the United States Congress conducts several thousand hearings which either analyze proposed legislation or examine existing laws. In the same way that the government seems to affect every part of our lives, Congress seems to get involved in almost every aspect of business. This makes it a unique source of low-cost investment information which is usually not taken advantage of. A recent review of subject areas covered under the letter M in the 99th Congress revealed such topics as: mail-order business, major league sports community protection, malpractice insurance, malt beverage interbrand competition, management buyouts, management consultants, management information system, manganese, manufacturing industries, marathon running, marine energy resources, marketing of farm produce, materials handling, meat packing industry, and medical corporations.

An important aspect of a congressional hearing is that the committee in charge is usually very thorough in covering a subject. Often the best experts in the world present testimony or submit written comments. Committee staffers identify all available information sources and collect the latest research. Many times the committee will even commission a research study on the subject.

Documentation from committee hearings normally exists in a number of formats.

- *Published Reports*—It often takes six months to one year after the date of the hearing before the report is published. Sometimes the printed committee or subcommittee hearings can be obtained free from the professional staffers or the full-committee documents clerk. More popular transcripts on controversial subjects are frequently for sale from the

Government Printing Office, Superintendent of Documents, Washington, DC 20402, 202-783-3238.

■ *Printed Transcripts*—These are normally available within days after the hearing from commercial reporting services for as much as $1 or more per page.

■ *Prepared Testimony Presented by Witnesses*—These formal statements sometimes are released before the hearing date but usually a limited number of copies is available at the hearings. If you are trying to get this documentation and cannot wait until the hearing is printed, contact the committee or subcommittee staffer responsible for the hearing or call the witness directly to request a copy. These statements will also show up as part of the published hearing record.

■ *Studies Commissioned by Congressional Committees*—Such studies are usually conducted by the Congressional Research Service (CRS) of the Library of Congress. If copies are available they can be obtained from the CRS through your member of Congress.

■ *Comments Sent to the Committee by Interested Parties*—Such comments may or may not be included in the published hearing. However, they are part of the committee files and can usually be viewed in the committee office.

There are three basic sources for finding out if hearings have been held on a specific topic.

■ *Bill Status Office*—This can be the fastest source because, by accessing the LEGIS computerized database, congressional staffers can tell you over the phone if a bill was introduced on a specific topic. In addition to telling you which committees are working on the legislation, they can give you the status of a bill, who sponsored it, when it was introduced, and if similar bills have been proposed and their status. Although this database is limited because it does not cover investigative or "oversight" hearings it is still quite inclusive since the information goes back to 1975. If a committee held a hearing on a subject because of proposed legislation it is also likely to be responsible for oversight hearings on that subject. Telephone assistance is free and printouts are available for ten cents per page. If you cannot arrange easily to have the printout picked up by messenger, you may want to ask your representative or senator's office to have it sent to you. For more information contact the Office of Legislative Information, House Office Building Annex 2, 3rd and D streets, NW, Room 696, Washington, DC 20515, 202-225-1772.

■ *The Committees*—Contacting a committee or subcommittee directly is another way to identify relevant hearings. The problem with this approach is that there are approximately 300 from which to choose. You must be prepared to make a few calls before landing on target. What is good about this approach is that if the committee you call does not cover a particular subject area they will probably be able to tell you who does. Keep in mind that the jurisdictions of many committees overlap so it is necessary to check with all those committees when searching for valuable market information.

For help in finding a relevant committee contact any or all of the following:

Capitol Hill Switchboard
202-224-3121

If your subject area is an easy one like energy, or transportation, for instance, they should not have trouble directing you because such words are also part of the name of key committees.

LEGIS
202-225-1772

This bill status office contains the computerized database described above. These staffers can often tell you off the top of their heads which committees deal with specific issues.

House Parliamentarian
202-225-7373

Senate Parliamentarian
202-224-6128

These offices are very knowledgeable about the jurisdictions of all the committees.

Your Representative or Senator's Office

Call the Capitol Hill switchboard listed above for the Washington office of your member of Congress. Legislators' aides should be able to get you started; remember it is their job to help constituents.

Congressional Information Service

This commercial firm indexes and provides copies of all published committee hearings. This service has its limitations because many hearings are never published or are published a long time after the hearing has been held. Remember that copies of unpublished documentation can be obtained by using the methods described above. The complete service costs approximately $2,200 per year or $630 for the annual index. Most libraries are subscribers to this service. For more information contact Congressional Information Service, Inc., 4520 East-West Highway, Bethesda, MD 20014, 301-654-1550.

■ *Congressional Caucuses*—The Steel Caucus, the Textile Caucus, and several dozen other "informal" study groups which are composed of house members and senators frequently produce reports on particular industries. There is no complete listing of these caucuses so it is best to contact your member of Congress and have his or her staff investigate whether specific reports can be obtained from these legislative groups.

International Trade Commission
Docket Room
Office of the Secretary
701 E Street, NW, Room 152   202-523-00471
Washington, DC 20436   202-523-5178—24-hour ordering

Part of the function of this agency is to study the volume of imports in comparison with domestic production and consumption. As a result, it produces close to one hundred free market studies each year on topics ranging from ice hockey sticks to clothespins. Some of the studies recently released included:

> fresh-cut flowers
> malts and starches
> floor coverings
> body-supporting garments
> glass mirrors
> computers and calculators
> sewing machines
> loudspeakers
> forklift trucks
> brooms and brushes

If you are interested in publications produced prior to 1984, this office can send you a free copy of "Publications and Investigations of the United States Tariff Commission and the United States International Trade Commission." You can also request to be placed on a list to be notified of future studies. Free copies of any of the above publications can be ordered twenty-four hours a day, seven days a week by calling 202-523-5178. For further information contact:

Congressional Research Service Reports
The Congressional Research Service (CRS) is an important research arm of the Library of Congress and conducts custom research for the members of Congress on *any subject*. When a congressional committee plans hearings on a subject such as the insurance industry, the Congressional Research Service will often churn out a background report on the industry. Here are examples of some current free studies which may be of interest to the investors and others in the business community:

> compensation in the airline industry
> information technology for agriculture in America

financial innovations and deregulation: nonbank banks
the shrinking market for foreign cars in Japan
Wall Street analysts' reasons for the decline in U.S. production of
 primary petrochemicals
health information systems
attorney-client privilege
discount brokerage of securities: a status report
top corporate executive compensation and economic performance
economic statistics: sources of current information
industrial robots in the United States
domestic crude oil production projected to the year 2000
foreign steel production and U.S. market

Free copies of these reports can be obtained only by contacting your senator or representative's office. The Congressional Research Service also publishes an index to all their reports. Although this index is free it can be difficult to obtain. Contact your member's office for a copy. If they say they cannot get extra copies ask to have a copy sent to the district office so you can visit the member's local office and review the available reports. Oddly enough, the reports are easier to get than the index. You can write or call your member of Congress at one of the two short addresses noted here:

US Senate
Washington, DC 20510
202-224-3121

US House of Representatives
Washington, DC 20515
202-224-3121

Congressional Research Service Issue Briefs

Each day the Congressional Research Service updates 400 reports, called Current Issue Briefs. These reports are designed to keep members of Congress informed on timely topics. Listed below is a sampling of subjects covered.

advertising of alcoholic beverages in the broadcast media
CBS takeover attempts
greenmail and the market for corporate control
backyard satellite earth stations
wind energy
commercial banking competition
the Fortune 500: name, address, and officers of the 500 largest
 industrial corporations in the United States
genetic engineering
U.S. automobile industry: issues and statistics

foreign investment in the United States: trends and impact
why some coporations don't pay taxes
biotechnology
problems facing U.S. petroleum refiners

To receive a complete list of all Current Issue Briefs you must contact the office of your representative or senator.

Every month the Congressional Research Service publishes "Update," which includes a list of new and updated issue briefs of current interest. Briefs that are no longer of intense public or congressional interest are listed in the "Archived Issue Brief List." These publications, along with copies of the Issue Briefs listed above are available free from your member of Congress in the same manner as described previously under "Congressional Research Service Reports."

International Trade Administration
Central Records Unit
U.S. Department of Commerce
14th Street and Constitution Avenue, NW, Room 2802
Washington, DC 20230   202-377-1248

Each year the International Trade Administration at the U.S. Department of Commerce investigates dozens of industries for possible violation of anti-dumping laws. These statutes have been established to protect domestic manufacturers from foreign competition. When the government conducts an investigation the resulting documentation contains a complete market study of the industry in question. The following is a listing of the some of the industries the ITA has investigated since 1978:

butter cookies
iron ore pellets
moist towelettes
photo albums
ceramic wall tile
electric golf carts
ice cream sandwich
motorcycle batteries
electronic tuners
thin sheet glass

A complete listing of industries studied is available upon request. Copies of documentation from any of the above investigations are available for ten cents a page. The first fifty pages are free.

General Accounting Office
Distribution Section
441 G Street, NW, Room 1000
Washington, DC 20548   202-275-6241

This office conducts special audits, surveys, and investigations at the request of Congress. It produces as many as 600 reports annually, many of which provide market information. Below is a sample of some GAO reports.

> assessment of new chemical regulation under the toxic substances control act
> electronic marketing of agricultural commodities: an evolutionary trend
> SEC's efforts to find lost and stolen securities
> natural gas profit data
> the U.S. Synthetic Fuels Corporation's contracting with individual consultants
> information on historic preservation tax incentives
> licensing data for exports to non-communist countries

Single copies of reports are available free of charge and additional copies can be obtained for $1 each. You can also receive a free annual index of available GAO reports, a free monthly catalog of current reports, and a free printout from a database containing all reports released since 1976.

Federal Trade Commission
Public Reference Division
6th Street and Pennsylvania Avenue, NW, Room 130
Washington, DC 20580   202-523-3598

Besides the activities of the Department of Justice, the Federal Trade Commission also has the authority to investigate certain industries for possible antitrust violations. Recent FTC investigations include:

> travel industry
> motion picture industry
> bail bond industry
> business opportunity companies
> dental laboratories
> mail-order stamp sales
> tuna industry
> buying clubs
> hearing aid industry
> fine paper industry

You can obtain a more complete list or inquire if a specific company has been investigated by the Commission. Documentation is available for ten cents a page.

Industry Subject Specialists

The world is full of free experts who are willing to help you get the latest information on a given industry. An expert is many times better than any market study, however expensive. If there are many studies on a subject an expert can tell you what is good or bad about each one and what studies are going to be released in the near future. Frequently an expert can give you the information you need off the top of his or her head, and, of course, can also send you copies of reports sitting on his or her desk or give you an interpretation of trends or opportunities for the future. Finding an industry expert on your subject can be your most rewarding source. They will work for you for free if treated correctly and can provide you with information opportunities that other investors never use.

The organizations listed below according to subject can not only supply you with free industry experts in their subject areas but can also refer you to other experts in the industry.

AGRICULTURE AND COMMODITIES

Office of Information
US Department of Agriculture
Room 402A
Washington, DC 20250
202-447-8005
A staff of research specialists is available to provide specific answers or direct you to an expert in any agriculturally related topic.

National Agricultural Library
10301 Baltimore Boulevard
Beltsville, MD 20705
301-344-3755
Serves as an information clearinghouse on agriculturally related subjects.

Economics Research Service and
Statistical Reporting Service
US Department of Agriculture
14th Street and Independence Avenue, SW
Washington, DC 20250
202-447-2122
Contacts for agricultural production, stocks, prices, and other data.

ARTS AND ENTERTAINMENT

Performing Arts Library
John F. Kennedy Center
Washington, DC 20566
202-287-6245

Offers reference services on any aspect of the performing arts.

BEST AND WORST INDUSTRIES

US Department of Commerce
Washington, DC 20230
202-377-1461

Over one hundred analysts who monitor all the major industries in the United States and the companies within these industries, ranging from athletic products to truck trailers.

Office of Industries
US International Trade Commission
701 E Street, NW, Room 254
Washington, DC 20436
202-523-0146

Experts who analyze impact of world trade on United States industries ranging from audio components to x-ray apparatus.

BUSINESS ADVICE

US Department of Commerce
14th Street and Constitution Avenue, NW
Washington, DC 20230
202-377-3176—Roadmap Program
202-377-5511—Library

The Roadmap Program and the Library of the Department of Commerce provide reference services on all aspects of commerce and business.

COUNTRY EXPERTS

Country Officers
US Department of State
2201 C Street, NW
Washington, DC 20250
202-632-9552

Hundreds of experts are available to provide current political, economic, and other background information on the country they study.

Office of Export Promotion
International Trade Administration
US Department of Commerce
Washington, DC 20230
202-377-2954
Staff of country experts can provide information on marketing and business practices for every country in the world.

International Agriculture
Economic Research Service and Statistical Reporting Service
Office of Information
US Department of Agriculture
14th Street and Independence Avenue, SW
Washington, DC 20250
202-447-8005
Provides information on agricultural aspects of any foreign country.

Branch of Foreign Data
Mineral and Materials Supply and Demand
Bureau of Mines
US Department of Interior
2401 E Street, NW, Room W614
Washington, DC 20241
202-632-8970
Foreign country experts monitor all aspects of foreign mineral industries.

CRIME AND SECURITY

National Criminal Justice Reference Service
National Institute of Justice
Box 6000
Rockville, MD 20850
301-251-5500
Offers a database and reference service that provide bibliographies and expertise for free or sometimes a nominal fee on industries related to criminal justice, such as security, alarms, etc.

Uniform Crime Reporting Section
FBI
US Department of Justice
9th Street and Pennsylvania Avenue, NW, Room 6212
Washington, DC 20525
202-324-5038
Statistics on eight major crimes against person and property.

DEMOGRAPHICS, ECONOMIC AND INDUSTRY STATISTICS

Data Users Services Division
Customer Service
Bureau of the Census
Washington, DC 20233
301-763-4100
   Staff will guide you to the billions of dollars' worth of taxpayer-supported data.

ECONOMICS: NATIONAL, REGIONAL, AND INTERNATIONAL

Bureau of Economic Analysis
US Department of Commerce
Tower Building
Washington, DC 20230
202-523-0777
   This offices houses the nation's economists, who can provide information and analysis at both macro and micro levels.

EDUCATION

Educational Resource Information Center
National Institute of Education
1200 19th Street, NW, Brown Building
Washington, DC 20208
202-254-7934
   A network of sixteen information clearinghouses that can identify literature, experts, and more on any educationally related market. For educational statistics contact the National Center for Education Statistics, 202-254-6057.

ENERGY

Energy Information Center
US Department of Energy
1F048 Forrestal Building
Washington, DC 20585
202-252-8800
   Provides general reference services on all aspects of energy.

Conservation and Renewable Energy
Inquiry and Referral Service
PO Box 1607
Rockville, MD 20850
800-523-2929
800-462-4983—in PA
800-523-4700—in HI and AK

Free help on how to save energy as well as information on solar, wind, or any other aspect of renewable energy.

Technical Information Service
US Department of Energy
PO Box 62
Oak Ridge, TN 37830
615-576-1301
Provides research and other information services on all energy-related topics.

HEALTH

National Health Information Clearinghouse
PO Box 1133
Washington, DC 20013
800-336-4797
703-522-2590—in VA
For leads to both public and private sector health organizations, research centers, and universities on any health-related topic.

National Center for Health Statistics
US Department of Health and Human Services
3700 East-West Highway, Room 1-57
Hyattsville, MD 20782
301-436-8500
For data on any aspect of health.

HOUSING

Program Information Center
US Department of Housing and Urban Development
451 7th Street, SW
Washington, DC 20410
202-755-6420
Provides information on all aspects of housing and staff will direct you to a program which meets your needs.

IMPORT AND EXPORT STATISTICS

World Trade Reference Room
US Department of Commerce, Room 2233
Washington, DC 20230
202-377-2185
For data on many aspects of United States trade.

METALS AND MINERALS

Assistant Directorate of Minerals Information
Bureau of Mines
US Department of Interior
Columbia Plaza, Room 1035
Washington, DC 20241
202-634-1187
Dozens of commodity specialists collect, analyze, and disseminate information on the availability of mineral and other aspects of the mineral industry.

PRICES, EMPLOYMENT, PRODUCTIVITY, AND LIVING CONDITIONS STATISTICS

Bureau of Labor Statistics
US Department of Labor
441 G Street, NW
Washington, DC 20212
202-523-1913
Subject specialists in such areas as plant closings, labor force projections, producer price indexes, and work stoppages can provide information on demographics affecting most industries.

WORLD IMPORT AND EXPORT STATISTICS

Harvey Schultz
World Trade Statistics
US Department of Commerce, Room 1323
Washington, DC 20230
202-377-4855
For numbers concerning most countries.

WHAT TO READ

If you want to begin with traditional published sources start with a local library that is oriented toward the business community. A nearby university with a business school or a large public library can be good starting places. Many business libraries offer free or low-cost telephone research service. For example, the Brooklyn Public Library's Business Library (280 Cadman Plaza West, Brooklyn, NY 11201, 718-780-7800) will answer brief questions over the telephone and hold your hand in identifying information sources if you visit in person.

If you are not familiar with traditional published information sources, using the services of a research librarian can be an efficient way to find out exactly what there is that will be useful to you. If you are in a hurry, see what you can get over the telephone. If time is not critical it is worth visiting the library to become acquainted with local resources; even if these reference sources are not useful to you now, they probably will be in the future. Many of the questions we answer for clients at a rate of $75 an hour can be answered for free by a local reference librarian.

FOR COMPUTER USERS

There are currently some 3,000 to 5,000 sources of computerized databases available to the public which may contain industry information. Some of the more popular publications describing these sources include:

- *Databasics: Your Guide to Online Business Information* —The authors are Doran Howitt and Marvin I. Weinberger. The cost is $16.95. It is available from Garland Publishing, Inc., 136 Madison Avenue, New York, NY 10016.
- *The Computer Data and Database Sourcebook*—The author is Matthew Lesko. The cost is $14.95. It is available from Avon Books, 1790 Broadway, New York, NY 10019.
- *Directory of Online Databases*—The cost is $95. It is available from Cuadra Associates, Inc., 2001 Wilshire Boulevard, Santa Monica, CA 90403, 213-829-9972

Nearly all the major database vendors maintain files that contain marketing data. A review of any of the books cited above will help you pinpoint databases that may be helpful, or you can call BRS, DIALOG, and other database vendors directly. Some of the more popular databases, which contain marketing information on a wide variety of industries, are basically indexes and abstracts of current trade and business periodicals. Included in this category are: ABI/INFORM, Management Contents, Predicasts, NewsNet, and HAR-FAX Industry Data Souces.

If you are using databases for the first time, it may be wise to have someone else do your searching. Companies called information brokers will usually handle this for you. The best way to find available brokers is to contact your local reference librarian. They are in a good position to tell you what is available locally. If you have trouble with this method you may find help by calling DIALOG Information Services' Customer Service at 800-334-2564. They keep a list, by city, of organizations that will provide this service for you.

Be sure to ask if a nearby public, academic, or specialized library performs on-line retrieval services. If they do, it is probably going to be *much cheaper.* For example, the Brooklyn Business Library will do database searches and charge only for direct out-of-pocket costs. An information broker is likely to cost you three to four times more.

If you have a PC with a modem but have been reluctant to access the more complicated business databases, you can call EASYNET with your modem. They can be reached at 14 North Narberth Avenue, Narberth, PA 19072, 800-841-9553 or 215-667-8942. Their modem number is 1-800-EASYNET. This firm will search some seven major vendors for you and send the results to your computer. EASYNET covers the traditional marketing databases and claims that their average search cost is $17.

Freebies from Accounting Firms, Brokerage Houses, and Stock Exchanges

Hundreds of additional freebies are identified throughout the other chapters of this book. This section is a result of a survey of the the big 8 accounting firms, major brokerage houses, and stock exchanges to see what free (or nearly free) services and publications each offer the public. Described here is a sampling of what we found. Some places, such as the accounting firm Coopers and Lybrand, offer far more material than we could list. So we suggest you use this chapter as a starting point and then contact offices in your community to see what else is offered. Also note that there are many more freebies scattered throughout other sections of the book.

ACCOUNTING FIRMS

Arthur Anderson & Co.
Marketing Group (FSI)
60 West Washington Street
Chicago, IL 60602   312-580-0033

By contacting the office above, you can get a complete list of Arthur Anderson's newsletters and publications. Here are a few of their more interesting titles.

- *Executive Financial Planning*—published in 1981, a four-page action plan encompassing personal economic goals, including building wealth, educating children, preserving capital for retirement, assuring family security, providing for orderly transfer of estate. Order No. AA3036, Item 1.
- *Commodities*—published in 1983, sixty pages on the futures and physical markets in London discussing the accounting, internal control, and tax implications of transactions in these markets. Order No. COMM.
- *Oil Futures: A Management Information, Accounting and Taxation Guide*—published in 1983, sixty-four pages on the oil futures market in London and the accounting, tax, and internal control implications for companies and individuals who use the market. Order No. 2420-45.

Coopers & Lybrand
PO Box 682, Times Square Station
New York, NY 10108   212-536-3367

In an effort to share its knowledge with the general public, Coopers & Lybrand puts out a great deal of printed literature. Order the free catalogue described below to see what's of interest to you.

■ *Compendium of Published Material 1985*—seventy-two-page booklet listing current Coopers & Lybrand literature with short descriptions and publication dates. Publications arranged according to subject and listed alphabetically by title in an index. Such subjects as obtaining venture capital, retirement planning for professionals, charitable giving to colleges and universities, taxes, a number of reports and surveys on specific industries, periodicals, and published books are included.

Deloitte, Haskins & Sells
1114 Avenue of the Americas
New York, NY 10036   212-790-0500

Contact the New York office of Deloitte, Haskins & Sells listed above, or any of its branches across the country, to obtain these free publications.

■ *Personal Financial Planning 1985*—this forty-nine-page book provides you with ideas for year-end personal tax and financial planning. It will help you better analyze your tax and financial situation, take appropriate action to reduce taxes, and achieve your financial objectives. There is a summary of tax law developments for the year, and a description of the potential impact of tax reform on investment decisions.

■ *Preserving and Transferring Wealth: A Guide to Estate Planning*—its thirty-four pages cover such topics as the necessity of having a will, recent estate and gift tax legislation, how the taxes are computed, the marital deduction, life insurance, pension, profit-sharing or stock options, lifetime gifts, closely held businesses, and community property.

■ *Questions at Stockholders Meetings 1986*—a fifty-two-page book comprised of probing questions that should be asked, ranging from those about operating results to concerns about social issues. The first section of the book deals with questions of general interest that concern company performance and the economy, management and the board of directors, mergers and acquisitions, stockholder matters, social responsibilities, financial accounting and internal control. The second section of the book deals with certain industries that merit special consideration such as financial institutions, public utilities, broadcasting, health care, transportation, insurance, health care, high technology, food service, oil and gas, and more.

■ *Entrepreneur's Guidebook Series*—a four-book series containing the following titles: *Expanding Your Business Overseas; Forming R & D Partnerships; Strategies for Going Public;* and *Raising Venture Capital.* These books contain a lot of pertinent information on each subject. Each book is from 100 to 150 pages long.

■ ■

FREE FILMS AND VIDEOS

If you get tired of *reading* about investments all the time, try *watching* some of these free films and videos for investors:

Hedging Speculating; 49 minutes, color.
> Audiences enter the Chicago Board of Trade for an entertaining look at the mechanics of risk management. Viewers are escorted through the definitions and practical applications of long and short hedging, price discovery, and margins. Available in ¾-inch videocassette and ½-inch VHS. (No. 18532, Chicago Board of Trade)

Where the World's Market Forces Converge: The Chicago Board of Trade; 14 minutes, color.
> Describes the functions of the Chicago Board of Trade, what futures are, the roles of the hedger and speculator/investor, price-risk transfer, and the role futures play in the world economy. Available in 16 mm, ¾-inch videocassette, and ½-inch VHS. (No. 16636, Chicago Board of Trade)

Trademarks: The Name Game; 15 minutes, color.
> The Eric Bass Puppets play the parts of a trademark expert and two business partners with a new product in this introduction to an important business subject. Helping to choose a name for the product, the expert explains all the basic information on trademarks/brand names: their function, history, selection, clearance, and protection. Available in 16 mm and ¾-inch videocassette. (No. 20345, US Trademark Association)

The Federal Home Loan Bank System; 14 minutes, color.
> This animated show presents the story of the savings and loan industry. Its structure and operation and how the Federal Home Loan Bank System regulates and assists the federal savings and loan associations throughout America are shown. It also explains in simple terms the flow of mortgage and its effect on the national economy. Available in 16 mm, ¾-inch videocassette, and ½-inch VHS. (No. 11096, Federal Home Loan Bank Board)

EFT at Your Service; 14 minutes, color.
> Electronic banking is here. Viewers are shown how they can deposit, withdraw, and save money conveniently, safely, electronically. Explained are everyday banking functions and how, with the help of Federal Reserve's Regulation E, this remarkable service is possible. Available in 16 mm only. (No. 20301, Federal Reserve Board)

Investment Strategy for Busy People: The Mutual Fund Method; 15 minutes, color.
> Shows how busy people can benefit from a mutual fund investment strategy. Available in 16 mm only. (No. 17689, Investment Company Institute)

Plan for Retirement; 30 minutes, color.
> The difference between a retirement that is disappointing and one that is rewarding is proper planning. This slide/tape presentation illustrates how two couples, one younger and one older, set goals, examine financial resources, and anticipate future needs. (No. 22373, American Council of Life Insurance)

Your Estate: Planning with Your Beneficiaries; 30 minutes, color.
Most Americans today are concerned about future financial security. This slide/tape program will help prepare for the orderly transfer of an estate after death. It considers such basic topics as wills, life insurance, pensions, and employee benefits, financial tools familiar to most people. (No. 15643, American Council of Life Insurance)

These films are available on a free loan basis. You pay return postage only. Contact: Modern Talking Picture Service, 5000 Park Street North, St. Petersburg, FL 33709, 813-541-5763.

■ ■

Touche Ross & Co.
1633 Broadway
New York, NY 10019   212-489-1600
Touche Ross publishes a number of free, beautiful glossy brochures describing its services, accounting-related careers, various types of businesses, taxes, and more. The company's Washington, D.C., Service Center offers expertise in all matters relating to the federal government. The New York office, listed above, can refer you to the branch office nearest you and will send you any publications available.
A sampling of brochures follows:
■ *Proven Professionals*—an eighty-page catalog describing the services the company offers and the variety of industries it serves.
■ *Tax and Investment Profile: United States*—last published in May 1985 and updated periodically, this sixty-five-page booklet has information on a number of topics. Examples are establishing a business, accounting and auditing, branches of foreign companies, price control and antitrust legislation, patents, trademarks, copyrights, and all types of taxation.
■ *Helping You Succeed in the Changing Telecommunications Industry*—one of a number of Touche Ross publications on individual industries, this twelve-page booklet discusses the issues arising from the evolution of telecommunications.
■ *Health Care Horizons*—this informative forty-page booklet for hospital administrators covers such areas as trustee liability, improving relationships between hospital trustees and their administrators, the hospital audit committee and the external auditor, trends in hospital operations, and an analysis of hospital revenues and expenses which can be used to evaluate your institution's internal operations and departmental costs, and to facilitate financial planning.

BROKERAGE HOUSES

E. F. Hutton & Company, Inc.
One Battery Park Plaza
New York, NY 10004

800-334-4636
800-422-0214—in New York City
212-742-5000

E. F. Hutton puts out a number of brochures on all aspects of financial planning and investing. In addition to literature covering various types of investments, it offers the following educational material of a more generic nature:

- *Managing Your IRA*—this twenty-page brochure groups together different kinds of IRAs according to their element of risk, from CDs and annuities to mutual funds and unit investment trusts to self-directed IRAs. IRA facts are presented through a question-and-answer format.
- *Personal Financial Planning: Choosing Your Critical Path*—this six-page brochure discusses such questions as the nature of financial planning and who needs it; whether your net worth is growing; and how to choose the right organization to do your financial planning.
- *Financial Alternatives for Today*—this thirty-eight-page booklet offers a lot of information on the following areas: helping today's investors prepare for tomorrow, growth of capital, more income with greater safety, reduced risk through diversification, capital appreciation with less risk, tax-free income, direct investments, professional financial planning, life insurance and annuities.

Dean Witter Reynolds, Inc.
130 Liberty Street
New York, NY 10006

800-221-2685
212-524-2222

Potential clients of this full-service brokerage house can get information from its branch offices nationwide. Look in your phone book or call the number above for your closest office. In addition to investing publications, the offices offer video tapes on particular sales vehicles and market letters on informational subjects. Prospective clients may obtain the following books and brochures free of charge:

- *Understanding Wall Street*—this 218-page basic book about Wall Street is for the beginning investor. It explains what a share of stock is, how a company is organized, how stock prices are determined, how to identify the best companies, and how to read the stock tables, financial page and earnings tables; it also gives a Wall Street glossary and history and an analysis of securities.
- *Understanding the New York Stock Exchange*—this forty-five-page booklet describes the organization of the Stock Exchange, tells how preferred stock, common stock, bonds, debentures and warrants work.
- *Understanding the Securities Market*—this twenty-four-page booklet tells you step by step how to buy and sell stocks or bonds. It covers selling

short, dollar cost averaging, stock splits, and commissions, and describes the various exchanges.

■ *Understanding Financial Statements*—put out by the New York Stock Exchange and distributed by Dean Witter, this twenty-six-page booklet will help you understand annual reports, balance sheets, and statements of change in financial position through description of terms and sample financial statements.

■ *Glossary*—Dean Witter distributes this thirty-page booklet for the New York Stock Exchange. It makes the special language of America's investment world clear.

■ *Understanding Options*—this thirty-five-page brochure explores why you should consider options, tells how they are traded, how to buy and sell put and call options, and basic option strategies.

Merrill, Lynch, Pierce, Fenner & Smith, Inc.

Marketing Communications
800 Scudder's Mill Road   800-637-7455
Plainsboro, NJ 08540-9019   212-637-7455

Merrill Lynch offers 150 free brochures, all available from its branch offices. Call the toll-free number above to obtain the address and telephone number of the nearest office. Call the local office to learn if they have the printed materials on hand that interest you. A sampling of brochures is given below:

■ *The Catalog of Investments*—this twenty-three-page catalog serves as an introduction to the topic of investing and how it can help you achieve your financial goals. Subjects covered include managing savings dollars, meeting college costs, tax savings tactics, getting rich, financial planning, and worksheets for calculating your net worth and cash flow.

■ *How to Read a Financial Report*—if you aren't an accountant, and you find that annual reports are over your head, this comprehensive and well-written thirty-page booklet can help you grasp the facts contained in such reports and become a better-informed investor.

■ *You and Your Money*—this forty-page brochure is written for the novice and beginning investor. Ideas and information are presented on budgeting, minimizing taxes, retirement income, your estate, deferred annuities, investment choices, reading stock and bond quotations, and balancing risk and reward.

■ *The Bond Book*—this twenty-page brochure discusses how to be a good bond buyer, bonds for capital gains, kinds of bonds, municipal bonds, corporate bonds, and how to use bonds.

■ *Strategies for Aggressive Investors*—a twenty-three-page brochure on techniques for the investor with a net worth of $50,000 or more and an annual income of $60,000 or more. Covered are stocks on margin, selling short, stock options, call options, put options, futures, bonds on margin, interest-rate options, interest-rate call options, and interest-rate put options.

■ *Double Income Couples*—this thirty-one-page booklet gives worksheets, definitions of terms, and various investment goals depending on your age, income, and dependents.

■ *Investing in Stocks for Capital Appreciation, Income, and Total Return*—this twenty-page pamphlet discusses stocks for different investment objectives, how to match the stock with the objective, and the importance of research when you invest.

■ *Investing in Municipal Bonds for Tax-Free Income*—this thirty-one-page booklet covers kinds of bonds, interest on bonds, marketability, yields and prices.

■ *Insured Certificates of Deposit*—this eight-page pamphlet discusses safety, yield, liquidity, and zero-coupon CDs.

■ *A Guide to Credit Management*—a ten-page pamphlet that reminds you that managing what you owe is as important as managing what you own. Save yourself money through the strategic use of credit.

Prudential-Bache Securities, Inc.
Marketing Department
One Seaport Plaza
199 Water Street
New York, NY 10292   212-791-1000
    Prudential-Bache has prepared the following brochures for investors:

■ *GNMA Securities*—a nine-page description of the safety, yield, pricing, and trading of GNMAs, this tells how GNMAs work.

■ *Preferred Stock*—an eight-page glossary of terms and explanation of preferred stock in a question and answer format.

■ *Municipal Bonds*—a nine-page description of the types of municipal bonds, bond forms, features of bonds, and reasons for considering municipal bonds in your investment program.

■ *Zero Coupon Bonds*—a one-page, fold-out definition of zero coupon bonds, explanation of how the money appreciates, and types of bonds.

■ *Mortgage Collateralized Bonds*—a one-page fold-out of facts in a question-and-answer format, details of investing, and an explanation of why MCBs are issued.

■ *Unit Investment Trusts*—a six-page explanation of unit trusts, and the types available, with a listing of benefits of unit trusts.

Broker's Exchange
6941 N. Trenholm Road   800-845-0946
Columbia, SC 29206   803-273-2828
    Broker's Exchange does not publish anything itself, but they will send you copies of articles and research reports on specific stocks they have collected.

Discount Brokerage Corporation (DBC)   800-522-7292—in NY State
67 Wall Street   800-221-8210
New York, NY 10005   212-806-2888

Call the toll-free number above to get a daily market report or to speak with Discount Brokerage Corporation staff members. Anyone filling out an account application will receive:

■ *Standard & Poor's Outlook: Annual Forecast*—the sixteen-page 1985-86 issue covered the 1986 market outlook, groups of stocks best situated for 1986, ten stocks for action, a list of recommended issues, rapid-growth stocks, speculations for aggressive investors, and high-yielding stocks and bonds for income.

Discount Investments of America, Inc.
PO Box 92181   800-346-0413
Long Beach, CA 90809   800-346-0405—in CA

DIOA is something of a blend of a full-service brokerage firm and a discount brokerage firm. It offers a variety of investments similar to full-service firms, but does not have a research department. It offers commission rates at 75 percent less than full commission firms charge.

Publications are limited to one folder-brochure:

■ *DIOA Brochure*—in addition to describing the company, this folder has loose-leaf sheets with good, basic investing information, definitions, and investment comparisons. Mutual funds, treasuries, IRA/Keogh plans, GNMAs, municipal bonds, and stocks, bonds, and options are covered.

Fidelity Brokerage Services, Inc.   800-544-6666
82 Devonshire Street   617-523-1919—call collect in MA, AL
Boston, MA 02109   617-570-7000

Fidelity publishes several free explanatory brochures full of information and definitions, which may be obtained by calling or writing the above address. When we went to press, Fidelity was preparing additional brochures on mutual fund basics, discount brokerage, fees and loads, and a glossary of financial terms.

A listing of current publications follows:

■ *Fidelity Guide to Investor Information*—prepared to help you become a better independent investor, this twenty-nine-page pamphlet is a list of books, periodicals, newsletters, and statistical services to consult with titles, publishers, years of publication, and descriptions. Subjects covered include the stock market, money markets, bond markets, financial planning, general securities, mutual funds, and economics. The title, publisher, year of publication, and a description are given.

■ *Guide to College Financing*—this twenty-five-page pamphlet discusses systematic savings and savings vehicles, tax planning, and various forms of financial aid, with suggestions for additional reading.

■ *IRA Owner's Guide*—a twenty-eight-page pamphlet giving information on evaluating IRA investments, opening the account, managing your investment, "rollovers," record keeping, and withdrawing money from your IRA, with suggested reading.

■ *An Updated Guide to Keoghs: Qualified Retirement Plans for Self-Employed Individuals*—a twenty-page pamphlet discussing basic information, investment choices, kinds of plans, contributing to the plan, taking distributions, and transfers and rollovers.

Quick & Reilly, Inc.

120 Wall Street	800-221-5220
New York, NY 10005	212-943-8686

Studies and pamphlets are published periodically by Quick & Reilly. Call or write to see what might be available. Examples are the following two studies reporting on selected stocks:

■ *NYSE Dividend Study*—this four-page study contains more than 250 NYSE stocks which have boosted their dividends every year for the last ten years. For each stock, the study shows dividends paid in 1975, dividends paid in 1985, overall percentage increase from 1975 to 1985, and the compounded annual percentage increase for the ten-year period.

■ *NYSE Worksheet*—this four-page worksheet includes more than 200 NYSE-listed stocks which have demonstrated the tendency to make sizable intra-year price moves. For every year of the last five years, the difference between each stock's low and high has been at least 50 percent (or at least 250 percent for the whole five-year span).

Spear Securities

626 Wilshire Boulevard, Suite 708	800-821-1902
Los Angeles, CA 90017	800-321-6116—in CA

This company operates a twenty-four-hour-a-day, seven-day-a-week computer investment center which may be accessed through a personal computer or communicating terminal. Using this center you can do trading, get up-to-the-minute quotes, and obtain analysis of public company securities. Contact Spear Securities for further details.

Unified Management Corporation

20 North Meridian Street	
600 Guarantee Building	800-233-4824
Indianapolis, IN 46204	317-634-3300

By obtaining a password, Unified clients can access the company's computer rating system on investments. Contact the office above for further information.

York Securities, Inc.
44 Wall Street   800-221-3154
New York, NY 10005   212-425-6400
    York Securities distributes the following sixty-two-page booklet providing
a good deal of information on standardized options:
        ■ *Characteristics and Risks of Standardized Options*—covers options no-
        menclature, tax considerations, risks of buying and writing options, stock
        options, index options, debt options, and foreign currency options.

STOCK EXCHANGES

    Most of the stock exchanges described below can provide you with
listings of the members and securities traded. Some also have general investment information. The New York Stock Exchange (NYSE) and the American
Stock Exchange (AMSE) are regarded as national securities exchanges. Both list
a large number of securities from firms dispersed across the country. The
regional exchanges, namely the Boston Stock Exchange, Midwest Stock Exchange, Pacific Stock Exchange, and Philadelphia Stock Exchange, operate in
much the same way as the NYSE and AMSE. Since small, local companies are
not listed on the national exchanges, the regional exchanges serve to provide
trading facilities for such companies. The regional exchanges also serve the
needs of local brokers who are not members of either of the national exchanges. Several other exchanges, as well as NASDAQ, the over-the-counter
quotations system, are also described below.

American Stock Exchange (AMEX)
86 Trinity Place
New York, NY 10006   212-306-1000
    AMEX conducts trading in a wide range of securities including common
stocks, warrants, put and call options on stocks, stock indices and U.S. Treasury securities. Additionally, AMEX conducts trading in corporate bonds, U.S.
government and government agency securities, and gold coins. It plans to start
trading options on gold bullion through a subsidiary market. You can obtain a
list of AMEX-listed companies as well as a list of member firms with seats on
the exchange from Delia Emmons, secretary and vice-president.
    AMEX has available a list of current publications, including options publi-
cations and several audiovisual materials. AMEX recommends that you obtain
options-related literature from your broker.

Boston Stock Exchange, Inc.
One Boston Place
Boston, MA 02108   617-723-9500
    As a participant in the Intermarket Trading System, which electronically
links all the nation's major exchanges, the Boston Stock Exchange provides all

of the same services of the larger national exchanges. The Exchange is an incorporated association of members providing facilities for trading in the equity securities of over 900 national and international corporations. To trade on the Boston Exchange, one must be a member. Currently there are 194 members representing specialist firms, regional retail firms, and large national retail firms with offices throughout the country. The retail firms, both regional and national, deal primarily with the public and offer a wide range of financial products. A listing of equities traded on the Boston Stock Exchange is available only to professional traders.

Chicago Board Options Exchange, Inc. (CBOE)
400 South LaSalle Street   312-786-5600
Chicago, IL 60605   312-786-7442—publications department
     CBOE currently trades solely in options. It can provide you with a listing of companies on the Exchange. It offers broker and customer seminars in cities across the country covering stock index options and stock options. For information about the seminars, call 312-786-7430. Publications include:

  ■ *Tax Considerations in Using CBOE Options*—this fifty-two-page booklet discusses the general tax rules applicable to stock options and nonequity options.

  ■ *Understanding Options*—an introductory guide to options. This twenty-six-page booklet provides a discussion of how options are traded, the language of options, and factors affecting options prices. Examples describe how buying and selling options help meet specific investment strategies.

  ■ *S&P One Hundred Index Options: The Index Edge*—explains how the S & P One Hundred Index is calculated. *The Index Edge* also explains the terms of the options contract and how it is traded. This 20-page booklet illustrates and explains index options strategies using examples.

Intermountain Stock Exchange (ISE)
373 South Main Street
Salt Lake City, UT 84111   801-363-3531
     This small stock exchange lists twenty-six companies, primarily involved in mining. The Exchange establishes market prices by having the executive secretary call out stocks and letting brokers answer with their bids. You can obtain information from the Exchange by telephone.

Midwest Stock Exchange, Inc.
Public Relations Department
440 South LaSalle Street
Chicago, IL 60605   312-663-2209
     This organization, trading in listed stocks, is the second largest stock exchange in the United States. It has several brochures for the public, including

one explaining trading floor operations and another explaining what happens in the clearing and settlement of a trade. Public relations staff can answer your questions.

NASDAQ, Inc.
National Association of Securities Dealers, Inc. (NASD)
1735 K Street, NW
Washington, DC 20006   202-728-8000
   This subsidiary of NASD operates the nationwide electronic NASDAQ System. An over-the-counter quotations system, it performs the same market functions as the stock exchanges. It collects price quotations from more than 450 dealers in over 4,700 NASDAQ securities and disseminates this data to NASDAQ subscribers and information vendors worldwide. Staff can provide you with listings of NASDAQ companies.

New York Stock Exchange (NYSE)
11 Wall Street   212-623-3000
New York, NY 10005   212-623-2089—publications
   NYSE offers a number of publications, and while most are directed toward new investors, a few are designed for the sophisticated investor. The latter group includes product promotion brochures. Contact the publications office for a complete list of free and fee publications.

The Pacific Stock Exchange, Inc.
618 South Spring Street
Los Angeles, CA 90014   213-614-8400

or

Pine Street
San Francisco, CA 91400   415-393-4100
   This stock exchange is an affiliation of member firms organized to provide facilities for conducting an auction market for the stocks, bonds, and options of the nation's leading corporations, as well as corporations in their formative years. It is the nation's largest market center outside New York City, based on the number of trades executed. The two divisions of the Exchange, located in San Francisco and Los Angeles, have technical information about the securities and options in which they trade. A directory listing members and member organizations and a directory of securities are also available.

Philadelphia Stock Exchange, Inc.
1900 Market Street
Philadelphia, PA 19103   215-496-5000
   The oldest stock exchange in the country, the Philadelphia Stock Exchange trades stocks, options on stock, an option on the Eurodollar, options

on stock indices, options on foreign currencies and other financial futures, and has begun trading options on over-the-counter stocks. A membership list and a list of all products traded are available. The staff can provide you with information about the Exchange and the products traded, including product-oriented brochures. Publications include:

> ■ *Foreign Currency Options*—published monthly, this six-page newsletter consists of one article and news relating to foreign currency options and their use by corporations, banks, and individual investors.

Spokane Stock Exchange
225 Peyton Building
Spokane, WA 99201   509-624-4632
   The exchange deals primarily in mining stocks, i.e., silver, gold, lead, and zinc, with thirty-seven issues listed. It also has an over-the-counter segment consisting of 100 mining issues. Staff will give you quotations by telephone.

Part Two

ECONOMIC RESOURCES

Monitoring the Economy

You don't have to be an economist to understand how the ups and downs of the economy affect your life. In fact, you probably know more about the economy than you think. But if terms such as consumer price index, rate of inflation, and fiscal policy leave you confused, read on. This chapter tells you how to get free or low-cost publications that will explain these terms, and free telephone recordings offering the latest economic data, as well as free bulletin boards you can hook into with a computer and modem.

Learning about the Consumer Price Index (CPI) and the rate of inflation is a good way to start to understand how economic trends affect you. One of the most widely used measures of inflation, the CPI calculates the average change in prices for major commodities such as food, clothing, shelter, fuels, and charges for dentists' and doctors' services. The Bureau of Labor Statistics (BLS) collects such data from 85 urban areas across the country and then publishes the CPI each month.

Monitoring changes in the CPI can tell you what to expect when you open up your heating bill, when you take your next trip to the grocery store, or when you get your next wage increase or social security check. Call BLS at the phone number given below for free information booklets about the CPI.

Interest rates are another popular economic statistic. If you are going to borrow money to buy a car, house, or boat, the total cost you will pay is directly dependent on current interest rates. And of course all investments or savings vehicles should be compared against the current interest rates paid on the likes of savings accounts, certificates of deposit, or treasury bills.

Whether you're a young entrepreneur, a shrewd investor, an economics teacher, a computer whiz, or all four, this chapter guides you to the information you need to hone your economic skills. By educating yourself in the basic economic facts of life you could be on your way to a more secure and profitable future.

AGENCIES, INSTITUTES, AND ORGANIZATIONS

The American Citizenship Center
Route 1, Box 141
Oklahoma City, OK 73111   405-478-5190

A nonprofit organization, the Center offers citizenship education programs for students and educators on the comparisons of economic systems. Seminars teaching the basics of economics and the free enterprise system are conducted in several states. The Center's president, Robert H. Rowland, speaks frequently on free enterprise subjects and is available to speak at meetings anywhere in the country. The Center rents films to anyone interested in economics. They also sell:

> ■ *Economic Truths and Myths*—an educational book, this discusses the many myths and truths of the free enterprise system. Cost is $2.50 plus postage.

Bureau of Economic Analysis (BEA)
U.S. Department of Commerce
Washington, DC 20230   202-523-0777—Public Information Office

BEA measures and analyzes United States economic activity through the development, preparation, and interpretation of the economic accounts of the United States. The Bureau provides basic information on key issues such as economic growth, inflation, interest rates, and the nation's role in the world economy. Staff members in the Public Information Office will answer your questions regarding interest rates and inflation, or they will refer you to the proper source of information.

The data that BEA analyzes comes directly from the Federal Reserve System. The following publications, available at the Government Printing Office, will help you understand and monitor the rate of inflation and interest rates. The address to write for these subscriptions is: Superintendent of Documents, U.S. Government Printing Office, Washington, DC 20402, 202-783-3238.

> ■ *Survey of Current Business*—published monthly, this survey contains estimates and analyses of United States economic activity. It includes tables that present more than 1,900 series from more than one hundred public and private sources, covering all aspects of the economy. Cost is $50 annually or $4.75 an issue.
>
> ■ *Business Conditions Digest*—a monthly digest, this is designed for business cycle analysis with tables and charts for 300 economic series, featuring the composite indexes of leading, coincident, and lagging indicators. Cost is $44 annually or $4 for a single copy.

Bureau of the Census
U.S. Department of Commerce
Data User Services Division
Washington, DC 20233   301-763-4100

The Bureau collects and publishes statistics on population, housing, business, agriculture, government finances, foreign trade and many other commercial areas. The Bureau's demographic and economic statistics reflect most aspects of American society and economy and are used by governments, businesses, trade associations, community organizations, students, farmers, researchers, and social scientists. Customer services staff and subject specialists at Bureau headquarters, as well as information services specialists in regional offices, are available to answer questions about census and survey data.

The Bureau conducts workshops for data users, and its College Curriculum Support Project (CCSP) provides lecture outlines, texts, practice exercises, and other instructional aids. For more information, including free lists or prices and ordering instructions, contact the Data User Services Division at the phone number above. The Bureau publishes a variety of guides, catalogs, indexes, fact finders, and other user aids. Most of these materials are available for reference as well as purchase; some are free. Bureau findings are available in most libraries across the country as printed reports and on microfiche. Current publications are kept for reference and order at the twelve Bureau of the Census regional offices and the forty-seven Department of Commerce district offices. Copies can be purchased by writing to the Superintendent of Documents, US GPO, Washington, DC 20402. Summary tape, public-use microdata, geographic reference files, flexible diskettes, maps, and publications not sold by GPO can be ordered directly from the Census Bureau.

There are also State Data Centers in almost all states. Private and public

■ ■

TOTAL FINANCIAL ASSETS OF AMERICAN HOUSEHOLDS

Total Financial Assets for Households, Personal Trusts, and Nonprofit Organizations in Billions of Dollars

	1970	Percent of total	1985	Percent of total
Checkable deposits and currency	118	5	428	4
Small time and savings deposits	408	16	1,829	18
Money market fund shares	0	0	208	5
Large time deposits	17	1	194	2
US savings bonds	52	2	80	1
Other Treasury/govt. issues	54	2	515	5
State and local obligations	46	2	249	2
Corporate and foreign bonds	36	1	54	1
Open-market paper	12	0.4	80	1
Mortgages	52	2	152	2
Mutual funds	47	2	283	3
Stocks/other corporate equities	682	27	1,666	16
Life insurance reserves	131	5	254	2
Pension fund reserves	239	9	1,737	17
Equity in noncorp. business	577	23	2,434	24
Miscellaneous	31	1	140	1
Total	**2503**	**100%**	**10,304**	**100%**

Source: Board of Governors, Federal Reserve System.

■ ■

■ ■

BEST AND WORST GROWTH INDUSTRIES

Listed below are those industries which have had the highest and lowest average growth rates from 1973 to 1986.

Best (top 10)	Rate of growth	Worst (last 10)	Rate of growth
Semiconductor devices	32.3	Turbine generator sets	−8.6
Computing equipment	18.0	Leather/lined clothing	−6.6
Optical devices/lenses	16.5	Silver and plated ware	−6.1
Biological products	11.3	Primary zinc	−5.7
X-ray apparatus and tubes	11.3	Women's footwear	−5.4
		Sewing machines	−5.3
Electronic connectors	10.7	Cigars	−5.2
Medicinals and botanicals	9.4	Building paper/board mills	−5.1
Electronic measuring devices	8.9	Wood TV, radio cabinets	−5.1
		Metal-forming machines	−4.4
Lithographic services	8.4		
Instruments	8.4		

Source: U.S. Department of Commerce, *U.S. Industrial Outlook*

■ ■

organizations located throughout the country are registered with the Bureau's National Clearinghouse for Census Data Services and are able to provide tape copies and related services to their customers.

Most Census and survey results are made available in statistical tables in printed reports. Since the amount of data that can be put in print is limited, greater detail, both statistical and geographic, may frequently be found on microfiche and on computer tape. The following are some Bureau of the Census publications:

■ *Data User News*—published monthly, this newsletter discusses activities and new products and services as they become available. Occasional descriptive articles highlight important features of particular statistics and/ or their application. Available from GPO, an annual subscription costs $21.

■ *Monthly Product Announcement*—this announcement lists every new report, computer tape, and microfiche produced by the Bureau and includes price and ordering information. Free.

■ *Statistical Abstract of the United States, 1985*—published since 1878, this book focuses primarily on national-level summary data for thirty one major subject areas. Statistics from fifty government agencies and 174 private organizations are presented. An appendix presents selected state rankings for fifty social and economic data items. Cost is $19.

■ *Population Profile of the U.S.: 1983/84, Current Population Reports*—this profile gives you an economic view of the population, with a discussion of the labor force and employment, occupation, income, earnings, noncash benefits, and poverty. Illustrated color charts and graphs are included. Available from GPO (S/N 003-001-91562-6), it costs $3.25.

Bureau of Economic Analysis (BEA)
Department of Commerce
Washington, DC 20230   202-523-0777

BEA produces a picture of the United States economy nationally, regionally, and internationally. This office does not collect data but it does provide the tools necessary for people to make their own forecasts. It provides basic information on key issues such as economic growth, inflation, regional development, and the nation's role in the world economy. BEA's Input/Output model tells you what industries are buying from one another. For instance, you can determine how much steel the automobile industry is buying from the steel industry. BEA classifies the economic indicators into leaders and laggers and draws the composite of leading indicators.

Experts at BEA can help you with general economic questions or they may refer you to relevant publications, but they will not analyze data for you. BEA's publications and databases on magnetic tapes include a complete selection of

■ ■

WHERE MILLIONAIRES KEEP THEIR MONEY

Millionaires don't keep all their eggs in one basket. They move their assets to achieve the greatest return in the prevailing economic climate. Here's where millionaires keep their money; where would you keep your millions?

Type of asset	1976	1982
Cash	5.7%	6.0%
Corporate stock	42.0	31.2
Bonds	12.3	7.8
Life insurance	0.5	0.6
Notes and mortgages	3.1	4.5
Real estate	14.7	23.6
Noncorporate business assets*	3.8	9.9
Other assets	17.9	16.4
Total	100.0	100.0

*From businesses that are not incorporated.

Source: Internal Revenue Service estate tax returns.

■ ■

data on GNP, income, personal consumer expenditures, capital goods, and imports and exports. BEA publications can be purchased from either Superintendent of Documents, Government Printing Office (GPO), Washington, DC 20402, 202-783-3238 or Department of Commerce, National Technical Information Service (NTIS), 5285 Port Royal Road, Springfield, VA 22161, 703-487-4600.

- *Survey of Current Business*—published monthly, this periodical contains estimates and analyses of United States economic activity. Features include a review of current economic development, and articles pertaining to BEA's work on the national, regional, and international economic accounts, and related topics. Available from GPO. Annual subscription costs $50.

- *Business Conditions Digest*—a monthly publication, this is designed for business cycle analysis with tables and charts for 300 economic series, featuring the composite indexes of leading, coincident and lagging indicators. Data sources are included. Available from GPO. Annual subscription costs $44.

- *Measuring Non-Market Economic Activity: BEA Working Papers*—a collection of working papers on GNP-related measures, these papers evaluate the national economic well-being. Six papers are presented, each one dealing with a topic involving measurement of nonmarket economic activity. Available from NTIS (#PB-83-167-395). The cost is $16.

- *An Introduction to National Economic Accounting*—this 119-page paper introduces the concepts, sources, and methods of the United States national income and product accounts. It shows the step-by-step derivation of a general national economic accounting system. Available from GPO, the cost is $1.

Bureau of Labor Statistics (BLS)

U.S. Department of Labor
Inquiries and Correspondence   202-523-1221
Washington, DC 20212   202-523-9658—hotline

The BLS hotline offers monthly information on economic trends for the United States on a four-minute taped recording. The CPI is given. For information not on the tape, including price movements of various commodities and the CPI for specific regions of the country, call 202-272-5160.

A staff person will assist you with any questions you may have about data published by BLS. Your inquiries may be made by telephone at the number above or in writing. This office also distributes free BLS publications. For any of the following publications for sale, send a prepaid order to: Bureau of Labor Statistics, Publications Sales Center, PO Box 2145, Chicago, IL 60690 (make checks payable to Superintendent of Documents).

- *Producer Price Index*—published monthly, this databook of producer price indexes and percent changes includes groupings by commodity line and stage of processing. Annual subscription costs $29.
- *BLS Handbook of Methods*—Volumes I and II present a detailed explanation of how BLS obtains and prepares the economic data it publishes. Information is included on concepts, definitions, sources, procedures, and limitations for all BLS programs. Cost of Volume I is $6.50 and Volume II $2.
- *Employment, Hours, and Earnings, States and Areas, 1939-82*—this databook contains monthly and annual data on employment, hours, and earnings for all states. Cost is $11.
- *Women at Work: A Chartbook*—focusing on women's economic activity, this booklet discusses labor force trends, occupational and industrial employment patterns, unemployment, and market worth of women in a family context (Bulletin #2168). Cost is $4.
- *Consumer Expenditure Survey: Interview Survey, 1980-81*—detailed income and expenditure data are presented in this ongoing consumer expenditure survey (Bulletin #2225). Cost is $6.
- *Relative Importance of Components in the Consumer Price Indexes, 1984*—this bulletin presents data on the expenditure or value weights of components in the consumer price indexes expressed as a percentage of all items. Cost is $1.75.
- *CPI Detailed Report*—published monthly, this report is a databook of consumer price indexes and percent changes. It includes data for twenty-eight cities. Annual subscription is $25.
- *Employment and Earnings*—a monthly databook, this survey details current employment, unemployment, and earnings statistics for the nation, individual states, and 200 selected regions. Subscription includes an annual supplement containing revised establishment data. Annual subscription costs $31.
- *Consumer Expenditure Survey Results from 1982-83*—this report contains the latest results of the continuing consumer expenditure survey. It describes the characteristics of the survey and includes detailed tables. Free.

Data Resources, Inc. (DRI)
24 Hartwell Avenue
Lexington, MA 02173   617-863-5100

Supported by a large collection of computer-accessible business and economic data, the staff at DRI develops customized applications using a range of software tools to help clients solve their business problems. DRI also offers hundreds of courses introducing clients to econometric theory, economic data manipulation and personal computer-based applications.

The following organizations are sources of information for DRI's economic databases: The Conference Board, Bureau of the Census, U.S. Department of Commerce, U.S. Department of Agriculture, U.S. Department of
Labor, U.S. Department of Interior, Bureau of Mines, and the Board of Governors of the Federal Reserve System. For more information on DRI services or
databases call the executive office above or one of the regional offices.

There are two pricing options for the services and databases described
below: an annual subscription fee and Information Plus. Call the office nearest
you for pricing specifics.

■ *The Conference Board (CBDB)*—a unique source or proprietary data,
both historical and forecasted, it measures activity in various sectors of the
economy.

■ *TRINET Establishment*—this database contains information on nearly
half a million business establishments with twenty or more employees. It
includes the name and address of the establishment, telephone number,
industry code and size factors, among other data.

■ *Flow of Funds*—statistics in this data bank relate to the financial activities
of the United States economy and indicators of nonfinancial activities that
generate income and production.

■ *DRI Interindustry*—this interindustry data bank provides historical information on production and deliveries by all industrial sectors of the United
States economy.

The Demographic Institute
PO Box 68   800-828-1133—outside NY
Ithaca, NY 14851   800-462-8686—in NY

The Demographic Institute trains people to use demographic data. Members of the Institute can use the American Demographics Referral Service,
which allows you to call an expert from the Institute for professional assistance
in finding and interpreting demographic information. The staff knows the Census Bureau and the private data and research companies, and can help you
understand current trends. The Institute holds an annual conference and conducts seminars around the country to give professionals in-depth information
about consumer trends. Some of the following publications are free or are
available at a reduced price for members:

■ *American Demographics Magazine*—published monthly, this publication provides a close look at how demographic trends shape specific
businesses' marketing strategies. It examines seven key areas including one
on the economy. Cost is $48 a year, free to members.

■ *Consumer Forecasts: Trends*—this package includes some valuable population projections and looks at current and future trends in employment,
income, families and industry. Cost is $10; $8.50 for members.

■ *What Lies Ahead for the Economy?*—author Frank Levy, School of
Public Affairs, University of Maryland, finds out which consumer trends

will be bringing us lower inflation, rising wages and spending, and new market opportunities. Cost is $7.50; $6 for members.

Economics Research Center (ERC)

National Opinion Research Center (NORC)
University of Chicago
6030 South Ellis Avenue   312-962-6072
Chicago, IL   312-962-1213—library

Founded in 1980, ERC is devoted to empirical studies in economics. Specifically, the Center has three objectives: (1) to conduct research on issues of long-run relevance to the economy and to social and private behavior; (2) to promote basic research by providing training and research procedures; and (3) to improve the tools of empirical research through efforts to provide better survey data and better statistical techniques of analysis. One of its major topics of study is the economics of the family.

ERC conducts regular workshops on current economic topics. You can call the Center for workshop locations and schedules. The library staff at NORC are available to answer your questions, within reason, about economic research and publication.

NORC publications include discussion papers on studies in applied economics, survey reports, and technical reports from various conferences.

- *Journal of Labor Economics*—published monthly, this journal presents theoretical and empirical articles pertaining to broadly defined labor economics. Annual subscription is $26.

Educational Service Bureau (ESB)

World Financial Center
200 Liberty Street, Tower A
New York, NY 10281   212-416-2000

Dow Jones established this service bureau to help serve the needs of educators by providing them with educational resources. ESB's Newspaper-in-Education Program has developed many innovative ways of using the *Wall Street Journal* to help students learn. It offers analysis of current happenings with a heavy economic content, written in such a way that students can see and understand how economic analysis can be used on a daily basis. The following publications are available for students and educators.

- *How to Read Stock Market Quotations*—this booklet will tell you how to interpret the daily activities of companies listed on a stock exchange. Free.
- *The Dow Jones Averages: A Non-Professional's Guide*—the method of calculation of the Dow Jones Average is explained in this pamphlet along with answers to some frequently asked questions. Free.
- *Understanding Financial Data in the Wall Street Journal*—this booklet will help you understand trading in stocks, bonds, commodities, currencies

and certain other financial instruments and how they are published in the *Wall Street Journal*. Free.

Federal National Mortgage Association (FNMA)   202-537-7100
3900 Wisconsin Avenue   202-537-6799—ARM hotline
Washington, DC 20016   202-537-7060—fixed rate hotline
The Commitment Operations Division of FNMA operates these mortgage interest rate hotlines twenty-four hours a day to give you up-to-date rates on FHA, VA, and conventional loan commitments. Questions concerning adjustable rate mortgages or any general information on FNMA should be referred to the corporate affairs office at 202-537-7113 or at one of FNMA's regional offices located in Atlanta, Los Angeles, Dallas, Philadelphia, Chicago, and Norcross, VA.

Federal Reserve System
Board of Governors
Division of Consumer and Community Affairs
Washington, DC 20551   202-452-3946
The Federal Reserve System was created by Congress to ensure a safe banking and monetary system and to encourage stable growth of the economy. The system implements statutes to protect you in your financial transactions. The Consumer and Community Affairs Office listed above will answer questions and will accept complaints about the practices of any bank and refer them to the appropriate bank regulator. The public information offices in the Federal Reserve Banks within the system also have staff available to help you with questions and complaints.

The Board makes available detailed statistics and other information about the system's activities through a variety of publications, some of which are listed below.

> ■ *What's All This About the M's?*—useful to the general public or students of economics, this six-page booklet defines the Federal Reserve System's various measures of money and relates them to the functions money performs. Free.
> ■ *Open Market Operations*—for amateur Federal Reserve System watchers, this forty-nine-page book describes how the Federal Reserve formulates and implements monetary policy. The book guides you through a typical day's open market operations to show how the effects of monetary policy are transmitted throughout the economy. Free.
> ■ *Two Faces of Debt*—a discussion of debt in the public and private sectors and its essential role in economic prosperity is given in this thirty-four-page booklet. Free.
> ■ *Selected Interest Rates*—published both weekly and monthly, this one-page chart gives current interest rates on: treasury securities; CDs; com-

mercial paper; prime rates; corporate, mortgage, and municipal bond rates. Free.

■ *Federal Reserve Bulletin*—this monthly report, available at university and most public libraries, contains financial tables, including interest rates. The cost is $20.

■ *The Transition to Low Inflation: Progress and Pressures*—this twenty-four-page booklet reviews macroeconomic policies over the past several years. It explores the resulting performance of the economy in the transition to low inflation, and proposes policies for continued growth. Free.

The staff economists in the research division of the Federal Reserve System monitor economic activities in the financial market by closely tracking interest rates and other economic indicators. The primary role of the economists is to serve the Board of Governors. However, they will accept limited telephone calls from the general public, although they will not read interest rates over the phone. They can be reached at the Division of Research and Statistics, Board of Governors of the Federal Reserve System, Washington, DC 20551, 202-452-2851.

The Federal Reserve Banks also offer several publications that are helpful in monitoring the economy. Each bank puts out a monthly or bimonthly publication (titles vary) that reviews monetary theory and policies, banking, and general economic topics. Check with the Federal Reserve Bank in your region for this and other publications. Some of the booklets available from Federal Reserve Banks are described below. You can order them from the banks indicated.

Many Reserve Banks have tape-recorded announcements of interest rates (updated by Tuesday morning). Since the Federal Reserve Board experts prefer not to give interest rates over the phone you should be aware of the availability of these numbers. In addition to interest rates, New York announces Fed Fund and CD rates; Washington, D.C., explains Treasury Constant Maturities and Federal Reserve Board meeting notices. Since not all branches offer this service call the nearest Reserve Bank:

■ Washington, DC: 202-452-3658; 202-452-3206 (for meeting notices)
■ New York: 212-791-6693
■ Chicago: 312-322-5112 (no recording)
■ Philadelphia: 215-574-6188
■ Cleveland: 216-579-2001
■ Richmond: 804-648-0880
■ Atlanta: 404-521-8657
■ St. Louis: 314-444-8590—Kathy Blumentritt (no recording)
■ Kansas City: 816-881-2364
■ Dallas: 214-651-6177
■ San Francisco: 415-974-2477

Information is also provided by the Treasury and the Bureau of Public Debt by recorded announcement:

> 202-287-4100—Auction results and rates
> 202-287-4091—Lesson on treasury bills
> 202-287-4088—Lesson on treasury notes
> 202-566-3734—Rate on 2 1/2-year certificate

Federal Reserve Bank of Chicago
Public Information Department
230 South LaSalle Street
Chicago, IL 60690
312-322-5112

> ■ *The ABC's of Figuring Interest*—the various ways of calculating interest are explained in this ten-page booklet. It also explains how this can affect the dollar amount paid. Free.

Federal Reserve Bank of Dallas
Public Information Department
400 South Akard Street
Dallas, TX 75222
214-651-6267

> ■ *Selected Interest Rates*—written for the general public, bankers, and real estate personnel, this pamphlet highlights interest rates of treasury securities, constant maturities, and prime rates since 1970 using tables and charts. Free.

Federal Reserve Bank of New York
Public Information Department
33 Liberty Street
New York, NY 10045
212-791-6134

> ■ *Debt and Deficits*—written for the general public and beginning students of economics, this eighteen-page publication examines the national debt and deficits, looks at their size and impact, and discusses various policy measures for bringing them under control. Free.
>
> ■ *A Primer on Inflation*—this booklet defines the inflationary process, identifies its root causes, examines how it is transmitted, and discusses some alternatives for dealing with the problem. Free.
>
> ■ *The Arithmetic of Interest Rates*—written for the general public, this book explains simple and compound interest and its effect on the yield of government securities and the cost of consumer credit. Free.

Federal Reserve Bank of Richmond
Public Services Department
PO Box 27622
Richmond, VA 23261
804-643-1250

■ *Economic Prosperity: An Eclectic View*—an examination of economic development over the recent past. Free.

■ *You and Your Money*—intended for high school students, this is a discussion of the causes of inflation and deflation and some possible remedies. Free.

■ *Borrowers, Lenders, and Interest Rates*— the process of determining interest rates is described in this pamphlet, along with definitions of credit terminology. Free.

■ *Essays on Inflation*—directed toward teachers and students, this 288-page book contains surveys of alternative explanations of the generation, propagation, and control of domestic and international inflation. Free.

Federal Reserve Bank of St. Louis
Bank Relations & Public Information Department
PO Box 442
St. Louis, MO 63166
314-444-8421

■ *Economic Activity and Markets*—for high school and college students, this thirty-page booklet relates how the nation's economic activity is coordinated to produce the goods and services the country demands. Free.

■ *Role of Government in U.S. Economy: Fiscal Policy*—the role of United States government fiscal policy and how it affects economic activity is examined in this booklet. Free.

Federal Reserve Bank of Kansas City
Public Affairs Department
925 Grand Avenue
Kansas City, MO 64198
816-881-2402

■ *Price Stability and Public Policy*—this is a 227-page book for the general public discussing the causes of inflation, the costs and benefits of stable prices, and the role of monetary policy in reaching price stability. Free.

Office of Prices and Living Conditions
Department of Labor
600 E Street, NW
Washington, DC 20212   202-272-5113

A team of economists from this office is available to answer any of your questions on the economy. Their areas of expertise include producer prices, price indexes, and industry-sector price indexes for the output of selected industries. This office operates a computerized database containing historical data on producer price indexes, and offers publications on consumer price indexes. If you need information on price indexes, wholesale prices, or machine-readable databases, call the experts at the number above.

Pacific Academy for Advanced Studies
1100 Glendon Avenue, Suite 1625
Los Angeles, CA 90024   213-208-7735
This nonprofit economics education organization is devoted to increasing economic literacy through seminars to educators. For the general public, the Center will try to answer specific questions or will make appropriate referrals. The following newsletter is available to teachers and, on written request, to the general public.

> ■ *Contemporary Economic Issues*—published quarterly, this four- to six-page publication discusses current economic issues and provides an objective economic analysis for each issue.

WHAT TO READ

The American Dictionary of Economics
Facts on File
460 Park Avenue South   212-683-2244
New York, NY 10016   800-322-8755
The definitions in this reference book are practical and easy to understand. It lists over 1,600 terms, concepts, organizations and individuals concerned with the field of economics. Cost is $17.95.

American Family and the Economy: The High Cost of Living
National Academy Press
2101 Constitution Avenue, NW
Washington, DC 20418   202-334-3313
Edited by Richard Nelson and Felicity Skidmore, this 307-page book discusses trends in the economic situation of the American family, and the housing trends of families with children. Cost is $18.75.

The Arithmetic of Interest Rates
Consumer Information Center-V
PO Box 100
Pueblo, CO 81002   303-948-3334

A handy guide, this thirty-three-page booklet will help you understand and calculate simple and compound interest rates. Order #418N. Cost is fifty cents.

The Brookings Institution
1775 Massachusetts Avenue, NW
Washington, DC 20036   202-797-6000

This private, nonprofit organization is devoted to research, education, and publication of important issues in domestic and foreign policy. The following is a sample of available publications:

■ *Economic Choices 1987*—written by a group of prominent economists, this concise, lively book discusses the outlook for the United States economy and appropriate fiscal and monetary policy for the next several years. Cost is $8.95 in paperback and $22.95 in hardcover.

■ *Trends in American Economic Growth*—author Edward F. Denison systematically distinguishes changes in the economy's ability to produce from changes in the ratio of actual output to potential output. Cost is $11.95.

■ *Brookings Papers on Economic Activity*—devoted exclusively to invited contributions, this journal, published twice a year, provides academic and business economists, government officials, and members of the financial and business communities with timely analyses of current economic developments. It offers authoritative, in-depth research studies relating to aspects of the current perrformance of the American economy. Annual subscription is $24.

Center for the Study of American Business
Washington University
Campus Box 1208
St. Louis, MO 63130   314-889-5630

This Center researches economic public-policy regulations. It conducts seminars only at Washington University. The Center's Contemporary Issues Series is available to the general public. Single copies are free. A sample of topics covered includes:

■ *Deficits and Dollars: The Effects of Government Deficits in an International Economy*—this is a discussion of how various international factors can be expected to influence the effects of large federal deficits in the domestic United States economy.

■ *An Economist in Government: Views of a Presidential Advisor*—Dr. Murray L. Weidenbaum discusses the policymaking role of the Chairman of the Council of Economic Advisors. He comments on a variety of issues, including supply-side economics and various policies of the Reagan administration.

■ *Confessions of a One-Armed Economist*—this collection of sixteen essays by Dr. Weidenbaum analyzes a variety of major economic issues facing the United States in four areas including economic change in the 1980s. The collection is designed as a "guide to a number of today's important economic questions."

Congressional Research Services (CRS)
First Street and Independence Avenue, SE
Library of Congress
Washington, DC 20540   202-287-5775

CRS reports are detailed accounts of issues large and small, foreign and domestic, social and political. You can request an index to these reports by calling the office of your Congressional Representative. CRS also publishes and records on cassette tapes hundreds of major issue briefs designed to keep members of Congress informed on timely issues. These briefs, written primarily for the layperson, provide a good deal of background information and are updated daily. Free hard copies may be obtained through your congressman's office. The following is a list of issue briefs relating to the economy.

■ *Gramm-Rudman-Hollings Legislation and Balanced Budget Issues*—this Info Pack contains material to help answer the many questions that are being raised in response to the Balanced Budget and Emergency Deficit Control Act of 1985 (PL 99-177). It includes a summary of the legislation, information on how the budget savings are to be achieved, preliminary analyses of anticipated effects on the budget process, federal expenditures, and the national economy. Order #IP0011G. Free.

■ *Federal Reserve System*—materials in this packet include comments by Chairman Paul Volcker on monetary policy and the state of the economy. It also includes a CRS report that provides answers to commonly asked questions about the Federal Reserve. Order #IP0105F. Free.

■ *The Consumer Price Index and the Rate of Inflation*—concepts such as "the purchasing power of the dollar" are discussed in this Info Pack. It also provides information on how the Consumer Price Index (CPI) is calculated and discusses alternative measures of the inflation rate. Tables are included showing index numbers and percentage changes in the CPI from 1800 to the present. Order #IP0025C. Free.

■ *Federal Deficits and Debt: Background and Statistics*—in response to numerous requests, CRS has put together this packet of information on the federal debt. It contains background information, material on the debt's effect on the United States economy, and historic, current and projected data. Bibliographies are also included for those interested in further research. Order #IP0274F. Free.

■ *Trade Issues and Trade Deficits: Background, Statistics and Proposed Legislation*—the reports and articles in this Info Pack discuss the causes and effects of the trade deficit and presents arguments for and against an import surcharge and other proposals designed to limit the volume of imports. Order #IP0263T. Free.

The Dow Jones-Irwin Guide to Interest: What You Should Know About the Time Value of Money
Dow Jones-Irwin
1824 Ridge Road   800-323-1717
Homewood, IL 60430   800-942-8881—in IL

This 263-page book makes complex mathematics simple by using concise graphs and formulas. Among the topics covered are: return on investment, discounted cash flow, mortgage points, personal financial planning, yield to call, and bond selection. Cost is $19.95.

Dow Jones and Company, Inc.
World Financial Center
200 Liberty Street, Tower A
New York, NY 10281   212-416-2000

A leading publisher of business news and information, Dow Jones publishes the following papers available at local newsstands or through subscriptions.

- *Wall Street Journal*—this newspaper, published each business day, is a major reference source for business, economic, and world news. Each day, *Journal* readers can find that day's most important economic and financial stories. It covers the federal government's impact on the market's interest rates, taxation, and economic growth. At least ten pages of data on financial markets are published each day. The majority of data relates to stocks and bonds. An annual subscription is $114; single copies are fifty cents.
- *Barron's*—published weekly, this magazine provides unbiased, incisive, and timely coverage of business and financial news written primarily for investors. Its aim is to help its readers raise their economic and investment IQs. *Barron's* is divided into features, sections, and columns covering the economic, financial, business, and investment scenes. An annual subscription is $77.

Economic Source Book of Government Statistics
Lexington Books
125 Spring Street
Lexington, MA 02173   617-860-1206

Written by Arline Hoel, this book will tell you where to find and how to evaluate official data on the United States economy. It is a guidebook to more than fifty separate sources of economic statistics compiled and issued by a variety of United States federal departments and agencies. Cost is $29.

Economics Department
Manufacturers Hanover Trust Company
270 Park Avenue
New York, NY 10017   212-286-7351

To receive the following publications and to be put on their mailing list, call or write to the Economics Department listed above.

■ *Economic Reports*—published monthly, this periodical contains articles on current economic subjects. It is written by bank economists. Free.

■ *Weekly Financial Digest*—this is a compilation of selected Federal Reserve data, bank loan figures, selected business indicators, and security markets. Free.

Economics Division
National Association of Home Builders (NAHB)
15th and M streets, NW
Washington, DC 20005   800-368-5242, ext. 434

The NAHB Economics Division staff are available to assist you in your publications needs. Call the toll-free number above if your need further information. NAHB offers a subscription service, *Economic News Notes* which includes *Current Housing Situation* and three newsletters. Cost for all three newsletters is $125.

■ *Monthly Report*—the report discusses the current housing outlook.

■ *Housing Starts Bulletin*—published monthly, this bulletin presents an overview of the current month's housing data along with detailed statistical tables.

■ *Quarterly Metropolitan Housing Starts Forecast*—this forecast provides extensive nationally published housing starts forecast data for about one hundred metropolitan areas.

■ *Current Housing Situation*—subscribers get an up-to-the-minute source of leading housing and economic indicators. It provides you with specific data on starts, sales, GNP, interest rates, CPI, housing prices, rents and much more. Cost is $75 annually.

The Handbook of Economic and Financial Measures
Dow Jones-Irwin
1824 Ridge Road   800-323-1717
Homewood, IL 60430   800-942-8881—in IL

Each chapter in this 517-page book is written by an expert in the field. It covers the major measures that dominate the analysis of economic and financial activities. Cost is $50.

Superintendent of Documents
U.S. Government Printing Office
Washington, DC 20402   202-783-3238

GPO distributes United States government publications through its twenty-five bookstores nationwide, or from the headquarters listed above. The following selected publications are about the economy. For a more comprehensive list of publications contact your nearest bookstore for a catalog.

■ *Technology, Innovation, and Regional Economic Development*—this report assesses the potential for local economic growth offered by high-technology industries. Order #S/N 052-003-00959-5. Cost is $5.50.

■ *Economic Analysis Procedures for ADP*—designed for the novice in the field of cost/benefit analysis, this guidebook establishes a procedural routine for conducting economic analysis. It develops material slowly from a few very basic economic and common-sense principles. Order #S/N 008-040-00091-5. Cost is $7.50.

■ *Monthly Labor Review*—this is the oldest government journal that provides up-to-date information on economic and social statistics. The *Review* publishes a forty-page section on current statistics covering employment and unemployment; wages, unit labor costs and output; consumer, industrial, and international prices; and economic growth and related topics. An annual subscription is $24.

FOR COMPUTER USERS

Economic Bulletin Board
U.S. Department of Commerce
Office of Business Analysis
Room H4887
Washington, DC 20230   202-377-4450
    You can get details of the latest releases on such subjects as the consumer price index, the leading economic indicators, and employment statistics by using your personal computer. Use your modem to call 202-377-3870 or 202-377-0433 and you will be provided with a weekly schedule of economic data from all government agencies. You will also receive files containing data from past releases issued by major government departments, information on data tapes and files you can get from the federal government, and descriptions of current marketing-related publications produced by federal agencies. Free.

CENDATA-The Census Bureau Online
CENDATA Program
Data User Services Division   301-763-2074
Bureau of the Census   800-334-2564
Washington, DC 20233   800-982-5838—CA only
    CENDATA offers current economic data in the areas of manufacturing, business, foreign trade, and construction on an on-line service for access from remote terminals or microcomputers. Demographic data include excerpts from the Current Population Reports and other population and housing information. Census Bureau data is available on-line through DIALOG Information Services, Inc., and the Glimpse Corporation. This service provides selected summary statistics from all Bureau programs. It also includes news releases and product

ordering information which is updated daily. Many data series are updated monthly. The charge is sixty cents a minute.

Dow Jones News/Retrieval

Dow Jones and Company, Inc.
World Financial Center
200 Liberty Street, Tower A   212-416-2000
New York, NY 10281   800-257-5114

News/Retrieval is an on-line financial news resource with exclusive electronic access to the *Wall Street Journal*. You can track past and present stock performance through Dow Jones quotes, or review economic and earnings forecasts in five minutes or less. This service includes a Weekly Economic Update, which is a review of the week's top economic developments. You will receive up-to-the-minute world, government, industry, or company news by using this service. All you need is a personal computer and a modem or time-sharing terminal. Staff is available to answer questions on how to use the system or to provide other information on the data. There are no communication costs, and there is no expensive equipment to buy. For more information on the data bases available call the toll-free number listed above. Membership kits include a password, five free hours of unrestricted usage, a user's guide, and discounts at Comp-u-Store. Cost is $29.95.

EXPERTS

Craig Howell

Department of Labor
Bureau of Labor Statistics
600 E Street, NW
Washington, DC 20212   202-272-5113

Mr. Howell has been with the bureau over twenty years and is currently the public affairs representative for the Producer Price Index. He regularly gives talks on the economic interpretation of PPI data. He has published several articles in the *Monthly Labor Review*.

Larry Moran

Public Information Officer
Bureau of Economic Analysis (BEA)
Department of Commerce
Washington, DC 20230   202-523-0777

As the Public Information Officer for five years, Mr. Moran assists the Bureau in informing the general public on BEA's estimates and programs. He has published several articles in the *Survey of Current Business* periodical and is currently writing an article for publication.

Alice M. Rivlan
The Brookings Institution
1775 Massachusetts Avenue, NW
Washington, DC 20036   202-797-6000

A former director of the Congressional Budget Office, Alice Rivlan is presently the Director of Economic Studies. She is the author of many economic publications, including *Economic Choices* (see write-up in preceding section).

Interest Rates and Inflation

See also:
Monitoring the Economy

You don't have to be a mover and a shaker to get an occasional jolt from the economy. Whether you're unemployed or have a six-figure annual income, you still have basic needs. And when the interest rates go up, prices do too. That's bound to affect you, one way or another.

So it's important to understand the relationship between inflation and interest rates, how they affect you, and what you can do about it.

The following section is a description of resources—publications and organizations, such as the Federal Reserve Banks and the U.S. Department of Commerce—that provide information to help you understand interest rates and inflation, how they affect the economy as a whole, and how they affect you as an individual. Also included, under Recorded Messages, are numbers you can call to get the latest interest rate data.

AGENCIES, INSTITUTES, AND ORGANIZATIONS

Bureau of Economic Analysis (BEA)
US Department of Commerce
Washington, DC 20230   202-523-0777—Public Information Office
BEA measures and analyzes United States economic activity through the development, preparation, and interpretation of the economic accounts of the United States. The Bureau provides basic information on key issues such as economic growth, inflation, interest rates, and the nation's role in the world economy. Staff members in the Public Information Office will answer your questions regarding interest rates and inflation or they will refer you to the proper source of information.

The data that BEA analyzes comes directly from the Federal Reserve System. The following publications, available at the Government Printing Office, will help you understand and monitor the rate of inflation and interest rates. The address from which to order these subscriptions is: Superintendent of Documents, U.S. Government Printing Office, Washington, DC 20402, 202-783-3238.

> ■ *Survey of Current Business*—published monthly this survey contains estimates and analyses of United States economic activity. It includes tables that present more than 1,900 series from more than a hundred public and private sources, covering all aspects of the economy. Cost is $50 annually or $4.75 an issue.

■ *Business Conditions Digest*—a monthly digest, this is designed for business cycle analysis, with tables and charts for 300 economic series featuring the composite indexes of leading, coincident, and lagging indicators. Cost is $44 annually or $4 for a single copy.

Board of Governors of the Federal Reserve System
Division of Research and Statistics
Washington, DC 20551   202-452-2851

The staff economists in this research division of the Federal Reserve System monitor the economic activities in the financial market by tracking interest rates closely. The primary role of the economists is to serve the Board of Governors. They can therefore accept only limited calls from the general public and will not read interest rates over the phone. For those interested in monitoring interest rates in the economy, the following publications are available from the publications office:

■ *Selected Interest Rates*—published both weekly and monthly, this one-page chart gives current interest rates for: treasury securities; CDs; commercial paper; prime rates; corporate, mortgage, and municipal bond rates. Free.

■ *Federal Reserve Bulletin*—this monthly report, available at university and most public libraries, contains financial tables, including interest rates. The cost is $20.

Federal Reserve Banks

The Federal Reserve System has publications about interest rates available to educators, bankers, economists, students, and the general public. Materials are free of charge unless otherwise indicated and may be ordered by contacting the reserve bank noted next to the publication. For further information on interest rates, or if you have questions on activities of the Reserve System, the public information offices have staff members available to help you. Direct correspondence should go to the Public Affairs Department.

■ *The ABC's of Figuring Interest*—the various ways of calculating interest are explained in this ten-page booklet. It also tells you how this can affect the dollar amount paid. Free from Public Information Department, Federal Reserve Bank of Chicago, 230 South LaSalle Street, Chicago, IL 60690, 312-322-5112.

■ *The Arithmetic of Interest Rates*—written for the general public, this book explains simple and compound interest and its effect on the yield of government securities and the cost of consumer credit. Free from Public Information Department, Federal Reserve Bank, 33 Liberty Street, New York, NY 10045, 212-791-6134.

■ *Borrowers, Lenders, and Interest Rates*—the process of determining interest rates is described in this pamphlet, along with definitions of credit terminology. Free from Public Relations Department, Federal Reserve Bank of Richmond, PO Box 27622, Richmond, VA 23261, 804-643-1250.

■ *Selected Interest Rates*—written for the general public, bankers, and real estate personnel, this pamphlet highlights interest rates of treasury securities, constant maturities, and prime rates since 1970 using tables and charts. Free from Public Information Department, Federal Reserve Bank of Dallas, 400 South Akard Street, Dallas, TX 75222, 214-651-6267.

■ *Essays on Inflation*—directed toward teachers and students, this 288-page book contains surveys of alternative explanations of the generation, propagation, and control of domestic and international inflation. Free from Federal Reserve Bank of Richmond. See address above.

■ *The Transition to Low Inflation: Progress and Pressures*—this twenty-four-page booklet reviews macroeconomic policies over the past several years. It explores the resulting performance of the economy in the transition to low inflation, and proposes policies for continued growth. Free from Board of Governors of the Federal Reserve System, Publications Services, Room MP-510, Washington, DC 20551, 202-452-3244.

Federal National Mortgage Association (FNMA)   202-537-7100
3900 Wisconsin Avenue   202-537-6799—ARM hotline
Washington, DC 20016   202-537-7060—fixed rate hotline

The Commitment Operations Division of FNMA operates these mortgage interest rate hotlines twenty-four hours a day to give you up-to-date rates on FHA, VA, and conventional loan commitments. Questions concerning adjustable rate mortgages or any general information on FNMA should be referred to the corporate affairs office at 202-537-7113 or at one of FNMA's regional offices located in Atlanta, Los Angeles, Dallas, Philadelphia, Chicago, and Norcross, VA.

Money Market Services, Inc. (MMS)
490 El Camino Real   800-227-7304
Belmont, CA 94002   415-595-0610

MMS is a multinational corporation specializing in financial and economic research. MMS offers the following products on interest rate trends:

   ■ MMS Fundamental Analysis—a comprehensive analytical service that presents forecasts and analysis of the supply and demand factors that affect short-term interest rates. The analysis focuses on federal policy and operations, monetary aggregates, economic conditions, treasury activity, and other interest-rate-sensitive topics. A popular feature of this service is the *Weekly Economic Survey,* which quantifies the expectations of over a hundred institutional market participants and leading economists for upcoming financial and economic releases, market tone, and market-sensitive events.

It offers subscribers unlimited, direct telephone access to analysts through a toll-free hotline. MMS encourages its clients to call with any questions they may have. Entire service cost is $275 a month.

■ FEDWATCH—a weekly newsletter which contains concise forecasts and interpretations of factors affecting debt market prices and short-term interest rates. Published every Thursday evening immediately following the release of relevant Federal Reserve data, the FEDWATCH newsletter is extremely timely. Topics discussed in the FEDWATCH newsletter include analysis of federal policy, international economics, treasury activity, and their respective impact on interest rate trends. The FEDWATCH newsletter is valuable to anyone who watches the financial markets, including the United States government securities market, financial futures, foreign exchange, and even the stock market. FED-WATCH is available on-line through CompuServe, NEXIS, and News-Net.

■ Ask Mr. Fed—in this on-line question-and-answer forum, participants discuss various topics related to interest rates and economic issues with analysts at MMS. The topics discussed include federal policy, debt market conditions, and other financial, economic, and political issues. This service is available only through the CompuServe system.

WHAT TO READ

The Dow Jones-Irwin Guide to Interest: What You Should Know About the Time Value of Money
Dow Jones-Irwin
1824 Ridge Road   800-323-1717
Homewood, IL 60430   800-942-8881—in IL
This 263-page book makes complex mathematics simple by using concise graphs and formulas. Among the topics covered are: return on investment, discounted cash flow, mortgage points, personal financial planning, yield to call, and bond selection. Cost is $19.95.

Income and Safety
The Institute for Econometric Research
3471 North Federal Highway   800-327-6720
Fort Lauderdale, FL 33306   305-563-9000
Published monthly, this consumer's guide to high yields is a survey of top-yielding federally insured accounts. The survey is restricted to banks and thrifts that do not charge extra account fees, which diminish actual

fees. Subscribers are automatically enrolled as members of the Institute. They will receive a free weekly hotline service. Annual subscription fee is $100.

ADDITIONAL RESOURCES

Interest Rates and Money Markets Made Easy
National Public Radio
Customer Service
PO Box 55417   800-253-0808
Madison, WI 53705   608-263-4892

With insight and humor, Robert Krulwich explains what causes interest rates to go up and how a money market fund actually works. Included are leading economists in "singing" roles. The cassette is twenty minutes long and costs $9.50.

Recorded Messages
There are several recorded messages you can dial to get current information about interest rates and related data.

Many Reserve Banks have tape-recorded announcements of interest rates (updated by Tuesday morning). Since the Federal Reserve Board does not give interest rates over the phone, you should call your nearest Reserve Bank listed below.

- New York: 212-791-6693
- Chicago: 312-322-5112 (no recording)
- Philadelphia: 215-574-6188
- Cleveland: 216-579-2001
- Richmond: 804-648-0880
- Atlanta: 404-521-8657
- St. Louis: 314-444-8590—Kathy Blumentritt (no recording)
- Kansas City: 816-881-2364
- Dallas: 214-651-6177
- San Francisco: 415-974-2477

The New York Fed provides daily Fed Funds and CD rates by recorded announcement. On Thursday the weekly Fed Funds average is also provided. The phone number is: 212-791-6693.

The Federal Reserve Board has two recorded announcements:

- 202-452-3206—Schedule of meetings and events
- 202-452-3658—Explanation of Treasury constant maturities and other general information pertaining to interest rates.

Constant maturities and bill rates that are used for adjustable rate mortgages (ARM) are provided by FNMA. See earlier in this section.

Information provided by the Treasury and the Bureau of Public Debt by recorded announcement:

      202-287-4100—Auction results and rates
      202-287-4091—Lesson on treasury bills
      202-287-4088—Lesson on treasury notes
      202-566-3734—Rate on 2 1/2-year certificate

Foreign Exchange Rates

Investing in overseas securities as well as foreign currency investing is becoming more and more popular as our world becomes smaller and smaller. A currency fluctuation can make or break an overseas investment opportunity, and such fluctuations appear to be increasing as countries increase competition in the trade wars.

Monitoring exchange rates can be as easy as checking your local newspaper or calling one of the toll-free numbers or recorded messages listed below. Other organizations listed can provide you with more detail and analysis if you have more than a passing interest in the subject.

AGENCIES, INSTITUTES, AND ORGANIZATIONS

Deak Perera   800-368-5683
1800 K Street, NW   202-872-8470
Washington, DC 20006   202-872-1630—recorded message

Known for expertise in the precious metal market, Deak Perera's nationwide offices also offer a full range of services in foreign currency exchange. The services include: buying and selling foreign currency for traveling or investment; issuing foreign currency traveler's checks (free of charge) and handling value-added tax refunds. Call the 800 or recorded message numbers above for current exchange-rate information. The following free publications are also available:

  ■ *Investing in Foreign Currency*—this brochure covers the ins and outs of investing in foreign currency.
  ■ *Foreign Exchange Rate Guide*—this monthly guide indicates the exchange rate of most of the major world countries.

Embassy
(Check with your local librarian for an address.)
The financial attaché of the country you are planning to visit, or from which you plan to purchase currency for an investment, can be of assistance in providing information on the exchange rate of their currency and the factors affecting it.

Foreign Exchange Division
Riggs National Bank
800 17th Street, NW   202-835-5125
Washington, DC 20006   202-835-5324—recorded message

The Foreign Exchange Division of Riggs can advise you, or refer you to an appropriate source, for all situations involving foreign currency exchange.

The phone number listed above is a daily updated recorded message giving the foreign currency exchange rate for the major countries of the world. (Remember these rates are the accounting rates with which banks exchange currency among themselves.)

Foreign Exchange and Gold Operations
Department of the Treasury
15th Street and Pennsylvania Avenue, NW, Room 5037
Washington, DC 20220   202-566-2773
   The Department of the Treasury monitors the foreign exchange market. For information contact Foreign Exchange and Gold Operations listed above.

Office of Data Management
Office of the Assistant Secretary for International Affairs
Department of the Treasury
1500 Pennsylvania Avenue, NW, Room 512
Washington, DC 20220   202-566-5473
   This office collects and analyzes data related to international portfolio investment and its effects on the national security, commerce, employment, inflation, general welfare, and foreign policy of the United States. It also reports on foreigners' portfolio investment in the United States.

Ruesch International   800-424-2923
1140 19th Street, NW   202-887-0990
Washington, DC 20036   202-887-0980—recorded message
   This foreign-exchange firm offers a variety of services to those services involving foreign currencies. Their recorded message will give you the current exchange rate for all major currencies. Pamphlets available from Ruesch are:
> ■ *Foreign Currency Guide*—this free guide contains currency conversion tables for twenty-four countries, and information on import/export restrictions and tipping customs for frequently visited countries. To obtain the pamphlet send a stamped, self-addressed envelope to the above address.
> ■ *6 Foreign Exchange Tips for the Traveler*—this free pamphlet offers a few simple tips for individuals traveling outside the United States that will help them save money and avoid hassles.

WHAT TO READ

Daily Newspapers
   Newspapers in large metropolitan areas carry a daily listing of foreign exchange rates for the major countries of the world. Check your local library for the *New York Times* and the *Washington Post.* Remember that these rates

are the accounting rates banks exchange among themselves and are lower than the actual figure an individual would be quoted.

Federal Reserve Bank of New York
Public Information Department
33 Liberty Street
New York, NY 10045   212-791-6134
   Two free publications address the topic of foreign exchange rates:
   - *Foreign Exchange Rates*—a weekly statistical release listing the currency exchange rates for thirty-two countries.
   - *Foreign Exchange Markets in the United States*—this booklet explores the foreign exchange markets structure, types of trades and how they are executed, commercial bank trading decisions, the economic factors determining exchange rates, and the dynamics of rate movements.

International Financial Statistics
International Monetary Fund
Publications
700 19th Street, NW
Washington, DC 20431   202-477-7000
   Published monthly, this periodical serves as a standard source of statistical information on all aspects of domestic and international finance. It lists foreign exchange rates for 149 countries and is available in major libraries. A single copy costs $10. An annual subscription with two supplements is $100.

Economic News from the Banks

Many banks offer newsletters, reports, and cassette tapes either free of charge or by subscription. Prepared by respected economists, these are excellent resources for tracking the economy and learning what future trends may be. Many include graphs and charts and most cover the national economy.

COMMERCIAL BANKS

Bank of America
World Information Services—3015   800-645-6667
Box 37000   800-645-4004—in CA
San Francisco, CA 94137   415-622-4120

The Bank of America publishes three reports in newsletter form on the economy. In each case, the December issue gives an analysis of the previous year and a two-year forecast:

- *California Economic Report*—a bimonthly covering agriculture, defense, energy, real estate, international banking, and other topics. It is four to six pages with the December issue running fifteen to twenty pages, and costs $12 a year.
- *U.S. Economic Report*—a monthly, covering such issues as budget debates in Congress, changing oil prices, the farm economy, and macroeconomic subjects. It is four to six pages, with the December issue running fifteen to twenty pages, and costs $12 a year.
- *World Report*—a monthly addressing issues of topical interest to the economic community. Subjects are of an international nature. It is four to six pages, with the December issue running fifteen to twenty pages, and costs $12 a year.

Chase Manhattan Bank
Energy Economics Department
One Chase Manhattan Plaza
New York, NY 10015   212-552-2222

Chase Manhattan puts out the following free publications on the petroleum industry:

- *Financial Analysis of a Group of Petroleum Companies: 1984*—published annually, this twenty-nine-page booklet is the result of a yearly study that Chase Manhattan conducts on the financial performance of nineteen of the larger non-OPEC petroleum companies. Because the aggregate operations of these companies constitute a significant proportion of the world-wide activities of the petroleum industry, an analysis of their combined financial performance provides an important part of the analysis of the entire worldwide industry. Nineteen companies are covered in this 29-page report.

■ *Capital Investments of the World Petroleum Industry: 1984*—published annually, this twenty-four-page booklet describes a Chase Manhattan study which extends the coverage of the above *Financial Analysis of a Group of Petroleum Companies* to an estimate for the entire industry worldwide except for centrally planned economies. The book goes into type and geographic location of these capital investments in considerable detail.

■ *The Petroleum Situation*—an eight-page newsletter of text and graphs published occasionally, each issue concentrating on a different petroleum topic.

First National Bank of Chicago
Business and Economic Research Division
One First National Plaza
Chicago, IL 60670   312-732-3779
  Two publications are offered:

■ *First Forecast Series*—this is a two-part publication. The monthly, entitled *First Forecast,* covers aspects of the domestic economy, rates and projections. The quarterly, *First Financial Forecast,* discusses factors determining fiscal and monetary policy. Each is four pages long. Free.

■ *International Update*—this quarterly looks at international economies and exchange rates by country. The length varies. About six pages are devoted to each country, with eight to ten countries represented in each issue. Free.

Harris Trust and Savings Bank
Economic Research Office
111 West Monroe Street   312-461-5322—*Barometer of Business*
Chicago, IL 60606   312-461-5552—*Sound of Business*
  The Harris Bank publishes the following newsletter and cassette tape on business issues:

■ *Barometer of Business*—this four-page, bimonthly report, written by Robert Genetski, the bank's economist, covers current economic and political topics valuable to both the serious investor and the household decision-maker. Topics have included gold, the stock market, tax reform, and the United States economic outlook. A look at the charts presented is enough to give any reader a snapshot of where today's economy stands in relation to its recent history.

■ *Sound of Business*—this monthly cassette tape features discussion and interpretation of current economic trends by Robert Genetski. It is an up-to-the-minute analysis of stocks, bonds, interest rates, monetary policy, tax reform, and more. Investment insight is provided by David Mead along

- -

> ## Where Most Americans Keep Their Money:
> ## Banks Are Most Likely to Get Your Account
>
> A CBS/*New York Times* poll showed that people are more
> likely to have an account in a commercial bank if they have
> any at all.

- -

with a rotating panelist from the Harris trust department. The program
is moderated by Larry Butler, an eminent Washington financial jour-
nalist. Each tape runs thirty-five to forty minutes. Annual subscription is
$150.

Manufacturers Hanover Trust Company
350 Park Avenue
New York, NY 10022   212-286-7359
   Two free newsletters are available by contacting the above address:
      ■ *Economic Report*—this four-to-six-page monthly, written by Irwin L.
      Kellner, Manufacturers Hanover Trust's chief economist, deals with current
      economic topics, both domestic and foreign, discussing the federal budget,
      projections for the future, and more.
      ■ *Financial Digest*—a four-page biweekly with about one and a half pages
      of tables, it contains selected Federal Reserve data, bank loan figures,
      business indicators, securities market information, and New York and inter-
      national money market information.

Morgan Guaranty Trust Company of New York
Economic Analysis Department
23 Wall Street
New York, NY 10015   212-483-2346
   You can get the following free publication by contacting the above ad-
dress:
      ■ *Monthly Economic Outlook*—a two-page newsletter containing a run-
      down on the GNP, consumer price index, United States economy, infla-
      tion, and interest rates.

Wells Fargo Bank
Economics Department
Box 44000
475 Sansome Street
San Francisco, CA 94163   415-396-0123

The Wells Fargo Bank puts out the following reports and newsletters:

■ *Wells Fargo Economic Monitor*—a monthly special series on business and finance, it covers current reports on: the nation, analyzing United States and international business conditions and trends; California, with an analysis similar to that in the national report; and money and credit markets, covering Federal Reserve and administrative policies, interest rate changes, and prime rate projections. Subscribers may telephone members of the economic department for answers to business and finance questions. A subscription costs $200 a year.

■ *Business Review*—published three or four times a year, this publication covers pertinent economic topics and business activities in California and the western United States. Free.

■ *Professional Business Reports*—issued periodically, these reports focus on various aspects of California, its markets, international trade, regional growth, agriculture, small business and more. The following are two samples.

■ *Small Business in California*—an outlook for the future which focuses on the importance of small business activity within the state. It is thirty pages long and costs $5.

■ *California 2000: A Business and Economic Appraisal*—a look ahead at the business and economic situation. It is thirty pages long and costs $5.

FEDERAL RESERVE BANKS

Each of the twelve district banks provides various weekly, monthly, quarterly, and yearly reports focusing on current economic issues, monetary policy, recent business activity, money and bond markets, and banking and finance. Most reports are offered free of charge. Those districts which publish newsletters are listed below.

Federal Reserve Bank of Atlanta
Research Department/Publications
104 Marietta Street
Atlanta, GA 30303   404-521-8788
The Federal Reserve Bank of Atlanta publishes the following:

■ *Southeastern Economic Insight*—a semimonthly, with brief, nontechnical articles relating current economic and financial news with emphasis on the Southeast. It is of particular interest to bankers, business executives, teachers, and the news media. Free.

■ *Economic Review*—issued every two months, this magazine informs the public, as much as possible in layman's terms, about Federal Reserve policies and the general economic environment. Free.

Federal Reserve Bank of Boston
Bank and Public Services Department
600 Atlantic Avenue
Boston, MA 02106   617-973-3459
The Federal Reserve Bank of Boston publishes the following:

- *Bank Notes*—published every Friday, this report condenses daily newspaper articles and regulatory agency press releases focusing on regional developments affecting banking structure. It would be of interest to New England financial executives.
- *The Ledger*—a bimonthly, with reports on economic education programs in New England, new publications, and games and films that can help teachers explain economic-oriented subjects. Features a simplified discussion of an economic topic. It is designed for high school economics teachers.

Federal Reserve Bank of Chicago
Public Information Center
230 South LaSalle Street
Chicago, IL 60690   312-322-5112
The Federal Reserve Bank of Chicago publishes the following:

- *Agricultural Letters*—a biweekly, this newsletter relates agricultural developments in the nation and in the 7th District. It is of interest to farmers, economists, bankers, business executives, college students, and teachers. Free.
- *Fed Wire*—a monthly, this publication summarizes developments in the Federal Reserve Bank system and the Chicago region of concern to district financial institutions. It is available to district financial institutions and others on request. Free.
- *International Letter*—a monthly letter which surveys international economic events. It includes foreign market interest- and exchange-rate charts. It is written for bankers, economists, business people, college students, and teachers. Free.
- *Midwest Update*—incorporates a summary of economic conditions, focusing on major sectors of the economy in the 7th District. It is of interest to bankers, press, business people, economists, college students, and teachers. Free.
- *On Reserve*—published in the fall, winter, and spring this report explores economic or consumer education topics, suggests supplemental reading materials and teaching activities, and relates news of regional economic education programs. It is of interest to high school economic teachers and consumer education teachers.

Federal Reserve Bank of Cleveland

Public Information
PO Box 6387
Cleveland, OH 44101   216-579-2048
The Federal Reserve Bank of Cleveland publishes:
   ■ *Economic Commentary*—a biweekly with articles on current economic
   developments. It is intended for bankers, economists, business people,
   college students, and teachers. Free.

Federal Reserve Bank of Dallas

Public Affairs Department
Station K   214-651-6289
Dallas, TX 75222   214-651-6266
The Federal Reserve Bank of Dallas publishes:
   ■ *Dallas*—a monthly which contains articles on operational developments,
   regulatory changes, and current events throughout the Federal Reserve
   System. It is available to depository institutions and the general public.
   Free.

Federal Reserve Bank of Kansas City

Public Affairs
925 Grand Avenue
Kansas City, MO 64198   816-881-2402
The Federal Reserve Bank of Kansas City publishes:
   ■ *Fed Letter*—a bimonthly which informs bankers about Federal Reserve
   issues and topics. It is available to bankers and the general public. Free.

Federal Reserve Bank of Philadelphia

Public Information Department
PO Box 66
Philadelphia, PA 19105   215-574-6115
The Federal Reserve Bank of Philadelphia publishes:
   ■ *Banking Legislation and Policy*—put out five times a year, this newsletter
   summarizes and updates pending banking and financial legislation at both
   the federal and state (Pennsylvania,New Jersey, and Delaware) levels. It is
   of interest to bankers, economists, corporate executives, libraries, and the
   general public. Free.
   ■ *Fed Briefs*—a bimonthly which reviews Federal Reserve Bank system-
   related news of interest to district financial institutions. It is available to
   bankers. Free.
   ■ *Regional Economic Highlights*—a monthly which summarizes business
   and economic news pertaining to Pennsylvania, New Jersey, and Delaware. It is available to bankers, economists, corporate executives, libraries,
   and the general public. Free.

Federal Reserve Bank of San Francisco
Public Information Department
PO Box 7702
San Francisco, CA 94120   415-974-3234

The Federal Reserve Bank of San Francisco publishes the following:

- *Federal Reserve Notes*—a monthly which reviews policy statements, Federal Reserve Bank operations, and regulatory (including consumer) issues. It is available to district bankers. Free.
- *Weekly Letter*—a weekly which highlights a single major issue each week. It is of interest to bankers, business executives, and teachers. Free.

Part Three

INVESTMENT VEHICLES

THE SECURITIES AND EXCHANGE COMMISSION
TEN RED FLAGS FOR INVESTORS

1. Reject high-pressure telephone solicitation from strangers.

2. Be very skeptical of promises of exceptional returns and profits. If an investment opportunity sounds too good to be true, it probably is.

3. Investment advisers and financial planners registered with the Securities and Exchange Commission are required to provide brochures that describe their qualifications and possible conflicts of interest. Read the brochure and ask about anything you do not understand. It is better to ask first than to be sorry later.

4. Before you invest, request and read the prospectuses and offering circulars that describe the investment. Get it in writing.

5. Be sure you understand the risks of loss. Don't invest in something you don't understand.

6. Be wary of extremely low-priced penny stocks. They often involve the greatest risk.

7. Don't put any more money into high-risk investments than you can afford to lose.

8. Don't tie up most of your money in nonliquid investments. You may not have access to cash when you need it.

9. Keep track of how your investments are doing. Make sure you know where your money and securities are. Get written statements and receipts.

10. If in doubt, or if your investment adviser, financial planner, or broker refuses to give you information about your investments or ignores your instructions, call your local Better Business Bureau, state securities regulator, or SEC office.

Source: U.S. Securities and Exchange Commission.

Stocks

"Stocks are like streetcars. If you miss one, another one will come along." So says experienced financial analyst Mel Wright of Dean Witter. Therefore, if you're eager to become a Wall Street wizard, be patient. Educate yourself first about the world of stocks and the particular company you got the "hot" tip on.

How do most of us make our stock decisions? A recent survey showed that 43 percent of us analyze companies on our own; 40 percent of us weigh a broker's advice against our own; and only 12 percent of us rely solely on a broker's advice in picking investments. So, a wise investor does a lot of homework before plunking down money on a stock.

Where do you start if you are new at this? A good way is to immerse yourself in any number of excellent financial publications and advisory newsletters. Many of the recommended resources are listed in this chapter. Most are available at your public library and, if not, check the library of a major brokerage house or a business school in your community. *Standard and Poor's Stock Guide* and the *Value Line Investment Survey* should help you evaluate companies. The *Wall Street Journal* and *Forbes* magazine are often recommended by experts as being especially comprehensive in their analyses of economic issues and trend forecasts.

Other chapters of this book, Company Information, Industry and Market Information, and Monitoring the Economy, will give you additional resources. Many brokerage firms recommend that their clients read *How to Buy Stocks* by Louis Engel and Brendan Boyd, as it is easy to read and understand. *Securities Analysis* by Graham and Dodd, considered the "bible" of the industry, is a good resource for the serious investor.

Most large brokerage firms provide free publications and seminars for prospective clients. And organizations such as the National Association of Investors Corporation and the American Association of Individual Investors provide excellent educational programs and services, usually for nominal fees. Community colleges also offer good, inexpensive courses.

There are many investment advisory services and newsletters out there and, according to the experts, you should think twice before you spend your

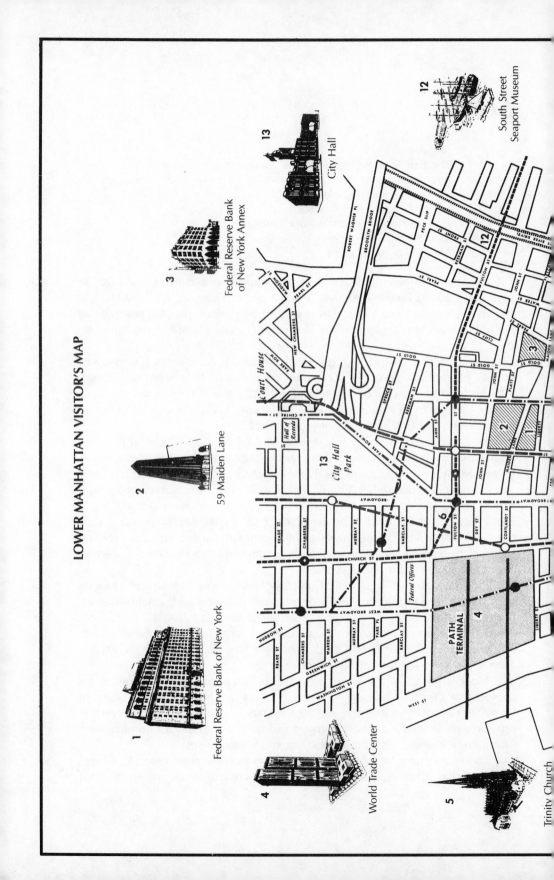

LOWER MANHATTAN VISITOR'S MAP

Federal Reserve Bank of New York

1

2

59 Maiden Lane

3

Federal Reserve Bank
of New York Annex

13

City Hall

12

South Street
Seaport Museum

4

World Trade Center

5

Trinity Church

PATH TERMINAL

City Hall Park

Court House

Hall of Records

Federal Offices

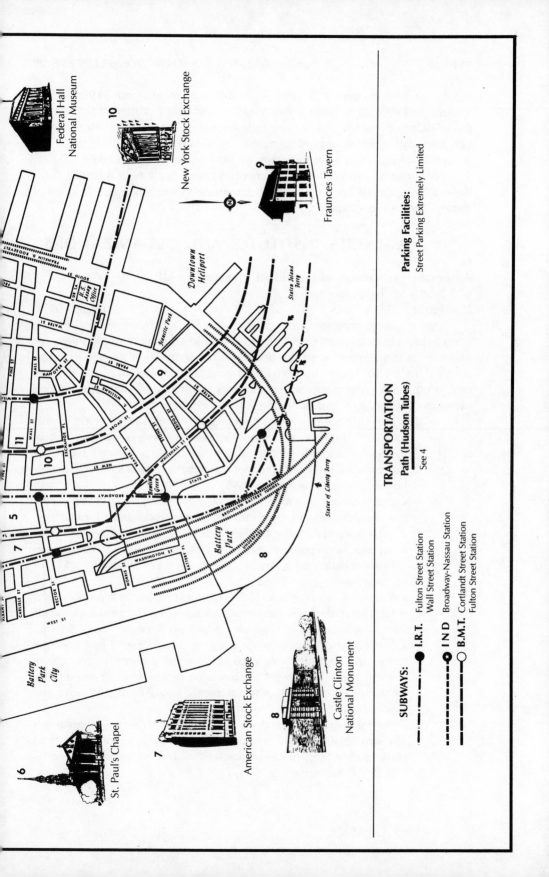

Federal Hall
National Museum

10
New York Stock Exchange

9
Fraunces Tavern

Battery Park City

St. Paul's Chapel

7
American Stock Exchange

8
Castle Clinton
National Monument

6

Parking Facilities:
Street Parking Extremely Limited

TRANSPORTATION
Path (Hudson Tubes)
See 4

SUBWAYS:

I.R.T. Fulton Street Station
        Wall Street Station

I N D   Broadway-Nassau Station

B.M.T. Cortlandt Street Station
        Fulton Street Station

money on them. Many are slanted, expensive (cost ranges from $100 to $900 a year), and difficult to understand. You can find many of them advertised in the *Wall Street Journal.* Ask for free sample copies of these newsletters *before* you part with your savings. Experts we consulted said you'd be better off putting your subscription money directly into stocks of your choice.

For those of you with home computers, there are lots of financial databases which provide updated daily stock quotations and other data. You'll find those listed in this chapter, too.

AGENCIES, INSTITUTES, AND ORGANIZATIONS

American Association of Individual Investors (AAII)
612 North Michigan Avenue
Chicago, IL 60611   312-280-0170

This national, nonprofit association, with 95,000 members nationwide and chapters in twenty-six cities, provides a solid education in investing—for all levels of experience, from the novice to the more sophisticated investor. AAII can help you set up your own investment club or refer you to an existing one in your area. The organization sponsors seminars, provides speakers on investment techniques and offers the following publications:

- *The AAII Journal*—a forty-page magazine, published ten times a year, the *Journal* features interviews with investment professionals, news about various financial products, evaluations of stocks, and stock screening. A subscription is included in the annual membership fee of $48; for nonmembers the annual subscription is $45.

- *Computerized Investing*—published every two months, this newsletter provides information on how to use your microcomputer for investing. Regular features include "how-to" articles, reviews of investment software, directory of public domain programs, book reviews, and evaluations of financial data systems. Annual subscription is $24 for members; $48 for nonmembers.

- *An Easy-to-Use Format for Selecting Stocks*—from the September 1985 *AAII Journal,* this reprint explains stock screening and provides a sample form by which you can judge any stock's performance. Cost is $4.

- *Home Study Curriculum*—for studying various types of investments at home, AAII offers this ten-chapter guide, which explains the concepts of risk and return and covers the basics on several kinds of investments, including common stock, debt instruments, mutual funds, currencies, real estate, and commodities. Cost is $38.

- *Individual Investor's Guide to No-Load Mutual Funds*—information is provided on 300 no-load mutual funds including historic returns, data on portfolio objectives, and risk characteristics. Free to members, the cost is $19.95 for nonmembers.

■ *The Individual Investor's Microcomputer Resource Guide*—this book provides basic information on selecting investment hardware and software, as well as book reviews and a discussion of on-line financial systems. In addition, the *Resource Guide* has hundreds of service listings for investment software programs and financial information systems. Cost is $9 for members and $11 for nonmembers.

■ *An Introduction to Shadow Stocks*—a listing of 440 "Shadow Stocks" (those smaller firms not in Wall Street's spotlight), along with screening information on how to pick them, is included in this four-page brochure. The cost is $4.

American Stock Exchange
86 Trinity Place
New York, NY 10006   212-306-1390
The American Stock Exchange conducts trading in a wide range of securities including common stocks, preferred stocks, warrants, put and call options, corporate bonds,and U.S.government securities. The Publication Services Division of the American Stock Exchange offers a number of free or low-cost publications, including:

■ *Amex Fact Book*—a statistical profile of the American Stock Exchange. Cost is $3.

■ *Amex Stats*—monthly statistical publication providing data on the Amex Market Value Index, equities, options, fixed income securities, top price percentage gainers, most active stocks and options, and new common stocks listed. Free.

■ *Poster*—color illustration of Amex trading floor activity. Cost is $3.

■ *Annual Report*—review of previous year's activity. Interim quarterly reports are also available. As the chairman's report to the Board of Governors, this document is ideal for learning the facts on membership, financial reports and tables, trading records, seat prices, new issues and all the information for the previous year. It is available in single copy only. Free.

■ *Listing of Foreign Securities on American Stock Exchange*—describes steps leading to listing of a company's issue on the Amex. Free.

■ *Requirements and Procedures for Additional Listings*—describes steps for a company to list additional shares. Free.

■ *Ten Years of Investment Returns*—a comparative study of rates of return on investment in the three major United States equity markets from 1974-1984: the New York Stock Exchange, the American Stock Exchange, and the NASDAQ over-the-counter market. Free.

Brokerage Houses
See also listings under THE FIRST STEP FOR BEGINNERS AND EXPERIENCED INVESTORS.

■ ■

SCRIPOPHILY: The Art of Locating Information
on Old Stocks and Bonds

If you ever cleaned out your attic and found an old stock certificate in your grandfather's trunk and wanted to know what it was worth, this is called *scripophily.* Here are sources to help you.

If you want to do it yourself:

Free Research Service
LaBarre Galleries Inc.
PO Box 746
Hollis, NH 03049
800-842-7000

Bond and Share Society
American Chapter
24 Broadway
New York, NY 10004
212-943-1880

*Scripophily: Collecting Bonds
and Share Certificates,* $14.95
Facts on File
Customer Service
460 Park Avenue South
New York, NY 10016
212-683-2244

Directory of Obsolete Securities, $200
Financial Information Inc.
30 Montgomery Street
Jersey City, NJ 07302
201-332-5400

If you want to have others do it for you:

Distinctive Documents
PO Box 1475
Orem, UT 84057
801-373-6790

Stock Market Information Service, Inc.
PO Box 120
Station "K"
Montreal, Canada H1N 3K9
514-256-9487

R. M. Smythe & Co., Inc.
24 Broadway
New York, NY 10004
212-943-1880

Tracers
39 Broadway
New York, NY 10006
212-558-6550

■ ■

Center for Research in Security Prices
University of Chicago
Graduate School of Business
1101 East 58th Street
Chicago, IL 60637   312-702-7275
   The Center for Research in Security Prices (sponsored by Merrill Lynch) was established in 1960. It maintains files of data on security prices and returns

and provides funds to support faculty and student research on related topics. It also maintains a library of financial publications.

The Center makes available to the general public a number of research papers on various securities-related topics. These papers are prepared by professors and financial experts. Topics include stock trading, inflation, executive stock options, components of investment performance, and more. A complete list of these papers is available free from the Center. To order a reprint of a particular paper, you must pay a $4 reprint charge, plus $2 postage and handling.

Investor Relations Departments

If you want to know exactly how your investment is being used, public companies have stockholders' representatives whose job it is to answer that kind of question. Call the company's headquarters and ask for the Investor Relations Department. Contact information can also be found in a company's annual report or *Moody's,* available at your library.

National Association of Investors Corporation (NAIC)
1515 East Eleven Mile Road
Royal Oak, MI 48067   313-543-0612

Here's an organization geared especially to beginning investors who are serious about educating themselves to manage their own investments or who wish to join with others to start or participate in an investment club. The National Association of Investors Corporation is a nonprofit, volunteer organization dedicated to helping investors since 1951 through various membership services. Your knowledge of common stocks and their place in your investment strategy will grow, and perhaps so will your stock earnings! You can get help from NAIC volunteers in over thirty cities through their regional council meetings.

NAIC's investment programs are *not* get-rich-quick programs; rather they are designed to help you build and accumulate, based on continuing experience and skill. Some individuals have built modest monthly investments into accounts over $200,000.

Membership in the NAIC also gives you information about and participation in Investors Fairs, held in more than fifty cities each year. There you can have the same one-on-one contact with top corporate officers that professional investors get. You'll learn about the National Congress, a yearly spectacular of investment information, with corporate exhibits, seminars, and speakers who are top investment personalities.

NAIC can refer you to an existing investment club or help you start one of your own. A club consists of a group of between ten and twenty people who meet once a month, deposit their monthly investment, review studies of stocks presented by members, and select a stock in which to invest. It isn't necessary

■ ■

THE REAL BOTTOM LINE:
What the Auditor's Statement Means

When reviewing financial statements, investors will encounter a number of different statements expressed by the auditors of the statements. Here is a description of what their expressed opinions stand for:

Unqualified: The audit was complete and statements were kept in accordance with generally accepted accounting principles. The auditor felt he did all he needed to do.

Unqualified Opinion: The audit was complete; perhaps the auditor did not do all he felt he needed to do; minor areas were not prepared according to generally accepted accounting principles; there were minor areas where the statements were not consistent with the preceding year, but these variations were not material.

Qualified Opinion: The audit was complete, but the omitted procedures and variations were sufficient to affect the opinion, which could be:

> *A Piecemeal Opinion:* Cash is correct, receivables have been confirmed, but an expression to the statement as a whole cannot be made.
> *Denial of an Opinion:* Nothing can be said for the fairness of the statement, either as a whole or in part.

Statements Prepared Without Audit: Statements were not audited and represent only the recordkeeping of management.

■ ■

to have investment knowledge before starting a club. As you attend each session and as your deposits grow (say $20-50 a month per member), so does your experience and skill.

In addition, NAIC members can participate in a low-cost stock purchase plan and receive special financial publications at a discount. Annual membership fee is $30 for individuals. NAIC offers the following publications:

> ■ *NAIC Investor's Manual*—for the individual investor or members of an investment club, NAIC's manual outlines investment principles to follow, a method for reviewing individual stocks, and an explanation of how to start an investment club. The cost is $12 and includes a $10 discount on your first year's membership should you decide to join.
> ■ *Better Investing*—the association's monthly magazine profiles selected stocks. Its monthly selections, "stocks to study," have beaten the Dow Jones Industrials in twenty-one of twenty-nine five-year periods since 1951. Free with membership, the annual subscription is $15 for nonmembers.

■ *Directory of Investor Contacts*—the investor contact, address, phone number, and ticker symbol for each company listed on the New York and American Stock Exchanges are provided in this annual directory. Price for members is $15, plus $1.50 postage and handling; price for nonmembers is $24 plus $2 postage and handling.

■ *NAIC Home Stock Study Course*—lessons to work on at home to educate yourself on stocks and investing are provided. Self-grading worksheets are included. The cost is $60 for members and $70 for nonmembers.

National Association of Securities Dealers
NASDAQ, Inc.
1735 K Street, NW
Washington, DC 20006   202-728-8000

Information about NASDAQ, which covers the over-the-counter (OTC) stock market, and help if you have a dispute with your broker are available from this trade association of security dealers.

NASDAQ, the acronym for the National Association of Securities Dealers Automated Quotes, is a nationwide electronic system that collects price quotes from more than 450 investment broker-dealers in more than 4,700 securities. The data is then distributed daily to NASDAQ subscribers and information vendors worldwide. NASDAQ is the main source on the OTC market as, unlike stocks traded on the New York Stock Exchange, American Stock Exchange, and regional stock exchanges, there is no central location trading floor for OTC stock. Common and preferred stocks are traded, and most bank and insurance company stocks are bought and sold over the counter. OTC trading isn't cheap. For a better understanding of how the OTC market works, check with your broker.

As the professional association for securities dealers, NASDAQ is concerned with maintaining the standards and ethics of the profession. If you should have a dispute with your broker, you're in luck; NASD has one of the best arbitration procedures of any profession. In fact, if you should file a claim (following NASD arbitration guidelines) statistics show you are most likely to win. To get an arbitration procedure going, call NASD for referral to one of its thirteen district offices.

In addition to a free arbitration guidebook, NASD publishes:

■ *NASDAQ Company Directory*—updated semiannually, this features a compilation of NASDAQ companies, with contact names and numbers. Cost is $5.

■ *NASDAQ Fact Book*—a 118-page annual report of statistics and information concerning the NASDAQ over-the-counter stock market. Free.

The New York Stock Exchange (NYSE)   212-656-3000
11 Wall Street   212-656-2089—publications
New York, NY 10005   212-656-5936—educational division

The New York Stock Exchange lists and trades over 1,500 stocks, almost 1,000 corporate bonds, nearly 400 convertible bonds, and over 200 convertible preferred stocks. The NYSE provides a public two-way auction market, supported by a multimillion-dollar computer execution system, giving orders from investors all over the world an equal footing. A film, teaching tools, and publications are available from NYSE:

- *The New York Stock Exchange Factbook*—this booklet contains information on fifty of the largest companies listed on the Exchange, their assets, and more. It also includes information on the stock exchange rules and miscellaneous statistics on member firms that are traded on the exchange. Call or write for current cost. (It was $3.70 as we went to press.)
- *Understanding Stocks and Bonds*—this eleven-page booklet explains in easy-to-read format the questions investors should ask before investing in a company; it outlines the rights and privileges of owning common stock. It defines preferred stocks, dividends, splits, etc., and it tells about the regulations governing the securities industry. It defines and describes different types of bonds, convertibles, and who should consider investing in stocks or bonds. Excellent basic information for beginning investors. This booklet is included in a set known as the Investors Information Kit. The kit also includes the following booklets: *Glossary, Understanding Financial Statements,* and *Getting Help When You Invest.* The complete set is available for $4 from NYSE's Publications Department.
- NYSE Film—the NYSE is distributing a new film, which was untitled when we went to press. Its purpose is to demystify the stock market. The viewer learns the workings of the modern trading floor. It is available to any educational group, in 16mm format, and runs ten to twelve minutes. Call the NYSE Educational Division for prices.

Securities Industry Association
120 Broadway
New York, NY 10271   212-685-5499
    See listing under KIDS AND MONEY.

The Securities Investor Protection Corporation (SIPC)
900 17th Street, NW
Washington, DC 20006   202-223-8400
    Suppose you invest in a company through a reputable broker-dealer or brokerage firm which goes under. What happens to your money? The SIPC is a federal corporation which insures the accounts of securities customers of member broker-dealers in case the brokerage firm fails. Customers are insured up to $500,000, of which no more than $100,000 can be for cash. Reimbursement to investors could take up to three months, after SIPC processes the claims. For more information on the services of the SIPC, write for a free eleven-page brochure, *How SIPC Protects You,* which may reassure you about

the protection of your stocks, bonds, and CDs (Certificates of Deposit). However, the SIPC doesn't insure commodities or interests in gold and silver.

Stockholders of America
1625 I Street, NW
Washington, DC 20006   202-783-3430

Founded in 1972, this organization represents more than 25 million stockholders in some of America's largest as well as smaller companies. It is a registered lobbying group for those who invest in stock, and it has successfully dealt with issues such as the repeal of the withholding tax on reinvested dividends. The organization periodically publishes a bulletin as needed. Annual membership in this organization costs only $15 a year.

U.S. Securities and Exchange Commission (SEC)
Publications Section, Reference Branch
450 5th Street, NW
Washington, DC 20549   202-272-7450

Created by Congress, the SEC administers laws that relate to the field of securities and finance and seeks to provide protection for investors and the public in their securities transactions. A company offering securities for public sale must register with the SEC, providing an accurate disclosure of the material facts concerning the company and the securities for sale. This is required by law so investors may make a realistic appraisal. The SEC does not give advice as to the merits of securities; that responsibility rests with the investor. If you are an investor who acquires 5 percent or more of a company's shares, you must report that to the SEC within ten days on a form called 13D. The SEC publishes a daily summary of these 13D filings in the *SEC News Digest,* which you can look at in the SEC's public libraries in Chicago, Los Angeles, New York, and Washington, DC.

For more information on the SEC, refer to the chapter How to Find Information on a Company. The SEC publishes the following booklet:

- *Investigate Before You Invest*—how to shop for securities and how to protect yourself against "con artists" are explained in this seven-page guide. Free.
- *What Every Investor Should Know*—a free booklet giving, in layman's terms, general information about various kinds of investments. Free.

WHAT TO READ

Dividend Reinvestment Plans
Want to save money in purchasing stocks? The Dividend Reinvestment Plan (DRP) is offered by hundreds of companies. A DRP allows shareholders to reinvest dividends—and often additional sums—in new stock shares without

incurring additional brokerage costs. Some companies even offer 3 to 5 percent discounts on any additional stock purchased for dividend reinvestors. The following directories can help you locate DRPs:

- *Duane E. Frederic's DRP Directory*—Mr. Frederic teaches finance at Notre Dame College in South Euclid, Ohio, and he tracks DRPs professionally. His directory lists over 940 companies arranged by industry group. Company name, stock symbol, and exchange are included. For a copy, send $8 to Duane Frederic, 8908 East Pilgrim Drive, Chagrin Falls, OH 44022.

- *Standard and Poor's*—a listing of DRP companies. Send $2 to Standard and Poor's, Public Relations Department, 25 Broadway, New York, NY 10004.

- *Evergreen Enterprises Directory*—a directory of more than 950 United States and Canadian companies that have DRPs. Listings include company addresses, discounts available and limits on optional cash investments. It is available for $14.75 from Evergreen Enterprises, Box 763, Laurel, MD 20707. (MD residents must add 70 cents sales tax.)

Dow Jones & Company, Inc.
The Educational Service Bureau
PO Box 300
Princeton, NJ 08540   609-452-2000
    See listing under KIDS AND MONEY.

Dun's Business Month
875 Third Avenue
New York, NY 10022   212-605-9400
    This monthly magazine, formerly *Dun's Review* and published by a subsidiary of Dun and Bradstreet Corporation, recaps the month's significant business news, forecasts economic trends, and analyzes companies' performances. Cost is $24 a year. A single copy is $2.50.

Forbes
60 Fifth Avenue
New York, NY 10011   212-620-2200
    See listing under NEWSPAPERS AND MAGAZINES FOR TRACKING NEWS AND TRENDS, AND FOR MANAGING YOUR MONEY.

Gaining on the Market
by Charles J. Rolo
Little, Brown, and Co.
34 Beacon Street
Boston, MA 02106   617-227-0730

This book, by the Wall Street columnist for *Money* magazine, describes investment strategy for stocks, bonds, options, mutual funds, and gold. Highly recommended for beginners. A 299-page hardcover, it costs $14.95.

High-Tech Directory
Barrington Research Associates
PO Box 860
Barrington, IL 60010   312-382-7788

For a descriptive listing of over 800 technology innovative companies whose stock is traded on various exchanges, send for a free copy of the *High-Tech Directory* at the above address.

How to Be Your Own Stockbroker
by Charles Schwab
Macmillan Publishing Co.
866 Third Avenue
New York, NY 10022   212-702-2000

This book, by the man whose discount brokerage firm is now the nation's largest, sets out a game plan for making your own investment decisions. Includes a review of stock market systems and how to apply principles of investing to IRAs, stocks, bonds, and mutual funds. Schwab also offers an introduction to market psychology, how to read cycles, and the author's ten secrets of success. A 228-page hardcover, it costs $15.95.

How to Buy Stocks
by Louis Engel and Brendan Boyd
Bantam Books
666 Fifth Avenue
New York, NY 10103   212-765-6500

This popular book on the stock market, for both new and seasoned investors, is now in its seventh edition. It explains how to open an account with a broker, read financial news, understand over-the-counter stocks, buy stock on margin, and much more. It has an especially thorough bibliography on stocks, and the recommendations of several investment experts. It has up-to-date information on trends in financial markets, and stock screening methods, and tells you how to make the computer revolution work for you. This 323-page book costs $4.50.

Investment Advisory Newsletters and Services
There are hundreds of advisory newsletters written for investors. Most are geared toward the intermediate to advanced and are difficult for the beginner. Described below is a sampling of the more popular ones. Before subscribing you should request several sample issues to determine if the service is for you.

The Astute Investor
Investors Analysis, Inc.
PO Box 988
Paoli, PA 19301

By Robert Nurock, a regular contributor to TV's *Wall Street Week*, it offers a consistently good, sophisticated analysis of the market and specific stocks and options. The newsletter is geared toward more advanced investors and not recommended for beginners. Published every three weeks. Annual subscription is $197.

Babson's Reports
Wellesley Hills, MA 02181
617-235-0900

A weekly advisory, this newsletter focuses on market/business trends, with some coverage of certain stock groups and recommendations on which stocks and bonds are best to buy or sell. This publication called the 1929 crash and has been around for years. Annual subscription is $96.

The Chartist
PO Box 3160
Long Beach, CA 90803
213-596-2385

This is a twice-monthly, eight-page advisory newsletter on the stock market. It reprints quotes from other selected advisory newsletters such as the *Zweig Forecast* and *Dick Davis Digest.* It also gives charts and outlines of top-rated stocks and follow-ups on previous reviews. Cost is $115 a year or $65 for six months.

Growth Stock Outlook
4405 East-West Highway
Chevy Chase, MD 20814
301-654-5205

A twice-monthly advisory, this features stock selections by Charles Allmon. According to *Hulbert's Financial Digest,* it provides good long-term results. This publication is for advanced investors. Cost is $175 a year.

The Hulbert Financial Digest
643 South Carolina Avenue, SE
Washington, DC 20003
800-227-1617, ext. 459
800-772-3545, ext. 459—in CA
202-546-2164—in DC area

This is a ten-page monthly publication which tracks and rates the performance of more than seventy-five investment advisory newsletters. According to Hulbert, the top three newsletters with the best five-year record

(1980-1985) were: *Prudent Speculator, Growth Stock Outlook,* and *Zweig Forecast.* In 1985, the best performer in terms of gain for the year was the *McKeever Strategy Letter.* A one-year subscription to the *Hulbert Financial Digest* costs $135.

The Hulbert Financial Digest Annual Review of Investment Newsletters—geared toward intermediate and advanced investors, this annual directory contains reviews of fifty investment newsletters, which are rated in terms of risk, tax considerations, and performance. There are also chapters on the place of such newsletters in your overall financial planning, which newsletters are best for stock market watchers, and answers to the most frequently asked questions about advisory services/ newsletters. Call or write for current price information, or check the financial reference section of your public library for a copy of the 342-page book.

Investment Horizons
Investment Information Services, Inc.
205 West Wacker Drive
Chicago, IL 60606
312-750-9300

This bimonthly, twenty-four-page newsletter recommends small company stocks—"shadow stocks"—based on their growth potential and price/earnings ratios. Annual subscription is $195.

Standard and Poor's Outlook
45 Broadway
New York, NY 10004

This weekly newsletter lists and rates best and worst performing stock groups and recommends issues on the basis of risk and investment goals. Reviews of economic trends and business/industry forecasts are included, along with appealing graphics. The newsletter is consistent and a little more conservative than others in its coverage. A one-year subscription to *Outlook* costs $195.

Timer Digest
PO Box 030247
Fort Lauderdale, FL 33303
305-764-8499

Unique among investment advisory newsletters, *Timer Digest* monitors over thirty advisory services and lists the top ten timers in timer standings. What, you may ask, is a timer? According to Robert E. James, editor of *Timer Digest* and a portfolio manager with over thirty years' experience, a "timer" is a financial analyst who is skilled in picking (predicting) the points at which the stock market will go up or down, and thus can aid you in your decisions of when to buy or sell. *Timer Digest* grew from a monthly letter which Mr. James originally wrote for his institutional clients. It is now read worldwide.

Published every third week, each issue gives you timing signals and a list of purchase recommendations. Every other issue spotlights one of the top ten advisers with an in-depth study of his or her work. Twice weekly (Wednesday and Saturdays), there is a recorded "hotline" message from Mr. James, with updated stock market information. *Timer Digest* costs $150 a year.

United Business and Investment Report
United Business Service
210 Newbury Street
Boston, MA 02116-9915
800-228-2028, ext. 431
617-267-8855

This is one of the oldest newsletters on stock market analysis and recommendations for buying different stocks. A general business forecast plus news from Washington is included each week. Personal financial planning information is also provided. Published each Friday, after the close of the markets for the week, *United Business and Investment Report* costs $170 a year.

Value Line Investment Survey
711 Third Avenue
New York, NY 10017
800-633-2252, ext. 281—credit card subscriptions

This is one of the largest, most comprehensive advisory services available to investors. Every week, its staff of economists, analysts, and statisticians reviews and evaluates 1,700 stocks. In the forty-page summary and index section, these stocks are listed with their performance, risk, estimated yields, latest earnings dividends, and other data. Each week there are full-page analyses of 130 stocks, and a section on especially recommended stocks. It is geared toward intermediate to advanced investors. A one-year subscription costs $395 and a ten-week trial offer is available for $50.

The Zweig Forecast
PO Box 5345
New York, NY 10150
212-644-0040

Rated a top performer among investment newsletters, *The Zweig Forecast* features a real portfolio and analyzes the strategy behind the choices. Published every three weeks, this newsletter costs $245 a year.

The Investor's Guide to Stock Quotations
by Gerald Warfield
Harper & Row
10 East 53rd Street
New York, NY 10022   800-638-3030

For novice and experienced investors, this is the most comprehensive reference available (and newly updated and revised) to demystifying the jargon of Wall Street. The author explains how to identify, read, and interpret stock, bond, mutual fund, money market, and commodity quotations and the stock symbols on cable TV. He covers important changes in these instruments as well as in financial futures and futures options. An appendix with 20,000 entries lists all major stock issuing companies and exchanges where they are traded. The 470-page paperback book costs $14.95.

Market Logic
Institute for Econometric Research
3471 North Federal Highway
Fort Lauderdale, FL 33306   305-563-9000

Market Logic is an eight-page, twice-monthly newsletter on stocks and options, with analysts' recommendations and ratings of current stock positions. Annual subscription fee is $200. (You can cancel within sixty days for a full refund if you're not satisfied.)

Media General
PO Box C-32333
Richmond, VA 23293   804-649-6000

For statistics-lovers and company analysts, Media General offers two publications:

- *The Media General Financial Weekly*—offers statistical information for stocks traded on the major exchanges. Annual subscription is $105.
- *The Media General Market Data Graphics*—provides in-depth graphics on individual companies. Annual subscription is $145. If you prefer, you can order both publications for a total of $180 a year.

Moody's Handbook of OTC Stocks
Moody's Investor Services
99 Church Street
New York, NY 10007   212-553-0300

Moody's Investor Services is a Dun and Bradstreet subsidiary with headquarters in New York City and branches in Boston, Cleveland, Dallas, Glendale (CA), Miami, and Philadelphia. In addition to *Moody's Manuals,* containing information on more than 23,000 companies, it publishes:

- *Moody's Handbook of OTC Stocks*—published quarterly, this is a compact, easy-to-use reference for investors. There is information on 561 companies whose common stock is traded over the counter (OTC). It features price score leaders, company stock selling below book value, ranking of stocks by various investment criteria, and low-price stocks. Annual subscription is $135. Your public library's financial reference section probably has copies of this publication.

The Moneypaper
2 Madison Avenue
Larchmont, NY 10538   914-833-0270
    See listing under NEWSPAPERS AND MAGAZINES FOR TRACKING NEWS AND TRENDS, AND FOR MANAGING YOUR MONEY.

The New York Times
Financial Section
229 West 43rd Street   212-556-1234—editorial
New York, NY 10036   800-631-2500—home delivery orders, nationwide
    The New York Times financial news is included in the "Business Day" section and contains information and charts on active stocks and stock trading, company information and profiles, and general economic news and forecasts. A one-year subscription (weekdays and Sunday) costs $185. Weekdays only, it costs $99.50; and Sundays only, it costs $94.

Security Analysis
McGraw-Hill Book Company
Princeton Road
Hightstown, NJ 08520   609-426-5254
    Considered the bible of the industry, this textbook by Graham and Dodd is used by colleges and universities nationwide. It is read, and reread, by professionals in the field. The basics of investing in common stocks, bonds, and other securities are covered. Information about the fundamental structure of companies and what to look for when analyzing companies for investment purposes is discussed. Although the current edition was updated in 1962 the book is still valuable. It can be found in most libraries or purchased for $41.95.

Shareholder Freebies: A Guide to Perks for Ownership of Common Stock
Buttonwood Press
41 Park Avenue
New York, NY 10016   212-689-4633
    Eamonn Fingleton has collected information about gifts and discounts that some companies offer their stockholders, such as fifty off rates for hotel corporation shareholders. Most of the gift and discount programs described in the forty-page paperback don't require ownership of a minimum number of shares. The cost is $7.95.

Standard and Poor's Corporation
25 Broadway
New York, NY 10004   212-208-8690
     Publications of interest are:
          ■ *How to Invest*—this handbook will tell you how to buy and sell stocks,
          as well as the advantages and disadvantages of investing in securities. It will
          make you familiar with the language of the financial community. Free.
          ■ *Standard and Poor's Stock Guide*—this is a monthly publication contain-
          ing pertinent financial data on more than 5,100 common and preferred
          stocks. A separate section covers over 380 mutual fund issues. The guide
          contains information for each stock on price ranges, dividends, earnings,
          financial position, institutional holdings, and ranking for earning and divi-
          dend stability. It is a quick and useful reference for almost all actively traded
          stocks. Cost is $84 a year.

The Stock Market Primer
by Claude N. Rosenberg, Jr.
Warner Books
666 Fifth Avenue
New York, NY 10103   212-484-2900
     This popular guide by a leading investment expert has been revised and
updated since 1981. It tells you how the stock market works, how to spot bull
and bear markets, how to tell which industries have the greatest potential, what
types of securities different corporations issue, when to buy, when to sell, and
where to invest. It is 357 pages and costs $4.95 in paperback and $5.95 in
hardcover.

The Thinking Investor's Guide to the Stock Market
by Kiril Sokoloff
McGraw-Hill Book Company
Princeton Road
Hightstown, NJ 08520   609-426-5254—order department
     A former commercial and investment banker and now managing editor of
a financial newsletter, Mr. Sokoloff offers a 234-page comprehensive guide
to participation in the stock market. It covers straightforward matters such
as how to evaluate the best stock, when to buy, when to sell, how to recognize bull and bear market cycles, and when to stay out of the market alto-
gether. The 1978 hardcover edition was revised in paperback in 1984. It costs
$9.95.

Understanding Wall Street
Liberty Publishing Company, Inc.
50 Scott Adam Road
Cockeysville, MD 21030   301-667-6680

Written by Jeffrey B. Little and Lucien Rhodes, this book is a readable and comprehensive guide for the layman to the complicated world of stocks and bonds. All major areas of investing in the stock market are covered. It is available for $7.95 plus $1 to cover shipping and handling.

Value Line OTC Special Situation Service
Value Line
711 Third Avenue   212-687-3965
New York, NY 10017   800-633-2252, ext. 281—order department
For the dedicated, experienced investor, the *Value Line OTC Special Situation Service* is an advisory newsletter published every two weeks. It provides expert recommendations on over-the-counter stocks, reviews, and quarterly follow-ups on previous recommendations. Statistics and charts are included in each issue. Issues are usually about twenty pages or more, and a binder is included to hold the year's copies. Subscribers also receive a reference library of selected back issues. A trial subscription of six issues is available for $35. One year's subscription is $350.

The Wall Street Journal
200 Liberty Street
New York, NY 10281   212-416-2000

Circulation and Customer Service:
200 Burnett Road   413-592-7761
Chicopee, MA 01021   800-628-9320—to arrange carrier deliver
The best-known daily newspaper specializing in business and investments, the *Wall Street Journal* is published Monday through Friday except for legal holidays. It publishes the latest stock market quotations from all exchanges as well as the over-the-counter market. Additionally, it contains market comment and analysis, as well as news about individual companies and economic developments. This paper probably gives more day-to-day statistics on stocks and stock trading than any other source. A six-month subscription is $56 and a yearly subscription is $107.

FOR COMPUTER USERS

If you're a serious investor with a home computer, you can access the same information your broker gets. With dedication and practice, you can begin to analyze financial data and make your own investment decisions via any number of databases and software systems. In 1985, almost 20,000 people were trading securities with their computers, while 58,000 were using financial databases on a regular basis. Dow Jones News Retrieval Service is the most popular database, followed closely by CompuServe and The Source. For your convenience, we've included information on these "big three" databases, plus information on some of the less well-known (and sometime less expensive) databases.

CDA Investment Technologies, Inc.
11501 Georgia Avenue
Silver Spring, MD 20902-1975   301-942-1700

Be your own stock market specialist with this database. CDA tracks and analyzes ownership data on over 6,000 companies as compiled from the SEC filings, updated daily. This information is available for access through the Spectrum Online System. Holdings can be accessed by stock or by owner. There is an analysis of voting authority and investment discretion. This information is available on a per report or unlimited basis. (Fees vary according to amount of information accessed.)

Through the Spectrum and Vista Online Package, you can compare any company with its competitors in terms of: current ownership, historical ownership and price performance over time (with color graphics), analysis, using thirty financial measures, and screening for institutions with specific investment styles (P/E yield, volatility, market cap, economic sector). Unlimited access is $1,800 a year. Also available on a per report basis, plus connect charge.

Hard-copy reports (loose-leaf bound volume) on United States and European Investment Company Stock holdings are available quarterly. Annual subscription is $195.

CompuServe Information Services
5000 Arlington Centre Boulevard
Columbus, OH 43220   800-848-8199

CompuServe offers current and historical price quotations on more than 40,000 stocks, bonds, and options; Standard and Poor's company reports; commodity news; Value Line reports; MicroNet (financial analysis programs and storage space for portfolio); and major newspapers and magazines. It is connected with Quick and Reilly brokerage.

Fees: No monthly minimum, except for "Executive Option" service which gives more detailed, professional information on specific companies, and more. Rates are approximately 20 to 25 cents a minute for "prime time" day use; and 10 to 20 cents a minute for "standard time." Sign up packages are available through computer stores.

Data Speed, Inc.
1900 South Norfolk Street, Suite 150
San Mateo, CA 94403   800-762-7538

How do you get stock quotes on the golf course or wherever else you're relaxing? A new portable device called Quo-Trek can deliver NYSE, AMEX, and NASDAQ share prices as well as commodity prices instantly. This investor's electronic cordless "toy" isn't cheap, but it's handy. Cost is $399.95 plus $10 shipping and handling. You can order by credit card through Data Speed's toll-free number.

Dow Jones News Retrieval Service
PO Box 300
Princeton, NJ 08543-0300   800-257-5114

Dow Jones offers the *Wall Street Journal, Barron's, Dow Jones News Wire,* transcripts of TV's *Wall Street Week* Securities and Exchange Commission filings by 8,500 companies, reports on 3,150 companies, stock price quotations, Fidelity Investor's Express (to trade stocks and options), and analysts' reports from 50 brokerages.

Fees: $29.95 signup cost includes five hours of free time; or $49.95 signup cost with eight hours of free time, plus an annual service fee of $12 (waived for first year). Day rates are 90 cents a minute and night rates are 20 cents a minute.

Investor's Express
Fidelity Brokerage Services
82 Devonshire Street
Boston, MA 02109   617-523-1919

Investor's Express allows investors to trade or obtain quotes on stocks and options listed on major exchanges. Quotes are delayed twenty minutes, and the system will automatically keep track of your investment portfolio.

Fees: Signup fee of $49.95; $15 a month charge which includes one hour of connect time. Rate for prime time is 40 cents a minute and rate for nonprime time is 10 cents a minute.

National Computer Network, Inc.
1929 Harlem Avenue
Chicago, IL 60635   312-622-6666

The National Computer Network, Inc. is now offering its major financial databases for home computer user access through its Nite-Line service. The service provides access to COMDAT (Commodity Data Base), OPTDAT (Options Data Base), FISCAL (Stock-Bond-Option-Index Data Base), and Media General (common stock on major exchanges as well as over-the-counter stocks). The commodity data include open, high, low, settle, volume, and open interest for major U.S. exchanges and London, with daily updates at 6 A.M. End of day stocks and options data include bid/low, ask/high, last sale, volume and open interest for all NYSE and AMEX and OTC stocks and all U.S. listed options. These updates are at 6 P.M. Historical information for stocks, bonds, indexes and options includes close, low, high, volume, shares outstanding, bid, ask, volume, and open interest figures. Prices are $9 an hour for 300 baud between 6 P.M. and 8 A.M. and on weekends, and $15 for 1200 baud. The prices go up to $20 and $26 an hour for daytime hours but the data are only updated at the close of the day, which means that during the day you will be receiving yesterday's prices. Communications charges are $4 at night, and $6 for 300 baud and $8 for 1200 baud during prime time on their Autonet system. There are no other surcharges, cpu charges, or monthly minimums.

PC Quote
401 South LaSalle Street, Suite 1600
Chicago, IL 60605   800-225-5657

For the experienced investor or trader who has a personal home computer (IBM or Compaq), a new piece of software that tracks real-time market activity is available. PC Quote will display the last sale or bid/ask prices for up to sixty-four stocks in your portfolio. Each computer screen will track up to eighteen securities. Press a single key to change screens. The system flashes price changes instantly. Also shown are the time of the last sale and that day's total change. You can program PC Quote to tell you when a stock reaches your upper or lower limit price. It can keep track of your portfolio value and can calculate your profit or loss. It will even run in a "background mode" while you use other software. It operates twenty-four hours a day.

The service is expensive. It costs $295 a month (includes satellite dish and decoder). For each stock exchange you subscribe to, you'll pay a user fee. The New York Stock Exchange charges nonprofessionals $7.50 a month for last-sale information. NASDAQ charges $8.75 a month for over-the-counter (OTC) bid/ask prices.

The Source
1616 Anderson Road   703-821-6666—in VA
McLean, VA 22102   800-336-3366

The Source offers market quotations updated every twenty minutes, options quotes, *U.S. News and World Report,* company reports, portfolio management, commodity news, investment adviser commentary, *Forbes, Harvard Business Review,* personnel network, major newspapers, and more. Connected with Spears Securities brokerage firm.

Fees: Sign up fee is $49.95 and the monthly user fee is $10. Day rates are 36 to 43 cents a minute and night rates are 14 to 18 cents a minute.

Warner Computer Systems
1 University Plaza   212-661-2860—in NY
Hackensack, NJ 07601   800-262-4634

Warner offers stock, bond, and options prices and financial data on 20,000 companies going back ten years; SEC filings; company earnings forecasts from 1,000 analysts; and commodity quotations only on gold.

Fees: one-time $48 sign up fee. Day rates are 85 cents to $1.50 a minute and night rates are 30 to 60 cents a minute.

PEOPLE TO TALK TO

Robert E. James
Publisher, *Timer Digest*
333 Sunset Drive, Suite 202
Ft. Lauderdale, FL 33301   305-764-8499
   A portfolio manager for individuals, institutions, and corporate clients for
more than thirty years, Robert E. James is the publisher of *Timer Digest,* a stock
market advisory newsletter which ranks the ten best market timers in terms of
intermediate timing. Mr. James has conducted courses in portfolio management for brokers and clients, and he is available to speak to groups on invest-
ment/portfolio topics. He has been a member of the New York Stock Exchange, Boston Stock Exchange, and the P-B-W Exchange.

ADDITIONAL RESOURCES

   Want to know the latest stock quotations and financial news? You don't
need to go to your broker. You can use one of these telephone hotlines:

DowPhone   609-452-2000
PO Box 300   900-976-4141—hotline
Princeton, NJ 08540   800-352-5378—DowPhone information
                                                          800-257-0437
                                                          800-345-NEWS
   Operated by Dow Jones and Co., DowPhone provides stock quotes on
over 6,500 companies from the New York and American Stock Exchanges,
plus market news and updates every half-hour. You need a touch-tone phone.
Cost is $1 a minute when you call one of the toll-free numbers. The charges
will go on your regular monthly phone company bill. If you call on the regular
phone line, the charge is fifty cents a minute, plus toll charges that apply from
your location. Or you can pay an initial fee of $12 and receive $25 worth of
time before being billed at the $.50 or $1 rates.
   You can also get more detailed information on particular industries, precious metals, interest rates, dealing with government agencies, and more. To
use this service, you must set up an account with DowPhone. You'll pay $1
a minute and can dial specific phone codes for the information you need.

Stock Fone   976-STOC
   This service is for stock quotes only. It is offered by local phone companies
in Washington, DC, Atlanta, Baltimore, Miami, Philadelphia, Pittsburgh, Los
Angeles, and San Francisco. The phone number is the same in each city. The
charges are fifty cents for three minutes of stock quotes. The service runs 24
hours a day. Quotes are delayed fifteen minutes during trading hours.

U.S. Quotes 212-687-7777

U.S. Quotes offers fifteen minute delayed prices on about 20,000 securities traded on the major exchanges and over the counter. Rates are twelve cents a minute when the market is open; half-price after hours. The user is charged a $45 up-front deposit, against which calls are deducted. U.S. Quotes is a local call for New Yorkers, but residents of other cities must make a toll call. Ten other United States cities, including Chicago, are soon scheduled for hookup.

COMEX Goldline 800-GLD-COMX

For this free call, you'll get the latest quotes on gold traded on the New York Commodity Exchange. A silver quote is scheduled to be added soon.

Bonds

See also:
The First Step for Beginners and Experienced Investors
Government Securities

When you purchase a bond, you are lending money at a fixed interest rate to the issuer for an agreed time. Bonds are classified according to who issues them, the specific types being municipal, corporate, government, and international. The sale of these bonds is heavily regulated by the federal government and individual states to ensure the purchaser gets complete and accurate information from the issuer about the investment.

While many people hold their bonds until the redemption date, bonds can be traded before that time. There is a thriving market in the United States in bond trading, and numerous bonds are listed and actively traded on stock exchanges. Their value fluctuates as interest rates rise and fall, and, in some cases, as the issuer gets into difficulties and is considered to be in greater risk of default.

How can you learn about and track bonds? The financial pages of the *New York Times* and the *Wall Street Journal* run a daily bond column and each Monday both papers print a calendar covering new bonds issued. The business section of your local paper may also carry similar information. Your county's designated business library and the libraries of major brokerage houses subscribe to many of the expensive rating services such as Moody's Investors Services, The Bond Record, Bond Survey, and Standard and Poor's Creditweek. Many libraries have bond handbooks and publications you can consult for general information. The Federal Reserve Board issues monthly statistical-reports, which are a good resource. The chapter on Government Securities gives you resources on that type of investment. For bond information from a company itself, go to the company's treasurer or legal department—but don't be surprised if you are referred to a company's investment banker who is their underwriter!

AGENCIES, INSTITUTES, AND ORGANIZATIONS

American Association of Individual Investors (AAII)
   See listing under STOCKS.

Board of Governors of the Federal Reserve System
Capital Markets Section
Research and Statistics Division
Washington, DC 20551   202-452-3631
This office compiles statistics on all corporate public bond offerings. These statistics are monitored monthly for volume changes. The research data are published in the *Federal Reserve Bulletin* described below. The board's research assistants will answer questions regarding published data.

- *Federal Reserve Bulletin*—published monthly, this official bulletin provides statistical and financial information on all types of Treasury, municipal, utility and corporate bond interest rates. Cost is $20 annually.

Bureau of Public Debt
Bond Consultant Branch
Parkersburg, WV 26106   304-420-6112
If you have lost a bond, this office will provide you with an application to receive a substitute. In order to file a claim you need to know the bond serial number and fill out form PD1048. If you do not know the serial number this office will search alphabetically through its files to try and find the number. If they are able to identify the serial number and the claim form is filled out you will receive a new bond with a new serial number with the original issue date on it.

Companies Trading Bonds
Listed below are some of the principal firms that buy and sell bonds. Although their interest is selling the public their particular product, the firms do offer a good deal of useful, free information about bonds. The companies often advertise their offerings in periodicals like *Barron's* and the *Wall Street Journal.* The ads frequently give a toll-free number you can call to get the companies' latest free publications and bond information. Contacts for these companies can be found by checking the yellow pages of your telephone book under Stock and Bond Brokers for a local office, or by calling the information operator in New York City at 212-555-1212.

- Salomon Brothers
- Goldman, Sachs and Co.
- Shearson, Lehman, American Express
- Merrill Lynch, Pierce, Fenner & Smith
- E. F. Hutton and Co.
- Dean Witter, Reynolds Co.
- Smith, Barney, Harris, Upham & Co.
- Paine Webber
- Kidder, Peabody & Co.

Municipal Bond Insurance Association (MBIA)

445 Hamilton Avenue
Box 788
White Plains, NY 10602   914-681-1300

MBIA insures new issues of municipal bonds and notes. It has insured tax-exempt offerings of municipalities and government units in every state and the District of Columbia. Each MBIA-insured issue automatically receives Standard and Poor's highest rating, Triple-A. To inform investment bankers, financial advisers and issuers about the general criteria used for insuring most types of municipal securities, MBIA introduced the *1985/86 Underwriting Guidelines* brochure. MBIA's concisely written brochures provide detailed information about its operations. They are:

- *Insured Municipal Bonds: Triple-A Protection for Investors*—information is provided about the benefits of municipal bond insurance. Free.
- *MBIA 1986 Underwriting Guidelines*—this brochure provides general underwriting guidelines for MBIA insurance programs. Free.
- *MBIA Insured Issues*—lists MBIA-insured bonds by state, including descriptions of each issue, par value, sale and dated dates. Free.
- *Investor Memorandum*—provides basic data necessary for a sophisticated evaluation of the financial strength of MBIA's companies, and covers legal and regulatory aspects of municipal bond insurance. Free.
- *Brokerfacts*—discusses how registered representatives can sell MBIA-insured obligations to clients. Free.
- *Investorfacts*—basic information for individual investors on the benefits of buying MBIA-insured tax-exempt obligations. Free.
- *The Glamour of Municipal Bonds*—information for individual investors on the attractive features of MBIA-insured bonds. Designed for enclosure with a securities firm's confirmation statements to clients. Free.
- *No Taxes. No Worries. No Kidding.*—highlights the size, reputation, and financial strength of the MBIA companies. Designed for registered representatives to use as a prospecting mailer. Free.
- *S & P Creditweek/Moody's Bond Record*—this is the latest review of MBIA's member companies by Standard & Poor's and Moody's. Free.
- *FastFacts*—highlights about MBIA are given in this brochure. It includes its guarantee, programs, andlatest statistics. Free.

The New York Stock Exchange (NYSE)

See listing under STOCKS.

Public Securities Association (PSA)
40 Broad Street, 12th Floor
New York, NY 10004-2373 212-809-7000

1000 Vermont Avenue, NW, Suite 800
Washington, DC 20005 202-898-9390

PSA is the national trade organization of banks, brokers, and dealers who underwrite, trade, and sell mortgage-backed securities, U.S. government securities, and federal agency securities. In addition to lobbying for the businesses it represents, PSA also educates the public on behalf of its members.

PSA answers inquiries, publishes informational materials, provides seminars, conferences, and meetings, and maintains a database of statistics on new issues of municipal bonds which can be accessed by computer through a timesharing service, MDCSS. If you receive information from the PSA, bear in mind that the principal purpose of the group is to represent the viewpoint of brokers and dealers. PSA publications available to the general public include:

- *Statistical Yearbook of Municipal Finance*—updated each year, this 120-page book is a comprehensive, definitive source of vital municipal securities industry information and statistics. It includes the ranking of the leading municipal underwriters in total volume, geographically, and by type of issue. It costs $45 plus $1.50 for postage and handling.
- *Fundamentals of Municipal Bonds*—an authoritative and definitive guide, this 208-page book details the basics of municipal securities. It describes the major market participants and how they interact. It discusses regulation, the secondary market, and credit analysis of general obligation and revenue bonds. It costs $14.95 plus $1.50 for postage.
- *An Investor's Guide to Tax Exempt Securities*—this twenty-page booklet covers types of bonds, effects of market fluctuations on price and yield, ratings, liquidity and basic facts about the mechanics of ownership. Cost is forty-five cents.
- *An Investor's Guide to Tax Exempt Unit Investment Trusts*—advantages of unit investment trusts are described in this booklet. It tells how they work, what to look for, and the mechanics of purchase and resale. It costs forty-five cents.
- *An Investor's Guide to Municipal Bond Swapping*—general information regarding federal tax consequences of swapping is given in this six-page booklet. Cost is forty-five cents.
- *How Will the Tax Reform Bill Affect Your Investments in Municipal Bonds*—chart showing the effects of the new tax laws on bond yields. Cost is 25 cents.
- *Tax-Free Bonds for Investors Worried About Inflation and Interest Rates (Put Bonds)*—this one-page flyer explains the advantages of option-tender, or put, bonds in clear and simple language. Free.

■ *Monthly Market Developments*—published monthly, this companion publication to the statistical yearbook contains updated municipal market statistics and underwriter rankings to help you stay abreast of developments in the new issue market. Cost is $45 annually.

Securities and Exchange Commission (SEC)
See listing under STOCKS.

The Securities Investor Protection Corporation (SIPC)
See listing under STOCKS.

WHAT TO READ

Barron's
200 Liberty Street
New York, NY 10281   212-416-2000

Subscriptions:
200 Burnett Road
Chicopee, MA 01021   800-628-9320

A leading weekly financial newspaper, *Barron's* is an excellent source of information about the bond markets and other investment markets. It includes articles, columns, statistics, and detailed records of transactions. It is intended for the general reader, although it is a standard source of information for professionals. A feature called "Government Bonds" covers weekly prices of U.S. Treasury bonds, notes, and bills, as well as other federal agency securities and tax-exempt revenue bonds. The "Listed Bonds" section reports bond trading on the New York and American Stock Exchanges, while "Bond Rating Changes" shows favorable and unfavorable changes in the rating of bonds. Subscription is $77 for one year and $136 for two years.

The Bond Buyer
One State Street Plaza
New York, NY 10004   212-943-8200

This publisher, which gears its material to dealers, bond counselors, and institutional investors, issues a weekly and a daily publication on bonds. Overall, its publications interpret international financial and economic news, and look at the stock market and money market as well as the bond market.

■ *The Bond Buyer*—a daily newspaper which concentrates on municipal and government bonds. Annual subscription is $1,295.

■ *Weekly Credit Markets*—deals with fixed-income securities, including municipal, government, and corporate bonds. Annual subscription is $525.

Business Week

1221 Avenue of the Americas   800-635-1200—subscriber relations
New York, NY 10020   800-257-5112—circulation

This weekly magazine, geared primarily to business people, includes, among broad coverage of financial matters, current information on bonds.

Dow Jones-Irwin   800-323-4560
Homewood, IL 60430   312-798-6000

This leading publisher of business books, a subsidiary of Richard D. Irwin, Inc., textbook publisher (itself a subsidiary of Dow Jones & Company, Inc.), will send a copy of its list on request. These titles are intended for persons interested in bonds:

- *The Dow Jones-Irwin Guide to Buying and Selling Treasury Securities,* by Howard M. Berlin—a step-by-step guide for the investor in U.S. government bonds, bills, and notes, this 210-page book covers a wide range of subject matter, including guidelines for dealing with the Federal Reserve Bank and the Bureau of the Public Debt. Cost is $25.
- *The Dow Jones-Irwin Guide to Interest: What You Should Know About the Time Value of Money,* by Lawrence R. Rosen—this book includes the topic of bond selection and uses concise graphs and formulas to make complex mathematics simple. Cost is $19.95.
- *The Handbook of Fixed Income Securities*—an extensive coverage of government, corporate, municipal, and international bonds is included in this 1101-page book, one of the most comprehensive works available on the subject. Each of the forty-nine chapters was written by an expert on the topic presented. Cost is $50.
- *The Dow Jones-Irwin Guide to Municipal Bonds,* by Feldstein and Fabozzi—a recent 250-page book addressing today's municipal bond market, this discussion is aimed at the general reader and offers practical guidelines for investment. Cost is $25.
- *The Municipal Bond Handbook*—in two volumes, this is an exhaustive coverage of tax-exempt bonds. Volume I provides a foundation of information about buying and selling such bonds. Volume II deals with credit analysis of municipal bonds. Each volume is over 700 pages long. Cost for the two volumes is $50.
- *No-Load Mutual Funds,* by William Droms—this publication includes information on tax-exempt bond funds. Cost is $25.
- *The Dow Jones-Irwin Guide to Personal Financial Planning,* by Fredrick Amling and William Droms—this book of more than 500 pages contains a chapter on bonds in a context of personal investment planning and financial management. Cost is approximately $24.95.

Farm Credit Administration (FCA)

Public Affairs Division
1501 Farm Credit Drive
McLean, VA 22102-5090   703-883-4056

Bonds are issued by the thirty-seven FCA banks and their affiliated associations, which are regulated by the Farm Credit Administration. FCA publishes the following:

- *FCA's Annual Report*—a description of the agency's operations during the year covered by the report, the free yearly report also contains statistical data. It is issued each year between April and August. Free.
- *Farm Credit Bank Report to Investors*—describing operations of the Farm Credit Administration and the securities issued under its regulation, this free publication is issued each April and is available from: Federal Farm Credit Banks Funding Corporation, 90 William Street, New York, NY 10038, 212-908-9400. Free.

Gabriele, Hueglin, and Cashman, Inc.

44 Wall Street
New York, NY 10005   800-422-7435

This brokerage firm specializes in bonds and has a reputation for making greater than ordinary efforts to inform the public on the subject. Its publications include:

- *News and Offerings*—this free monthly newsletter discusses interest rate trends and offerings of municipal and government bonds. Free.
- *Hueglin's Bond Market Report*—a special analysis of the bond market and related subjects, this free newsletter is published once a month. Free.
- *Guide to State and Local Taxation of Municipal Bonds*—this is a book containing tax information of use to those interested in municipal bond investment. Cost is $10.
- *Guide to Federal, State and Local Taxation of Fixed Income Securities*—a new book on taxation of bonds. Cost is $20.

Income Without Taxes: An Insider's Guide to Tax-Exempt Bonds

Carroll & Graf Publishers, Inc.
260 Fifth Avenue
New York, NY 10010   212-889-8772

Written for the beginner investor, this book by Hildy and Stan Richelson has useful information on the mechanics of saving with municipal bonds. Cost is $16.95.

An Insider's Guide to the Wall Street Journal
Wall Street Journal
200 Liberty Street
World Financial Center
New York, NY 10281   212-416-2000
    Helpful hints on how to read the *Wall Street Journal* are provided in this booklet. In addition to an overview of the newspaper, there is a special section on understanding financial data in the *Journal.* Call or write the above address and it will be sent to you free.

Inside the Yield Book
Prentice-Hall, Inc.
Book Distribution Center
Route 59W
Nyack, NY 10995
    Written by Homer and Liebowitz, this workbook gives information about how a bond gets priced. It is available for $19.95.

Investment Companies
Wiesenberger Financial Services
1633 Broadway
New York, NY 10019   212-977-7453
    This widely distributed annual publication has a section on tax-exempt bond mutual funds. It also contains information of corporate bond funds, listed under "Senior Securities." The full subscription includes monthly and quarterly performance updates and costs $295 a year.

Investors Information Kit
New York Stock Exchange
Publications Department
11 Wall Street
New York, NY 10005   212-623-2089
    The largest exchange on which bonds are traded, the New York Stock Exchange does not deal directly with the public, but it does distribute a package entitled *Investors Information Kit.* Among about seven informational items, this kit includes a pamphlet called "Understanding Stocks and Bonds." It is useful primarily as a very general introduction to the subject for beginners. Cost is $7.

Magazines and Newspapers
    Reading publications such as the *Wall Street Journal, Forbes, Barron's,* and *Changing Times* will teach you investment jargon and keep you abreast of stock market trends and financial news in general. Refer to the chapter

Newspapers and Magazines for Tracking News and Trends and for Managing Your Money.

McGraw-Hill Book Company
Princeton Road
Hightstown, NJ 08520   609-426-5254
This company publishes some of the classic works on bonds and bond-related subjects. Books now in print include:

■ *How to Invest in Bonds,* Hugh C. Sherwood—published in 1983, this broad introduction to the subject of bond investment is good for beginners. Cost is $5.95.

■ *The Complete Bond Book,* David M. Darst—although not revised since 1975, this still provides a thorough coverage of bonds and is recognized as a valuable reference work. This book is $39.95.

■ *Security Analysis,* Graham and Dodd, 4th ed. 1962—probably the foremost book on analysis of securities, with very useful discussions of bonds. It is of the nature of a textbook on the subject, and describes detailed methods of analysis which the investor can use in order to make his/her own decisions. Cost of this book is $41.95.

Moody's Investors Services, Inc.
99 Church Street
New York, NY 10007   212-553-0450
This and Standard and Poor's Corporation are the two organizations most widely known for rating bonds. Investors use the ratings to judge the relative security of a bond investment. Moody's bonds publications include:

■ *Bond Record*—a comprehensive source of statistical data of 40,700 corporate, convertible, government, municipal, and international bonds, this monthly publication includes such facts as offering and maturity dates, interest rates, redemption features, and yields to maturity. It gives Moody's ratings. Cost is $125.

■ *Bond Survey*—appearing weekly, the *Bond Survey* highlights new and prospective bond offerings and presents commentary on economic and market conditions, such as interest rate levels, which are relevant to bonds. Annual subscription is $895.

■ *Municipal and Governments Manual*—this manual covers over 14,000 bond-issuing municipalities and state and federal government agencies. It is issued yearly and supplemented with *News Reports* twice weekly, including recent developments and any changes in Moody's bond ratings. Annual subscription is $1175.

Standard and Poor's Corporation (S&P)
25 Broadway
New York, NY 10004   212-248-2525

One of the two major bond-rating services (Moody's Investors Service is the other), S&P also publishes a lot of information about bonds and other financial matters. Its ratings are widely relied on by professionals and the public as a guide to the safety of investment in any particular bond. S&P provides advice to the public mainly through its publications, but staff will answer general inquiries. S&P publications include:

- *CreditWeek*—an in-depth analysis of credit markets, this weekly updates bond information and reviews new bonds coming to market. It contains commentary on trends that will affect the bond markets, along with information about criteria used. Includes new ratings and revised ratings. Oriented toward large institutional investors. Annual subscription is $1,125.

- *CreditOverview, Corporate and International Ratings*—updated as needed, this publication highlights S&P's rating processes, methodology, organization, and related subjects. Includes rating worksheet forms which can be used by the reader. This is a free supplement to *CreditWeek*.

- *Bond Guide*—a reference for ratings and key status of bonds. Published monthly, it features descriptive and statistical data on corporate, state, municipal, general obligation and revenue bonds, convertible bonds, and foreign bonds. Annual subscription is $138.

- *Blue List*—issued daily, this list records 12,000 to 18,000 bond offerings, with prices. Annual subscription is $605.

- *CreditWeek International*—published six times a year, this gives S&P's coverage of the international bond market. It offers information on United States companies issuing bonds overseas as well as foreign companies selling bonds in the United States. Annual subscription is $215.

- *Called Bond Record*—a report on bonds subject to calls, tenders, default, and related situations, this record is published twice a week. Annual subscription is $720.

- *Corporate Records*—this six-volume set, updated constantly, contains information on over 10,000 publicly held United States companies. For the bond purchaser or seller, it is a good reference for those wishing to know more about specific companies which issue bonds. The latest developments are reported five days a week in a Daily News Section. Annual subscription is $1,960.

- *Registered Bond Interest Record*—a weekly compilation of cumulative information on interest payments on registered bonds. Separate editions are published for corporate bonds and for municipal bonds. Annual subscription is $1,800 for the corporate bond edition and $4,000 for the municipal bond edition.

- *How to Invest*—a handbook for buying and selling stocks and bonds, this booklet will tell you how to start investing, its strong points and shortcomings. It also describes different types of bond obligations. Free.

■ *How the Bond Market Works*—this booklet will provide you with some insights into fixed-income investing. It describes how bonds are issued, evaluating a bond, yields and maturities, and dos and don'ts when purchasing bonds. Free.

PEOPLE TO TALK TO

Timothy Cowling
Vice President
The Milwaukee Company
250 East Wisconsin Avenue   800-558-1015
Milwaukee, WI 53202   414-347-7000
   A Certified Financial Planner, Mr. Cowling has been active in the investments industry for nine years. He gives advice on bond investments and is available to speak at management or civic group conferences. Mr. Cowling is also a columnist for a local business newspaper.

William G. Droms
Georgetown University School of Business Administration
Washington, DC 20057   202-625-4273
   A professor of finance and the author of books on bonds and other investment vehicles, Dr. Droms is a specialist in personal financial planning. He is willing to respond to brief inquiries without charge. A fee would be required for more extensive consultations.

Steve Hueglin
44 Wall Street
New York, NY 10005   212-422-1700
   One of the principals in the bond firm of Gabriele, Hueglin, and Cashman, Inc., Mr. Hueglin has gained a reputation among his colleagues as an expert on bonds who communicates well with the public. He lectures frequently, and in certain cases will speak free of charge to a group of potential investors. In other situations he may charge a fee. He speaks on fixed-income investment strategies, interest rate forecasting, and taxation in relation to investment in bonds.

Byron Klapper
Vice President and Publisher
Standard and Poor's Corporation
25 Broadway
New York, NY 10004   212-208-1710
   Mr. Klapper publishes all of Standard and Poor's (see Agencies, Institutes, and Organizations) bond-rating publications, and his expertise covers all as-

pects of bonds and bond markets, as well as such related areas as banking and commercial paper.

John Markese
612 North Michigan Avenue
Chicago, IL 60611   312-280-0170
   A finance professor as well as director of research for the American Association of Individual Investors (see Agencies, Institutes, and Organizations), John Markese is well informed in the general area of bonds and bond markets. He is a frequent public speaker, and he is willing to answer brief questions about bonds.

ADDITIONAL RESOURCES

Bonds
Morris Video
413 Avenue G, Suite #1
Redondo Beach, CA 90277   213-374-4984
   Your host, Roma Simm, will show you how to save bonds or trade them. This video offers an understanding of bonds and acquaints you with short-term money-market saving instruments. It covers the types of bonds available, terminology, and the basic market principles that affect their value. Cost is $24.95.

Securities Data Company, Inc.
62 William Street
New York, NY 10005   212-668-0840
   A computerized database firm, Securities Data Company provides twenty-four-hour on-line service to commercial banks and other consulting firms on corporate securities and municipal bonds. Individual investors may use their service, paying on an "as-use" basis. The office above can provide more detailed pricing information for individual use. The following is a sample of database services available:
   ■ *New Issues of Corporate Securities*—this database includes information
   on each new issue, such as coupon, offering price, maturity, call, sinking
   fund provision, trustee and Dun & Bradstreet number for debt. It also
   includes underwriters and fees, data from financial statements, law firms,
   and ratings. The statistics can be used to evaluate the performance of
   managing underwriters, agents, and advisers in various market segments.
   ■ *New Issues of Municipal Debt*—the following descriptive information
   on each new issue is included in this database: offering price, maturity, call
   and sinking fund provisions, underwriters and fees, trustee, and geographical location of issuer.

Options

If you are interested in an investment with attractive profit possibilities and limited risks, an investment in which you can share in the upside potential of a stock without risking more than a fraction of its market value, or a way of balancing downside risk with premium income, take a look at options. But take a close look; the strategy combinations and wide variety of considerations involved make careful study a must for intelligent investing with this unique and versatile instrument.

Options are the most overlooked and misunderstood financial planning tool. The reasons for this are twofold: options are complex, and they are new. Options were not a practical investment vehicle for individuals until 1973, when the Chicago Board Options Exchange started listing options. Before that time only the very wealthy could make use of options by trading over the counter with large blocks of money. Nor were options on commodities regulated until 1985. So the whole field is relatively new, and many experts hesitate to recommend them since they themselves are still learning about the various ramifications of this investment medium.

Intimidating though it may seem, it is wise to become familiar with the concept behind options. This type of trading is becoming more popular, and it is likely that you will receive solicitations by phone or mail from companies extolling the virtues of options.

A simple way to look at options is to use real estate as an analogy. Buying a call option is very much like writing a contract with an option to purchase a house. The prospective buyer makes a down payment and in return the owner agrees to sell the house at an agreed price by a certain deadline. If the buyer decides not to buy the house after all, she/he forfeits the down payment.

In the case of a stock or commodity option, a call gives the buyer the right to purchase a hundred shares of a specific commodity at a fixed price at any time before the option expires. For example: you have been watching X stock, which sells for $50, and you expect it to rise in value. For a price of $500 you buy an option on a hundred shares of stock. Let us assume that the stock hits $80 within the option period. You exercise your option, buy the 100 shares at $50, and then turn around and sell the shares for $80. You receive $8,000 from the sale of the shares; from that you subtract the $5,000 you paid for them, the $500 premium, and about $150 for the brokerage fees. Your profit is $2,350.

Using the same example, assume that the stock fell to $30. You do nothing; the option expires and you are out only $500.

A put option is the reverse of a call. You now have the privilege of selling 100 shares of stock at a fixed price within the option period. These usually cost a bit less than calls and are not as popular. Generally, a put is viewed as an "insurance policy" to protect against a fall in the price of stocks which you own.

It is possible to buy a put and a call on the same commodity. This is called a "straddle" and is a somewhat more conservative approach to options buying.

An individual may choose to be either a buyer or a writer of calls, and she/he may choose to be either a buyer or a writer of puts.

Orders to buy and sell options are handled through brokers in the same way as orders to buy and sell stocks. But there are significant differences in the management of stocks versus options. Common stock can be held indefinitely in the hope that it will have lost the entire premium paid for the option. The advantage to options buying is that the investor knows in advance that the most she/he can lose is the premium—a fraction of the cost of buying the stock outright. The sophisticated investor can utilize strategies for times when securities prices are rising, and others for periods when prices are declining; the options can be as conservative or as speculative as the investor wishes.

As with other types of investment, knowledge is power, and before using options you need to immerse yourself in the jargon involved. This first step should be followed by investigating the tax implications, the risks involved, transactions costs, and how to screen a broker or company dealing in options. The final step is to contact a broker who can further clarify the options field and set up your first transaction for you. The Commodities Futures Trading Commission cautions that you get all the details in writing before you buy, and that you resist pressure to make hurried, uninformed decisions.

When pursuing profits via option trading, use the resources described in this chapter to understand the risks and potentials, strategies and variations.

AGENCIES, INSTITUTES, AND ORGANIZATIONS

American Stock Exchange (AMEX)
86 Trinity Place
New York, NY 10006   212-306-1390

AMEX conducts trading in a wide range of securities: common stocks, warrants, put and call options on stocks, stock indices and U.S. Treasury securities. In addition, the AMEX provides a market in corporate bonds and U.S. government and government agency securities, and trades options on gold bullion through a subsidiary market.

For individual investors, AMEX recommends that all options-related literature be obtained from your broker. The following booklets are free for single copies except where cost is indicated:

- *Call Options: Versatile Investment Tools*—a review of fundamental call option trading strategies is included in this sixteen-page booklet. Illustrations are given of actual trading situations.

■ *Put Options: Versatile Invesment Tools*—fundamental put and combination put-and-call option trading strategies are reviewed in this twenty-page booklet.

■ *Versatile Options Mailer*—a customer mailer to determine interest in learning more about options and receiving the "Versatile Options" booklets.

■ *AMEX Options Seminar System*—a comprehensive modular system for qualified investors. Consisting of slide shows, flip charts, and audio presentations with accompanying scripts. Each modular covers three main objectives: (1) gaining extra income; (2) protecting investments; and (3) seeking profit potential. Rates available.

■ *Buying Options for Profit Opportunities*—a sixteen-page, basic customer information booklet about the potential risks and rewards of buying puts and calls.

■ *Increasing Your Income with Options*—an eight-page information booklet about covered call writing.

■ *Protecting Your Investments with Options*—this twelve-page booklet explains how to buy protective puts and write covered calls to reduce downside risk.

■ *Options for Institutions*—five booklets written specifically for the professional investor: Charitable Organizations, The Prudent Man Rule, ERISA and Bank Trust Accounts, Insurance Companies and Mutual Funds, and Public Employee Retirement Systems.

■ *Stock Options Strategy Sheets*—each information sheet provides a concise explanation of an options strategy, detailing the potential profit and possible loss under various market conditions. The strategies being offered are: Selling Puts, Covered Call Writing, Buying Stock and Puts Simultaneously, and Buying a Put to Protect a Profit in Stock. Each pad contains fifty sheets. Cost is $2 per pad (discounts available).

■ *Options on U.S. Treasury Bills*—an informational brochure about AMEX options on U.S. Treasury bills, as well as detailed contract specifications.

■ *Interest Rate Options Study Guide*—this comprehensive study guide details contract specifications on AMEX Interest Rate Options, as well as various strategies under certain market conditions.

■ *Major Market Index Options*—consumer information is provided in this twenty-four-page booklet on cash-settled index options. It explores the investment benefits and risks of various major market index options.

■ *Expand Your Options Universe Index Options Slide Show Package*—this audiovisual package covers broad market indices and industry indices: the "markets" they measure, their component securities, and method of calculation. The presentation includes a twenty-minute audio cassette, sixty-seven slides, and a script, plus an add-on section introducing industry index options. Cost is $35.

■ *Gold Options*—an introduction to AMEX gold options, this informational brochure points out the contract's key advantages, similarities to index options and contract specifications.

■ *Gold Options Videotape*—a comprehensive introduction to gold options, this videotape contains strategies for speculating and hedging. It is available in VHS, Beta and 3/4" formats. Cost is $25.

The Chicago Board of Trade (CBOT)

Market Information	312-435-3500
141 West Jackson Boulevard	312-922-9120—daily recording
Chicago, IL 60604	312-922-7885—weekly recording

CBOT provides a daily recorded message with information on highs, lows, closing settlement, and net changes. Each Friday it provides a recorded message summarizing options trading statistics. Those numbers are listed above.

A variety of new educational and customer-oriented audiovisual programs are available through CBOT. The presentations are suitable for the investment/ brokerage community, prospective market users, educators, and students. In addition, publications are available that explain options trading opportunities for hedgers and speculators. For more information contact Education Publications at 312-435-7208.

■ *1983 Interest Rate, Options on T-Bond Futures, and Metals*—a daily historical record of interest rate futures, options futures, and metals traded at the CBOT, this annual report covers contract rules and regulations. It also covers daily cash and futures prices, daily volume, open interest, and government securities yields and rates, among other relevant data. Cost is $17.

■ *CBOT Options on Futures Members' Manual*—this manual offers a guide to trading options on futures at the Chicago Board of Trade. Tabbed for easy reference, the manual includes options basics, information on clearing and exercise procedures, margins, strategies, and more. Cost is $75.

The Chicago Board Options Exchange (CBOE)

The Chicago Board Options Exchange (CBOE)	800-621-5499
LaSalle at Van Buren	312-786-7503
Chicago, IL 60605	800-332-CBOE—currency options information

CBOE pioneered listed options and is the nation's largest options market. Sixty-five percent of all options trading takes place on the CBOE floor; an average of 600,000 contracts change hands each day. CBOE has made the listed option a practical investment vehicle for individuals and institutions seeking profit or protection. The Board, which is regulated by the Securities and Exchange Commission, developed the trading procedures that today assure rapid, reliable, and fair execution of all customer orders in a continuously competitive marketplace.

Prior to buying or selling an option, an index option, or an option on a debt instrument, a person must receive a copy of the supplemental disclosure document pertaining to that option. Copies of these documents may be obtained from this office or from your broker.

The CBOE's Marketing Services Department has several publications available on option products and trading strategies. A sample includes:

- *Understanding Options*—an introduction to buying and selling listed options, this thirty-one-page booklet answers many questions that investors may have about options. This booklet has been updated to include changes in the new tax law. Free.
- *Tax Considerations in Using CBOE Options*—federal income-tax principles governing exchange-listed options as they apply to investors are reviewed in this booklet. There are a number of examples to clarify these principles. Free.
- *S & P 100 Index Options: The Index Edge*—this booklet describes the three components of risk: market risk, industry risk, and firm-specific risk. It also describes and gives examples of index option strategies. Free.
- *Call Option Spreading*—the risks and potential rewards of spreading are presented in this brochure in such a way that you may decide for yourself whether it is a useful strategy for your investment objectives. Free.
- *Buying Puts, Straddles, and Combinations*—necessary precautions that should be observed when trading in puts are discussed and illustrated in this thirty-two-page booklet. Free.
- *Writing Puts, Straddles, and Combinations*—a number of ways in which puts can be employed in pursuit of profit are described in this twenty-four-page booklet. Free.

CME-IMM-IOM Information Bulletins
Chicago Mercantile Exchange (CME)
30 South Wacker Drive
Chicago, IL 60606   312-930-3457

This daily subscription package includes five daily information bulletins: *CME Daily,* on livestock futures; *IMM* [International Monetary Market] *Foreign Exchange Daily,* on currency futures; *IOM* [Index Option Market] *Futures Daily,* on lumber futures; *IMM Precious Metals and Interest Rates Daily; IOM Options Daily;* and four monthly information bulletins: *CME Monthly; IMM Foreign Exchange Monthly; IMM Precious Metals and Interest Rates Monthly;* and *IOM Monthly.* For further information call or write to the above address. Cost is $75 annually.

Coffee, Sugar and Cocoa Exchange, Inc. (CSCE)
4 World Trade Center
New York, NY 10048   212-938-2800

CSCE is the leading international marketplace for trading both domestic and world sugar future contracts, world sugar options and both coffee and cocoa futures contracts. This exchange has been at the forefront of the drive to obtain government approval for options trading on commodity futures. Options trading broadens the Exchange's trading base by providing existing users of the futures markets with new trading opportunities and by offering new hedging and speculative strategies to a broad spectrum of additional market participants. CSCE provides daily recorded messages at various times of the day. It gives the estimated and final open, interest, and volume. (The number is listed above.)

Each option has its own contract specifications and each underlying futures contract its own market characteristics. More detailed information can be obtained from your broker or tax adviser. The information your broker will provide should be read and understood. The following publications will help you understand the mechanics of option trading:

- *Understanding Options on Futures*—a thirty-six-page brochure defining options, explaining how they are traded, the concept of premiums and strategies for options trading, both alone and in combination with futures positions. Specifications for the options trading on the Sugar No. 11 (World) Contract are included. Free.
- *Strategies for Buying and Selling Options on Cocoa Futures*—a brief introduction to options trading strategies is given in this thirty-seven-page booklet. It includes a chapter on options on cocoa futures and option strategies. Free.

The Options Clearing Corporation (OCC)
200 South Wacker Street, 27th Floor
Chicago, IL 60604   312-322-6239

As a clearinghouse for the financial services industry, OCC offers its member organizations broad access to its clearance settlements and information services. It works to promote the financial integrity of the market it serves. The Clearing Corporation settles the account of each member firm at the end of the trading day, balancing quantities of commodities bought with those sold.

OCC provides brokers with disclosure documents pertaining to each option. Prior to buying or selling an option a person must receive a copy of the appropriate document. A prospectus on the Corporation is also available giving a brief description of OCC and options. The following publications are available:

- *Characteristics and Risks of Standardized Options*—anyone trading options should read this booklet. It gives basic information on options, including foreign currency options and other debts. Free.
- *The Options Clearinghouse Corporation Monthly Statistical Report*—a set of four reports, published monthly, provides statistical data on options

traded on all the option exchanges. It includes equity, index, foreign currency, and interest rate options. The annual cost of $200 includes a weekly service.

WHAT TO READ

The ABC's of Option Trading
Educational Service Bureau
Dow Jones and Company, Inc.
Box 300
Princeton, NJ 08540   609-452-2000
   Written specifically to give you the basics, this booklet examines the uses of puts and calls and describes the sophisticated use of options in easy-to-understand language. Free.

Barron's
Dow Jones and Company
200 Liberty Street
New York, NY 10281   212-416-2000
   A weekly national business and financial newspaper, *Barron's* was the first to carry options listings. Its complete list of all options traded carry a variety of information useful for both options buyers and sellers. *Barron's* is available in most public libraries. Annual subscription cost is $77.

Cotton Futures Options
New York Cotton Exchange
4 World Trade Center   212-938-2702
New York, NY 10048   212-432-7274—options info and futures recording
   The basics of cotton futures options are explained in this booklet. It describes a few strategies available for capitalizing on the advantages presented by cotton options. A trading guide is also available. Free.

The Dow Jones-Irwin Guide to Put and Call Options
1824 Ridge Road   312-798-6000
Homewood, IL 60430   800-323-1717
   Written by Henry K. Clasing, Jr., this 223-page guide describes different strategies to use with combinations of puts, calls, spreads, hedging, and other factors. It includes easy-to-use timing tools. Cost is $24.95.

Investor Publications, Inc.
Box 6   800-553-1789
Cedar Falls, IA 50613   800-772-0023—in IA

A publisher of investment publications, Investor Publications offers the following books on options:

- *Winning the Interest Rate Game: A Guide to Debt Options*—thirteen industry experts contributed to this guide on debt options. It provides the fundamentals on strategies that can be used. Cost is $30.
- *Options as a Strategic Investment*—helpful strategies for any level of trader are given in this book by Lawrence G. McMillan. Cost is $27.95.
- *Inside the Commodity Options Markets*—a complete guide to the commodity options market, this book explores every market and every method used to trade options successfully. Dozens of diagrams, graphs, and tables make option strategies easy to understand. Cost is $29.95.

Commodities and Futures Trading

When you inquire about commodities investments, don't be offended if you're interrogated by the broker before you can open an account. Good brokers are careful about whom they do business with. This is a very high-risk, high-anxiety field that requires a certain psychological profile of its investors.

As one Paine Webber broker put it, "A commodities investor should be a gambler, an entrepreneur who doesn't mind losing money. A young person just starting out is a better prospect than a retired person who can't afford to start over."

Starting over is the key phrase here, as it isn't uncommon to lose an entire investment in days. And novices sometimes make the mistake of gambling on money they can't afford to lose. The first rule of commodities investing is that your financial house is in order in terms of other savings and investments, so that you can afford to lose whatever investment you make. Most commodities firms require its investors to have a minimum net worth of $50,000 with a minimum account of $10,000.

Commodities include the future delivery of raw materials such as wheat, cotton, soybeans, pork bellies, and gold. Financial commodities include treasury bonds and notes, GNMAs, and foreign currencies. Prices of these items fluctuate rapidly due to the rate of inflation and the up and down demand for agricultural and industrial products. The futures contract specifies the quantities, grades, where, when, and at what price the goods are to be delivered, even though they rarely are. So the futures speculator must know a lot to be able to predict what the prices will be at a certain time. While only a small percentage of futures contracts are profitable, the good news is that you can win big—and fast. That's why more and more investors are jumping into the commodities market.

If you are a risk taker and can afford to gamble at least $10,000, experts advise you first to find a good broker. When selecting a firm, consider:

- how comfortable you are with the broker
- how diversified the firm is—one with limited focus could end up bankrupt, taking your money with it
- its experience in your particular area of interest (e.g., meat, soybeans, or silver)
- how good the firm's market analysis is, by comparing its research reports with other firms' reports

Before commiting any money in the market, commodities expert Paul Wilcox (described in this chapter) advises: (1) read as much as possible about the market you want to get into; (2) paper trade first for practice—watch the market and decide what you would do; and (3) start very small and ease into it.

Following is a list of government agencies, organizations, publications, and experts to help you educate yourself before you get into this exciting and risky field. Under Additional Resources you'll find many experts and telephone numbers you can call for the latest information. But don't stop there. Be sure you choose some specific publications to read regularly, as you'll need to stay up on the changes in your particular market. The Department of Agriculture does an enormous amount of research and has a staff of specialists to answer your questions. You can get plenty of printed information from them, too. The commodity exchanges are another good information resource and many offer recorded messages you can call for the latest news. The Commodity Futures Trading Commission (CFTC) is the consumer agency that protects you and regulates the industry, so contact the CFCT for information on a specific broker or with any complaints. To find a broker, try the American Association of Commodity Traders and the Future Industry Association.

AGENCIES, INSTITUTES, AND ORGANIZATIONS

American Association of Commodity Traders (AACT)
Ten Park Street
Concord, NH 03301   603-224-2376
A professional association, AACT is biased in favor of spot and spot-deferred markets rather than futures markets. It advises its members and non-members through its major publication, the *Commodity Journal,* and through published special reports which are of technical matters and only of interest to commodity traders. AACT has annual meetings and published proceedings are available for a fee to nonmembers.

> ■ *Commodity Journal*—published six times a year. This is the official publication of the American Association of Commodity Traders. It contains philosophical and technical information on spot and spot-deferred markets. Back issues are available to nonmembers. Cost is $20 a year.

Bureau of Mines
U.S. Department of Interior
Division of Non-Ferrous Metals
2401 E Street, NW
Washington, DC 20241   202-634-1004
The Bureau of Mines collects, organizes and analyzes daily developments in the major commodity metals market. It publishes statistical and economic information on all phases of mineral resource development, including exploration, production, shipments, demand, stocks, prices,imports, and exports. The Bureau's commodity specialists can give you information about the precious metals they are responsible for (see People to Talk To and Additional Resources in this section). The Bureau publishes many items. Of particular interest are:

■ *Bureau of Mines Minerals Yearbook*—an annual report explaining the domestic production of aluminum, copper, gold, palladium, platinum, and silver month by month in the United States. Also covered are refinery production, consumption, and foreign trade. Free.

■ *Mineral Availability—Market Economy Conditions*—a yearly circular is published for each of the following metals: aluminum, copper, gold, palladium, platinum, and silver. Each circular analyzes the availability of a specific metal from both domestic and foreign sources. Free.

■ *Mineral Commodity Profile*—an annual report on aluminum, copper, gold, palladium, platinum, and silver. It covers problems, technology trends, supply and demand, and world production and consumption. Free.

■ *Mineral Commodity Summaries*—published annually, this provides an up-to-date summary of nonfuel mineral commodities. The book contains information on the domestic industry structure, government programs, tariffs, and five-year salient statistics for individual metals. Free.

■ *Mineral Facts and Problems*—chapter reprints from this regularly up-dated book are available for each precious metal: aluminum, copper, gold, palladium, platinum, and silver. Each reprint covers the industry structure, reserves,technology, and the outlook for a specific metal. Free.

■ *Mineral Industry Surveys*—this monthly leaflet gives mine production, price structure, reported consumption and the trading activity of aluminum, copper, gold, palladium, platinum, and silver. Free.

Commodity Futures Trading Commission (CFTC)

Office of Communication and Education
2033 K Street, NW
Washington, DC 20581   202-254-6387

Charged with protecting both the rights of customers and the financial integrity of the marketplace, CFTC regulates trading on all United States futures exchanges as well as the activities of some 5,724 commodity exchange members, 461 public brokerage houses, about 55,000 commission-registered futures industry salespeople and associated persons, and 4,100 commodity trading advisers and commodity pool operators.

Staff members can answer your questions about commodities and supply you with information about brokers, brokerage house, stock exchanges, and investments. They will also help you determine the questions you should ask before you engage in trading and the various considerations you should take into account. Staff members cannot, however, recommend brokers or advise about the frequency of customer complaints. Consumers with a complaint to file can do so by contacting the office listed above, or one of CFTC's regional offices.

The following publications explain the basics and are useful to anyone who is considering investing in one of the commodity markets.

■ *Before Trading Commodities Get the Facts*—shows how to deal with a commodities broker and how to investigate a broker's background. Free.

■ *Basic Facts About Commodity Futures Trading*—this twenty-four-page booklet provides a primer in commodities investing. It shows you how to read and understand the various figures that are published and where to get additional sources of information. Free.

■ *Glossary of Trading Terms*—lists and defines over 350 terms used by investors and traders in the commodities market. Free.

■ *A Spotter's Guide to Commodity Fraud*—this brochure highlights the more common elements presented by today's fraudulent commodities operators. Free.

■ *Economic Purposes of Futures Trading*—the competitive market system of futures trading is discussed in this thirteen-page booklet. Free.

Crop Reporting Board
USDA, Room 5829-S
Washington, DC 20250   202-447-4020

The Statistical Reporting Service collects data on crops, livestock, poultry, dairy, prices, and labor, and publishes the official USDA state and national estimates through the Crop Reporting Board. The forty-four field offices serve all states and collect and publish local information on these topics.

This information, gathered by mail and telephone surveys, personal interviews, and field observations, is used by virtually every agriculture-related group, from farmers to commodity buyers. Computerized data are available through the Crop Reporting Board and private computer networks. For details, contact the secretary of the Crop Reporting Board at 202-447-7017.

The Crop Reporting Board issues over 300 reports annually covering domestic agriculture, such as estimates of production, stocks, inventories, prices, disposition, utilization, farm numbers and land, and other factors. A sample includes:

■ *Crop Reports*—this monthly report provides estimates of acreage farmers intend to plant, the acres planted and harvested, production, marketings, and storage of the crop. Forecasts of yield and output are issued during the growing season. Cost is $30.

■ *Price Reports*—prices received by farmers for products, and prices paid by them for production or family living items, are published here monthly. Reports present indices of prices received and paid, parity prices, and season average prices of crops, livestock, poultry, and dairy products. It costs $27.

■ *Agricultural Statistics*—issued annually, this is a comprehensive presentation of tabular data, both current and historical, for all elements of agriculture. Available from GPO. Cost is $12.

Chicago Board of Trade   312-435-3500
Market Planning and Support   312-922-9110—agriculture hotline
141 West Jackson Boulevard   312-922-9120—financial update hotline
Chicago, IL 60604   312-922-7885—commentary hotline

The Chicago Board of Trade is a commodity exchange, marketplace, meeting place for buyers and sellers. Here is where information is assembled that bears on the supplies of commodities and the demand for them. Hotline recordings announcing the latest information are offered throughout the day. The Board was established to maintain a commercial exchange and to acquire and disseminate valuable commercial and economic information. It provides futures markets in wheat, corn, oats, soybeans, soybean oil and meal, silver, and gold. In the financial area, futures are traded in GNMA mortgage certificates, U.S. treasury bonds, ten-year treasury notes, and the Major Market Index, as well as options on U.S. treasury bond features.

A variety of new, general-educational and customer-oriented audiovisual programs are available through the Education Department. The presentations are suitable for the investment/brokerage community, prospective market users, educators, student associations, and the media. Leaflets and booklets that offer a wide range of information in varying amounts of detail are available. Frequently discussed topics include futures and/or options trading opportunities for hedgers and speculators, underlying commodity specifics, and CBOT contract specifications. Publications available include:

- *Introduction to Hedging*—describes principles of hedging and basic trading, with examples of hedging activities by producers, handlers, and users of commodities. Free.

- *Action in the Marketplace: Trading Commodity Futures*—a basic introduction to the marketplace, its history and activities, with a description of the use and functions of futures trading at the Chicago Board of Trade. Free.

- *Speculating in Futures*—describes the fundamentals of speculating including a basic introduction to the commodity futures markets, techniques of trading, the sources of market information. Free.

- *A Guide to Financial Futures*—a booklet which provides a general introduction to the CBT financial futures markets. Free.

- *Financial Futures: The Delivery Process*—a booklet which provides a summary of the delivery process for each CBT interest rate futures contract, along with an example of the invoice calculation and a diagram showing the delivery sequence. Each of the following leaflets provides a brief introduction on the energy and metal instruments behind the CBT futures contract and highlights the specifications of the energy and metal futures contracts traded at the exchange. Free.

- *GNMA II Futures: Cash/Market, Basis & Spread Charts*—this brochure presents an overview of the mortgage market and how GNMA II futures contracts relate to this market. The brochure also discusses hedging uses for the contract and includes complete contract terms and conditions. Free.

■ *GNMA II Futures*—this leaflet discusses the contract's advantages, the criteria for deliverable coupons, and the distinctions between GNMA II futures and GNMA CDR futures. It also includes a sample delivery schedule, contract highlights, and conversion factors. Free.

■ *GNMA II Futures: The Mortgage Industry's Comments and Questions*—this booklet contains the mortgage professionals' evaluations of and questions about the GNMA II futures contract, which are based on talks with mortgage originators, cash dealers, savings and loan institutions, pension funds, insurance companies, and institutional investors. It discusses the effectiveness of GNMA II as a current production hedge and explains contract applications. Free.

■ *Contract Specifications and Vendor Guide*—information included in this brochure covers contract highlights for all contracts traded at the Chicago Board of Trade as well as noncustomized quote services and vendor access codes. Free.

■ *Financial Futures Active Professional* and *Agricultural Futures Professional*—both are CBT newsletters published monthly for market professionals, participants, and prospective market users. Each issue covers a variety of topics, including new contract data, regulatory information, prospecting ideas, margin information, delivery experience, opinions of market leaders, and news of upcoming events. Free.

■ *Commodity Trading Manual*—this includes a comprehensive discussion of supply-demand factors affecting the most active futures contracts on the major United States exchanges. It covers the history of futures trading, theories of price forecasting, hedging, and speculation. Cost is $18.50.

■ *Gold Futures*—this is a descriptive leaflet which explains how gold is traded. It also describes the uses of gold and how the supply and demand factors affect its prices, and the Chicago Board of Trade specifications for contracts. Free.

■ *Silver Futures*—this is a descriptive leaflet which explains how silver is traded, the uses of silver, how the supply and demand factors affect its prices, and the Chicago Board of Trade specifications for contracts. Free.

Chicago Mercantile Exchange (CME)
30 South Wacker Drive
Chicago, IL 60606   312-930-3457

The International Monetary Market Division of the Chicago Mercantile Exchange trades precious metals in the daily futures metal market. They publish:

■ Information Bulletins—ten bulletins are published daily covering all items traded on the Chicago Mercantile Exchange. A subscription for one year is $75 in the United States, Canada, and Mexico, and $260 elsewhere.

Coffee, Sugar and Cocoa Exchange, Inc. (CSCE)

4 World Trade Center   212-938-2800
New York, NY 10048   212-938-2847—recorded message

CSCE is the world's leading marketplace for futures trading in these three international agricultural commodities. Members of the exchange include floor brokers and traders, and major domestic and international brokerage houses, plus the largest commercial users and producers of coffee, sugar, and cocoa in the world. The exchange itself does not participate in the trading of futures contracts. It is designed to provide an orderly, fair trading environment and a detailed system of rules and regulations to govern conduct of business. CSCE ensures that trading data are processed properly and prices are disseminated rapidly. CSCE provides daily recorded messages at various times during the day. It gives the estimated and final open, interest, and volume.

As part of its program to improve understanding of, and interest in, the commodities markets, CSCE offers the following booklets:

■ *Trading in Coffee Futures*—an eight-page brochure describing the details of the Exchange's coffee "C" contract. It also contains an overview of supply and demand factors affecting the international marketing of coffee and the role of the futures exchange in that process. Free.

■ *Trading in Sugar Futures*—a twelve-page brochure describing the contract specifications for the sugar no. 11 (world) and sugar no. 12 (domestic) contracts traded on the exchange. It outlines the economics of world and domestic sugar markets, current developments affecting the marketing of sugar, and the functions of the Exchange.

■ *Trading in Cocoa Futures*—an eight-page brochure outlining the contract specifications for the Exchange's cocoa futures contract. It gives a basic overview of cocoa production and demand and the role of the Exchange in the international marketing of cocoa. Free.

■ *Economic Index Futures: An Introduction to the Concept of Shifting Microeconomic Risk*—a forty-four-page booklet introducing the hedging potential of the CSCE's four proposed economic index contracts—the CPI-W, Housing Starts, Retail New Car Sales, and the CSCE Earnings Index. Hedging inflation, industrial output, corporate profitability, and variability in real estate interest rates are discussed. Includes contract specifications. Free.

Commodities Educational Institute (CEI)   800-221-4352—outside IA

219 Parkade   800-772-0023—in IA
Cedar Falls, IA 50613   319-277-6341

CEI training courses will help you sharpen your trading skills and understanding of the dynamic futures and options markets. These courses are directed toward producers who use futures markets to control price risks; bankers, money manager and corporate purchasing agents who need to use commodity futures to lock in raw material prices, as well as commodity traders and speculators. Call the toll-free number above for a course schedule.

Commodity Exchange Center, Inc. (COMEX)

4 World Trade Center   212-938-2937

New York, NY 10048   212-938-9020—gold and silver prices

COMEX is the world's largest metal futures exchange. Its gold and silver price hotline listed above is updated as soon as trading occurs. A daily and weekly market report is published through the COMEX statistical department. For further information and assistance in interpreting the following COMEX publications, contact the telephone number listed above.

- *COMEX Copper Futures*—a booklet describing the commodity, the industry structure, and the uses of copper, and how its uses affect the supply and demand of the commodity. It also explains how COMEX trades futures contracts. Free.
- *COMEX Gold Futures*—an illustrated booklet explaining the importance of gold, how COMEX trades in gold futures, hedging strategies and trading gold futures for profit. Free.
- *COMEX Silver Futures*—an illustrated booklet explaining the importance of silver, trading silver futures, hedging strategies, and trading silver futures for profit. Free.
- *Daily Market Report*—a daily report which provides the opening, highs, lows, closing, opening interest, and settlement data for the previous day. This report is available for $125 a year.
- *Statistical Yearbook*—an annual two-volume publication. Volume I summarizes all aluminum, copper, gold, silver, and other metals trading statistics for the year, and Volume II deals with options. The two-volume set is available for $15.
- *Weekly Market Report*—a weekly report which provides statistics on aluminum, copper, gold, and silver. The report is available for $35 a year.
- *The World Metals Market*—an illustrated booklet, updated periodically, describing the market and trading processes, and behind-the-scenes information, along with illustrations of the trading floor. Free.

Economic Research Service (ERS)

U.S. Department of Agriculture

1301 New York Avenue, Room 228

Washington, DC 20005   202-786-1494

ERS researches the production and marketing of major agricultural commodities; foreign agriculture and trade; economic use, conservation, and development of natural resources; and performance of the United States agricultural industry. It provides objective and timely information to farmers, farm organization members, farm suppliers, marketers, processors, consumers, and others who make production, marketing, and purchasing decisions.

Staff specialists can answer questions on agriculture production and stocks estimates. They can also refer you to the state statistician's office in individual states for additional information on state agricultural production, stocks, prices, and other data. A listing of ERS experts is provided in the People to Talk To section of this chapter.

ERS research, analyses, and forecasts are documented in a wide variety of publications. ERS offers a free series of fourteen commodity papers written for the general reader. These provide information on the structure of each industry, trends in domestic use and exports, and farm prices and returns. For more information or to order the series, contact the office above. Also available is the free *Reports* newsletter. It lists current agency research reports and other publications and their prices. Call the Information Office at 202-786-1512 to order a copy. Summaries of all *Outlook and Situation* reports and abstracts of research reports may be accessed electronically. For details call the office above.

ERS publications are available from the Government Printing Office (GPO), Washington, DC 20402, 202-783-3238; and the National Technical Information Service (NTIS), 5285 Port Royal Road, Springfield, VA 22161, 703-487-4650. Below is a sample of these publications. For a more complete listing contact ERS for a publications list:

- *The Distribution of Daily Changes in Commodity Futures Prices* (S/N 001-019-00393-6)—agricultural futures prices are discussed in this forty-page book. It describes economic models used in analyzing and forecasting price changes of commodity futures. Order from GPO. Cost is $1.50.

- *Farmers' Use of Cash Forward Contracts, Futures Contracts, and Commodity Options* (S/N 001-019-00386-3)—different types of forward contracts are described in this book along with factors a farmer should consider in forward selling and the major pitfalls involved. Order from GPO. Cost is $1.50.

- *Farmer's Guide to Trading Agricultural Commodity Options* (S/N 001-019-00331-6)—this manual explains the concept of options, the terminology of option contracts, and factors influencing option prices. Order from GPO. Cost is $1.50.

- *Agricultural Outlook*—published eleven times a year, this is USDA's official outlet for farm income and food price forecasts. It emphasizes short- and long-term analyses of issues ranging from international trade to United States land use and availability. Regular coverage includes the outlook for commodity supply and demand. Cost is $36 a year.

- *Agricultural Economics Research*—a quarterly journal, this reports the latest in technical research in agricultural economics, including econometric models, and statistics focusing on methods employed and results of USDA economic research. Articles discuss commodity studies, functional analyses, and new areas of research. Cost is $36 a year.

■ *Farmline*—published eleven times a year, this journal provides practical economic information covering farm economics. It covers such issues as production and marketing of major farm commodities, world agriculture and trade, cost and price trends. It costs $24 a year.

■ *1985 Agricultural Chartbook* (S/N 001-019-00428-2)—a 996-page overview of the agricultural sector, it contains 278 charts illustrating data and trends for agricultural subjects from farm income to consumer costs, and commodities to agricultural trade. Order from GPO. Cost is $3.50.

Future Industry Association (FIA)

1825 Eye Street, NW, Suite 1040
Washington, DC 20006   202-466-5460

FIA collects and publishes data about commodity futures exchanges and trading. The Association will answer inquiries, provide a correspondence course, disseminate data compilations, and make referrals. Monthly and yearly subscriptions containing statistics on volume of commodity trading are available to members only. The Association has one free report available to nonmembers. Contact the office above to be put on the mailing list.

Gold Institute

1001 Connecticut Avenue, NW, Suite 1140
Washington, DC 20036   202-331-1227

The Gold Institute is comprised of gold companies in thirteen gold-producing countries, excluding South Africa and the U.S.S.R. These companies are involved in mining, refining, and manufacturing products using gold; serving banking needs; and making gold bullion. The Institute serves as the arm of the gold industry helping keep track of all gold-producing countries and detailing the physical movement of all gold and gold coins among countries. It publishes:

■ *World Mine Production of Gold*—an annual leaflet with statistics on the total worldwide production of gold at year's end. A five-year projection is also provided. Free.

■ *The Gold News*—a bimonthly newsletter that reports on the uses of gold, the meetings of the Gold Institute, and new members of the Institute. Free.

Government National Mortgage Association (GNMA)

451 7th Street, SW, Room 6224
Washington, DC 20410   202-755-8772

The GNMA program offers investors government-guaranteed securities which are designed to attract nontraditional investors into the residential mortgage market. GNMA mortgage-backed securities are purchased and sold through financial institutions that trade government securities. GNMA securities are issued by private firms and cannot be purchased directly from the government. The securities are traded within the United States in the over-the-counter market as government-guaranteed securities. Interests in them are also traded in futures and options markets.

Information concerning trading and pricing of GNMA securities can be obtained by contacting a securities dealer active in the market for mortgage-backed securities. A list of such dealers can be obtained by writing to the Public Securities Association, 40 Broad Street, New York, NY 10004.

International Precious Metals Institute (IPMI)
Government Building
ABE Airport
Allentown, PA 18103   215-266-1570
The largest precious metals association in the world, IPMI is a nonprofit organization designed to serve the technical, economic, and educational needs of the precious metals community. It is composed of miners, refiners, producers, users, research scientists, bankers, government representatives, and private individuals. IPMI encourages the exchange of information concerning precious metals on an international level by publishing data and statistics and a newsletter, and through its library and information center. IPMI provides a common information forum throughout the world by conducting international conferences and publishing proceedings of these meetings. Annual technical conferences and periodic seminars are conducted and are open to all persons, but members receive a fee reduction. IPMI publishes:

  ■ *Precious Metals News and Review*—this monthly newsletter provides member industry information, news concerning government regulations, notices of upcoming events, seminars, and/or conferences. Free to members and $15 a year to nonmembers.

  ■ *A Practical Guide to the Commodities Markets*—this book provides a complete in-depth look at all aspects of commodities futures trading. It includes chapters on speculating in financial futures, metals, energy futures, and tropical commodities. Cost is $20.

International Trade Administration (ITA)
Department of Commerce
Primary Commodities Division
14th Street and Constitution Avenue, NW, Room 4412
Washington, DC 20230
Commodity experts in this office collect and analyze economic data for industrial raw materials, both domestic and international, to specific industrial commodities. They also focus their attention on international commodity agreements between producing and consuming countries. General economic information, including trade and production figures, is available for copper, tin, lead, zinc, and rubber, as well as agricultural commodities. ITA's major publication, *U.S. Industrial Outlook,* is a major channel through which the Department of Commerce makes its data and analytical resources readily available.

Staff specialists can answer inquiries and give referrals to other government and industry sources.

■ *U.S. Industrial Outlook*—updated each year, this provides analyses of American businesses competing in the world markets. It contains a "snapshot" of each industry, relating current import and export data as well as historical trends. It is available from the Government Printing Office, Washington, DC 20402, 202-783-3238 (SN 003-008-00197-1). Cost is $21.

Kansas City Board of Trade (KCBT)

800-892-KCBT
4800 Main Street, Suite 303
816-753-7500
Kansas City, MO 64112
816-753-1101—daily recording

KCBT is one of the nation's oldest commodity exchanges. It is the largest cash wheat trading center and the largest hard winter wheat futures market in the world. KCBT initiated trading in Value Line stock index futures. Value Line futures are the most sensitive to overall market movements, and outpace all imitators by advancing or declining to a greater extent, thus providing the greatest potential for profit or loss. For inquiries about Value Line futures and for assistance interpreting KCBT data, contact the Executive Office at the phone number above.

Financial sections of major newspapers and financial papers provide daily future statistics on Value Line futures. By calling 816-753-1101 you can reach KCBT's daily recording, which provides opening, noon, and closing prices. The following items are available to assist individual investors and brokers.

■ *Value Line "The Year of the Bull Run"*—this wall chart compares the Dow Jones and the Value Line composite index on a weekly high, low, and close from August 1982 to August 1983. It costs $3.

■ *Wheat Brochure*—basic information and specifications for the hard red winter wheat contract. Free.

■ *Value Line Futures*—this pamphlet provides basic information and specifications for the original stock index contract. Free.

■ *Annual Statistical Report*—published each year, it provides daily open, high, low, and close for futures and cash prices for KC Wheat and Value Line, plus annual grain market statistics. Free.

■ *Grain Market Review*—this daily publication covers grain market news and prices. Cost is $60 a year.

MidAmerica Commodity Exchange (MACE)

444 West Jackson Boulevard
312-341-3000
Chicago, IL 60606
800-572-3276

MidAmerica is managed and operated in the same manner as other United States exchanges, in that it is a federally designated market regulated by the Commodity Futures Trading Commission. It offers novice traders the flexibility and precision of minicontracts (contracts begin at one fifth to one half the size of those traded on other exchanges). It also extends trading hours ten to fifteen minutes after corresponding contracts at other exchanges have closed, which allows the investor to realize profit opportunities unavailable elsewhere. The exchange provides the following three recorded messages which are updated several times a day:

- Agricultural Price Update: 312-922-9110
- Financial Update: 312-922-9120
- Financial and Agricultural Commentary: 312-922-7885

As a commodity futures exchange, it cannot recommend a broker but can provide you with a list of member brokerage firms. The following guide is available:

- *Options on Grain and Soybean Futures*—provides an introduction to the mechanics of options and explores some basic option hedging strategies. Free.
- *Mini-Contracts in Precious Metals*—a leaflet which outlines the trading of copper, gold, platinum, and silver, describing their uses and sources, trading hours, trading units, delivery months, daily price limit, exchange policies, and specifications.

National Futures Association (NFA)
200 West Madison Street, Suite 1600
Chicago, IL 60606   312-781-1300

NFA ensures, through self-regulation, its members' high standards of professional conduct and financial responsibility. It is responsible for the screening, testing, and registration of commodity futures professionals.

Through its arbitration program, NFA provides a mechanism for the settlement of disputes. Decisions of the arbitrator(s) are final and can be enforced in any court of competent jurisdiction. NFA maintains a list of qualified arbitrators in every section of the country. Contact the office of the NFA General Counsel for more information. The following publications are available:

- *Understanding Opportunities and Risks in Futures Trading*—this brochure is intended to provide a better understanding of the opportunities and risks in futures, what futures markets are, how they work, who uses them, and their vital economic function. Free.
- *Arbitration: A Way to Resolve Futures Related Disputes*—NFA's nationwide arbitration system is described in this booklet. Free.
- *The Need for a Coordinated Campaign Against Commodity Fraud*—the scope and nature of commodity fraud is presented in this booklet by Robert K. Wilmouth, president and chief executive officer of NFA. Free.
- *Before You Say Yes: 15 Questions to Turn Off an Investment Swindler*—questions that swindlers don't want to hear are given in this leaflet. It tells you how to avoid fraudulent investment schemes. Free.

New York Mercantile Exchange (NYME)
4 World Trade Center
New York, NY 10048   212-938-2222
   This exchange is the futures trading place for the high-tech metals platinum and palladium. It welcomes inquiries from the public. NYME's publications include:

> ■ *Hi-Tech Metals*—a booklet explaining the supply, the demand, and the pricing structure of its contracts. The booklet explains the valuable uses of platinum and palladium in today's society. Free.
>
> ■ *The Daily Futures Report*—a paper which provides trading statistics summaries for palladium and platinum. It includes opening prices, highs, lows, volume traded, and other data. The paper is available for $60 a year.

Oster Communications, Inc.
219 Parkade   800-772-0023—in IA
Cedar Falls, IA 50613   800-221-4352—elsewhere
   Oster Communications publishes a variety of specialized newsletters and *Futures Magazine.* It also provides electronic news services for agriculture and the commodity futures industry. A sample includes:

> ■ *Commodity Closeup*—published weekly, this newsletter recommends trades only if they show a high reward-to-risk ratio. It provides specific trade recommendations covering twenty-three key markets and a telephone hotline with daily updates. Annual subscription fee is $180.
>
> ■ *Commodity Price Charts*—depending on the service you need, weekly or biweekly, you'll receive as many as 200 charts tracking all active contracts, for the most popular commodities, on all major markets. All charts are grouped by commodity, allowing you instant comparison of active contracts on each big, easy-to-read spread. Annual subscription to the weekly costs $369 and to the biweekly $205.
>
> ■ *Futures Update*—an information database, this source provides the latest market news, prices, technical data, commentary and statistics on futures and options. As a subscriber, you can call the data bank whenever you wish. Cost is forty cents per 1,000 characters, plus a low monthly access fee.

Professional Farmers of America
219 Parkade   800-772-0023—in IA
Cedar Falls, IA 50613   800-221-4352—elsewhere
   This marketing advisory service, a division of Oster Communications, is designed to help farmers better understand market forces and trends. It gives seminars at convenient locations around the country. Topics include: financial management, marketing, land buying, and farm computer applciations. Cassette tapes and books are available at the organization's Home Learning Center.

Professional Farmers of America newsletter editors are available to speak at conventions, seminars, or training sessions. Subscribers to the newsletter automatically become members of this organization and have access to crop and livestock telephone hotlines.

■ *Pro Farmer*—this four-page weekly newsletter is filled with marketing news, and management advice alerts readers to important developments affecting their income. Annual subscription fee is $80.

The Silver Institute
1001 Connecticut Avenue
Washington, DC 20036   202-331-1227

The Silver Institute is comprised of silver companies in twenty silver-producing countries. These companies are involved in mining, refining, and fabrication of products using silver. The purpose of the Institute is to provide assistance to people who use silver in technical industries. The Institute details the physical movement of silver and silver coins among countries. It publishes:

■ *The Silver Institute Letters*—a bimonthly newsletter that reports on the Institute's meetings and the uses of silver, and announces new members. Free.

■ *Mine Production of Silver*—an annual leaflet listing the total worldwide production of silver for the year. Projected totals are also provided for the upcoming five years. Free.

Securities Dealers
Your local securities dealer can provide information on the various ways to invest in aluminum, copper, gold, palladium, platinum, and silver; aluminum, copper, gold, palladium, platinum, and silver futures; gold bullion and silver bars, gold and silver certificates, gold and silver coins, gold options, and gold mutuals; and stock in mines producing aluminum, copper, gold, palladium, platinum, and silver.

WHAT TO READ

Annual Data (1987)
Copper Development Association, Inc.
Greenwich Office Park 2
Box 1840
Greenwich, CT 06836   203-625-8210

This twenty-page booklet covers statistics on copper supply and consumption in five major markets. Consolidates data from many sources for 1962-1986. It costs $11.

Commodity Research Bureau (CRB)

75 Montgomery Street   301-451-7500
Jersey City, NJ 07302   800-524-0850

CRB publishes commodity reference materials for professional traders, brokers, analysts, and investors, such as:

- *CRB Futures Chart Service*—this weekly provides you with more than 200 daily action price charts, covering all active futures markets in the United States, Canada, and London, including the newest markets in interest rates, currencies and stock index futures. Cost for three months is $136.50; annual subscription fee is $385.

- *Futures Market Service*—an eight-page weekly, this gives a market-by-market analysis of the factors that influence price movements. It provides traders with current fundamental (supply/demand) information on the futures markets. It costs $135 a year.

- *Commodity Index Report*—this weekly report follows twenty-seven major futures markets. It also presents futures price indices for all commodities. Subscribers to this report can phone daily for updates on any one or several of the indices. Annual cost is $75.

- *Commodity Yearbook*—updated each year, this reference book provides the information you need to assess the impact of supply/demand reports, evaluate production and consumption estimates, and gauge price trends in the futures markets. Cost is $44.95.

The Dow Jones-Irwin Guide to Commodities Trading

Dow Jones-Irwin
1824 Ridge Road   312-798-6000
Homewood, IL 60430   800-323-1717

Bruce G. Gould's book will give you the necessary knowhow to enter the commodities market with confidence. It is a step-by-step guide to the fundamentals of successful trading. It costs $27.50 plus $1.75 for postage and handling.

Gold

Gold Fields American Corporation
230 Park Avenue, 32nd Floor
New York, NY 10169   212-880-5128

Updated annually, this booklet explains the investment demand for gold, lists secondary sources of gold and details the supply of gold for the previous year. Free.

Import Bulletin

445 Marshall Street   212-425-1616
Phillipsburg, NJ 08865   800-221-3777

Published each Wednesday, this lists incoming cargoes entered at all leading United States ports reported by commodity group. Each cargo is described by nature, quantity, port of origin, the vessel, and the name of its authorized agent. Cost is $308 a year.

An Introduction to Investing in Gold
Gold Information Center
645 Fifth Avenue
New York, NY 10022   212-688-0474
This booklet provides a good background for the novice investor. It deals with some of the major investment issues in concise and fundamental language. Free.

Investor Publications, Inc.
Box 6
Cedar Falls, IA 50613   800-553-1789
The following books are available from this publisher:
   ■ *How to Use Interest Rate Futures Contracts*—a primer on the fundamentals of commodity trading, this book by Edward W. Schwarz explains the concept of interest rate futures contracts and how to use them. Cost is $27.50.
   ■ *Charting Commodity Market Price Behavior*—revised and updated, this book provides traders with a practical, nontechnical guide to chart trading and tells you how to analyze markets by using price, volume, and open interest indicators. It costs $30.
   ■ *Trading in Commodity Futures*—the basics of sound commodity tradings are given in this book. It includes fundamental and technical analysis. Cost is $27.95.

The Journal of Commerce
110 Wall Street   212-425-1616
New York, NY 10005   800-221-3777
A daily international business paper, the *Journal of Commerce*'s up-to-date news includes information on commodities.

Metals Bulletin, Inc.
703 Third Avenue
New York, NY 10017   212-490-0791
This twice-weekly publication covers world steel and metals news, including aluminum. It focuses on analysis, supply, and modeling programs of metals. Cost is $344 a year.

Mocatta 1684-1984
Mocatta Futures Corporation
4 World Trade Center
New York, NY 10048   212-938-8220

This illustrated booklet, along with some free brochures, describes the history of Mocatta in the gold and silver futures market, as well as mining, refining, fabrication, and industrial marketing of gold and silver. Free.

North American Gold Industry News
PO Box 662
Wilsonville, OR 97070   800-547-3428

Published twenty-six times a year, this gold trade industry paper has 170 mines as associate members. It is available for $45 a year bulk mail or $470 a year first class.

The Spector Report
PO Box 467
Hewlett, NY 11557   212-309-8310

This monthly publication on aluminum follows production, shipment, consumption, supply and demand, balance payments, and prices. It is available for $2,000 a year.

U.S. Mineral Resources
Superintendent of Documents
US Government Printing Office
Washington, DC 20402   202-783-3238

This book covers all metals, including those traded in the futures market. Updated sporadically, it describes the geology of the metals, where they occur and the United States reserves and resources of those metals. Its order number is 24-0100-307, and it is available for $8.50.

The Wall Street Journal
Dow Jones and Company
200 Burnett Road
Chicopee, MA 01021   800-228-6262—subscriptions

This is a daily financial newspaper that provides the daily cash and futures prices data for the previous day. A subscription is $56 for six months and $107 for a year.

Weekly Weather and Crop Bulletin

U.S. Department of Commerce
NOAA/USDA Joint Agricultural Weather Facility
South Building, Room 5844
Washington, DC 20250   202-447-7917

A weekly review of national and international weather reports, this Bulletin uses maps and charts to analyze how weather has affected crop conditions. It costs $25 a year.

World Bank Publications

1818 H Street, NW
Washington, DC 20433

The World Bank offers a wide range of its papers and publications for sale. A free catalog that lists titles of more than 600 staff working papers published since 1967 is available upon request. These papers, published every week, cover a broad range of subjects, including commodities. The following book is distributed for the World Bank by the Johns Hopkins University Press.

> ■ *Commodity Trade and Price Trends*—provides historical information on the trade of developing countries and eighty market price quotations for fifty-one commodities that are important in international trade. Actual current and constant dollar prices are shown in tabular and graphic form to indicate commodity price movements relative to the international price level. The 175-page book costs $25.

FOR COMPUTER USERS

AgriData Network

Midwestern Continental Telephone Company (Contel)
PO Box 146
Wentzville, MD 63385   314-327-3600

Subscribers can call a toll-free number that provides access to information on the agribusiness market, commodity news, state agriculture news, futures price quotation and trading data, market analysis and advisories, agricultural weather management and forecasts, United States government agricultural reports, agricultural chemical information, and livestock auction and sales reports. Cost is $199 for six months plus an on-line charge.

Ag Data Network

Purdue University
Cooperative Extension Service
Smith Hall, Room 105
West Lafayette, IN 47907   317-494-8333

This professional bulletin board provides the latest news and answers to questions in the area of agriculture. It also provides access to a number of agricultural newsletters. For more information on the database and how to use your modem, call the office above.

PEOPLE TO TALK TO

Below are experts who can provide much of the information you'll need to make wise commodities decisions. All are federal employees, and they spend their workday tracking the latest trends and developments in their particular area of expertise. While they won't tell you how to invest, they can give you invaluable insight, and there's no charge for their services!

Agricultural Specialists
U.S. Department of Agriculture
Economic Research Service (ERS)
1301 New York Avenue, Room 228
Washington, DC 20005   202-786-1494
Generally, the experts listed with an S can give you the latest production and stocks estimates, and those identified with an E can help with supply-demand-price relationships and other economic factors. All can be reached by phone or writing the address listed above.

Broilers
Ron Sitzman   S   202-447-3244
Allen Baker   E   202-786-1830

Catfish
Paul Hurt   S   202-447-3237

Cattle
Steve Pavlasek   S   202-447-3040
John Nalivka   E   202-786-1830
Linda Bailey (world)   E   202-786-1691

Coffee and Tea
Fred Gray   E   202-786-1769

Cold Storage
Bernie Albrecht   S   202-382-9185

Corn and Feed Grains
Gary Nelson   S   202-447-9526
Dave Hull   E   202-786-1840
Jim Cole (world)   E   202-786-1692

Cotton
Radley Edwards   S   202-447-5944
Terry Townsend   E   202-786-1840
Richard Cantor (world)   E   202-786-1691

Dairy Products
Dan Buckner   S   202-447-4448
Clifford Carman   E   202-786-1830
Jerry Rector (world)   E   202-786-1691

Eggs
Al Drain   S   202-447-6147
Allen Baker   E   202-786-1830
Linda Bailey (world)   E   202-786-1691

Fibers
John Lawler   E   202-786-1840

Fruits and Nuts
Doyle Johnson   S   202-447-5412
Ben Huang   E   202-786-1767

Hay
Steve Kellogg   S   202-447-7780
Dave Hull   E   202-786-1840

Hogs
Steve Wyatt   S   202-447-3106
Leland Southard   E   202-786-1830
Linda Bailey (world)   E   202-786-1691

Milk
Dan Buckner   S   202-447-4448
Clifford Carman   E   202-786-1830
Jerry Rector   E   202-786-1691

Peanuts
Radley Edwards   S   202-447-5944
Duane Hacklander   E   202-786-1840
Jan Lipson (world)   E   202-786-1693

Potatoes
Arvin Budge   S   202-447-4285
Glenn Zepp   E   202-786-1768
Shannon Hamm   E   202-786-1767

Poultry
Paul Hurt   S   202-447-3237
Allen Baker   E   202-786-1830
Linda Bailey (world)   E   202-786-1691

Rice
Clif James   S   202-447-7960
Janet Livezey   E   202-786-1840
Scott Reynolds (world)   E   202-786-1693

Sheep
John Cole   S   202-447-3578
Leland Southard   E   202-786-1830

Slaughter
John Cole   S   202-447-3578

Soybeans and Oilseeds
Craig Hayes   S   202-447-7310
Roger Hoskin   E   202-786-1840
Jan Lipson (world)   E   202-786-1693
Duane Hacklander   E   202-786-1840

Sugar and Sweeteners
Rose Petrone   S   202-447-2555
Robert Barry   E   202-786-1769
Luigi Angelo   E   202-786-1769

Tobacco
Darwin Ransom   S   202-447-7621
Verner Grise   E   202-786-1840

Turkeys
Ron Sitzman   S   202-447-3244
Allen Baker   E   202-786-1830

Vegetables
Jim Brewster (fresh)   S   202-447-7688
Arvin Budge (processing)   S   202-447-4285
Shannon Hamm   E   202-786-1767

Wheat and Food Grains
Vaughn Siegenthaler   S   202-447-8068
Allen Schienbein   E   202-786-1840
Scott Reynolds (world)   E   202-786-1693

Wool
John Cole   S   202-447-3578
John Lawler   E   202-786-1840
Terry Townsend   E   202-786-1840

Africa and Middle East
Cheryl Christensen   E   202-786-1680

Agricultural Development
Lon Cesal   E   202-786-1705

Asia
Carmen Nohre   E   202-786-1610

China
Fred Surls   E   202-786-1616

Commodities
Ed Overton   E   202-786-1620
Jerry Rector   E   202-786-1691

Eastern Europe and USSR
Kathryn Zeimetz   E   202-786-1710

Economic and Trade Policy
Vernon Roningen   E   202-786-1630
Richard Kennedy   E   202-786-1688

Food Aid
Ray Nightingale   E   202-786-1705

International Monetary and Finance
Art Morey   E   202-786-1687
Dave Stallings   E   202-786-1624

Western Europe
Reed Friend   E   202-786-1720

Western Hemisphere
Ronald Trostle   E   202-786-1668

U.S. Exports and Imports
Thomas Warden (statistics)   E   202-786-1621

Food: Commodity Policy
Leroy Rude   E   202-786-1790
Cathy Jabarra   E   202-786-1636

Other Topics: Commodity Programs and Policy
Keith Collins   E   202-786-1880

Industrial Specialists

US Wood Products Industry
Office of Forest Products and Domestic Construction
US Department of Commerce, Room 4045
Washington, DC 20230
Donald Butts   202-377-0382
Adair Mitchell   202-377-0377
Walter H. Fausel   202-377-0378

Pulp, Paper, and Board
Office of Forest Products and Domestic Construction
US Department of Commerce, Room 4045
Washington, DC 20230
Donald Butts   202-377-0382
Mary Anne Smith   202-377-0375
Leonard S. Smith   202-377-0376
Iris A. Dean   202-377-0132

Coal
Office of Energy
US Department of Commerce
14th Street and Constitution Avenue, NW, Room 4413
Washington, DC 20230
Erast N. Borissoff   202-377-1466

Energy Information Administration
Department of Energy, CNEAF
1000 Independence Avenue, SW
EI—521 Forrestal Building
Washington, DC 20585
Charles C. Heath   202-252-6860

Energy Information Administration
Department of Energy, CNEAF
1000 Independence Avenue, SW
EI—521 Forrestal Building
Washington, DC 20585
Gerard L. Lagace   202-252-1452

Petroleum
Energy Information Administration
Department of Energy, CNEAF
1000 Independence Avenue, SW
EI—521 Forrestal Building
Washington, DC 20585
Gregory P. Filas   202-252-1347

Chemicals and Allied Products
Office of Chemicals and Allied Products
14th Street and Constitution Avenue, Room 4031
Washington, DC 20230
David H. Blank   202-377-0128
Sobhag Narain   202-377-0128
Leo McIntyre   202-377-0128

Rubber and Plastics
Office of Chemicals and Allied Products
14th Street and Constitution Avenue, Room 4031
Washington, DC 20230
David H. Blank   202-377-0128
David G. Rosse   202-377-0128

Non-Ferrous Castings
Office of Minerals, Metals and Commodities
US Department of Commerce
14th Street and Constitution Avenue, Room 4059
Washington, DC 20230
Robert A. Ricciuti   202-377-0610

Tobacco
Office of Automotive Affairs and Consumer Goods
Cornelius F. Kenney   202-377-2428

Textiles
Office of Textiles and Apparel
Kim Ilich   202-377-4058

Ferrous Metals
Office of Basic Industries
US Department of Commerce
14th Street and Constitution Avenue, Room 4045
Washington, DC 20230
Ralph Thompson   202-377-0606

Precious Metals Experts
Office of Minerals, Metals and Commodities
14th Street and Constitution Avenue, Room 4059
Washington, DC 20230

For information on precious metals phone the following experts or write to the address listed above. Additional information is given for those experts marked with an asterisk following this listing.

Aluminum
James S. Kennedy   202-377-0575
Frank X. McCawley   202-634-1080
*Joann Santangelo   212-938-2937

Copper and Zinc
David Stonfer   202-377-0575
Robert C. Reiley   202-377-0575
*Janice L. Jolly   202-634-1071
*Joann Santangelo   212-938-2937

Gold
*John Lucas   202-634-1070
*Joann Santangelo   212-938-2937

Nickel
Graylin W. Presbury   202-377-5158

Palladium
*J. Roger Loebenstein   202-634-1058

Platinum Group
James J. Manion   202-377-5157
*J. Roger Loebenstein   202-634-1058

Silver
*Robert Reese   202-634-1054
*Joann Santangelo   212-938-2937

Titanium
James J. Manion   202-377-5157

Tungsten
Seward L. Jones   202-377-5125

Jeffrey Christian
Vice President, Commodities Research
J. Aron and Co./Goldman Sachs
160 Water Street
New York, NY 10038   212-902-7872

Mr. Christian produces research on the white group of metals—silver, platinum, and palladium. His research includes tracking the amounts mined in various countries, the amounts sold and the demand from various industries around the world.

Richard Davies
Managing Director, Gold Institute
1001 Connecticut Avenue, NW Suite 1140
Washington, DC 20036   202-331-1227
    Mr. Davies is an industrial chemist by profession, as well as an expert in international money and banking. He is chairman of the firm Klein and Saks, which oversees the operation of the Gold Institute and many large central banking operations. Mr. Davies has served central banks and many ministers of finance in finance and technical fields in his career.

Janice L. Jolly
US Department of Interior
Bureau of Mines
Division of Non-Ferrous Metals
2401 E Street, NW
Washington, DC 20241   202-634-1071
    An expert in copper, Ms. Jolly has experience in the lead/zinc/copper area. She has spent four years in Zambia as a copper research geologist, and is currently the copper specialist with Bureau of Mines.

J. Roger Loebenstein
US Department of Interior
Bureau of Mines
Division of Non-Ferrous Metals
2401 E Street, NW
Washington, DC 20241   202-634-1058
    Mr. Loebenstein has specialized in the platinum group metals as a commodities expert. He is interested in following the mining and the supply and demand of the platinum group metals in the United States, as well as worldwide.

John Lucas
US Department of Interior
Bureau of Mines
Division of Non-Ferrous Metals
2401 E Street, NW
Washington, DC 20241   202-634-1070
    Mr. Lucas is an expert in the mining of gold and in following its supply and demand in the United States. A trained geologist, he is keenly aware of gold operations.

Frank McCawley
US Department of Interior
Bureau of Mines
Division of Non-Ferrous Metals
2401 E Street, NW
Washington, DC 20241   202-634-1080
    Mr. McCawley has done research in metals and metallurgy for about twenty-five years. His work in aluminum is following the finished product, supply and demand, production, shipment, and consumption, including the use of scrap aluminum.

Jeffrey Nichols
President
American Precious Metals Advisors, Inc.
707 Westchester Avenue
White Plains, NY 10604   914-681-4412
    Mr. Nichols, an expert in precious metals, has been an adviser to mining companies, industrial users, central banks, and other institutions for the past several years.

Robert Reese
US Department of Interior
Bureau of Mines
Division of Non-Ferrous Metals
2401 E Street, NW
Washington, DC 20241   202-634-1054
    Mr. Reese follows silver mining through the refining process for the Bureau of Mines. He publishes statistics and follows the supply and demand of silver.

Joann Santangelo
Statistics Department
Commodity Exchange Center, Inc. (COMEX)
4 World Trade Center
New York, NY 10048   212-938-2937
    Ms. Santangelo is in charge of the statistics and market information for COMEX. She is able to chart the trends for the commodity exchange and the futures of any of the commodities traded by COMEX.

Money Market Funds

See also:
Mutual Funds

A very popular type of mutual fund, money markets accounted for approximately 33 percent of all money invested in mutual funds during 1986. This totaled approximately $260 billion.

Money market funds generally put contributors' money into low-risk, short-term investments of a year or less, such as certificates of deposit and treasury bills. When interest rates are high, money markets allow the small investor to participate in a diversified portfolio at a substantially greater interest rate return than is possible from savings accounts. Fund investors can withdraw their money on demand similar to regular bank accounts, but the investment isn't guaranteed by the federal government. However, funds have a high degree of safety as there is no risk of principal.

You'll find the Investment Company Institute, the Donoghue Organization, and the other resources described in this section helpful as you research money market funds to decide if such an investment is right for you. Funds are advertised daily in the *Wall Street Journal* and many other newspapers. But the best source of data about a particular fund is the fund itself. Most have toll-free numbers you can call for information. Call 800-555-1212 to get this number for any fund you are interested in.

In addition to this section, be sure to check the Mutual Funds chapter. It covers many of the essential resources on money markets, such as Wiesenberger's directory and the American Association of Independent Investors.

AGENCIES, INSTITUTES, AND ORGANIZATIONS

The Donoghue Organization, Inc.
360 Woodland Street   617-429-5930
PO Box 540   800-343-5413
Holliston, MA 01746   800-445-5900—for free samples

This financial research organization serves consumers as well as institutional investors. It publishes various newsletters and books for those who need a timely analysis of the financial market. Subscribers who have questions on a particular service or who require additional information can call the toll-free number above; a newsletter editor will provide answers.

Below are samples of available publications. For more information on Donoghue's full line of service call the toll-free number listed above.

■ *Donoghue's Money Fund Report*—Money market and municipal bond traders consider this monthly and weekly report their bible. It features insightful commentary and statistical data pertaining to trends in the money markets. The cost for weekly reports is $595 a year and the cost for monthly reports is $345 a year.

■ *Donoghue'$ Money Letter*—Geared to consumers or the individual investor, this bimonthly newsletter focuses on topical financial matters and gives information on the money market and mutual fund industries and investment switches between them. An annual subscription costs $87.

■ *Donoghue's Mutual Fund Almanac*—updated annually, this book contains information on 850 money market and other mutual funds. It gives the names, addresses and phone numbers for each of the funds, and a ten-year past performance record. It includes their checking policies. It costs $23.

■ *Donoghue's Money Fund Directory*—updated and revised twice a year, this directory lists all of the money funds and details their services. The cost is $19.95. (You can also obtain this information direct from each money market's toll-free number. Call your toll-free number operator at 800-555-1212.

Investment Company Institute (ICI)
1600 M Street, NW
Washington, DC 20036   202-293-7700

The staff in the Public Information Office will answer your questions on money market mutual funds or will find an expert to help you. The Investment Company represents 90 percent of all mutual funds. For further information about its services, see the chapter Mutual Funds. ICI's membership directory is available to the public free of charge. The following brochure on money market funds is also available:

■ *Money Market Mutual Funds—What Are They?*—in easy to understand language, this brochure explains what money market mutual funds are all about and how to take that important first step. Free.

Money Market Funds
The funds themselves are a good resource. You can get a company prospectus, financial reports, information about its investment objectives, and more.

Most funds offer a toll-free number you can call for information and publications. Call the toll-free operator on 800-555-1212 to see if a specific fund has such a number. The Investment Company Institute (ICI), *Wiesenberger's Investment Company Service Directory,* and the Securities Exchange Commission are other sources for contact information. ICI is described in this chapter, the other two in the Mutual Funds chapter.

United Business Service Company
210 Newbury Street
Boston, MA 02116   617-267-8855
   One of the oldest and largest advisory services in the country, United
Business Service provides a full range of investment advisory and investment-
related information services. Questions regarding mutual funds and money
markets are answered through the following newsletter:

> ▪ *United Mutual Fund Selector*—issued twice a month, this newsletter
> presents short- and long-term performance records on over 500 funds. The
> *Selector* tracks seventy money market funds with favorites indicated. Con-
> tinuing commentary on the mutual fund industry, including personal inter-
> views with top managers of selected funds, appears regularly. Annual
> subscription costs $98.

WHAT TO READ

Instruments of the Money Market
Federal Reserve Bank
Public Services Department
PO Box 27622
Richmond, VA 23261   804-643-1250
   Ten major money market instruments are reviewed in detail in this 148-
page book. It emphasizes the interaction of the various market sectors. Free.

Money Market Calculations: Yields, Break-Evens and Arbitrage
Dow Jones-Irwin   312-798-6000
1824 Ridge Road   800-323-1717
Homewood, IL 60430   800-942-8881—in IL
   A series of formulas for determining the true yield of money market
instruments under varying conditions is presented. The authors, Marcia Stigum
and John Mann, also cover how to annualize daily yields, dollar price, and how
to calculate the yield of U.S. treasury bills at the time of purchase. The cost
is $35.

100 Highest Yields
Advertising News Service Inc.
Box 088888   800-327-7717
North Palm Beach, FL 33408   305-627-7330
   Published weekly, this newsletter reports the highest yields on nationwide
federally insured banks and thrifts. It will provide you with up-to-the-minute
information on your best money market investment opportunities. You learn
the institution's name, address and phone number as well as the minimum

deposit required, stated rate and method of compounding, and annual effective yield. The cost is $84 a year or $19 for six weeks.

PEOPLE TO TALK TO

William E. Donoghue
President
The Donoghue Organization, Inc.
360 Woodland Street
Holliston, MA 01746   617-429-5930
    A pioneer in the money fund industry, Mr. Donoghue is the publisher of a variety of materials considered required reading for those who desire timely analysis of the financial markets. He has been called the "do-it-yourself investment guru." Mr. Donoghue is a nationally syndicated personal finance columnist in over thirty newspapers reaching 70,000 readers.

ADDITIONAL RESOURCES

Interest Rates and Money Markets Made Easy
National Public Radio
Customer Service
PO Box 55417   800-253-0808
Madison, WI 53705   608-263-4892
    With insight and humor, Robert Krulwich explains what causes interest rates to go up and how a money market fund actually works. Included are leading economists in "singing" roles. The cassette is twenty minutes long and costs $9.50.

Mutual Funds

See also:
Money Market Funds
IRAs and Keogh Funds

Want the benefits of portfolio management without spending a lot of time or money? Consider mutual funds. Introduced in the United States more than fifty years ago, a mutual fund is an investment company. Its money managers take the combined dollars of the shareholders—individuals and institutions—and invest them in a diversified list of securities thereby giving each shareholder a proportionate interest in many individual companies. Several types of mutual funds exist, each with a different investment objective: growth funds, income funds, growth-income funds, balanced funds, bond funds, money market funds, and municipal bond funds.

Since a mutual fund can't go bankrupt, it is a relatively safe investment. It can, however, decide to dissolve, at which time the fund's assets are dispersed among current shareholders. Another advantage is that mutual funds require no monthly minimum or time commitment. Depending on the fund, your initial investment can be as little as $25 or as much as $1,000.

One of the best ways to get information about a mutual fund is to contact the specific fund you are interested in. Most have a toll-free number you can call for information and to get free copies of the fund's quarterly and annual reports. All are required by law to send you a company prospectus. It is important to note that if you go to a broker you will get biased advice, as she/he will try to steer you into one of the funds his/her firm deals with. To decide which fund to invest in, the Investment Company Institute (ICI), a trade association representing 90 percent of the funds, recommends that you:

First, answer the question: Why do I want to invest? Is it for retirement, educating my child, saving for a house? Depending on your purpose you will want to select a mutual fund that is long-term or short-term, high-risk or no-risk, one that supplies immediate income, etc.

Next consult *Forbes* Annual Mutual Fund Survey and Wiesenberger's *Investment Company Service Directory* (the bible of the industry) at your library. Both are described in this chapter. *Forbes* rates the funds, and Wiesenberger gives you a historical perspective. It is important to go back over the past ten years and see what the performance has been for a particular fund. Do not judge a fund solely by how it is performing today.

Next select several funds—half a dozen or so—that you think you'd like to invest in and contact them *directly* for a prospectus. By law the fund must send you one so that you can evaluate whether or not it would be a good investment. You might also want to check with the SEC if you can't find the address of a new fund, as all mutual funds must register with this federal agency. Go through the prospectus for each fund, compare what each has to offer, and decide which fund you want to invest in. Then go directly to the fund and apply. You do not need a broker and you will save yourself money.

To track a mutual fund, look under Mutual Funds in the *New York Times, Wall Street Journal,* and other papers. When the market closes at 4 P.M., every money market fund must figure out what the fund has done in terms of "net asset value," and this gets reported the next day in the business section of major newspapers. To arrive at net asset value, a fund takes all shares in the portfolio and what they are worth and then divides that figure by the number of shareholders. Keep current on the investment scene by reading periodicals such as *Money, Changing Times,* and *Fact.* Many financial magazines review mutual fund performance every year; check with the individual publications. Some are described in this chapter. Also, you will find several mutual fund newsletters described here. Most offer a free trial period of one to three months; try several and compare, then decide if you want to subscribe. There are books in many libraries that review newsletters and do a good job analyzing investments. Check with your librarian.

Lots of options exist for the money market investor. ICI will send you a free list of more than 1,300 funds, their addresses, phone numbers, and investment objectives. You can find out about "no-load" funds, those sold directly to the public without a commission fee, by checking ads in financial magazines or newspapers. You can also contact the No-load Mutual Fund Association for information, or purchase their $2 directory describing more than 100 such funds. Or you can contact your broker for information.

Mutual funds are very popular because with one investment you can buy into a diversified group of stocks and bonds *and* accomplish your own unique investment objectives, including the degree of risk that's comfortable for you. However, to make a wise choice you'll need to do some homework. The sources here will get you started.

AGENCIES, INSTITUTES, AND ORGANIZATIONS

American Association of Individual Investors (AAII)
See listing under STOCKS.

Investment Company Institute (ICI)
1600 M Street, NW
Washington, DC 20036   202-293-7700
The trade association for the mutual fund industry, ICI represents more than 1,300 funds, or about 90 percent of the industry. In addition to representing the interests of its members, the Institute also serves as a clearinghouse for

the public. Staff members will answer your questions, refer you to experts, and give you contact information for a specific fund. Speakers are also available from the Institute.

ICI holds an annual meeting, conferences, and regional meetings. These are open to the public and a good way to get insights into the industry. Cassette tapes and proceedings are available.

Publications and films designed to keep investors informed on the issues are offered by the Institute. In addition to ICI's free membership directory, you can obtain:

- *Investment Company Institute's Guide to Mutual Funds*—over 1,400 mutual fund companies are listed in this 1986 publication, with information on each fund company including what size investment they require to start, the assets, the year the fund began, and toll-free numbers to call. Fourteen of the eighty pages are devoted to consumer text explaining what mutual funds are, how they are regulated, how to read a prospectus, and other basic information. Cost is $1.
- *Women: Active Money Managers*—the Institute, in 1984, conducted a national survey of 2,000 women and their attitudes toward investing. Findings published in this report revealed that women prefer to make their own financial decisions and are knowledgeable and venturesome investors willing to assume moderate or substantial risk in return for a higher yield on their investments. The study costs $100.
- *Mutual Fund Fact Book*—a publication which includes a five-year analysis of load and no-load mutual funds. The hundred-page fact book provides statistical information on funds, performance, and other relevant data. The cost is $4.
- *A Translation: Turning Investmentese into Investment Ease*—a twenty-page brochure containing general information on mutual funds. The publication is written for the general public and it helps consumers who want to learn about mutual funds by providing explanations of technical terminology and information on services and objectives of various funds. Cost is thirty cents.

Does the Average Investor Really Have a Chance Against Institutional Investors?

Most Americans don't seem to think so. Fewer than a third of those surveyed felt the individual investor gets treated fairly on Wall Street.

- *Money Market Mutual Funds—What Are They?*—this ten-page pamphlet tells you how these funds work, and gives you a list of questions you should ask when you are comparing one fund with another. Free.
- *Free List of More Than 1,200 Mutual Funds*—this includes names, addresses, phone numbers, and investment objectives of each fund.
- *How Will You Ever Scrape Up the Money When Your Child's Ready for College?*—major types, services, and advantages of mutual funds are outlined in this brochure. It gives compelling reasons why you should plan in advance for your children's higher education. Free.
- *Discipline. It Can't Really Be Good For You, Can It?*—the strategy for buying mutual funds shares is explained in this well-illustrated brochure. Free.
- *Investment Strategy For Busy People: The Mutual Fund Method*—this fifteen-minute film shows how a typical family's household, job, and personal demands point to a mutual fund strategy. It is available on loan free for three days.
- *Monthly Statistics*—this is a monthly statistical service that shows industry sales, redemptions, net assets, cash holdings, and total portfolio transactions of the mutual fund activity for the current month, previous month and comparable periods of the previous year. The annual cost is $36.

Money Concepts
1523 King Street
Alexandria, VA 22314   703-684-1277

This financial planning center is a franchise of International Financial Services, Inc. Money Concepts offers many types of informational seminars, all free to the public. Seminar workshops cover IRAs, Keoghs, mutual funds, annuities, money management, and personal finance. The purpose of these seminars is to help individuals and organizations to better understand money management, financial planning, and investments. As a free service, a staff person will analyze your personal financial situation and after three interviews will prepare a written plan with specific investment recommendations. To find out if there is a member company of International Financial Services in your area contact their headquarters: 1 Golden Bear Plaza, U.S. Highway One, North Palm Beach, FL 33408, 305-627-0700.

No-Load Mutual Fund Association, Inc.
1 Penn Plaza, Suite 2204
New York, NY 10001   212-563-4540

Publications:
PO Box 1010
South Orange, NJ 07079   Written requests only

Founded in 1971, the No-Load Mutual Fund Association is a nonprofit organization consisting of 370 no-load and low-load mutual funds from ninety different management companies. It seeks to educate investors about the distinctive features that mutual funds offer. Staff members will answer questions, make referrals to experts, and investigate problems you may be having with a particular fund. The association provides speakers (such as portfolio managers from some of the nation's largest financial institutions who have the responsibility of investing billions of dollars annually) who may address your group on topics such as: how to pay for your children's college costs, the no-load mutual fund's role in estate planning, what you need to know about IRAs and Keogh plans, ways to boost current income, and how to be your own investment counselor. The association publishes:

- *Investor's Directory: Your Guide to Mutual Funds*—an annual forty-eight-page directory that explains mutual funds and how they work and lists over a hundred such funds, including their investment objective/policy, assets, purchase requirements, redemption procedures/check writing privileges, and services provided. A glossary of terms is included. The directory costs $2.

- *Bibliography*—the association also offers a one-page bibliography of books, magazines, newsletters, and financial advisory services which provide information to beginning investors. Free.

Schabacker Investment Management
8943 Shady Grove Court
Gaithersburg, MD 20877   301-840-0301

This company offers an investment service called Discretionary Managed Accounts to investors who have a minimum of $100,000 to invest in mutual funds. Individuals get advice about evaluating investment goals and determining appropriate investment activity. The fee is one to two percent of the investor's account balance. The following publications are available:

- *No-Load Low-Load Mutual Fund Directory*—this directory provides the name, address, and phone number of a mutual fund and tells you the minimum deposit required. Free.

- *Switch Fund Advisory*—this monthly twenty-page newsletter offers performance ratings and analysis of various load and no-load mutual funds, as well as investment advice on these funds. The publication includes model portfolios and switching advice based on stock and economic forecasting. Finally, the newsletter analyzes sector mutual funds and highlights fund families every month. The cost is $135 annually; a weekly update bulletin is also available for the aggressive investor for an additional $129 a year.

- *Retirement Fund Advisory*—a monthly six-to-eight-page retirement-planning newsletter which advises mutual fund investors on investment techniques to prevent loss in retirement and capitalize on new opportunities. The publication specifically analyzes Keogh and IRA funds and offers performance guidelines and advice on these funds. The cost is $59 annually.

■ *Mutual Fund's Quarterly Performance Report*—a twenty-page quarterly report which evaluates over 500 mutual funds and provides composite ratings of good hold, buy, or sell funds. The cost is $25 for a single issue or $70 for four.

Securities and Exchange Commission (SEC)
Office of Consumer Affairs
450 5th Street, NW
Washington, DC 20549   202-272-7460—publications
If you are trying to get contact information for a new fund and can't find it, contact the SEC. All funds must register with it, and staff will have the information for you. SEC publishes:

■ *Investigate Before You Invest*—a seven-page free booklet, this explains how to shop for securities and how to protect yourself against con artists.

WHAT TO READ

NoLOAD Fund
DAL Investment Co.
235 Montgomery Street
San Francisco, CA 94104   415-986-7979
This monthly newsletter covers the entire no-load and low-load industry. The publication identifies top-performing funds, new funds, changes, and mergers. Fund comparisons are made within the six fund categories into which all market funds are divided, thereby increasing analysis accuracy. Finally, a question-and-answer section and capital gains and dividend information are provided for the reader. The annual subscription costs $95 a year. A three-month trial membership is available for $27.

Expanding Your Investments With Mutual Funds
Mutual Fund Services
The OLDE Building
735 Griswold Street   800-225-FUND
Detroit, MI 48226   313-963-FUND
This booklet helps you identify the mutual funds that are most suited to your immediate and future investment needs. Free.

Investment Information Services (IIS)
205 West Wacker Drive
Chicago, IL 60606   312-750-9300

This company's book publishing division, Investment Information Services Press, offers a diverse spectrum of financial publications written in a style that is clear and understandable for all investors, novices and experienced alike.

■ *The Mutual Fund Letter*—published monthly, this advisory letter recommends top-rated no-load and low-load mutual funds for various investment strategies (aggressive, conservative, fixed income, etc.). Subscribers also receive the comprehensive book, *Mutual Funds and Your Investment Portfolio.* The annual subscription cost is $72.

■ *The Individual Investor's Guide to No-Load Mutual Funds*—in its fourth edition, this annual guide contains descriptions and six-year operating histories on 446 no-load mutual funds and a text section featuring a five-factor model for selecting funds. It includes summary descriptions of the fifty largest money market funds and thirty-eight tax-exempt money funds. The cost is $19.95.

■ *Mutual Fund Newsletter*—a twelve-page monthly publication providing recommendations on no-load funds in various risk categories. Although past performance data is provided on various funds, recommendations are made on the funds' future potential. The publication includes model portfolios based on risk, as well as academic studies that are used in investment recommendations. A news column and commentary section are provided on mutual funds and the funds industry. An annual subscription to the fund newsletter costs $75 and includes a directory of mutual funds.

■ *Mutual Funds and Your Investment Portfolio*—a 140-page directory of mutual funds which includes data and information on no-load funds. The directory is provided free of charge with a subscription to the IIS newsletter.

Extraordinary Investments for Ordinary Investors
Putnam Publishing Group
200 Madison Avenue
New York, NY 10016   212-576-8811

Written by Wayne F. Nelson, this book provides some suggestions for obtaining important information before investing in mutual funds. It includes advice on how to pick mutual and IRA funds, and important facts for fund investors. An appendix in the back of the publication describes over 1,000 mutual funds. The cost is $16.95 plus $1.50 for postage and handling.

Forbes Magazine
60 Fifth Avenue
New York, NY 10011   212-620-2200

Each fall *Forbes* magazine publishes a survey of mutual funds. It lists, ranks, and provides the names and addresses for the top funds. *Forbes* subscribers automatically receive the survey. It may be purchased separately on newsstands. The cost is $4.

Mutual Fund Forecaster
Institute for Econometric Research
3471 North Federal Highway   800-327-6720
Ft. Lauderdale, FL 33306   305-563-9000—FL only, collect calls accepted
This monthly newsletter, which has a large circulation, aids consumers in making mutual fund investment decisions. The newsletter contains information on performance forecasts, profit projections, risk ratings, and service evaluations for over 450 funds. Each issue provides specific best-buy recommendations for different categories of funds, as well as "avoid" recommendations for those funds which are expected to lower in value. Finally, the *Forecaster* provides switching recommendations, coverage of penny gold, sector, and international stock, and a review of newly isssued funds.

For newsletter subscribers, the Institute provides a telephone hotline report on mutual funds. It is updated weekly. Annual subscription fee is $49 for the newsletter and hotline service. A free two-month trial subscription is also available.

Magazines
Many finance and business magazines publish charts and analyses of the performance of major mutual funds during the previous year.

Forbes, described previously, does its annual mutual fund wrap-up each August. *Changing Times* publishes its review in October. *Money* reviews mutual fund performance twice a year, in the spring and fall. These publications are all described in the Newspapers and Magazines chapter.

Mutual Fund Investing
Phillips Publishing
7811 Montrose Road
Potomac, MD 20854   301-340-2100
Published monthly, the eight-page newsletter provides a general narrative description of economic strategies for investment in mutual funds. The newsletter, which is written for the general public, offers two portfolios each month which are appropriate for the safe and moderate investor. In addition to investment advice, the publication analyzes sector funds, newly issued funds, and fund categories, and features a question and answer section in each issue. The cost is $95 annually. This includes a directory and special reports which are issued throughout the year to subscribers.

Handbook for No-Load Fund Investors
PO Box 283
Hastings-on-Hudson, NY 10706   914-478-2381

The publications below can be purchased either individually or as a set:

■ *Handbook for No-Load Fund Investors*—a comprehensive 320-page book which provides information on no-load, low-load, and closed-end mutual funds. The book contains three major sections: how to invest in mutual funds, ten-year performance data on funds, and a directory with over twenty-eight points of interest on various funds. The cost is $32 if purchased alone. For $49 you can receive the handbook and quarterly issues of the following newsletter. For $79 you can receive the handbook and a twelve-month subscription to the newsletter.

■ *The No-Load Fund Investor*—a supplement to the *Handbook for No-Load Fund Investors,* this monthly newsletter provides current information on various mutual funds. The primary focus of the newsletter is in making recommendations and forecasts for no-load funds. The publication also contains data on fund performance and objectives. The cost is $63 annually if purchased separately.

The Telephone Switch Newsletter
PO Box 2538
Huntington Beach, CA 92647   714-898-2588

In its tenth year of publication, the *Telephone Switch Newsletter* has over 27,000 subscribers and is one of the largest mutual fund investment newsletters. Dick Fabian, its editor, recommends moving 100 percent in or 100 percent out of diversified equity funds, gold funds, international funds, and sector funds. Over one hundred mutual funds are monitored.

The goal of the *Telephone Switch Newsletter* is a 20 percent compounded return over every five-year period. Since its inception, the newsletter has achieved this goal for every five-year period while only switching an average of 1.2 times a year. An eight-month subscription costs $87 and an annual subscription costs $117.

Wiesenberger's Investment Co. Service
c/o Warren, Gorham and Lamont   212-977-7400—in NY
1633 Broadway   617-423-2020—in MA
New York, NY 10019   800-922-0066

Several publications are available from this company. The first described below is the most noteworthy, experts having described it as "the bible of the field."

■ *Wiesenberger's Investment Co. Service*—a mutual fund sourcebook, geared toward the individual investor, provides a thorough review of mutual funds, their histories, and updates on current activity. The 800-page sourcebook offers a ten-year history of the funds' performances and a five-year capsule of price changes. The services provided by various funds are also discussed in the publication. Included in the investment service are a monthly and quarterly publication. The sourcebook may be found in libraries. The cost is $295.

■ *Current Performance and Dividend Records*—a monthly publication which reports prices, dividends, and capital gains for various funds. The resource also contains an address directory for major funds. The cost is $150 annually if purchased separately; otherwise, the publication is included in the investment service.

■ *Management Results*—a quarterly publication which describes the long-term performance of mutual funds through a quarterly analysis of various funds. The cost is $100 annually if purchased separately; otherwise the publication is included in the investment service.

PEOPLE TO TALK TO

Burt Berry
DAL Investment Co.
235 Montgomery Street
San Francisco, CA 94104   415-986-7979
Mr. Berry, an investment adviser, is the pioneer of the use of no-load funds for investment. Mr. Berry specializes in utilizing no-load funds as investment vehicles, particularly for the management of pension plans.

Dick Fabian
Telephone Switch Newsletter
PO Box 2538
Huntington Beach, CA 92647   714-898-2588
Editor of the *Telephone Switch Newsletter,* Dick Fabian came into prominence with the publication of his investment manual, *How to Be Your Own Investment Counselor: Through the Use of No-Load Mutual Funds* in 1976. Mr. Fabian has been called "the father of mutual fund trading." *The Telephone Switch Newsletter* is the largest mutual fund newsletter published with over 7,000 subscribers.

Norman G. Fosback, President
Institute for Econometric Research
3471 North Federal Highway   800-327-6720
Ft. Lauderdale, FL 33306   305-563-9000—in FL, collect calls accepted
Mr. Fosback, president of the Institute for Econometric Research, is an expert on the money and stock markets. Mr. Fosback is very knowledgeable about the mutual fund industry, as he serves as the editor of the Institute's newsletters: *The Insider, New Issues, Market Logic, Money Fund Safety Ratings,* and the *Mutual Fund Forecaster.*

Sheldon Jacobs
PO Box 283
Hastings-on-Hudson, NY 10706   914-478-2381
    Mr. Jacobs, the editor of various publications related to no-load mutual funds, is an expert in the entire field of no-load funds. He edits the *Handbook for No-Load Fund Investors* and *The No-Load Fund Investor,* publications useful to consumers making no-load investment decisions.

Erick Kanter
Vice President, Public Information
Investment Company Institute
1600 M Street, NW
Washington, DC 20036   202-293-7700
    Mr. Kanter has spent twenty years with news reporting and public information offices at national and international levels. He has been a senior public affairs official for presidential commissions as well as for federal government agencies and has written many articles for the *Wall Street Journal* and the *New York Times.* He and his staff will refer you to mutual fund experts and will answer questions relating to mutual funds and IRAs.

Kathleen Q. Lantero
Wiesenberger's Investment Co. Service
c/o Warren, Gorham and Lamont
1633 Broadway
New York, NY 10019   212-977-2067
    Ms. Lantero is editor of the publications available from Wiesenberger's Investment Company Service. She is an expert in the area of mutual funds, particularly measuring mutual fund performance.

John Markese, Ph.D.
American Association of Individual Investors
612 North Michigan Avenue
Chicago, IL 60611   312-280-0170
    Dr. Markese has a Ph.D. in finance and is an expert in investment analysis. He is knowledgeable about mutual funds and their selection by investors.

Gerald W. Perritt
President
Investment Information Services, Inc.
205 West Wacker Drive
Chicago, IL 60606   312-750-9300
    Author of the *Individual Investor's Guide to No-Load Mutual Funds,* and editor of the *Mutual Fund Letter,* Dr. Perritt follows and analyzes mutual funds. He conducts research on various market trends and theories. As an

informative and entertaining lecturer and a trusted source of investment knowledge, Dr. Perritt is always available to share his views and critiques with the financial press.

Jay Schabacker
President and Publisher
Schabacker Investment Management
8943 Shady Grove Court
Gaithersburg, MD 20877   301-840-0301
    Mr. Schabacker is the editor of numerous publications on mutual funds and market timing.

Lisa F. Swaimann
Investment Company Institute (ICI)
1775 K Street, NW
Washington, DC 20006   202-293-7700
    Assistant vice president of the ICI, Ms. Swaimann writes and edits articles and other publications for the Institute. She is an expert on no-load and load mutual funds.

ADDITIONAL RESOURCES

Mutual Funds
Morris Video
413 Avenue G, Suite 1
Redondo Beach, CA 90277   213-374-4984
    This tape offers expert training on how mutual funds work. It describes the types of funds and features available for investors, as well as the protection the industry provides. The cost is $24.95.

Government Securities

See also:
Bonds

In addition to collecting taxes, the U.S. Treasury raises money for the federal government by selling marketable securities to the general public. And since Uncle Sam has a history of repaying his loans on time, with interest, buying U.S. savings bonds, treasury bills, notes, and bonds is a risk-free investment. Cities and states also raise money by offering securities. However, tax-free municipal bonds are somewhat riskier since cities and states have (although rarely) defaulted on their obligations. In the case of the latter securities, you definitely need to do some research before you invest.

If you decide U.S. government securities are for you, contact your nearest Federal Reserve Bank (or see Federal Reserve below), as they will sell you a government security—without a service charge. Commercial banks and other financial institutions also sell these securities, but they usually charge a fee based on each transaction.

Your Federal Reserve Bank is also a good information resource, as personnel will answer your questions about the purchase, exchange, or redemption of treasury securities. Many of these banks also offer free publications and recorded messages you can call for the latest details about new offerings, auction dates, minimum purchase ($25 as we go to press), and more. The Bureau of the Public Debt is another excellent resource. Staff members will answer your questions, send you free publications, and help you if you want to replace a lost, stolen, or destroyed security. The Bureau also operates several recorded messages you can call for the latest news on government securities.

In terms of securities, the Public Securities Association represents 95 percent of the nation's municipal securities underwriting and trading activity. Educational materials and information are available from the organization.

AGENCIES, INSTITUTES, AND ORGANIZATIONS

Department of the Treasury   202-287-4113—general info
Bureau of Public Debt Information Center   202-287-4091—T-bills
13th and C streets, SW   202-287-4088—T-notes and bonds
Washington, DC 20228   202-287-4100—procedures and auction results
    While staff members cannot offer investment advice, they will answer questions and assist you with any problems you may have regarding government securities. Staff members also handle claims about lost, stolen, destroyed,

or mutilated securities. If you are self-employed or not covered by any other retirement plan, this office will sell you individual retirement bonds. Call the general information number above for assistance, or write to Department X at the above address for information about treasury bills and Department A for information about treasury notes or bonds.

This office also provides several recorded messages you can call for the latest information about government securities. For general information dial 202-287-4113. By calling 202-287-4091 you can get the discount rate on thirteen-week, twenty-six-week, and one-year bills. For notes and bonds you can call 202-287-4088 for the latest on security terms, auction dates, maturity dates, minimum purchase, closing time for the offering, and payment instructions. And if you want particulars on procedures for buying treasuries, or auction results, call 202-287-4100.

A variety of written materials are available. A listing can be obtained by writing Department C at the above address. Examples of publications are:

■ *50 Q & A on U.S. Savings Bonds*—a general description of savings bonds is given in this question and answer booklet.

■ *Series EE & HH Savings Bonds*—this pamphlet tells you about where to buy bonds, their tax status, and how interest accrues.

Federal Reserve Bank of New York
Public Information Department
33 Liberty Street
New York, NY 10045   212-791-6134

This public information office, or a similar office at any other Federal Reserve Bank, can answer your questions about government securities or refer you to a bank member who can provide an answer. However, bank personnel are not permitted to offer investment advice. To find a branch near you contact the office above or your local banker. The following publications on government securities are offered by the above Federal Reserve Bank:

■ *Estimating Return on Treasury Issues*—how to calculate the yield on treasury bills, notes, and bonds is explained in this four-page pamphlet. Free.

■ *How to Read U.S. Government Securities Quotes*—written for the general public, this four-page booklet explains how to read the published daily price quotations of government securities. Free.

■ *A Primer on Treasury Securities*—New York's investors can learn the basic facts about buying and owning U.S. treasury bills, notes, and bonds in this booklet. Free.

■ *Basic Information on Treasury Bills*—primarily intended for investors living within the New York Bank's district, this pamphlet offers general explanation of how investors may buy new issues of U.S. treasury bills. Free.

■ *Basic Information on Treasury Notes and Bonds*—although directed to the New York investors, this brochure explains how any investor may buy new issues of U.S.treasury notes and bonds. Free.

■ *A Capital Adequacy Standard for U.S. Government Securities Dealers*—for those engaging in repurchase transactions, this pamphlet summarizes the government's voluntary capital adequacy guidelines for unregulated government securities dealers, and suggests how customers can determine compliance by unsupervised dealers. Free.

■ *Special U.S. Government Securities (Fedpoints 24)*—for historical purposes, this four-page booklet reviews the types and uses of nonmarketable treasury securities issued to foreign governments. Free.

Federal Reserve Bank of Texas
Public Affairs Department
Station K
Dallas, TX 75222   214-651-6289

The staff at this office will answer your questions about government securities or will refer you to member banks. Bank personnel can answer questions on the purchase, exchange, or redemption of securities, but are not permitted to offer investment advice. The following publications are available from the address above.

■ *United States Savings Bonds*—this twenty-four-page booklet provides basic information on purchasing and redeeming savings bonds at Federal Reserve Banks. Free.

■ *United States Treasury Securities*—basic information concerning investment in U.S. treasury bills, notes, and bonds is provided in this twenty-page booklet. Free.

Government National Mortgage Association (GNMA)
451 7th Street, SW
Washington, DC 20410   202-755-7141

The GNMA program offers investors government guaranteed securities designed to attract nontraditional investors into the residential mortgage market. GNMA daily future statistics are available in the financial sections of major newspapers, as well as the financial newspapers. GNMA statistics are also available on the Chicago Board of Trade prerecorded message: 312-922-9120. For more information, contact your broker or the Chicago Board of Trade.

Public Securities Association (PSA)
40 Broad Street
New York, NY 10004   212-809-7000

PSA is the national organization of banks, dealers, and brokers who underwrite, trade, and sell municipal securities, mortgage-backed securities, and U.S.

government and federal agency securities. PSA's member firms collectively account for approximately 95 percent of the nation's municipal securities underwriting and trading activity.

PSA publishes educational materials, provides seminars, conferences, and informational meetings on topics of current interest, maintains a database of municipal finance statistics, and periodically provides surveys of members of the government and mortgage-backed securities markets. These efforts are aimed at raising public awareness of the importance of the markets served by the Association. The following public education materials are available:

- *Fundamentals of Municipal Bonds*—an authoritative and definitive guide to the municipal securities industry, this 208-page book describes the major market participants and how they interact. It covers economic, financial, and special market factors that shape and determine bond rates. Cost is $14.95.

- *Statistical Yearbook of Municipal Finance*—a comprehensive, definitive source, this 128-page book contains thousands of facts not available elsewhere. It includes the ranking of the leading municipal underwriters in total volume, geographically, and by type of issue. Cost is $45.

- *An Investor's Guide to Tax-Exempt Securities*—this twenty-one-page brochure describes the tax advantages of owning municipal securities. Types of bonds, effects of market fluctuations on price and yield, ratings, liquidity, and basic facts about the mechanics of ownership are covered. Cost is forty-five cents.

- *Municipal Market Developments*—published monthly, this newsletter contains updated municipal market statistics and underwriter rankings to help you stay abreast of developments in the new issue market. An annual subscription costs $45.

Dow Jones-Irwin

1824 Ridge Road 800-323-1717
Homewood, IL 60430 800-942-8881—in IL

The following financial books on government securities are available through this Dow Jones Publishing Company:

- *The Municipal Bond, Volume 1 and 2*—this is a two-volume set, sold separately. Volume 1 provides information about the buying and selling of tax-exempt debt. Volume 2 fills the need for state-of-the-art information on the credit analysis of municipal bonds and notes, and on the many new financing structures. Cost is $50 each.

- *The Dow Jones-Irwin Guide to Buying and Selling Treasury Securities*—this 245-page guide leads investors step by step through all aspects of buying and selling the various treasury securities, and offers guidelines for dealing with the Federal Reserve Bank and the Bureau of Public Debt. The cost is $25.

Government Guaranteed Investments
Publications International, Ltd.
3841 West Oakton Street
Skokie, IL 60076   312-676-3470
   A basic guide for consumers, this book will help you make an informed
investment decision. It covers treasury bills, notes and bonds, treasury zero-
coupon bonds, municipal bonds, and tells you where to go for more information. It is available in most book stores and libraries. Cost is $3.50.

▪ ▪

WHO INSURES YOUR INVESTMENTS?

Although you cannot insure that all of your investments will not lose money,
you should be aware that the federal government will insure that your money
in some investment institutions will not be lost in the case of bankruptcy or
failure. Listed below are the organizations which provide this coverage.

   The Securities Investor Protection Corporation (SIPC)
   900 17th Street, NW
   Washington, DC 20006
   202-223-8400
Security broker-dealers—up to $500,000 per customer.
Covers only securities (stocks, bonds, CDs, etc.) for broker-dealers registered with
Securities and Exchange Commission

   Federal Deposit Insurance Corporation
   Information Office
   550 17th Street, NW
   Washington, DC 20429
   800-424-5448 or 202-389-4221
Banks—up to $100,000 maximum of $100,000 per depositor.
Coverage can be greater than $100,000 if additional accounts are in joint names,
Keogh accounts, trust accounts, etc.

   Federal Savings and Loan Insurance
   Public Information
   1700 G Street, NW
   Washington, DC 20552
   202-377-6934
Savings and loan institutions—maximum of $100,000 per depositor.
Coverage can be greater than $100,000 if additional accounts are in joint names,
Keogh accounts, trust accounts, etc.

▪ ▪

Income without Taxes: An Insider's Guide to Tax-Exempt Bonds
Carroll and Graf Publishers, Inc.
260 Fifth Avenue
New York, NY   212-889-8772
Written for the average investor, this book by Hildy and Stan Richelson has useful information on the mechanics of investing with municipal bonds. The new paperback edition reflects recent changes in the tax laws. Cost is $9.95.

An Introduction to Zero Coupon Bonds
Thomson McKinnon Securities, Inc.
1 New York Plaza
New York, NY 10004   212-482-7000
The mechanics and language of zero-coupon fixed-income securities are examined in the booklet. It also tells you the pros and cons of investing in these U.S. government bonds. Free.

Standard and Poor's Corporation
25 Broadway
New York, NY 10004   212-208-8690
To help you learn how to invest in government securities, Standard and Poor's offers the following free handbooks.
  ■ *How to Invest*—this handbook for buying and selling stocks and bonds describes the advantages and disadvantages of investing in securities. It includes a section on types of bond obligations, and bond terms and features, and makes you familiar with the language of the financial community. Free.
  ■ *How the Bond Market Works*—this booklet can give you some insights into fixed-income investing. These investment instruments include bonds, mutual funds, treasury bills, and money market funds. It answers general questions normally asked when purchasing bonds. Free.

Treasury Bulletin
Division of Government Accounts and Reports
Bureau of Government Finance Operations
Department of the Treasury
441 G Street, NW
Washington, DC 20226   202-566-4531
Published quarterly, this publication provides information and data on: federal obligations, U.S. savings bonds and notes, ownership of federal securities; market quotations on treasury securities; and the average yields of long-term bonds. Subscriptions are available from the Government Printing Office (GPO). Cost is $50 a year.

REITs

REITs, real estate investment trusts, offer small investors the opportunity to pool their resources for the purchase of real estate. They are bought and sold like stocks; when you want your money out, you sell. REITs are listed with the New York and American Stock Exchanges. There are three types:

1) Equity: invest in real property
2) Mortgage: make mortgage funds available
3) Hybrid: a combination of equity and mortgage

REITs are either "infinite life" or a self-liquidating trust. The latter type has a time limit (for example, between seven and ten years), after which it liquidates its assets, with investors receiving both dividends and stock appreciation.

REITs are beginning to specialize in geographical areas (Northeast or South) and types (health care facilities, raceways). When investigating a REIT for investment, experts advise that you examine its focus, management and leverage opportunity. You should also look at the past three years for financial stability and proven track record. This information can be obtained from the company's annual report, available from the REIT or through a broker. Your local stockbroker is always available to help you choose a REIT and determine how many shares of stock to purchase. However, keep in mind that a broker is biased toward what his/her company invests in. The National Association of Real Estate Investment Trusts is a good resource for general information on the subject.

AGENCIES, INSTITUTES, AND ORGANIZATIONS

Bechtel Information Services
15740 Shady Grove Road   301-258-4300
Gaithersburg, MD 20877-1454   800-231-DATA
As a contractor for the Securities and Exchange Commission (SEC), Bechtel Information Services has the SEC database of REITs on microfiche. If you can't get the information you need directly from the REIT company, you may want to use Bechtel. You can call the above toll-free number to order a particular prospectus. There are three rates available for getting REIT information: seven-day service is twenty cents a page plus postage; twenty-four-hour service is twenty-five cents a page plus postage; and one-hour service is thirty cents a page plus postage.

Consolidated Capital Equities Corp.
Mortgage Division
2000 Powell Street
Emeryville, CA 94608   415-652-7171

As one of the nation's largest sponsors of public real estate investment programs, Consolidated Capital provides short-term finances for existing income-producing real estate. Staff within the Mortgage Division will answer questions. A free brochure is available upon request.

National Association of Real Estate Investment Trusts, Inc. (NAREIT)
1101 17th Street, NW, Suite 700
Washington, DC 20036   202-785-8717

A nonprofit organization, NAREIT represents the great majority of all REITs in the United States, with assets of almost $7 billion. NAREIT provides a forum for its membership of qualified and nonqualified REITs, lawyers, accountants, and organizations with an interest in real estate and mortgage finances.

The organization monitors, reports on, and seeks to influence activities in the following areas: mortgage credit, property management, investment and commercial banking, IRS, HUD, and SEC activities, real estate concepts and practices, and more. NAREIT staff members will answer questions concerning the organization's services. NAREIT produces numerous industry publications, some of which are sold to nonmembers. Examples include:

- *REIT Fact Book*—an annual historical, legislative, and technical review of the REIT industry. Annual subscription is $15 for members and $40 for nonmembers.
- *Directory of Members*—an annual alphabetical listing of all voting and associate members. Annual subscription is $35 for members and $75 for nonmembers.
- *Compendium of Public and Private IRS Rulings*—updated yearly, this loose-leaf binder gives tax rulings and other legislative information (1934 to present) of interest to REIT-related organizations. Annual subscription is $225 for members. This is not available to nonmembers.
- *The REIT Report*—a sixteen-page bimonthly newsletter reporting on industry news and performance. This is only for members.
- *How to Form a REIT*—a useful source package updated annually for the newcomer. Cost is $325 for members and $325 for nonmembers.

REITs in Your Community
Many communities now have REITs owning interest in local real estate. In general a REIT provides an investor with a long-term financial growth with a fairly even guaranteed yield. To find out if there is a REIT in your community, check the yellow pages under Real Estate. The National Association of

Real Estate Investment Trusts located in Washington, DC (202-705-8717) can also tell you if there is a REIT in your area. Here are three examples of local REITs:

Washington Real Estate Investment Trust (WRIT)
4936 Fairmont Avenue
Bethesda, MD 20814
301-652-4300

WRIT is a self-administered equity real estate trust investing principally in income-producing properties in the Washington, D.C., metropolitan area. Mary Dean is the staff expert who will answer questions on REITs. WRIT regularly sends press releases to shareholders and members, and will make them available to the public. The press releases are free.

Federal Realty Investment Trust
5454 Wisconsin Avenue, Suite 1100
Chevy Chase, MD 20815
301-652-3360

As an equity real estate investment company, Federal Realty Investment Trust specializes in owning, leasing, and renovating shopping centers, primarily on the East Coast. Staff is available to answer questions. An annual report is available upon request. Free.

Sierra Capital Companies
1 Maritime Plaza
San Francisco, CA 94111
800-902-4141
215-982-4141

This investment company specializes in providing commercial and industrial real estate services to its public and institutional clients. Sierra Capital Companies is an adviser to a series of "self-liquidating finite life" commercial equity real estate investment trusts. Its extensive sales staff will answer questions at the above toll-free telephone number. In addition to an annual and quarterly report, Sierra Capital Companies publishes:

- *REIT's, Ultimate Investment Vehicle for the 80's*—a publication defining REITs in easy terms. Free.
- *Sierra Update*—a monthly newsletter for brokers, reporting new acquisitions, market conditions, and including special articles on investment strategies. Free to brokers.

Securities and Exchange Commission (SEC)
450 5th Street, NW
Washington, DC 20549   202-272-7450

SEC is an independent federal agency charged with protecting the public and investors regarding securities transactions. It maintains financial and other information on all REITs offered for public sale. Private offerings are not required to file with the SEC.

The SEC Public Reference Room, located in Washington, D.C., maintains files on all public REITs. Listings are in alphabetical order, without subject indexing. Copies are fifteen cents a page and staff will help you find a specific prospectus.

Bechtel Information Services, under contract with the Securities and Exchange Commission, has the entire SEC database on microfilm. See the entry on Bechtel earlier in this section.

WHAT TO READ

Communications Channels, Inc.
6285 Barfield Road
Atlanta, GA 30328   404-256-9800
Publications covering REITs include:
■ *National Real Estate Investor*—issued monthly, this is a professional periodical serving the fields of investment and management of commercial real estate or income-producing properties and its allied fields. It reports on new projects, recent sales, financial transactions, and market studies of specific cities. Subscription includes a free copy of the directory described below. Annual subscription fee is $45.
■ *The National Real Estate Investment Directory*—an annual publication giving a geographical/alphabetical listing of firms in seventeen categories of real estate, including a chapter on REITs. Annual subscription fee is $29.95. The publication is free to subscribers of the above periodical.

Questor Strategic Real Estate Letter
Stephen E. Roulac & Co.
103 Post Street, Suite 1900
San Francisco, CA 94014   415-433-0300
Published monthly, this professional periodical covers the latest growth trends for all types of commercial real estate transactions nationwide. Annual subscription fee is $197.

Review of the Real Estate Investment Trust Industry
Merrill Lynch and Co.
155 Broadway
New York, NY 10080

A pamphlet describing how REITs, dividends, and stock performances work. Available through your local Merrill Lynch sales office. Free.

PEOPLE TO TALK TO

Kenneth D. Campbell
Audit Investments, Inc.
230 Park Avenue
New York, NY 10169   212-661-1710
    Mr. Campbell is very active in the area of real estate securities. His company, Audit Investments, Inc., is a research investment company in real estate stock.

Bob Frank
Alex, Brown & Sons, Inc.
135 East Baltimore Street
Baltimore, MD 21202   301-727-1700
    A chartered financial analyst and an officer in numerous organizations, Mr. Frank has been following real estate for ten years. His expertise is in Equity REITs.

Gary Gordon
Merrill Lynch and Co.
155 Broadway
New York, NY 10080
    Mr. Gordon is assistant vice president industry specialist in the real estate industry of Merrill Lynch. In addition to advising Merrill Lynch's brokers about REIT opportunities, he also provides investment advice to real estate companies and savings and loan associations.

Sheldon A. Noble
Vice President Finance and Treasurer
Federal Realty Investment Trust
5454 Wisconsin Avenue, Suite 1100
Chevy Chase, MD 20815   301-652-3360
    A CPA with thirty-five years' public accounting experience, Mr. Noble is a specialist in REITs. His special interest is buying and renovating shopping centers.

Thomas B. Swartz
Chairman and Chief Executive Officer
The Sierra Capital Companies
1 Maritime Plaza
San Francisco, CA 94111   415-982-4141

A founder of the Sierra Capital Companies, Mr. Swartz, is a pioneer in developing the self-liquidating finite life equity real estate investment trust. He has been active in the real estate industry for over twenty years and is a member of several professional institutes.

Socially Responsible Investing

See also:
The First Step For Beginners and Experienced Investors
Mutual Funds

Did you know you can meet your ethical requirements and still make money? People have done it for a long time, but given today's highly diversified conglomerates it's becoming more and more difficult to know exactly where your money is going. You may invest in a restaurant franchise and learn later that you are supporting the clubbing of baby seals for the fur industry. The newly minted term "ethical investing" refers to the activities of the growing number of people who are taking the extra time and effort not only to avoid stocks in companies they feel negative about, but also to seek investments that actively promote causes they believe in.

What is socially responsible investing? It's keeping your investments in synch with your integrity. First you decide what operations you don't want your money to support; then you direct your investments toward a community, a business or a product you believe in. The next step is deciding how far you'll stick to these parameters. Some investors set limits or percentages on the amount of a particular type of business they will tolerate in their portfolio. Others draw up a list of definite no-nos, such as cigarettes, alcohol, nuclear energy, or repressive political regimes, to name a few of today's most frequently avoided stocks.

According to Bill Sena, an expert in socially responsible investing, smaller investors often select "ethical" stocks in the retail, health care, and education fields.

There are organizations, publications, and even entire investment management companies devoted to investing in companies and products that meet certain social and ethical requirements. But before you rely on their wisdom, make sure their idea of socially responsible investing is the same as yours. Some mutual funds are geared toward investing in, or staying away from, particular social concerns. The group is limited, and we have identified many of the major ones in this chapter.

If you decide to use an "ethically" oriented broker or financial adviser, you should be prepared to do a bit of shopping around. Although the term "ethical investing" is coming into more frequent use, you could be explaining yourself more than you expected. Also, it takes extra effort to follow ethical stocks as closely as needed, and if your investment is small, brokers may not be eager to handle your account.

You can do a lot of research into companies yourself. This chapter describes several resources the socially responsible investor can consult for information. After you've researched and found a company that sounds right to you, contact them and ask to be sent a prospectus and other relevant materials. A company's annual report is a good, although glamorized, source for the kind of information you want. Check and see if any lawsuits have been filed against the company.

This book's chapter HOW TO FIND INFORMATION ON A COMPANY will give you additional resources for investigating a company.

Once you've invested your money in what you believe to be a suitable stock, your homework is not done. Companies' priorities change. Or maybe yours will. It's important to keep checking. Most public companies have stockholder's representatives who can answer questions related to your investment.

While it is probably not possible to be 100 percent sure that your money is doing only what you want it to do, the resourceful, educated investor can achieve results that satisfy the soul as well as the bank book.

AGENCIES, INSTITUTES, AND ORGANIZATIONS

Center for Corporate Public Involvement
American Council of Life Insurance
1850 K Street, NW
Washington, DC 20006-2284   202-862-4047

The center serves as a clearinghouse for corporate social responsibility in the life and health insurance businesses. It acts as a liaison between organiza-

---

CRITERIA SOCIALLY RESPONSIBLE INVESTORS SEEK:
How to Align Your Conscience with Your Portfolio

The authors of "Rating American Corporate Conscience" suggest using the following criteria when looking to invest in socially responsible companies:

- No activities in South Africa
- No contracts involving nuclear arms
- No contracts involving conventional arms
- A board of directors with minority or women representatives
- Charitable giving of at least 1 percent net earnings before taxes
- A pattern of disclosing information to the public
- No PAC contributions to elected officials who are not sympathetic to the items above

tions and individuals interested in socially responsible investments. The following publications are available free of charge:

> ■ *Response*—published quarterly for the life and health insurance businesses, it outlines and highlights what the industry has done in the area of social responsibility.
>
> ■ *Understanding Social Investment*—an overview of social investing is given in this nine-page booklet. It also includes definitions, criteria, and a listing of the different types of social investing.

Clergy and Laity Concerned
198 Broadway, Room 302
New York, NY 10038   212-964-6730

This nonprofit organization will mail you a free packet of magazine articles that address the issue of socially responsible investing. The articles contain tips on social investing and lists of resources to help you make informed decisions.

Council on Economic Priorities
30 Irving Place
New York, NY 10003   212-420-1133

As a public-service research organization, CEP's primary goal is enhancing corporate performance as it affects society in areas such as the consequences and costs of military spending, energy, fair employment practices, political influence, and environmental impact. CEP acts as a clearinghouse on corporate responsibility issues, documents corporate activities, and monitors the role of government as it relates to these issues. The staff of CEP is often called to testify before Congress on these issues. The Council will send you a free publications list and offers the following:

> ■ *CEP Newsletter*—the Council's newsletter focuses each month on one of the areas of corporate responsibility research. Members receive all studies, reports, and newsletters for $100 annually. A single copy is free on request.
>
> ■ *Better Buying: Everybody's Guide to Socially Responsible Companies*—this guide will help consumers concerned with social responsibility make informed decisions on investments, where to shop, and consumer products. It costs around $20.

Data Center
464 19th Street
Oakland, CA 94612   415-835-4692

The Data Center is a nonprofit public-interest resource center and library, collecting and organizing information on political and economic issues. It monitors 400 magazines and newspapers from the daily, business, labor, church, and political press, and maintains clippings files on over 7,000 corporations. Their library contains 3,500 books and 400 periodicals. This information may be obtained in a variety of ways. The library is open to the public for an annual membership fee, or a custom research service is available, billed on an hourly basis through which staff searches the files, retrieves documentation, photocopies articles, and mails the material to the client. Two regular clipping services on business issues are also published. They are:

- *Corporate Responsibility Monitor*—a monthly clipping service of a hundred pages of full-text reprints of articles pertaining to corporate responsibility and socially responsible investing. A subscription is $420 a year.

- *Plant Shutdowns Monitor*—a monthly clipping service of full-text reprints of articles identifying plant shutdowns and the initiatives being taken to deal creatively with the after-effects of plant closures, as well as legislative efforts to address the problem. Each issue also contains a directory of all the shutdowns, layoffs, and cutbacks reported in the press during the previous month. A subscriptions costs $90 a year. A single issue can be obtained for $7.

Ethics and Public Policy Center
1030 15th Street, NW
Washington, DC 20005   202-682-1200

As an independent, nonprofit educational corporation, the center conducts a program of research, writing, publication, and conferences designed to encourage reflective debate on major domestic and foreign policy problems. In reaffirming the necessary bond between basic Western values and public policy choices, the Center publishes studies and essays that combine empirical analysis and moral reasoning. The following publications are available:

- *Ethics and Public Policy Center Catalog*—this is a complete listing of titles available from the Center. Free.

- *Ethics and Public Policy Center Newsletter*—the Center's monthly newsletter features articles on public issues. Free.

- *Conscience and Dividends: Churches and the Multinationals*—the church-led corporate-responsibility movement, which has tried to influence the operations of multinational companies, particularly in the third world, is examined in this 176-page report. The author assesses the behavior of transnational enterprise and distinguishes between critics seeking reform and those attempting to destroy the market system. He offers guidelines for church involvement in social issues. Cost is $9.

- *The Politics of Sentiment: Churches and Foreign Investment in South Africa*—written by Richard E. Sincere, this book is an examination of the proposal, supported in some United States church circles, that American corporations should withdraw their investments from South Africa in order to fight apartheid. Sincere has found that many South African religious, political, labor, and business leaders of all racial groups believe divestment would hinder rather than help constructive change. Cost is $8.

Franklin Research and Development Corporation
711 Atlantic Avenue
Boston, MA 02111   617-423-6655

This is the largest investment management company specializing in socially responsible investing. It maintains a database on the social impact of 1,200 companies. The minimum account is $250,000, and individuals needing information on stocks they own can receive consultation for an hourly fee. The following publication is available:

- *Insight: The Advisory Letter for Concerned Investors*—stock recommendations and detailed profiles of specific industries are included in this monthly newsletter, designed to assist you in making knowledgeable choices for ethical investing. The cost is $87.50 for one year and $45 for six months.

Good Money
Box 363   802-223-3911
Worcester, VT 05682   800-535-3551

Formerly the Center for Economic Revitalization, Good Money is a worker-owned business providing information, research, and networking services for socially concerned investors and business people. The following publications are available:

- *Guide to Investing in Social Change*—this forty-page booklet is an introduction to the world of alternative investing. It contains descriptions of the kinds of organizations and projects involved in alternative investments. The price is $5.
- *Socially Responsible Stock Guide*—you are given economic and social information on fifty publicly traded companies in this forty-page guide. It demonstrates how investors can seek higher income and, more security or capital gains while still remaining true to their social goals and principles. Included are "how to" articles, such as how to replace offending "black hats" in your portfolio with desired "white hats" without sacrificing economic goals. It costs $5.
- *Guide to the Social Investment Community*—this is a listing of brokers, revolving loan funds, nonprofit organizations, financial planners, money managers, and responsive banks and credit unions involved in social investing. The price is $10.
- *Good Money: The Newsletter of Social Investing*—a twelve-page bimonthly newsletter reporting on the ethical behavior of publicly traded corporations, the social investment movement, and the relationship between corporate responsibility and financial return. It is offered as a package deal with the next two publications described below. The cost is $49 for one year and $26 for six months.
- *Catalyst: Investing in Social Change*—another bimonthly newsletter, Catalyst provides detailed profiles of businesses and organizations,

both profit and nonprofit, that offer investment and partnership opportunities. It links people who wish to invest for the purpose of social change with those whose goods and services provide such opportunities.

■ *Netback*—this "bulletin board" newsletter informs socially sensitive investors of special events and services of interest to them. Each subscriber is entitled to a free hundred-word listing to announce meetings, a project, a business opportunity, or even just an idea. It is published as often as needed.

Interfaith Center on Corporate Responsibility (ICCR)

475 Riverside Drive, Room 566
New York, NY 10115   212-870-2936

ICCR is an organization of church and religious institutional investors concerned about the social impact of corporations and the application of social criteria to investments. To reflect their theological and programmatic concerns, ICCR member agencies initiate and participate in a number of activities, such as public hearings, testimony before government and other agencies, on-site research, open letters, litigation, and publishing information, and providing resources for church constituencies. Issues receiving attention include community reinvestment, domestic equality, energy and environment, international health, infant formulas, pharmaceuticals, international justice, militarism, and systemic analysis. Publications available are:

■ *ICCR Publications List*—a listing of all publications available from ICCR. Free.

■ *The Corporate Examiner*—published ten times a year, this newsletter examines United States corporate policies and actions on environment, foreign investment, minorities and women, military production, health, hunger, energy, human rights, alternative investments, and corporate responsibility. The annual subscription rate is $25.

■ *The Financial Implications of Divestment*—written by Fantu Chery, this booklet discusses the financial impact divestment has had on several states and universities that have carried it out. It also discusses several different approaches to divestment, and answers some of the most frequently asked questions on the subject. The cost is $6.50.

■ *A Shareowners' Manual: For Church Committees on Social Responsibility in Investments*—written by Eleanor Craig, it is the most complete handbook on church shareholder action ever assembled. The cost is $4.30.

■ *What the Banks Say on South Africa*—this directory deals only with American banks involved in South Africa. It provides a short statement of banks' policies in South Africa, and includes quotes from the banks themselves. It also contains more limited information on Canadian banks. The cost is $3.

International Council for Equality of Opportunity Principles, Inc.
1501 North Broad Street
Philadelphia, PA 19122   215-236-6757
Composed primarily of educators and clergy, the Council acts as an advisory
board, with the purpose of promoting adherence to the Sullivan Principles by
companies operating in South Africa. The Council has the following publications available:

> ■ *The Sullivan Statement of Principles*—the six Sullivan principles for
> promoting racial equality in employment practices for United States firms
> operating in the Republic of South Africa are described in this pamphlet.
> Free.
>
> ■ *Annual Report on the Signatory Companies to the Sullivan Principles*—
> this booklet tells the reader how the companies are evaluated, and explains
> the Sullivan principles and ratings. It also gives a list of the signatories, their
> ratings, and analyzes the results. A useful book that explains the principles
> in a coherent, easy-to-read way. Cost is $15.

Investor Responsibility Research Center Inc. (IRRC)
1319 F Street, NW, Suite 900
Washington, DC 20004   202-833-3727
    IRRC is an independent nonprofit corporation that conducts research and
publishes impartial reports on contemporary social and public policy issues and
the impact of those issues on major corporations and institutional investors.
Periodic studies available from ICCR analyze economic, social, and political
issues. Recent studies have covered the top eighty-four United States defense
contractors, the debate about nuclear power, the future of alternative energy
sources, the nuclear weapons industry, the growing pressures on pension fund
managers to use nontraditional criteria in making investments, and the public
pressure directed against United States companies doing business in South
Afica. The following publications are available:

> ■ *Publications List*—a complete list of published studies conducted by
> ICCR. Free.
>
> ■ *Foreign Investment in South Africa*—a complete guide to foreign invest-
> ment in South Africa, this directory lists the United States, British, and
> Canadian companies that have investments there, and describes the South
> African lending policies of the hundred largest United States banks. Cost
> is $100.
>
> ■ *Stocking the Arsenal: A Guide to the Nation's Top Military Contrac-
> tors*—this unique survey provides detailed information on the major de-
> fense programs of the eighty-four largest publicly held United States sup-
> pliers of equipment and support services for national defense. Cost is $75.

Investor Relations Departments

If you want to know exactly how your investment is being used, public companies have stockholders' representatives whose job it is to answer that kind of question. Call the company's headquarters and ask for the Investor Relations department. The annual report for each company will name the contact, or you could consult Moody's at your local library.

Media Network

The Alternative Media Information Center
208 West 13th Street
New York, NY 10011   212-620-0877

If your group would like to learn about the various social issues of the day, you may want to get in touch with Media Network. It is a national membership organization that offers programs and services designed to introduce the public to quality, independently produced social-issue media. Services include an information center that recommends films, videotapes, and slide shows on a wide range of issues. Subject headings include banks and banking, consumer issues, economic and industrial development, employment, multinational corporations, taxes, and worker-owned businesses. Searches for more than one title are done for a nominal charge and users are encouraged to become members. The Information Center is open Tuesday and Thursday from 2 to 6 P.M.

National Action/Research on the Military Industrial Complex (NARMIC)

1501 Cherry Street
Philadelphia, PA 19102   215-241-7175

A project of the American Friends Service Committee, NARMIC does research on who does business with the military and has a wide range of information on the military-industrial complex. It offers the following publications:

- *Investing in Apartheid*—this listing of companies provides the United States company name, address, South African affiliate, affiliate address, and the product or service of the affiliate. Companies that adhere to the Sullivan principles are identified. It is easy to read and understand. Cost is $2.
- *Defense Department Top 100 Military Contractors*—updated annually, this pamphlet ranks contractors by the dollar amount received from the Pentagon. The price is $1.
- *Invasion: A Guide to the U.S. Military Presence in Central America*—United States weapons and arsenals in Central American countries are listed in this guide. Manufacturers and purchasing countries are identified. Cost is $2.

■ *Literature List*—a complete listing of all publications available from National Action. Free.

Nuclear Free America (NFA)
2521 Guilford Avenue
Baltimore, MD 21218   301-235-3575

A nonprofit organization, NFA serves as an international clearinghouse and resource center for the Nuclear Free Zone Movement, which urges communities to adopt nuclear-free zone legislation banning nuclear weapons industries. Several NFA publications, and an audio cassette, address socially responsible investing:

■ *The New Abolitionist*—published six times a year, this newsletter is committed to the abolition of nuclear weapons through the proliferation of nuclear-free zones. It contains news on the Nuclear Free Zone Movement and highlights socially responsible investing information. The subscription price is $10.

■ *Top 50 Nuclear Weapons Contractors*—this list of the top fifty United States corporations involved in the production of nuclear weapons is free.

■ *NFA's Guide to Socially Responsible Investing*—an annotated listing of alternative investment funds, resources, and advisers and a bibliography on pension fund investments are provided. Cost is $2.50.

■ *Consumer Brand Names of the Top 50 Nuclear Weapons Contractors*—NFA's list of the top fifty nuclear weapons contractors and several hundred of their consumer product brand names including corporate addresses. Cost is $3.

■ *Nuclear Free Investments*—sample legislation for cities and counties and notes on campaign organizing, alternatives, and resources are provided in this handbook. It includes the NFA Guide and list of brand names described in the above publication. Cost is $6.

■ *Divestment: The Offensive Against Apartheid and Nuclear Weapons*— a forty-minute audio cassette discusses consumer boycotts and divestment as tactics for confronting corporations involved in South Africa or in the production of nuclear weapons. Cost is $5.

Social Investment Forum
711 Atlantic Avenue
Boston, MA 02111   617-423-6655

The Forum is a national professional association of individuals and institutions interested in social investment. Its members include financial advisers, bankers, analysts, and investors. It provides regular access to the people and organizations involved in social investing and defining the field. The following publications are available:

■ *Social Forum Vendor's Guide*—the Forum members who have services to offer are given one-page descriptions in this book. It includes ethical investment advisers, financial services, money funds, and other resources. Free.

■ *Social Forum Folder*—this threefold pamphlet describes what the Forum is and gives brief information about the newsletter and member services. Free.

South Shore Bank
71st Street and Jeffery Boulevard
Chicago, IL 60659-2096   312-233-1000

Designed as the nation's first private neighborhood development bank, South Shore Bank is one of the pioneers of social investing through its Development Deposit and lending programs. Development Deposits are linked to the bank's innovative urban lending program, which is the primary tool for neighborhood renewal. Investors can choose from several financial vehicles to participate in this program. The minimum investment amount is $200, which can be deposited in a one-year Certificate Savings Account.

Major Mutual Funds and Investing Companies
Some mutual funds and investment companies are geared toward investing in, or staying away from, particular social concerns. The group is limited but growing, and we've identified some of the major ones in this section. Check with the associations listed above for more leads. If a company here sounds interesting to you, contact it and ask to be sent a prospectus and any other relevant materials. If socially responsible investing is your goal, be sure to ask the company anything you need to know to make sure its idea of socially responsible investing is the same as yours. And remember, organizations' priorities change, so after you invest you'll need to follow the company to make sure it stays on track.

Amana Mutual Funds Trust
Unified Management Corporation
Guaranty Building   317-634-3300
Indianapolis, Indiana 46204   800-UMC-SAVE

Amana Mutual Funds Trust is a series trust that offers several separate mutual funds designed to meet the special needs of Muslims by investing in accordance with Islamic principles. The fund manager will not invest in companies with pork, liquor, gambling, or pornography interests. On-line computer service is available.

Calvert Social Investment Fund
1700 Pennsylvania Avenue, NW   301-951-4800—in DC
Washington, DC 20006   800-368-2748

This investment fund is designed to direct investments toward enterprises that make a significant contribution to society through their products and services and the way they do business. The fund will not knowingly invest in companies that are primarily engaged in weapons manufacture, generate electric power from nuclear fuels, or actively support and expose their assets to repressive regimes such as the current government of South Africa.

Dreyfus Third Century Fund

666 Old Country Road	212-895-1206
Garden City, NY 11530	800-645-6561

Dreyfus is a socially responsible mutual fund whose primary investment objective is capital appreciation through investment in companies that give priority to individual well-being in America's third century. Each company is screened for social impact on equal employment, consumer protection, and occupational health and safety. You can open an account with as little as $2,500 and add to your investment at any time in amounts as small as $100.

New Alternatives Fund, Inc.

295 Northern Boulevard, Suite 300
Great Neck, NY 11021   516-466-0808

New Alternatives is a mutual fund which invests its shareholders' funds in the common stocks of companies concentrating in solar energy, alternative energy, and energy conservation. Social criteria for the fund includes solar cells production, natural gas, fuel cells, passive and active solar architectural products, forest products, conservation systems, and energy efficient motors and systems. Atomic energy and petroleum resources are excluded as areas for investment. The minimum initial investment is $2,650, with minimum subsequent investments of $1,000.

Parnassus Fund

1427 Shrader Street
San Francisco, Ca 94117   415-664-6812

Following a "contrarian" policy of investing in stocks that are out of favor with the financial community, this "low load" mutual fund also prefers to invest in companies that practice corporate responsibility. This fund is for investors who want to make money but want to do it in a way that will have a positive impact on society. The minimum initial investment is $5,000, except for IRA and Keogh plans, which have a $2,000 minimum.

Pax World Fund, Inc.

224 State Street
Portsmouth, NH 03801   603-431-8022

Pax World is a social responsibility fund that stresses investment in non-military industries. It invests in firms producing life-supporting goods and services. Pax also avoids any investment in the liquor, tobacco, and gambling industries. Initial investment must be $250 or more and additional shares may be purchased in amounts of $50 or more at any time.

The Pioneer Group
60 State Street   617-742-7825
Boston, MA 02109-1975   800-225-6292
   Pioneer offers socially responsible mutual funds. The funds do not invest in South Africa, defense, tobacco, or alcohol. Accounts can be tailored to an individual's concerns. An initial investment of $25 is necessary to open an account and there is a $25 minimum investment each month thereafter. The following publication is available free of charge to clients:

   ■ *Pioneer Quarterly Report*—this quarterly report provides updates on the contents of the funds portfolios.

Roger Stephen Scott Financial Adviser, Inc.
2033 6th Street, Suite 1030
Seattle, WA 98121   206-448-7865
   This is a for-profit, SEC-registered investment advice and financial planning firm. Clients determine the social criteria they wish to subscribe to and Scott Financial Adviser, Inc., provides investment options and information. It assists in making investments in mutual funds, stocks, bonds, venture capital, oil and gas, real estate partnerships and limited partnerships of all kinds. The minimum investment is $1,000. The following publication is available free of charge to clients:

   ■ *Financial Freedom Newsletter*—published quarterly, this newsletter addresses general financial planning. Complimentary copies may be requested.

Strategic Investment Advisors (SIA)
142 Lincoln, Suite 781
Santa Fe, NM 87501   505-984-9370
   SIA is a registered investment advisory firm that specializes in balancing traditional investment objectives with contemporary social concerns. It makes every effort to help the conscientious individual, group, and institutional investor achieve their financial objectives through socially responsible investment opportunities. The fee for consultation is $50 an hour.

United States Trust Company
Asset Management Division
PO Box 373
Boston, MA 02101   617-726-7254
   The Socially Sensitive Investment service offered by United States Trust provides comprehensive portfolio management to individuals and institutions whose investing is governed by social concerns. The approach varies with the

goals of the client. The minimum account size is approximately $300,000. The following publication is available:

> ■ *Socially Sensitive Investing*—this nine-page booklet describes three useful approaches to the problems of socially sensitive investing. Free.

Working Assets
230 California Street
San Francisco, CA 94111   415-989-3200

Working Assets is a socially responsible money market fund. It consciously avoids investing in companies that manufacture weapons, produce nuclear power, or support apartheid in South Africa. Instead, they invest in top-rated securities that finance housing, small business, renewable energy, higher education, and family farms. Their quarterly publication, *Money Matters,* which is available only to shareholders, reports on investments that have been made by the fund.

WHAT TO READ

Clean Yield
Fried & Fleer Investment Service
PO Box 1880
Greensboro Bend, VT 05842   802-533-7175

Written for the socially concerned investor, money manager, and broker, this monthly newsletter highlights specific companies that are socially concerned and provides functional and technical information. His column "Night School" provides information on investment techniques. The yearly subscription price is $65.

Concerned Investors Guide
Resource Publishing Group, Inc.
Order Department B
PO Box 390
Arlington, VA 22209   703-524-0815

This hard-bound, easy-to-read volume is a valuable reference book for nonfinancial corporate data on 1,400 companies listed with the New York Stock Exchange. The companies' socially responsible policies and performance have been researched, and a five-year history of each company is included, covering antitrust, environment, South Africa, nuclear issues, product safety, fair labor practices, weapons contractors, and occupational safety and health. The guide will help the investor make more knowledgeable and responsible investment decisions. The unique topic-to-company and company-to-topic indexes make it easy to look things up quickly. The cost is $147 for the complete volume, but reports may be obtained on individual companies. The rates are $5.50 for 1-5 companies, $8.50 for 6-10 companies, $12 for 11-15 companies and $15.50 for 16-20 companies.

Directory of Socially Responsible Investments
Funding Exchange
135 East 15th Street
New York, NY 10003   212-260-8500
    For the individual and institutional investor, this directory is an up-to-date listing of investment opportunities and resources. It catalogues fifty organizations, firms, and individuals who have demonstrated a broad commitment to socially responsive investing, who offer investors bona fide social investment opportunities, and who can serve a national or broadly regional clientele. The cost is $5.

Ethical Investing
Addison Wesley Publishing
1 Jacob Road
Reading, MA 01867   617-944-3700
    Written by Amy Domini, this book shows how to profit in investing without sacrificing personal ethics. It is for the beginner or the experienced investor who wants to bring investments in line with conscience. The cost is $10.53.

Rating Corporate America
Council on Economic Priorities
30 Irving Place
New York, NY 10003   212-420-1133
    One hundred thirty major suppliers of products we consume every day are covered in brief profiles that describe their general performance as corporate citizens. Topics covered range from minority hiring practices to involvement in South Africa. Clear charts help you decide among different companies. The cost is $16.95.

Research in Corporate Social Performance and Policy
JAI Press, Inc.
36 Sherwood Place
PO Box 1678
Greenwich, CT 06836-1678   203-661-7602
    This research annual is edited by Lee E. Preston. It is a compilation of new research by both established and new scholars on corporate social performance and policy. There are seven volumes available. The cost is $23.75 a volume. They may be available at your local library.

U.S. Corporations and Banks in South Africa
Committee on Mission Responsibility Through Investment
Presbyterian Church
475 Riverside Drive, Room 1020
New York, NY 10115   212-870-3015
The names of the United States corporations and banks currently operating in South Africa (addresses not included) are listed here. The booklet also includes a directory of the fifty most strategically important companies in South Africa. It costs $2.

PEOPLE TO TALK TO

Richard T. DeGeorge
Department of Philosophy
University of Kansas
Lawrence, KN 66045   913-864-3976
Richard T. DeGeorge is University Distinguished Professor of Philosophy at the University of Kansas. He has written extensively and led seminars on corporate social responsibility and general business ethics. He is the co-editor of *Ethics, Free Enterprise and Public Policy* (Oxford, 1978), and the author of *Business Ethics* (2nd ed., New York: Macmillan, 1985). His articles have appeared in *Best of Business,* the *Business & Professional Ethics Journal,* and the *Journal of Business Ethics,* as well as in newspapers and popular journals.

Bill Sena
Sena, Weller, Rohs and Williams
105 East 4th Street
Cincinnati, OH 45202   513-621-2875
Mr. Sena is chairman of Sena, Weller, Rohs, and Williams, a financial counseling firm. He is enthusiastic about socially responsible investing and believes you can meet your ethical requirements and still make money. He will be happy to answer your questions on this issue.

Antiques and Collectibles

See also:
Coins and Paper Money

There are at least seventy recognized categories of collectibles and some experts would argue that there are more than a hundred! Instead of trying to cover every category, we have compiled a listing of antique dealer associations, appraiser organizations, publications, and experts who deal with the antique and collectible field in a general manner. Most of these resources will be able to refer you to organizations, publications and experts covering your particular area of interest.

There are some encouraging stories, such as the one of the handyman who took old toys for payment and ended up with $30,000 worth of antiques, and the little old lady who filled her tiny house with five-dollar pieces of majolica pottery that years later were worth $50,000. But most collectors do it for love, not money.

Experts suggest that you choose one type of collectible and learn all you can about it. It doesn't matter whether it's perfume bottles, handbags, or folk art, as long as you have a genuine interest and it hasn't already become a trend. The handyman and the little old lady acquired their collections for the joy of it when few others were doing it. If you follow a trend rather than precede it, you'll pay a high price. Once something has caught on and dealers know the value, there are few bargains.

There are some rules to follow if you're a beginning collector:

- Buy the best you can afford. It's better to get one item in good condition than three damaged or worn ones. Experts can usually tell if something has been restored or repaired, even though you probably can't at first.
- If possible, buy regional pieces. Every area has something that was made in the region, and if you live there, you have a better chance of finding it at a garage sale or in someone's home. For example Van Briggle pottery is fairly easy to find in Denver. In Virginia, there is considerable interest in regional silversmiths.
- And get there before the museums do, because by that time the trend has probably peaked. Look for the beginnings of a trend by reading the trade papers and newsletters (many are listed in the following section) and by talking to collectors and dealers.

Ralph and Terry Kovel, antiques and collectible experts who have written fourteen books and published a monthly newsletter, suggest that you go to the oldest and most expensive antique dealer in your area and browse around often until you develop an interest in something. Then talk to the dealer about it at length before you buy.

Other experts suggest that you find out everything you can about a piece, remembering that family history of an item is not good documentation. There is the story of a collector who asked a dealer what kind of history a piece of glass had. The dealer said, "What kind of history do you want it to have?" The point is, know what you're doing and find dealers and appraisers you respect before making a major purchase.

AGENCIES, INSTITUTES, AND ORGANIZATIONS

American Society of Appraisers (ASA)
PO Box 17265
Washington, DC 20041   703-478-2228
ASA is a professional appraisal testing/certifying society concerned with all property. It publishes several pamphlets to help consumers understand more about the appraisal profession. The following titles are available at no cost by sending a stamped, self-addressed business-size envelope:
> ■ *Information on the Appraisal Profession*—Contains a series of questions (and answers) to ask the appraiser before you retain his or her services.
> ■ *1987-88 Directory of Certified Professional Personal Property Appraisers*—Lists tested/certified members of the Society who are qualified to appraise personal property.

Antique Appraisal Association of America (AAAA)
11361 Garden Grove Boulevard
Garden Grove, CA 92643   714-530-7090
A national organization, AAAA initiates, promotes, and sponsors any activities that improve or maintain the ethical standards of antiques appraising. Their staff will refer you to members in your area who specialize in particular types of antiques. The organization publishes a newsletter and membership directory available only to members.

Appraisers Association of America (AAA)
60 East 42nd Street
New York, NY 10165   212-867-9775
AAA is a professional society of appraisers of personal property that maintains a computerized referral service. The following publications are available:
> ■ *The Appraiser*—a monthly newsletter featuring articles about issues and items affecting appraisers. It is available only to members.
> ■ *AAA Membership Directory*—a worldwide directory of AAA members which lists members' appraising speciality. It may be purchased for $4.

Art & Antique Dealers League of America

c/o E. J. Frankel, Ltd.
1020 Madison Avenue
New York, NY 10021   Written inquiries only

The League is the oldest trade association for art and antique dealers in the United States. It will serve as an arbitrator in any dispute that arises between member dealers and their customers. Two publications are available:

■ *Membership Directory*—a complete listing of members and their specialties. Free.

■ *The Clarion*—a quarterly publication containing news of the League, general information about antiques, and reports about antique auctions. The subscription fee is included the League's $300 yearly membership dues.

Indiana University

Division of Professional Development
School of Continuing Studies
Owen Hall 204
Bloomington, IN 47405   812-335-5323

Several antiques and collectibles courses are offered by the university. Home study courses on the evaluation of specialty areas (antiques, residential contents, gems, jewelry, and others) are available. In conjunction with the International Society of Appraisers (mentioned in this section), the university offers certified appraisers two-and-a-half-day courses which cover the basics of evaluation theory, ethics, authentication, identification, and many other subjects of importance to appraisers. These courses are given several times a year at various metropolitan sites throughout the United States.

Industry Council for Tangible Assets (ICTA)

1701 Pennsylvania Avenue, NW, Suite 533
Washington, DC 20006   202-785-8600

ICTA is a nonprofit trade association. It was organized to promote the interests of those individuals, partnerships, firms, associations, and corporations engaged in the business of manufacturing, importing, distributing, or selling at retail any tangible assets. This includes precious and other metals, coins, antiques, and art objects. ICTA tracks legislation that affects its members at national, state, and local levels and often testifies before congressional committees. The following publications are available:

■ *ICTA Washington Wire*—a bimonthly newsletter that keeps its members informed about government legislation and what ICTA is doing to protect their interests. Subscription fee is $100 for nonmembers.

■ *ICTA Membership Directory*—a listing of ICTA members indexed alphabetically, geographically, and by specialty. Free.

International Society of Appraisers (ISA)
PO Box 726
Hoffman Estates, IL 60195   312-882-0706

ISA is the largest society of certified personal property appraisers in the country. The professional association recognizes over 130 specialties in appraising personal property, and its members have all completed an educational certification program. If you are trying to find an expert appraiser in a particular specialty, ISA will refer you to one. ISA will also send you a free copy of its membership directory so that you can locate a qualified appraiser in your specialty and geographical location.

In conjunction with the University of Indiana, ISA offers the Certified Appraisers of Personal Property (CAPP) Program. This includes three-, two-, and one-half-day courses covering the basics of evaluation theory, ethics, authentication, identification, and many other subjects of importance to appraisers. The courses are offered several times a year at various metropolitan sites throughout the United States.

ISA publishes the following:

■ *Consumer Information Pamphlet*—this free pamphlet gives a general description of the field of appraising and the reasons for appraisals.

■ *Appraisers Information Exchange*—a bimonthly newsletter providing an exchange of general information among members. It is available free to anyone interested.

■ *Journal of Appraisers*—a quarterly journal which contains four or five in-depth technical articles on specialty areas of appraising. Contact the society for subscription information.

The National Antique & Art Dealers Association of America, Inc. (NAADAA)
15 East 57th Street
New York, NY 10022   212-355-0636

A nonprofit organization whose members pledge to safeguard the interests of those who buy, sell, or collect antiques and works of art. Members of the Association are available for lectures; requests for speakers must be made in writing to the secretary. The following publication is available free of charge:

■ *Membership Directory*—contains a list of members and their specialties. A compilation of some synoptical tables of historical periods is also included in the directory.

National Association of Dealers in Antiques (NADA)
5859 North Main Road
Rockford, IL 61103   919-929-1338

NADA is an association of professional antique dealers, both show and shop. The association offers a referral service to collectors searching for reputable dealers. It also maintains an 800-volume reference library on antiques. NADA offers an annual decorative arts seminar that is open to public registration, dealers or collectors. The seminar is a three-day series of lectures and hands-on demonstrations that explore various aspects of the field of antiques. NADA publishes the following:

- *Roster of National Association of Dealers in Antiques*— the roster includes a geographic survey of members and their specialties and information on NADA's speakers bureau. Free.
- *The Bulletin*—an eight-page monthly newsletter that contains educational articles, news of the association, and news of legislative issues pertaining to antiques. The newsletter is available to members only, but reprints of educational articles are available to the public.

WHAT TO READ

Americana Magazine
29 West 38th Street
New York, NY 10018   212-398-1555
Published bimonthly, this national magazine explores America's enduring traditions. It offers readers a chance to recreate history with tips for travel to historic places, traditional recipes, how-tos for old-time crafts, decorating ideas, and marketplace information for collecting antiques. The column "In the Marketplace" concentrates on a different category of collectible in each issue. "The Queries" column gives readers a chance to write to *Americana* editors about their own specific collectible. Editors research the collectible and give information about the particular piece, including its current value. Each issue also has a column giving tips on caring for antiques.

Antique & Collecting Hobbies
Lightner Publishing Company
1006 South Michigan Avenue
Chicago, IL 60605   312-939-4767
Written for collectors, this monthly magazine carries regular feature articles about glass and china, dolls, toys, miniatures, firearms, numismatics, and philately. A regular question-and-answer column entitled "Information Desk" handles written inquiries. Every month feature articles focus on specific antiques and collectibles. The yearly subscription fee is $14.

Antique Monthly
PO Drawer 2
Tuscaloosa, AL 35402   205-345-0272
Published monthly, this national color tabloid is aimed at the collector. It covers collecting trends, market news, current options, exhibitions and antique

shows from San Francisco to London. Collecting tips are given in each issue. Cost is $14.

Babka Publishing Co.
PO Box 1050
Dubuque, IA 52001   319-588-2073
The following publications on antiques and collectibles are available:
■ *The Antique Trader Weekly*—a weekly tabloid designed to provide a public mail-order marketplace for dealers and collectors. Seventy-six categories of antiques and collectibles are listed, from automobiles to musical instruments. Feature articles on specific antiques are included, as well as advertisements and reports on auctions and shows. A sample copy of this publication may be obtained for fifty cents if you mention the title of this book with your request. Annual subscription price is $22.
■ *Antique and Collectible Price Guide*—a 960-page annual price guide to antiques and collectibles. It covers more than 70,000 items and contains 1,400 photographs. Cost is $10.95.
■ *Antique Trader Price Guide to Antiques and Collectibles*—published bimonthly, this hundred-page guide provides up-dated prices for antiques and collectibles. A sample copy of this guide may be obtained for $1 if you mention the title of this book with your request. Annual subscription price is $10.50.

Collector Books
PO Box 3009
Paducah, KY 42001   800-626-5420
More than 130 books covering a wide variety of collecting categories are published by this firm. Upon request, the company will send you a free catalog describing its books. One of its most popular books is:
■ *Schroeder's Antiques Price Guide, 1988 4th Edition*—a 608-page price guide reporting on over 500 categories. Each subject is represented with histories and background information. In addition, hundreds of sharp original photos are used to illustrate not only the rare and unusual, but the everyday "fun-type" collectibles as well. Cost is $11.95.

Crown Publishers, Inc.
225 Park Avenue South   800-526-4264
New York, NY 10003   212-532-9200
Fourteen books on antiques and collectibles, all by Ralph and Terry Kovel, are published by Crown. A free pamphlet describing each book is available. Four books of general interest are:
■ *The Kovels' Antiques & Collectibles Price List*—contains current recorded prices for more than 50,000 antiques and collectibles. The seventeenth edition of this price guide has detailed section headings, warnings

about reproductions, and updated market information, including new trends in collecting. It is available for $9.95.

■ *The Kovels' Collectors' Source Book*—a comprehensive, illustrated A-to-Z directory of resources for collectors. It is an alphabetically arranged catalog of more than eighty kinds of collectibles and contains everything collectors need to know to keep their collection alive, secure, and growing. Cost is $13.95.

■ *Kovels' Know Your Antiques*—written especially for the novice, this contains information about recognizing and determining the value of virtually every type of antique, and provides updated bibliographies, price guides, clubs, and other lists. Cost is $14.95.

■ *Kovels' Know Your Collectibles*—416-page up-to-date illustrated guide to the most fascinating collecting trends. It focuses on silver, glass, furniture, and other objects that are not old enough to be officially called "antiques" but nonetheless are rapidly increasing in value. It contains information about value, origin, availability, storage, and buying and selling, and costs $16.95.

House of Collectibles

Orlando Central Park
1904 Premier Row
Orlando, FL 32809   305-857-9095

This company publishes ninety guide books to antiques and collectibles. A free list of all publications is available by calling the company's toll-free number. Three current best sellers are:

■ *The Official Price Guide to '86 Antiques and Other Collectibles*—a comprehensive price guide to antiques and collectibles. It costs $9.95.

■ *The Official Encyclopedia of Antiques*—this guide contains description of articles without prices. It includes information about identification marks. Cost is $9.95.

■ *The Official Guide to Buying and Selling Antiques*—an advisory book. Cost is $9.95.

The Knopf Collectors' Guides to American Antiques

Alfred A. Knopf
201 East 50th Street
New York, NY 10022   212-751-2600

The Knopf Collectors' Guides to American Antiques is a series of practical guides that measure a handy 4 1/2 by 8 1/2 inches so they can be taken along on visits to antique shops and museums. Each 480-page volume covers the entire range of its subject, from early Colonial to Modern, and is carefully designed to enable the collector to readily identify, evaluate, and buy authentic pieces. When complete, the series will run to ten volumes or more.

The 1980s—A Decade for Financial Assets
(Compound Annual Rate of Return, 1980-86)

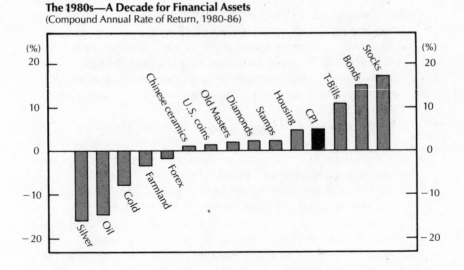

The 1970s—A Decade for Collectibles and Commodities
(Compound Annual Rate of Return, 1970-80)

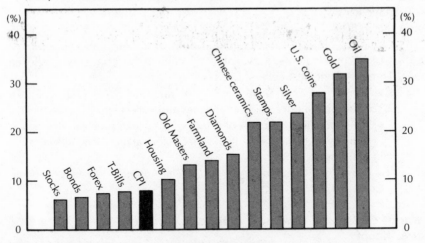

WHAT A DIFFERENCE A DECADE MAKES

The best investments for the 1980s have been stocks and bonds, which have been giving returns to investors of 17 percent and 15 percent respectively. All tangible assets did not even keep up with the rate of inflation (Consumer Price Index, CPI). However, during the 1970s it was a different story. Stocks and bonds were the decade's worst-performing investment vehicle.

Eight volumes now in print are:
- *Chairs, Tables, Sofas and Beds* by Marvin D. Schwartz
- *Chests, Cupboards, Desks & Other Pieces* by William C. Ketchum, Jr.
- *Quilts, Coverlets, Rugs & Samplers* by Dr. Robert Bishop.
- *Glass Tableware, Bowls & Vases* by Jane Shadel Spillman.
- *Folk Art: Paintings, Sculpture & Country Objects* by Robert Bishop and Judith Reiter Weissman.
- *Dolls* by Wendy Lavitt
- *Glass 2: Bottles, Lamps & Other Objects* by Jane Shadel Spillman.

The Lyle Official Antique Review
Putnam Publishing Group
200 Madison Avenue
New York, NY 10016   212-576-8910
Completely revised and updated each year, this guide to antiques brings you current value for every type of collectible. The 672-page identification and value guide contains more than 5,000 illustrations compiled by Anthonly Curtis. It is available in paperback for $10.95.

The Magazine Antiques
Grant Publications
980 Madison Avenue
New York, NY 10021   212-734-9797
The oldest of the antique magazines, this was first published in 1922. It is a monthly publication and features articles about American fine and decorative arts and architecture. Annual subscription price is $38.

Prentice Hall, Inc.
Mail Order Division
200 Old Tappan Road
Old Tappan, NJ 07675   201-592-2000
Examples of books on antiques and collectibles available from this publishing firm are:
- *Field Guide to Antiques and Collectibles*—this guide focuses on articles made between 1880 and 1930. It covers all areas of interest to collectors including furniture, glass, pottery, china, clocks, photographs, and jewelry. The guide is available for $8.95.
- *Christie's Pictorial History of Collecting*—a guide to the pleasures and pitfalls of collecting, by Robert Cummings, contains over 100 illustrations. It offers advice on how to develop a collector's eye and how to start your own collection. The cost is $15.95.

Wallace-Homestead Book Co.

PO Box 6500
Department 04
Chicago, IL 60680   800-328-1000

This firm publishes numerous antique books. Call its toll-free 800 number for a complete list. Two of its most comprehensive books are:

■ *Confusing Collectibles: A Guide to the Identification of Contemporary Items*—a 208-page guide to collectibles containing 1,500 photos. Cost is $12.95.

■ *Wallace-Homestead Price Guide to Antiques and Pattern Glass*—the tenth edition of this guide contains new categories, new prices, and news about the market. It also has an extensive pattern-glass section. Cost is $11.95.

Warman Publishing

PO Box 26742
Department H-10
Elkins Park, PA 19117   215-657-1812

Warman's offers the following publications about antiques and collectibles:

■ *Warman's Antiques and Their Prices*—published annually, this guide gives representive prices for different categories of antiques. Historical information about specific antiques is also included. Cost is $10.95.

■ *Warman's Americana and Collectibles*—a price guide to fun collectibles—"the things you wish you hadn't thrown out." It costs $12.95.

Web Publishing

PO Box 12830
Wichita, KS 67277   316-722-9750

Two magazines on antiques and collectibles are available from Web Publishing:

■ *Antique Market Report*—a bimonthly magazine that reports on: current prices paid for thousands of auctioned and gallery sale items throughout the United States and market trends, with indicated highs and lows, as reported from major auction houses. It features interviews with specific galleries on undervalued art. Yearly subscription fee is $18.

■ *Collector's Mart*—a bimonthly all-color magazine focusing on limited-edition art. Artists' profiles are covered in feature articles. Annual subscription fee is $18.

PEOPLE TO TALK TO

Ralph and Terry Kovel
PO Box 2200
Beachwood, OH 44122   Written inquiries only
   For thirty years, the Kovels have been leading antiques and collectibles
experts. Together they have written more than forty informative books and
price guides. (See publications entry in this chapter for a partial list. You can
order a complete list of their books by sending a stamped, self-addressed
envelope.) The Kovels write a nationally syndicated newspaper column, "Kovels: Antiques and Collecting," and a monthly column for *House Beautiful*
called "Your Collectibles." They also host a syndicated television series called
"Kovels on Collecting." Publications available directly from them are:

   ■ *Kovels on Antiques and Collectibles*—a twelve-page monthly newsletter which carries no advertisements. It features reports of the antique and
   collectible market, articles about antique identification marks, and reviews
   of new antique price books. Annual subscription fee is $25 a year.

   ■ *Current Antique Clubs and Publications*—a leaflet listing current antiques clubs and publications. It costs $2. A stamped, self-addressed enve-
   lope must accompany your order.

Precious Metals and Stones for the Small Investor

See also:
Commodities and Futures Trading

A potential investor in pork bellies, fortunately, doesn't touch or feel them before buying. And few investors would want to feast their eyes on AT&T stock certificates before purchasing shares. Not so with precious gems and metals.

The "fondle factor" is a term used in the field to describe the attraction most people feel when they touch gold, silver, platinum, and diamonds and other gems. Experts say we are nine times more likely to buy if we're allowed to see and touch first. It's called "emotional buying," and the same experts warn that it's one of the biggest mistakes inexperienced investors make.

As with coins, paper money, and other collectibles, the emotional buy is fine if the investment value is secondary. But if you're considering an investment in precious metals or stones, the first thing you should know is that such an investment is considered high risk and recommended only for those who already have solid investments in real estate, stocks, bonds or other more secure, easily liquidated investments.

If you do decide to go with this type of investment, experts advise you to have several consultations, read as much as you can, and take the time to invest properly. Precious metals expert Glen Kirsch of International Financial Consultants in Rockville, Maryland, says that many first-time investors in this area demonstrate the "self-destruct syndrome" by working all their lives to save money and then making a poorly thought-out investment and losing it. "The irony is that if people spent more time learning how to invest money properly, they wouldn't even have to work," he said.

Kirsch recommends that before you buy you should know (1) why you're buying, (2) how much money you can risk, and (3) how long you intend to hold it. He also suggests that you stagger in and stagger out, which means, simply, to buy a little at a time and sell a little at a time.

Kirsch illustrates this with the story of a client who invested several thousand dollars in silver and six months later had made $350,000. In the process, he became emotionally attached, refusing advice to sell half of it. He was soon $10,000 in the hole. Luckily he could afford to lose his original investment, and said, "I took the win; now I'll take the loss."

Always check with the Better Business Bureau before buying or taking advice from anyone. The credibility test for a mail-order dealer insist that delivery is made to and paid by your bank.

The following section lists a publication called *The Role of Gold in Con-*

sumer Investment Portfolios, by the Salomon Brothers Center for the Study of Financial Institutions, which discusses gold in detail. You'll also find in this section a description of the American Gem Society that will help you learn more about gems and the Jewelers Vigilance Committee, which helps guard against fraudulent jewelry appraisals. There are numerous companies that will appraise or sell you precious metals and stones and others that will store them for you. And many publications are listed here to help you educate yourself before you make this important investment or purchase.

AGENCIES, INSTITUTES, AND ORGANIZATIONS

American Gem Society (AGS)
5901 West 3rd Street
Los Angeles, CA 90036-2898   213-936-4367
AGS is a nonprofit, professional association of jewelers pledged to protect the buying public. The Society is the only organization that awards the titles of Registered Jeweler, Certified Gemologist, and Certified Gemologist Appraiser. These designations require special courses at the Gemological Institute of America and the passing of rigorous examinations.

AGS offers a free AGS consumer kit to all those interested in learning more about gems, jewelry, and jewelers. The kit contains a roster of American Gem Society jewelers located across the United States and Canada; brochures on a variety of topics including diamonds, colored gemstones, precious jewelry appraisals, gold and silver buying tips; and a fact sheet on the AGS Accredited Gem Lab.

Donald S. McAlvany's International Collectors Associates
2696 South Colorado Boulevard, Suite 430
Denver, CO 80222   303-758-8536
Specializing in precious metals of all kinds, International Collectors Associates is a brokerage and consultation firm assisting brokers and conservative investors in the preservation of assets against the ravages of inflation and monetary instability. A South African Investment Tour is offered each year for investors. For more information call the number above. Staff members in this organization will answer questions from the public on gold, silver, rare coins, and gemstones. The following newsletter is available to nonmembers:
- *McAlvany Intelligence Advisor*—published monthly, this financial newsletter provides an in-depth, monetary, economic, geopolitical analysis of trends that offset the precious metals marketplace. Annual subscription is $95.

Federal Trade Commission (FTC)

Pennsylvania Avenue & 6th Street, NW
Washington, DC 20580   202-523-3598

The FTC monitors the jewelry industry for unfair or deceptive trade practices but it does not intervene in individual disputes. The following consumer publications are available free of charge:

- *Gemstone Investing*—this fact sheet gives sound advice on the steps to take before purchasing.
- *Gold Jewelry*—a fact sheet defining the terminology used to describe gold jewelry.
- *Bargain Jewelry*—an informational circular to aid the consumer in interpreting jewelry ads with bargain prices.
- *Guides for the Jewelry Industry*—a pamphlet containing administrative interpretations of laws administered by the FTC for the jewelry industry.

The Gemological Institute of America (GIA)

1660 Stewart Street   213-829-2991
Santa Monica, CA 90404   800-421-7250

GIA is dedicated to educating the world's professional jewelers. Its courses cover three major areas of the jewelry industry: gemology, jewelry manufacturing arts, and business. The gemology curriculum includes courses on diamonds, colored stones, gem identification, colored stone grading, and pearls. The Institute offers a variety of educational programs. A free course catalog, available upon request, describes the extension courses, the residence program, and the home study program.

GIA's 4,000-volume library contains one of the largest, most comprehensive collections on gems and jewelry in the world. A free catalog is available listing the 350 titles on gems and jewelry in stock at the GIA bookstore.

Gold Information Center

900 Third Avenue
New York, NY 10022   212-688-0474

The Center was formed to increase consumer knowledge and awareness of gold and to stimulate the buying and wearing of gold jewelry. It also provides the jewelry industry with information as well as trends in jewelry, fashion, and promotional programs. GIA maintains a library housing a complete range of photos, books, data, statistics and films about gold. The following publication is available free of charge:

- *An Introduction to Investing in Gold*—this ten-page guide is designed to assist new investors in understanding the characteristics of gold as an investment medium.

The Gold Institute
1001 Connecticut Avenue, NW, Suite 1140
Washington, DC 20036   202-331-1227
The Gold Institute is comprised of gold companies in the thirteen major gold-producing countries (except South Africa and the U.S.S.R.). These companies are involved in mining, refining, and manufacturing products using gold; serving banking needs; and making gold bullion. The purpose of the Gold Institute is to assist people who use gold in technical industries and to assist the central banks issuing of gold coins. The Institute serves as the arm of the gold industry helping keep track of gold-producing countries and detailing the physical movement of all gold and gold coins among countries. It publishes:

- *Modern Gold Coinage*—an annual publication listing the details of gold coins issued in sixty-five countries. It costs $7.
- *The Gold News*—a bimonthly newsletter that explains the uses of gold, reports on the meetings of the institute, and announces its new members. Free.
- *How to Invest in Gold*—a twenty-page booklet for the individual investor who plans to invest in gold. Free.
- *The Languages of Gold*—a useful fact sheet for every person who buys or sells gold in any form. It provides data on purity, weight, and thickness. Free.

International Precious Metals Institute (IPMI)
Government Building
ABE Airport   215-266-1570—general information
Allentown, PA 18103   212-679-6383—information center
IPMI is the largest precious metals association in the world. It is a nonprofit organization designed to serve the technical, economic, and educational needs of the precious metals community. The Institute is composed of actively involved miners, refiners, producers, users, research scientists, bankers, governmental representatives, and private individuals. IPMI encourages the exchange of information concerning precious metals on an international level by publishing data and statistics and a newsletter, and by running a library and information center. It provides a worldwide information forum by conducting international conferences and publishing their proceedings. Its annual technical conferences and periodic seminars are open to all, but members pay a reduced fee. The following publications are available:

- *Precious Metals News and Review*—published monthly, this newsletter provides members with industry information news concerning government regulations, notices of upcoming events, seminars, and conferences. Annual subscription price is $15.
- *A Practical Guide to the Commodities Markets*—this book provides a complete in-depth look at all aspects of commodities future trading. It

includes chapters on speculating in financial futures, metals, energy futures, and other topical commodities. Cost is $20.

Jewelers of America, Inc.
Consumer Program
1271 Avenue of the Americas
New York, NY 10020   212-489-0023

The trade association will send you free consumer-oriented fact sheets on the following subjects: colored gemstones, cultured pearls, platinum jewelry, karat gold jewelry, fine watches, jewelry appraisals, diamonds, care and cleaning of fine jewelry and jewelry discounts. You can also get the following free packet that includes:

■ *What You Should Know About Platinum Jewelry*—this two-page booklet tells you how to choose the best platinum, where to buy it, what to wear it with, and how it compares with other metals.

■ *What You Should Know About Buying a Diamond*—two pages, including a glossary of terms, about buying diamonds.

■ *What You Should Know About Jewelry Bargains and Discounts*—another small brochure that warns you about buying cut-rate jewels, watches, and gold by mail order or in discount stores.

National Committee for Monetary Reform (NCMR)
4425 West Napoleon Avenue
Metairie, LA 70001   800-535-7633

NCMR was originally founded as the National Committee to Legalize Gold in 1971. Through an intensive effort of lobbying, political activity, and education, it was successful in its campaign for permission for private citizens to own gold by January 1975. NCMR is now an economic and educational think tank which publishes hard-money-oriented newsletters and sponsors economic, educational and investment conferences. It works on a long-term educational campaign in favor of an eventual return to the gold standard. It publishes:

■ *Aden Analysis*—a monthly investment newsletter, written by the famous Aden sisters. It regularly covers a broad range of markets, bonds, commodities, currencies, and their specialty, precious metals. Subscriptions include a periodic special report, a telephone hotline, and a free emergency mailgram service. The annual subscription fee is $195.

■ *Gold Newsletter*—published monthly, it is the country's oldest and largest privately circulated economic and investment newsletter specializing in gold. The world's top analysts and authorities on precious metals are featured in in-depth articles, interviews, and summary news coverage. The annual subscription fee is $95.

The Old Mint of San Francisco
5th and Missouri streets
San Francisco, CA 94103   415-974-0788

The museum area is open to the public free of charge. It houses a collection of U.S. silver commemorative coins, the famous Kagin Collection of pioneer gold coins, western art and many other antiques, mining equipment and artifacts, western memorabilia and graphics displays. A million dollars in gold may be viewed in the form of a pyramid of twenty-eight bars of gold surrounded by a collection of 1,000 gold nuggets on loan from Sierra County, CA. The gold is encased in a cylinder of Plexiglas in a steel walk-through vault. The museum also has a Numismatic Library, open to the public by appointment, and a Numismatic Sales Room. The Old Mint Museum is open Monday through Friday.

Professional Numismatics Guild (PNG)
PO Box 430
Van Nuys, CA 91408   818-787-4020

PNG is an association of professional numismatists. It restricts its membership to dealers who possess and demonstrate three essential qualifications: knowledge of the subject arising from extensive experience; responsibility to sell only fully authenticated and accurately described items of numismatic value; and integrity in assuring the buyer of a safe, honest, and mutually satisfying transaction. All members of PNG will provide a certificate of authentication of items purchased from them. To aid the consumer in finding a qualified dealer in numismatics the Guild will provide a free copy of their membership directory.

The Silver Institute
1001 Connecticut Avenue
Washington, DC 20036   202-331-1227

The Silver Institute is comprised of silver companies in twenty silver-producing countries. These companies are involved in mining, refining, and fabrication of products using silver. The purpose of the Institute is to provide assistance to people who use silver in technical industries. The Institute details the physical movement of silver and silver coins among countries. It publishes:

- *The Silver Institute Letters*—a bimonthly newsletter that announces new members and reports on the Institute's meetings, and the uses of silver. Primarily an educational publication, this newsletter is free.
- *Mine Production of Silver*—a free annual leaflet listing the total worldwide production of silver for the year. Projected totals are also provided for the next five years.
- *Modern Silver Coinage 1983*—complete data on all silver coins issued in the world, with names and addresses of mints from which they can be

acquired. This information is prepared with the cooperation of the monetary authorities, central banks, and mints of each country. It costs $15.

APPRAISALS

In addition to resources in this section also see ANTIQUES AND COLLECTIBLES.

Jewelers Vigilance Committee (JVC)
1180 Avenue of the Americas, 9th Floor
New York, NY 10036   212-869-9505
JVC is a nonprofit organization founded to promote, monitor, and guard against unfair competition by maintaining the highest ethical principles governing the jewelry industry. Its sole purpose is to protect the jewelry industry's prestige and maintain public confidence in it. JVC will take corrective action when abuses and violations of laws that regulate the jewelry industry are brought to its attention. Its monitoring service will test any questionable merchandise for accuracy. Before sending JVC the merchandise you can get a form from them to fill out. The following free publication is available:
> ■ *What You Should Know About Jewelry Appraisals*—this pamphlet describes the different types of appraisals and purposes they serve.

Ledoux & Company
359 Alfred Avenue
Teaneck, NJ 07666   201-837-7160
This is an independent laboratory that uses accurate and impartial methods for the sampling and analysis of base and precious metal materials. Ledoux will provide analysis on bullion bars or wafers whose markings are not recognized. Minimum fee is $25.

STORAGE COMPANIES: HOW TO PROTECT YOUR INVESTMENT

Do you need a place to store your precious metals and diamonds? A safe-deposit box may not be adequate, depending on the quantity and size of your cache. Try a storage company that offers high-security confidential vaults that specialize in these valuables.

You'll find some that are tax-free and climate-controlled and many that offer shipping services. Ask your bank for a referral to a storage vault or contact the National Association of Private Security Vaults described here. Some of the storage companies are listed below. (Note that many gold and silver brokers will also store your purchase for you.)

National Association of Private Security Vaults
PO Box 1416
Claremont, NH 03743   Written inquiries only
   This national membership organization of private security vaults will send you a list of members offering open vaults for storage of precious metals.

Bank of Delaware
300 Delaware Avenue
Wilmington, DE 19899   302-429-1210
   The Bank of Delware is one of the largest precious metals depositories in the United States. Just about every major dealer, bank, and brokerage house engaged in precious metals activity maintains a relationship with Bank of Delaware, because precious metals purchases are tax-free there. In the bank's storage, all a client's precious metals are physically segregated from all other clients' metals. Each time you release metal from or receive metal into your account, the material is physically moved (except 1,000-ounce silver bars, which are separately controlled).
   The Bank of Delaware will ship precious metals anywhere in the world. Each shipment is mailed first class via the U.S. Postal Service and is fully insured: it is registered and contains a return receipt. Trained storage professionals of the bank can conduct authentication tests on any gold coins received into a client's account.

Guardian Safe Deposit, Inc.
2499 North Harrison Street
Arlington, VA 22207   703-237-1133
   Guardian specializes in storing precious metals and is one of the largest private security vaults in the United States. It offers its clients twenty-four-hour access to their valuables, 365 days a year. It maintains an armed guard on the premises twenty-four hours a day in order to protect the valuables stored and to better serve its worldwide clientele, which includes individuals, companies, and banks. Guardian protects your personal or corporate privacy. Since it is a nonbanking depository, complete anonymity can be arranged through a numbered account. Storage fees are based on volume displaced, not value of items stored. Guardian is fully protected by vault liability insurance.

Perpetual Storage, Inc.
3322 South 300 East
Salt Lake City, UT 84115   801-942-1950
   Perpetual Storage is vault is tunneled 300 feet into a solid granite mountain just half an hour east of Salt Lake City. The vault specializes in precious metal storage. It offers complete twenty-four hour retrieval service 365 days of the year. A client's precious metals are not subject to sales tax or inventory tax.

Perpetual Storage will also ship anywhere on a moment's notice twenty-four hours a day.

The Security Center
147 Carondelet Street
New Orleans, LA 70130   504-522-1254
    Located in the heart of New Orleans central business district, the fortress-like Security Center was built originally as the Federal Reserve Bank. It specializes in the storage of gold and silver bullion and coins. Storage areas are available for jewelry or larger valuables such as paintings, silverware, and objects of art. The vault is climate-controlled for protection and preservation of valuables. It is accessible twenty-four hours a day, 365 days a year. Numbered accounts for more confidential service are available. The Center is not subject to state or federal banking authorities.

DEALERS AND BROKERS

    Described in this section are some of the companies through which you can buy and sell precious metals. Staff, although biased toward what their company offers, should be able to provide helpful information about precious metals. Learn as much as you can about the market and purchase plans available *before* you do business.

Dean Witter Reynolds, Inc.
1 World Trade Center
New York, NY 10048   212-524-3744
    Account executives at branch offices nationwide can offer advice about investing in precious metals. Clients can purchase precious metals in two ways. You can buy actual gold and silver coins and bars, which Dean Witter will either store and insure or deliver. The second method is the Precious Metals Portfolio Plan. For a nominal minimum investment, you can get a diversified portfolio of the most liquid precious metals—gold, silver, and platinum in $1,000 units. Each unit contains approximately 40 percent gold, 40 percent silver, and 20 percent platinum, subject to prevailing market pricing conditions, and can be stored, segregated, and fully insured. The following free publication is available to clients:
> ■ *Precious Metals Newsletter*—published every other month, this newsletter reports on current trends in the precious metals market.

Dreyfus Gold Deposits
666 Old Country Road   718-895-1330
Garden City, NJ 11530   800-544-4424
    This is a gold buying and selling program whereby a client may purchase the gold bullion or coins and take physical possession. Dreyfus will also arrange

storage and insurance for a nominal fee. Out-of-state residents are not subject to sales tax. Dreyfus is in the process of developing a silver purchase program. The following publication is available to clients free of charge:

- *Letter of the Line*—published quarterly, this general investment newsletter provides information on the precious metal market.

E. F. Hutton & Company, Inc.
1 Battery Park Plaza
New York, NY 10004   212-742-5000

This company offers several programs for buying gold and silver. It also provides storage for the gold you purchase at a nominal fee that includes insurance. A small investor may purchase as little as one ounce of gold or ten ounces of silver. E. F. Hutton has free information brochures on buying silver and gold. For example:

- *A Practical Guide to Gold Coins*—a ten-page guide to the history and value of gold coins and their place in your financial planning.

International Financial Consultants (IFC)
966 Hungerford Drive, #5-A
Rockville, MD 20850   301-424-9430

IFC is a consulting general partnership specializing in the areas of precious metals, foreign exchange, and overseas banking. It provides consulting services for individuals, corporations, and institutions. It also acts as broker/dealer in buying and selling precious metals and foreign exchange. IFC publishes:

- *Information Line*—a monthly newsletter reporting on the precious metals market.

Merrill, Lynch, Pierce, Fenner & Smith, Inc.
1 Liberty Plaza
165 Broadway
New York, NY 10006   212-709-2418

Merrill Lynch offers two financial vehicles by which an investor may buy gold. Share Builder is an accumulated metal program requiring an investment of $100 and subsequent investment amounts of as little as $50. Gold may also be purchased in the form of the Canadian gold coin, the maple leaf, or by the ounce in gold bars. Merrill Lynch offers potential clients the following publication:

- *Precious Metal Monthly*—this monthly newsletter is designed to keep the investor informed of fluctuations in the precious metals market.

Shearson/American Express
2 World Trade Center
New York, NY 10048   212-321-4577

Financial consultants in all Shearson branch offices can advise an investor on purchasing gold or silver. The company offers two separate programs for purchasing these precious metals. The Purchase Plan consists of outright purchase of gold or silver in the form of bullion bars or coins. The Precious Metal Accumulation Plan is a one-dollar cost-averaging plan. An initial $500 investment is made and an automated or occasional purchase agreement is arranged. The minimum on these additional purchases is $100.

Sunshine Bullion Company
PO Box 214509   214-922-0162
Dallas, TX 75221   800-527-5769
Sunshine Bullion Company, a wholly-owned subsidiary of Sunshine Mining Company, was formed to sell Sunshine silver direct to investors. It provides choices in silver to match your taste and portfolio. The company offers a guarantee to buy back your Sunshine silver at the current market price. Sunshine also offers sight draft deliveries wherein your metal is shipped to your banker and only after receiving your shipment does the bank release your payment to Sunshine Bullion. Sunshine will also store silver bullion for a fee of ten cents an ounce a year.

WHAT TO READ

Analysis and Outlook
PO Box 1167
Port Townsend, WA 98368   206-385-5097
This monthly newsletter is a review of the precious metals market. Annual subscription is $32.

Consumer's Guide to Buying & Selling Gold, Silver & Diamonds
Doubleday & Co.
501 Franklin Avenue
Garden City, NJ 11530   516-294-4000
Written by I. Jack Brod, an internationally acknowledged authority on precious metals, gems, and jewelry, this consumer guide provides solid, reliable advice on whether or when to invest, and how to do so wisely. A discussion of the pluses, minuses, and strategies involved when investing in commodities is included. The book contains a brief history of each metal or gem, an explanation of why it is valuable, how its price is determined, and what the future looks like. This is followed by a section covering an individual's investment choices. Cost is $15.95.

Deak Perera
Precious Metals Department
29 Broadway
New York, NY 10006   212-635-0515

A variety of publications are available from Deak including:

- *Deak Speaks on Gold*—a brochure containing data on gold bullion, gold coins, and gold certificates. Free.
- *Deak Speaks on Silver*—a descriptive brochure about silver bars, silver coins, and silver certificates. Free.

Dick Davis Digest
PO Box 2828
Ocean View Station
Miami Beach, FL 33140   305-531-7777

Published every two weeks, the digest is a twelve-page summary of over 300 of the leading market letters. Coverage includes specific stock recommendations from the best known advisers on Wall Street. Though not a precious metals newsletter, the digest carries reports on precious metals in each issue. It is easy to read and cuts through the mass of typical Wall Street verbiage. A one-year subscription costs $95.

Green's Commodity Market Comments
PO Box 174
Princeton, NJ 08542   609-921-6594

Published twice a month, this newsletter is considered the world authority on gold and silver. It covers precious metals and monetary matters exclusively. A one-year subscription is available for $240. A three-month trial subscription is $65.

Metals Week
1221 Avenue of the Americas, 43rd Floor
New York, NY 10020   212-997-6248

This weekly newsletter gives a quick, concise briefing on the market for all nonferrous (non-iron) metals. It carries a separate column which reports on the precious metals market. The newsletter also contains reports on worldwide market prices, production data, corporate news, government actions, technological breakthroughs, and labor activities. Annual subscription fee is $527.

Investor's Notebook
2400 Jefferson Highway   800-535-7633
Jefferson, LA 70121   504-837-3010—in LA

This sixteen-page monthly advisory newsletter focuses on investing in gold, silver, and international coins. Recent articles have identified five top stock market advisers, four investment megatrends for the year, and ten tested rules for successful tax-shelter shopping. Information on how to receive a 10 to 20 percent discount on gold bullion and the most common error that mutual fund investors make has also been outlined for readers. Publisher James U. Blanchard III has been selected as "Investor's Best Friend" by the editor of *Forecasts and Strategies.* A yearly subscription costs $78.

Mocatta 1684-1984
Mocatta Futures Corporation
4 World Trade Center
New York, NY 10048   212-938-8220
　　　This booklet describes the history of the gold and silver industry, the gold and silver market operations, and the trading of gold and silver coins. Free.

The New World of Gold
Walker and Company
720 Fifth Avenue
New York, NY 10019   212-265-3632
　　　Timothy Green captures all the romance of the gleaming metal in *The New World of Gold.* The full story of this most precious and sought-after commodity is told, including the inside story of the mines, the markets, the politics and the investors. It contains chapters on the United States gold markets, the Hong Kong scene, a first-hand account of the great new gold rush in Brazil, plus a full analysis of the London and Swiss markets. It also covers the roles of the central banks, speculators, and small investors in today's volatile gold business. The price of the paperback edition is $12.95.

The Official Investors Guide: Buying & Selling
　　Gold, Silver & Diamonds
House of Collectibles, Inc.
Orlando Central Park
1900 Premier Row
Orlando, FL 32809   305-857-9095
　　　This 197-page investment guide, written by Marc Hudgeons, tells what you need to know to make money in the precious metals and gems market. The book features a history of gold, silver, and diamonds. The diamond market is covered extensively, including tips on diamond grading, clarity characteristics, types of diamond substitutes, and diamonds as investments. The book costs $9.95.

The Role of Gold in Consumer Investment Portfolios
Salomon Brothers Center for the Study of Financial Institutions
Graduate School of Business Administration
New York University
Washington Square
New York, NY 10003   212-285-6000
A sixty-seven-page study by Lawrence S. Ritter and Thomas J. Urich, this booklet examines how the price of gold is and has been determined in the financial marketplace. The study also examines the risk and return characteristics of gold in an investment portfolio and its future possible role. A conclusion is reached on what percentage of one's total investment portfolio in gold is warranted and prudent. The price is $5.

Silver & Gold Report
PO Box 40
Bethel, CT 06801   203-748-2036
The following publications are available:
- *Silver & Gold Report*—an independent and impartial precious metals newsletter published twenty-two times a year. Some of the regular features are: exclusive interviews with the world's leading silver and gold experts; analyses of silver and gold price trends and investments; and dealer price surveys and other "how-to" articles, filled with money-saving tips and techniques for buying and selling silver and gold. The yearly subscription fee is $144.
- *Insider's Guide to Buying Silver & Gold*—written by Daniel Rosenthal, this book is full of dozens of valuable nitty-gritty tips, hints, angles, and techniques for saving and making money on your silver and gold investments. It costs $78.
- *Silver & Gold Investor's Checklist*—this book is written by Daniel Rosenthal in an easy-to-read format. It organizes the questions used in checking out a dealer before you buy. A simple, usable system to help you buy silver and gold safely. The price is $49.95.

PEOPLE TO TALK TO

R. W. Bradford
PO Box 1167
Port Townsend, WA 98368   206-385-5097
A pioneer in the investment precious metals business, Mr. Bradford writes regularly about rare coins and precious metals for numerous investment publications. He is editor of the precious metal market newsletter *Analysis & Outlook*. Mr. Bradford has served as a consultant on counterfeit coins and on precious metals.

Peter C. Cavelti
Guardian Trustco International
74 Victoria Street
Toronto, Ontario M5C 2A5
Canada   415-863-1100
    Peter C. Cavelti, one of the world's foremost experts on the metals market, is presently president and chief executive officer of Guardian Trustco International of Toronto, Ontario. He is also a consultant to the Royal Canadian Mint and an adviser to the Ontario Securities Commission on Foreign Exchange and Precious Metals. Mr. Cavelti is the author of the following book, which is currently available from McGraw-Hill Book Company, 1221 Avenue of the Americas, New York, NY 10020, 212-512-2000:

> ■ *New Profits in Gold, Silver & Strategic Metals: The Complete Investment Guide*—filled with the latest advice on how and when to (or when not to) invest in gold, silver, and strategic metals. The cost is $15.95.

Donald S. McAlvany
President
International Collectors Associates
2696 South Colorado Boulevard
Denver, CO 80222   303-758-8536
    Mr. McAlvany is a former national salesman for International Investors, Inc.'s $6 million mutual fund for gold shares. He is the editor and publisher of the *McAlvany Intelligence Advisor,* a monthly financial newsletter (see the entry in the What to Read section, above). He lectures throughout the United States on gold inflation and conducts an annual investment tour to South Africa.

John P. Norris
Credit Suisse
100 Wall Street
New York, NY 10005   212-612-8276
    Mr. Norris has extensive experience in precious metals and marketing. He is presently manager of precious metals marketing, including gold and silver, for Credit Suisse in the United States. In the past, Mr. Norris worked as a staff economist for Commodity Exchange, Inc., the largest metals market in the world for gold, silver, copper, and aluminum futures transactions.

Coins and Paper Money

See also:
Antiques and Collectibles
Precious Metals and Stones for the Small Investor

Our fascination with coins and money goes back to the first hammerstruck piece created in 600 B.C. But don't assume that because a coin is old it is valuable. Experts say the biggest mistake collectors make is not knowing how to grade an item. In estimating the value, the condition and date are not the only considerations. Most novices assume, for example, that if a coin is shiny, it's more valuable than if it is tarnished. Yet tarnish may attest to the fact that it is an authentic piece.

To assume that the mere fact of age makes a piece more valuable is also a common error on the part of novice coin collectors. Some 1,500- or 2,000-year-old coins are not very valuable because they were stored in hoards or caches and thus there are a great many of them. On the other hand, a 1927-D (Denver Mint) twenty-dollar gold piece has sold for more than $300,000 because it is a very scarce coin. In coin and paper money collecting, as in all collecting, supply and demand is the key to value.

Paper money collectors should consider specializing in a specific type of paper money, such as obsolete bank notes, checks, stock certificates or war bonds. The geographic area in which you live is also important because it may be conducive to collecting certain type of money. For instance, Washington, D.C., would be a good place to collect national bank notes or pre-Civil War bank notes. If you live in California, consider old Bank of California or Wells Fargo Bank checks.

The following list of museums, publications, and organizations will help you in your search. Consider subscribing to one of the newsletters or magazines listed here so you can stay up on what other collectors are doing. A good place to start educating yourself is the American Numismatic Association Library, where you can borrow innumerable books to help you. The professional Currency Dealers Association is a good organization to keep in mind if you have a dispute with one of its members. The organization provides mediation services.

Described in this section are sources to give you information about ancient and modern coins. They can be gold, silver, bronze, or a mixture of metals. The resources here include authentication services, museums, publications, experts, and places to purchase collectors' coins.

AGENCIES, INSTITUTES, AND ORGANIZATIONS

The American Numismatic Association (ANA)
PO Box 2366
Colorado Springs, CO 80901   303-632-2646

This is a membership organization that promotes study and research of coins, coinage, and the history of money. ANA sponsors workshops, seminars, and coin shows and provides a "second opinion" service to authenticate purchases. Its seminars cover topics such as grading, counterfeiting, investment pitfalls, and investment advice. Membership in ANA is $18 a year, plus an additional $5 the first year to cover application fees. ANA publishes:

- *The Numismatic Monthly*—a monthly magazine listing current summaries and statistics of both U.S. and foreign coins. Current prices are also given and the magazine subscription price is included in the membership fee.

The ANA Library is the largest circulating numismatic library in the world. The library's 30,000 circulating items are lent directly to ANA members anywhere in the world. The books here cover all aspects of numismatics, including coins, paper money, tokens, medals, orders, decorations and stocks and bonds. Holdings include books on how to collect, on economics, and on banks and banking. Aspects of world numismatics, both ancient and modern, are also represented.

The library's collection of auction catalogs documents the numismatic items that have sold at auction throughout the United States and Europe, and is an invaluable research tool. The library staff maintains a collection of slide programs featuring different aspects of numismatics. These visual education programs are available to member clubs for use at meetings and may also be borrowed by individual members for presentation to school and civic groups.

A complete list of the programs offered, and specific instructions for ordering, are available from the library, which is open from Tuesday through Saturday. Anyone, member or nonmember, may write, call, or come in to use library materials.

The ANA museum includes extensive and growing collections of coins, medals, tokens, and paper money housed and displayed at American Numismatic Association (ANA) headquarters for viewing by visitors. Members of ANA may study the items on display, and, by prearrangement, other available museum material for research purposes. It is open from Tuesday through Saturday. Admission to the museum is free.

American Numismatic Society
617 West 155th Street
New York, NY 10032   212-234-3130

■ ■

If Given an Extra $10,000, People Would Rather Give to Charity Than Put It into the Stock Market

When *Money* magazine asked household financial decision makers what they would do with an unexpected $10,000, 12 percent said that they would give it to charity and only 11 percent said they would buy stocks. But the first choice of the majority of those responding was to put the money into savings.

■ ■

An educational organization, this society supports a museum with a large collection of coins and a library with one of the largest collections of numismatic literature in the world. It also offers an eight-week summer seminar on numismatics for doctoral candidates. The society is staffed by experts in coins dating back to the beginning of time, who can be used as reference sources. Membership in the society, which includes a quarterly newsletter, is $20 a year. The society periodically publishes books about coins, as well as:

- *Museum Notes*—an annual publication containing illustrated plates of unusual coins as well as articles on numismatics. Articles covering new items and reprints of older works are provided.

Check Collectors Roundtable
PO Box 65
Scandinavia, WI 54977   Written requests only

Members of this organization are interested in collecting, preserving, and researching old and new drafts, money orders, deposit receipts, notes, stocks and bonds, engraving and protectographing methods. As a unique service to its members, the Roundtable answers questions, submitted in writing, relating to the collecting of checks and other banking instruments. A panel of experts answers all questions. The following publications are available:

- *Checklist*—a quarterly publication which carries articles primarily on checks and other banking instruments. The subscription fee is included in the $10 annual membership fee.
- *Membership Roster*—a complete list of members and their area of collecting interest. A copy of the roster is included in the $10 annual membership fee.

Early American Numismatics
PO Box 2442
La Jolla, CA 92038　　　　　　　　　　　　619-273-3566
　　This dealership specializes in colonial coins and currency. It offers an appraisal service. For $10 a year you can be placed on its quarterly mailing list which provides current price lists and information on buyer-bid sales.

Eric P. Newman Numismatic Education Society
PO Box 14020
St. Louis, MO 63178　　　　　　　　　　　Written requests only
　　A cultural organization, the Society was established to research Colonial coins and currency. A museum containing early American numismatics is maintained at Mercantile Towers, 7th Street and Washington Avenue, St. Louis, MO 63102. It is open to the public on weekdays from 10 A.M. to 4 P.M.

The Gold Institute
　　See listing under PRECIOUS METALS AND STONES FOR THE SMALL INVESTOR.

International Bank Note Society (IBNS)
c/o Milan Alusic
PO Box 1222
Racine, WI 53405
　　This is a worldwide organization of paper-money enthusiasts who collect, study, and share information and educate others about bank notes from all over the world. It has 1,400 members from more than sixty countries, who contribute to its publications and attend auctions and regional meetings. There are several publications available to members only, including the quarterly *IBNS Journal, Bank Notes of the 20th Century* (a continuing book project with two volumes completed), *IBNS Quarterly Newsletter,* and *Membership Directory* with members listed alphabetically and geographically. Society by-laws and auction rules are included in the directory. You can request a free copy of the IBNS membership brochure with a description of the society and a membership application. Annual membership costs $9 in the United States.

International Gold Corporation, Ltd.
900 Third Avenue
New York, NY 10022　　　　　　　　　　　212-688-0005
　　International Gold Corporation, Ltd., is involved in marketing Krugerrand gold coins and advising the public as to where they may be purchased. It publishes:

　　　　■ *The Krugerrand: Today's Golden Investment Opportunity*—a free
　　　　booklet describing Krugerrands, South Africa's gold coin. The booklet ex-
　　　　plains the physical properties of the Krugerrand, how it is produced, and
　　　　how it is priced.

■ *What You Should Know About Gold and the Family of Krugerrands*—a free leaflet explaining why gold is so precious, the amount of gold mined a year, what is karat gold and what Krugerrands are.

■ *The Sure and Steady Way to Accumulate Gold*—this free leaflet explains the advantage of Krugerrand investment, how to store Krugerrands, and how to accumulate gold.

■ *The Investment Performance of Gold*—a free leaflet detailing how gold has performed in relation to other investments, how supply and demand affect gold prices, and what the experts say about gold.

■ *Gold Coins for the Collector*—a seven-page booklet that reveals the history of gold coins from ancient times to the present. There is a section on numismatic and bullion coins. Free.

The International Numismatics Authentication Bureau
PO Box 66555
Washington, DC 20035   202-223-4496

The bureau provides an authentication service to anyone who wants to find out if a coin is genuine. It will check any U.S., foreign, or ancient coin and provide you with a certificate containing a photograph of the front and back of the coin and a statement of authenticity. A fee is charged according to the value placed on your coin. The minimum charge is $15, plus a $4.50 return postage fee.

International Numismatic Society (INS)
PO Box 66555
Washington, DC 20035   202-223-4496

This society is open to anyone interested in coins, currency, and tokens. The goal of the society is to put coin collectors and dealers in contact with each other. Membership is $18 a year, which entitles members to a 10 percent discount on authentication service, and the following publications:

■ *Numorum*—a magazine with articles written by members along with reprints of timely articles from the past. The magazine is published irregularly, generally once or twice a year.

■ *INS Newsletter*—a bimonthly publication designed to keep members up-to-date on new coins issued, grading of coins, new counterfeiting locations, and news about upcoming INS conventions.

James U. Blanchard & Co.
4425 West Napoleon Avenue   504-456-9034
Metairie, LA 70001   800-535-7633

This company is one of the top coin retailers in the United States and the world's largest dealer in uncirculated United States and world silver dollars. It has one of the most respected numismatic staffs in the country. It offers the following publication:

■ *Market Alert*—published monthly, this is the world's largest newsletter covering investment grade coins. It regularly features the views of editor James U. Blanchard III, covering the outlook for precious metals, the world economy, issues such as inflation and deflation, and the world debt crisis. Each issue includes in-depth coverage of the world's coin markets, including a specialty in "semi-numismatic" coins. In addition, *Market Alert* covers the United States rare coin market. Annual subscription is $95.

The Old Mint of San Francisco
See listing under PRECIOUS METAL AND STONES FOR THE SMALL INVESTOR.

Professional Currency Dealers Association
PO Box 589
Milwaukee, WI 53201   414-282-2388
This is an association of the forty-five leading rare currency dealers in the United States. It will mediate disputes between the consumer and member dealers. The following publication is available free:
■ *Membership Directory*—contains a complete listing of members and their specialties.

Professional Numismatic Guild (PNG)
See listing under PRECIOUS METAL AND STONES FOR THE SMALL INVESTOR.

The Silver Institute
See listing under PRECIOUS METAL AND STONES FOR THE SMALL INVESTOR.

Society for International Numismatics
4214 West 238th Street
Torrance, CA 90505   213-375-2646
This educational numismatic organization was formed to help collectors of foreign coins gain more knowledge about their coins. As part of its educational program, the society will provide speakers for groups, answer the public's questions about foreign coins, and rent out its audiovisuals. The group also offers youth-oriented educational programs. Members receive a newsletter and other information on a quarterly basis.

WHAT TO READ

Coin Collectors Survival Manual
Arco Publishing Company
215 Park Avenue
New York, NY 10003   212-777-6300

A guide for collectors and investors, this book deals with detecting counterfeit coins, gives advice on grading coins, and tells how to preserve them. It also provides advice about how to deal with coin dealers. The paperback manual is available from some coin dealers, at bookstores, and from the above address for $9.95 plus $1 to cover postage and handling.

The Coin Dealer Newsletter
PO Box 11099
Torrance, CA 90510   213-370-5579
Widely known as the "gray sheet," this weekly newsletter is aimed at dealers but is also available to investors and collectors. Complete weekly dealer-to-dealer bid/ask prices for all United States coins, plus market analysis, gold and silver bullion reports and discussions of current market trends are included in the newsletter. A monthly summary is part of the subscription price. The supplement covers the previous month's activity in specific dates and mint marks of United States coins not covered in the weekly issue, plus in-depth analysis of various aspects of the United States coin market by experts in the field. It costs $27 for a three-month subscription or $89 for one year.

Coin World
PO Box 150
Sidney, OH 45367   513-498-2111
This weekly newspaper covers various aspects of coin investments. The paper also includes sections on price summaries and is available for $23.95 a year.

Currency Dealer Newsletter
PO Box 11099
Torrance, CA 90510-1099   213-370-5579
A monthly newsletter reporting on the national currency market, including in-depth articles and analyses by the most respected experts in this field. Annual subscription fee is $35.

David Hall's Rare Coin Study
PO Box 8521
Newport Beach, CA 92660   714-756-8164
This study is a price history of all coins for the past thirty-five years, with statistical breakdowns and charts. The study also includes coin market forecasts. It costs $25.

Deak Perera
See listing under PRECIOUS METAL AND STONES FOR THE SMALL INVESTOR.

A Guide Book to U.S. Coins
Whitman Coin Products
Western Publishing Company
Racine, WI 53404   414-633-2431
This annual catalogue summarizes statistics on coins in the United States. The book is available in coin bookstores or directly from the publisher.

Krause Publications
700 East State Street
Iola, WI 54990   715-445-2214
This firm publishes four research books for the collector of paper money. They are:

> ■ *Standard Catalog of National Bank Notes*—a 1,216-page catalog containing valuations and facts for approximately 50,000 National Bank notes. This book is written by veteran researchers John Hickman and Dean Oakes. It is available for $75.
>
> ■ *Standard Handbook of Modern United States Paper Money*—a comprehensive catalog of small-size currency for the collectors. It gives complete listings and market values for all small-size issues from 1928-1981. This catalog costs $15.
>
> ■ *Auction Prices Realized: U.S. Paper Money*—this 360-page catalog offers coverage of almost 20,000 paper-money lots from 140 public auctions and mail-bid sales. Listings cover the period from 1978 through 1982. The catalog costs $40.
>
> ■ *Standard Catalog of United States Paper Money*—compiled by Chester Krause and Robert Lemke, this gives a comprehensive overview of all currency issues of the United States. It costs $14.50.
>
> ■ *Bank Note Reporter*—this monthly is the only newspaper in the world not sponsored by a society or dealer that is exclusively devoted to paper money. It contains news, advertising, a market value guide, new issue listings and historical features—all focusing on world and U.S. paper money, On the U.S. side, coverage includes military currency, bonds, stock certificates, Confederate currency, and state banknotes, along with U.S. large- and small-size notes. Annual subscription is $11.

Mocatta 1684-1984
See listing under PRECIOUS METAL AND STONES FOR THE SMALL INVESTOR.

The New International Green Sheet
Carson City Publishers
PO Box 36
Midland Park, NJ 07432
This newsletter reports on many aspects of coin investment, and contains a weekly update of foreign coin price summaries. It costs $25 a year.

Numismatic News
Krause Publications
700 East State Street
Iola, WI 54990   715-445-2214

This weekly publication reports on many phases of gold and silver coin investments. Price summaries for U.S. coins are included, and the paper is available for $23 a year.

The Official Blackbook Price Guide to U.S. Paper Money
House of Collectibles
Order Department
Orlando Central Park
1904 Premier Row   305-857-9095
Orlando, FL 32809   800-327-1384

This price guide gives values for collectible U.S. paper money. It is published annually and costs $3.95.

The Rare Coin Investor Newsletter
Liberty Rare Coin Consultants, Inc.
PO Box 324
Lawrence, NY 11559   516-569-6905

This newsletter is for those who have the interest but lack the knowledge of rare United States coins. It offers independent, unbiased, and impartial information and investment advice, plus reviews of every major rare coin advisor. Also offered with each yearly subscription is personal consultations by phone (all questions answered). Cost for a one-year subscription is $80.

Standard Catalogue of World Coins
Krause Publications
700 East State Street
Iola, WI 54990   715-445-2214

This annual catalogue summarizes statistics on all foreign and U.S. coins. It gives a listing of prices, coin sizes and other data prized by numismatists. It is available for $35 in coin stores, or $35 plus $2 postage from the publisher.

Superintendent of Documents
U.S. Government Printing Office
Washington, DC 20402   202-783-3238

The following publications about coins are available:

> • *Domestic and Foreign Coins Manufactured by Mints of the United States, 1793-1980*—a 178-page book that presents a complete historical record of coins manufactured by United States Mints from 1793 through 1980. It costs $6.50.

■ *Our American Coins*—a twenty-three-page booklet that gives brief biographies of the United States presidents pictured on six of our coins. It shows the front and back of each coin, explains the symbols on each, and tells who designed them. Cost is $3.25.

■ *World's Monetary Stocks of Gold, Silver and Coins in 1979*—a 178-page book that presents coinage statistics arranged alphabetically by country, a list of government coinage mints, and numerous photographs of coins from the annual report of the Director of the Mint. Cost is $5.50.

■ *Facts About United States Money*—a twenty-eight-page booklet that explains how money is coined and paper currency printed. It explains important features on paper currency, gives specifications for United States coins, and tells how unfit money is destroyed. It sells for $3.50.

■ *Know Your Money*—a twenty-page booklet that describes and illustrates how to recognize counterfeit bills and forged United States government checks. It sells for $3.25.

World Coin News

Krause Publications
700 East State Street
Iola, WI 54990   715-445-2214

This weekly newspaper devoted to foreign coins has a calendar of shows, conventions and auctions, as well as advertisements and price lists from dealers nationwide. The paper is available for $20 a year.

PEOPLE TO TALK TO

Gerald Bauman

Manfra, Tordella & Brookes
59 West 49th Street   800-235-7241
New York, NY 10112   212-621-9502—in NY

Mr. Bauman has been interested in coin collecting for twenty-five years and has worked as a professional numismatist for thirteen years. His field of expertise is numismatic investments and he is quoted on this subject in numerous nationwide publications. He has contributed to several well-known coin guide books. Mr. Bauman has frequently consulted on authentication of rare coins. He is available for speaking engagements for a fee.

Col. Grover C. Criswell

Ft. McCoy, FL 32637   904-685-2287

For the past twenty-five years Colonel Criswell has lectured and written books on Confederate money, about which he is considered the world's top authority. He has served on the Board of Governors of the American Numismatics Association and also as president. He has published:

■ *Confederate Money & Civil War Tokens*—Lists all major types of Confederate government notes and many Civil War tokens. Available from author for $2.95.

Richard Davies
Managing Director, Gold Institute and Silver Institute
1001 Connecticut Avenue, NW, Suite 1140
Washington, DC 20036   202-331-1227

Mr. Davies is an industrial chemist by profession, as well as an expert in international money and banking. He is chairman of the firm Klein and Saks, which oversees the operations of the Gold Institute and many large central banks. Mr. Davies has provided financial and technical advice to central banks and many ministers of finance.

Dana Linett
PO Box 2442
La Jolla, CA 92038   619-273-3566

Dana Linett is an expert in Early American numismatics. He is a contributor to *Yeoman's Red Book: Guide to U.S. Coinage* and *Krause's Standard Catalog of U.S. Currency.* He is now a consultant to the American Numismatic Association Certification Service.

Jeffrey Nichols
President, American Precious Metals Advisors, Inc.
707 Westchester Avenue
White Plains, NY 10604   914-681-4412

Mr. Nichols, an expert in precious metals, has been an adviser to mining companies, industrial users, central banks, and other institutions for the past several years.

Larry Adams
PO Box 1
Boone, IA 50036   515-432-1931

Larry Adams is a document examiner and forensic consultant with a specialty in local National Bank notes, bank history, checks, and tokens. His general interest is in paper money, banking, stocks, bonds, checkwriters, and security printing. Adams maintains an extensive reference library on numismatics, document examination, forensic science, photography, graphic arts, banking, history, research, and related subjects. A lecturer on paper money, checks, and banking, Adams is presently in charge of the Check Collectors Round Table slide program on checks. He has contributed articles to *Paper Money, The Check List,* and *Collectors News.* Adams serves, at this writing, as president of the Society of Paper Money Collectors, described earlier in this section.

Trey Foerster
Route 2, Box 1
Iola, WI 54945   715-445-2214
    Trey Foerster is presently the managing editor of *Goldmine Magazine,* a
record collector's magazine. In the past, he has been the editor of three
numismatic publications—*World Coin News, Standard Catalog of World
Coins,* and *Bank Note Reporter.* Mr. Foerster is a recognized authority on
media presentation of numismatic material.

Fred Schwan
PO Box L
Fort Leavenworth, KS 66027-0351   913-651-2878
    Fred Schwan is an authority on and one of the leading collectors of military
currency. He has written three books on the subject. His first book, *World War
II Military Currency,* is a comprehensive book on all issues of military money
with history, price guide, and illustrations. Mr. Schwan is willing to give advice
and share information on the subject of paper money.

ADDITIONAL RESOURCES

Educational Videos
31800 Plymouth Road
Lavonia, MI 48150   313-661-0163
    The following videos on coin collecting are available:

> ■ *Coins: Genuine, Counterfeit & Altered*—a fifty-minute program on coin
> collecting, the tape tells how to perform a point-of-purchase examination,
> how to find a trustworthy coin dealer, and what equipment to buy. It also
> demonstrates the "cartwheel" pattern of the way a coin reflects light. A
> list of authentication services and their addresses is given at the end of the
> tape. The cost is $59.95. (This video is also available from the American
> Numismatic Association Library—see the entry in this section for address.)
>
> ■ *Collecting & Grading U.S. Coins*—a sixty-minute program which de-
> scribes the various factors that influence the value of a coin: supply, de-
> mand, and condition. Since condition is the most inportant variable, the
> bulk of the program focuses on this aspect. (This video is also available
> from the American Numismatic Association Library—see entry in this sec-
> tion for address.)

Real Estate

We have all seen those television salesmen telling us how we can become millionaires in real estate by investing $300 in their courses. A better investment would be to take the $300 and add it to a down payment for a piece of property. The techniques being promoted in these seminars have been questioned by real estate experts for a variety of reasons: some of the techniques taught are illegal and can result in prosecution; the primary commodity being sold is motivation, not real estate experience; the techniques promoted are unrealistic. Almost every no-money-down property is either a bad investment or an occurrence that cannot be duplicated often because it is either a bad loan for the financing institution or an unethical deal for the seller. If you are still convinced that you need such a seminar, investigate the Seminar Library described in this chapter. For the price of one seminar, you can have access to virtually all those available by borrowing the tapes from this library.

The best courses you can take on real estate will be given by your local community college or by the Commercial Investment Real Estate Council described in the listing below.

Although there are sources described in this section to help you locate and maintain investment property, the bulk of the material is dedicated to the financial aspects of the investment. Also listed here are those federal programs which have been established to assist the real estate investor. Sometimes the seminar salemen will charge you $300 for this information alone.

AGENCIES, INSTITUTES, AND ORGANIZATIONS

American Bar Association (ABA)
Information Services Department
750 North Lake Shore Drive
Chicago, IL 60611   312-988-5000
ABA's Information Services Department will help direct you to the proper legal resources pertaining to real estate. The staff suggests you first contact your local Bar Association for advice or for an attorney referral. If you still have questions, call the Chicago Office for additional information. The following free booklets are available:

> ■ *Buying or Selling Your Home*—a pamphlet pointing out the principal considerations involved and their significance to the home buyer or seller. It also explains the essential steps in every home purchase or sale. Free.
> ■ *Residential Real Estate Transactions: The Lawyer's Proper Role-Services-Compensation*—this paper explores whether the parties to the home-buying transaction receive adequate legal services, whether they

pay more for these services, and if these procedures can be modified to provide necessary services at a reasonable cost. Free.

The American Institute of Real Estate Appraisers
430 North Michigan Avenue
Chicago, IL 60611-4088   312-329-8559

You can contact the Appraisers Institute and its chapters across the country for answers to your home appraisal questions. If the staff cannot help you, they will refer you to a member organization that can. You can also contact the Institute if you have a complaint against an appraiser and want the Institute to examine the problem. To use the service, put your complaint in writing and send it to the Professional Standards Office at the address listed above.

A publisher of professional textbooks, the Institute also issues a membership directory available free to the public and the following free consumer pamphlets:

- *Estimating Home Value*—a pamphlet which looks closely at how a real estate appraiser determines the value of your home. Free.
- *Analyzing Rehab Potential*—gives a description of rehab cost components and a before-and-after analysis. Free.
- *Understanding the Appraisal*—the pamphlet is designed to educate the general public on the nature, purpose, and uses of real estate appraisals. Free.

Companies Offering Computer Searches
Several companies maintain computerized systems which they will search for clients in order to provide the latest information on loans and mortgages suitable to each client's financial situation. In some cases your real estate broker can have the database searched for you. Examples of these services are described below.

CompuFund
National Mortgage Network
3720 South Susan Street, Suite 100
Santa Ana, CA 92704
714-979-0783

CompuFund is a computerized loan origination and mortgage brokerage network. Searches for new funding sources are conducted regularly to expand and update the network database. Instant information is provided on rate changes, underwriting guidelines, and fees. CompuFund calculates the maximum fixed and adjustable-rate loan you can afford based on how much cash you have available for a down payment,closing costs, your income, and your other debts. Your realtor has access to the CompuFund network and can provide you with a computer printout of available mortgage programs.

■ ■

Thar's Gold in Them Thar Hills

Or so many Americans believe. When asked to state a preference, respondents to a Louis Harris survey chose real estate as the best investment to make by three to one over the next most popular response, government bonds.

■ ■

Computerized Search Bibliography
Credit Research Center
Krannert Center, Room 206
Purdue University
West Lafayette, IN 47907
317-494-4380

The Credit Research Center maintains a computerized bibliography of research citations on consumer and mortgage credit. Submit a search request form (available from the address listed above) with a short description of the purpose and subject area of the search and any key words that can be identified so that the operators may best define the parameters of your search. The maximum output of searches is 400 citations. Searches will be made and mailed within five days of receipt of request. Addresses of publishers listed in the bibliography search can be obtained from your local library reference desk. Cost is $10 per search.

Shelternet
First Boston Capital Group, Inc.
The First Boston Corporation
Tower Forty-Nine
12 East 49th Street
New York, NY 10017
212-909-2000

Shelternet is a computer-driven mortgage origination network that links mortgage lenders with mortgage originators nationwide through a technology-based delivery system. The Shelternet system evaluates for consumers the appropriateness of certain mortgage plans based on the consumer's financing needs, the consumer's present financial position, and competitive market conditions. Consumers get a "take home kit" or home purchase analysis that describes the individual's calculated buying decision based on various financing options. Shelternet processes the loan application, verifies all credit information, and performs the preliminary underwriting function, according to specified lender criteria. Call the telephone number above to find out which lenders participate in the Shelternet network. The First Boston Capital Group will also send you a free booklet that provides an overview of the Shelternet network.

Commercial Investment Real Estate Council
430 North Michigan Avenue   800-621-7035
Chicago, IL 60611   312-670-3780

Part of the National Association of Realtors, this professional organization is for commercial-investment specialists: brokers, managers, financial service managers, developers, attorneys, bankers, and practitioners in allied fields. In its efforts to achieve its goal of enhancing the professional competence of its members through education, it has become known as the "commercial-investment real estate industry's university of higher learning." Courses are provided throughout the country. They are open to nonmembers and include: fundamentals of real estate investment and taxation, fundamentals of location and market analysis, advanced real estate taxation and marketing tools for investment real estate, financing income properties, business opportunity brokerage, making money buying discount mortgages, and successful negotiating.

Counseling Services Branch
Office of the Secretary
Single Family Servicing Division
U.S. Department of Housing and Urban Development
451 7th Street, SW, Room 9186
Washington, DC 20410   202-755-6664

Staff at more than 600 HUD-approved counseling agencies nationwide can help you with questions about mortgage default, financing and maintaining your home, conserving energy, budgeting money, and more. The agencies can also tell you about HUD programs. Contact the office above to find out where your closest center is.

Division of Credit Practices
Federal Trade Commission (FTC)
6th Street and Pennsylvania Avenue, NW
Washington, DC 20580   202-326-3167

This office enforces the Truth-in-Lending Act, which requires mortgage companies to disclose certain cost information, such as the annual percentage rate (APR), before consumers enter into a mortgage contract. It will assist consumers with complaints against mortgage companies or mortgage brokers. It does not, however, have jurisdiction over mortgages from banks, savings and loans, and federally chartered credit unions. A duty officer is available to help you interpret legal mortgage contract terms and to refer you to local consumer agencies where you can get individualized assistance.

The staff in this office cannot give specific advice on the type of mortgage a consumer should obtain, but they will explain the implications of each type of mortgage. You can contact the office above or any of FTC's regional offices for the services described above. On request FTC will send you:

- *The Mortgage Money Guide*—this popular guide serves as a handbook for all available forms of creative real estate financing. It explains the basic concepts needed when shopping for real estate.

Federal Home Loan Bank Board (FHLBB)
Office of Communications
1700 G Street, NW
Washington, DC 20552   202-377-6677
Each month the FHLBB surveys 1,500 lenders in thirty-two of the largest metropolitan areas. A monthly chart lists the average conventional mortgage rate that lenders charged the previous month. You can call the Office of Communications to be put on their mailing list. Free.

Federal National Mortgage Association   202-537-7000
3900 Wisconsin Avenue, NW   202-537-6799—ARM hotline
Washington, DC 20016   202-537-7060—fixed rate hotline
Fannie Mae is a private corporation with a public purpose: to enhance the efficient flow of funds to America's low, moderate, and middle-income housing markets. It does business in the secondary mortgage market in all economic environments, providing mortgage lenders and investors with a variety of products and services. Fannie Mae is the largest single source of mortgage funds in the United States. The Adjustable Rate Mortgage (ARM) was developed to meet the needs of home buyers and lenders for an economy experiencing wide swings in interest rates.

The Commitment Operations Division of FNMA operates a twenty-four-hour hotline service providing current mortgage loan commitment rates on ARMs and conventional fixed rate mortgages. The following publication is available:

- *Fannie Mae's Consumer Guide to ARMs*—an explanation of ARMs is given in this booklet that will also help you understand the many options available in home mortgages. Free.

Federal Trade Commission (FTC)
Correspondence Branch
6th Street and Pennsylvania Avenue, NW
Washington, DC 20580   202-523-1642
If you have a complaint against a real estate broker or a problem with a real estate transaction you can file a complaint with the FTC. Your complaint must be in writing and if the staff think you have a case they will investigate, keeping the case strictly confidential.

The FTC offers several real estate publications, all available from its Bureau of Consumer Protection at the address listed above. Available booklets include:

■ *Using Ads to Shop for Home Financing*—home credit advertising questions are answered in this brochure. Free.

■ *Real Estate Brokers*—a brochure for consumers. This tells you the professional role of the real estate broker and the buying/selling relationship necessary to sell a home. Free.

Housing Costs and Benefits Analysis Program (HCBAP)
Cooperative Extension/Consumer Economics and Housing Department
Cornell University
Ithaca, NY 14853

What is the house you are thinking of buying really worth to you? You can get an answer by filling out an HCBAP questionnaire which you return to the service for analysis. You'll then receive a financial comparison between the house you are considering and a known amount of rent. As many of the considerations associated with purchasing a house come into play over a long period of time, the analysis includes consideration of expected rates of inflation, house value appreciation, and the rate of return you could receive if you did not buy the house in question and invested the money elsewhere. You'll also receive a five-page computer printout and an explanatory booklet to help you with your housing investment decision. Cost is $25.

HUD Program Information Center
U.S. Department of Housing and Urban Development (HUD)
Program Information Center
451 7th Street, NW   202-755-6420—information center
Washington, DC 20410   202-755-5111—HUD program locator number

HUD administers approximately sixty government programs that provide grants, loans, loan guarantees, direct payments, and mortgage insurance programs to help individual homeowners and real estate investors.

Under the Urban Homesteading program, HUD gives to municipalities any single-family homes that the government has insured but which the owners have abandoned, reneging on their loans. Rather than let these homes stand empty, the government then turns these houses over to local communities, which in turn sell them to lower-income families for a small amount of money (usually only one dollar). To find out whether your community is participating in the program and whether you qualify, contact your local government officials at the Department of Housing and Urban Development office nearest to you, or: Urban Homesteading Division, Office of Urban Rehabilitation, Community Planning and Development, Department of Housing and Urban Development, 451 7th Street, SW, Room 7168, Washington, DC 20410, 202-755-6880.

In addition to the Urban Homesteading programs, each week HUD publishes, in local newspapers nationwide, a list of houses that have been foreclosed on. These can be great bargains—some have been sold for as little as

$1—but you must act quickly as the houses go quickly. Contact your local HUD office or the office above for further information.

Because of the large number of financial assistance programs offered by HUD, you could be eligible for one or more of them. Listed below are those programs which are specifically aimed at the real estate investor. Remember, HUD has additional programs aimed at the individual homeowner which can also be used by an investor. For more information on individual homeowner programs contact your local HUD office or the office above. Details about each of the programs listed below include: 1) a short interpretation of what the money is given for, 2) the official name of the program, 3) the official number given to the program in the "Catalog of Federal Domestic Assistance," 4) the type of financial assistance available, and 5) the name and address of the main government office responsible for the program:

- **Free Money to Real Estate Investors Who Rent to Elderly or Handicapped**—Interest reduction payments (14.1030), direct payments. Contact: Director, Office of Multifamily Housing Management, Dept. of Housing and Urban Development, Washington, DC 20410, 202-426-3968.

- **Loans to Real Estate Investors Who Want to Improve or Purchase 1-4 Unit Dwellings**—Rehabilitation mortgage (14.108), loan guarantees. Contact: Director, Single Family Development Division, Office of Single Family Housing, Dept. of Housing and Urban Development, Washington, DC 20410, 202-755-6720.

- **Loans to Condominium Developers**—Mortgage insurance: construction or substantial rehabilitation of condominium projects (14.112), loan guarantees. Contact: Insurance Division, Office of Insured Multifamily Housing Development, Dept. of Housing and Urban Development, Washington, DC 20410, 202-755-6223.

- **Loans to Developers of New Coop Apartments**—Mortgage insurance: development of sales-type cooperative projects (14.115), loan guarantees. Contact: Insurance Division, Office of Insured Multifamily Housing, Dept. of Housing and Urban Development, Washington, DC 20410, 202-755-6223.

- **Loans to Investors Who Develop Coop Housing**—Mortgage insurance: investor-sponsored cooperative housing (14.124), loan guarantees. Contact: Insurance Division, Office of Insured Multifamily Housing Development, Dept. of Housing and Urban Development, Washington, DC 20410, 202-755-6223.

- **Loans for Land Developers**—Mortgage insurance: land development (14.125), loans and loan guarantees. Contact: Director, Single Family Development Division, Office of Single Family Housing, Dept. of Housing and Urban Development, Washington, DC 20410, 202-755-6720.

- **Loans to Management-type Coop Housing Projects**—Mortgage insurance: management-type cooperative projects (14.126), loan guarantees. Contact: Insurance Division, Office of Insured Multifamily Housing Development, Dept. of Housing and Urban Development, Washington, DC 20410, 202-755-6223.

- **Loans to Investors in Mobile Home Parks**—Mortgage insurance: manufactured home parks (14.127), loan guarantees. Contact: Insurance Division, Office of Insured Multifamily Housing, Dept. of Housing and Urban Development, Washington, DC 20410, 202-755-6223.

- **Loans to Investors in and Builders of Nursing Homes**—Mortgage insurance: nursing homes, intermediate care facilities and board and care homes (14.129), loan guarantees. Contact: Insurance Division, Office of Insured Multifamily Housing Development, Dept. of Housing and Urban Development, Washington, DC 20412, 202-755-6223.

- **Loans for Investors, Builders, and Developers of Rental Housing**—Mortgage insurance: rental housing (14.134). Contact: Insurance Division, Office of Insured Multifamily Housing Development, Dept. of Housing and Urban Development, Washington, DC 20410, 202-755-6223.

- **Loans for Investors, Builders, and Developers of Rental Housing for Moderate Income Families**—Mortgage insurance: rental housing for moderate income families (14.135). Contact: Insurance Division, Office of Insured Multifamily Housing Development, Dept. of Housing and Urban Development, Washington, DC 20410, 202-755-6223.

- **Loans for Investors, Builders, and Developers of Rental or Coop Housing for Moderate Income Families**—Mortgage insurance: rental and cooperative housing for moderate income families, market interest rate (14.137), loan guarantees. Contact: Insurance Division, Office of Insured Multifamily Housing Development, Dept. of Housing and Urban Development, Washington, DC 20410, 202-426-3968.

- **Loans for Investors, Builders, and Developers of Rental Housing for the Elderly**—Mortgage insurance: rental housing for the elderly (14.138), loan guarantees. Contact: Insurance Division, Office of Insured Multifamily Housing Development, Dept. of Housing and Urban Development, Washington, DC 20410, 202-755-6223.

- **Loans to Investors, Builders, and Developers of Rental Housing in Urban Renewal Areas**—Mortgage insurance: rental housing in urban renewal areas (14.139), loan guarantees. Contact: Insurance Division, Office of Insured Multifamily Housing Development, Dept. of Housing and Urban Development, Washington, DC 20410, 202-755-6223.

■ **Free Money to Investors, Builders, and Developers of Rental Housing for Lower Income Families**—Rent supplements: rental housing for lower income families (14.149). Contact: Management Information Chief, Program Support Branch, Office of Multifamily Housing Management, Dept. of Housing and Urban Development, Washington, DC 20410, 202-755-5654.

■ **Loans to Investors to Improve Rental Apartment Buildings**—Supplemental loan insurance: multifamily rental housing (14.151). Contact: Insurance Division, Office of Insured Multifamily Housing Development, Dept. of Housing and Urban Development, Washington, DC 20411, 202-755-6223.

■ **Loans to Investors to Purchase or Refinance Rental Apartment Buildings**—Mortgage insurance for the purchase or refinancing of existing multifamily housing projects (14.155). Contact: Office of Insured Multifamily Housing Development, Dept. of Housing and Urban Development, Washington, DC 20410, 202-755-6223.

■ **Free Money for Investors in Rental Apartment Buildings Who Are in Financial Trouble**—Operating assistance for troubled multifamily housing projects (14.164), grants and direct payments. Contact: Chief, Program Support Branch, Management Operations Division, Office of Multifamily Housing Management, Dept. of Housing and Urban Development, Washington, DC 20420, 202-755-5654.

■ **Loans for Investors Who Purchase, Repair, or Refinance Rental Apartment Buildings**—Coinsurance for the purchase or refinancing of existing multifamily projects (14.173). Contact: Director, Office of Insured Multifamily Housing Development, Coinsurance Branch, Dept. of Housing and Urban Development, Washington, DC 20410, 202-426-7113.

■ **Loans to Home Builders Who Use Experimental Housing Construction Techniques**—Mortgage insurance: experimental homes (14.507), loan guarantees. Contact: Assistant Secretary for Policy Development and Research, Building Technology Division, Dept. of Housing and Urban Development, Washington, DC 20410, 202-755-6900.

■ **Loans to Investors or Builders in Group Medical Practices or Subdivisions Which Use Experimental Construction Techniques**—Mortgage insurance: experimental projects other than housing (14.508), loan guarantees. Contact: Assistant Secretary for Policy Development and Research, Building Technology Division, Dept. of Housing and Urban Development, Washington, DC 20410, 202-755-6900.

■ **Loans to Investors, Builders, and Developers of Rental Housing Using Experimental Construction Techniques**—Mortgage insurance: experimental rental housing (14.509), loan guarantees. Contact: Assistant Secretary for Policy Development and Research, Building Technology Division, Dept. of Housing and Urban Development, Washington, DC 20410, 202-755-6900.

There are hundreds of free publications available from HUD with general or specific information about individual programs. Contact your regional field office to obtain publications such as the following:

■ *Programs of HUD*—updated periodically, this booklet contains information on HUD programs that help people and communities improve housing standards. It covers community planning and development, public and Indian housing, access to housing for the handicapped, and the Government National Mortgage Association. Free.

■ *GNMA Mortgage-Backed Securities*—intended for investors, the pamphlet summarizes the GNMA mortgage-backed securities programs. Free.

■ *A Guide to Housing Rehabilitation Programs*—this guide gives a summary of property rehabilitation programs that are administered by HUD. It also guides you to the appropriate office for further details and application forms. Free.

■ *Settlement Costs and You—A HUD Guide for Home Buyers*—available at all HUD Regional Area and Service Offices throughout the country, this booklet provides you with information that will take the mystery out of the settlement process so that you can shop for settlement services and make informed decisions. Free.

■ *Home Buying Members of the Armed Services*—discusses how a member of the armed services can finance the purchase of an existing home. Free.

■ *Move In . . . With a Graduated Payment Mortgage (GPM)*—explains this popular HUD program, allowing a reasonable down payment and lower initial monthly payments. Free.

■ *Fact Sheet—Should You Rent or Buy a Home?*—that decision may be influenced by a number of factors. This pamphlet discusses financial conditions and responsibilities of owning a home. Free.

■ *Let's Consider Cooperatives*—cooperative housing programs of the Federal Housing Administration are outlined in this pamphlet. Free.

■ *Questions About Condominiums*—to help potential owners buy wisely, this booklet warns of possible pitfalls of condominium ownership and suggests safeguards for avoiding a potentially poor investment. Free.

■ *Wise Home Buying*—a consumer guide on shopping for a house, this brochure has tips on selecting a new or existing house. Free.

Land Sales—Reports and Complaints
Office of Lender Activities and Land Sales Registration
Department of Housing and Urban Development (HUD)
451 7th Street, SW, Room 6278
Washington, DC 20410   202-755-0502
Did you get cheated in a land purchase? File a complaint with the above office and staff members will investigate your claim. They will also send you a copy of the property report which a developer offering fifty or more unimproved lots must file with HUD. The developer is required to give you this report which describes in detail the facts about the land you are buying. Try to get it from him/her first—but if that fails contact the office above or your local HUD office. HUD will also send you:

> ■ *Buying Land. . . Get the Facts*—written for consumers, this tells you what to watch out for when you buy land. Free.

Local Government Agencies
The are two major local government agencies you should get to know when investing in real estate. At the local county clerk or recorder of deeds office you can find the sale price for any piece of real estate. These data enable you to compare the selling prices of properties similar to that which you are investigating. Also check into the local economic development agency. Regional planners can show you what kinds of developments are anticipated for almost any area of the city. Future developments will certainly have an impact on future real estate values.

Mortgage Bankers Association of America (MBA)
1125 15th Street, NW
Washington, DC 20005   202-861-6500
MBA has more than 2,300 members involved in real estate finance, including mortgage companies, savings and loan associations, savings and commercial banks and life insurance companies. The public relations department will answer your mortgage questions. The Association has a wide variety of publications and correspondence courses, all described in a free catalog available to the public. Examples of publications are:

> ■ *What You Should Know About ARMs*—this booklet gives brief definitions of the various features of ARMs that will help you determine which ARM, if any, is right for you. Cost is forty-five cents.
>
> ■ *Consumer Handbook on Adjustable Rate Mortgages*—a reference guide, prepared by the Federal Reserve Board and the Federal Home Loan Bank Board, this informative brochure helps the consumer make the best mortgage choice. Cost is twenty cents.
>
> ■ *How to Save Half on Mortgage Interest Costs*—a consumers guide to fifteen-year fixed-rate mortgages. The pamphlet costs twenty-two cents.

Mortgage Survey Reports
In many metropolitan areas nationwide, there are companies that survey the most popular types of mortgage programs available in their geographical area and publish their findings in a weekly report that is available to the public. These reports are quite useful as they tell you at a glance who the lenders are and what they offer. It is then up to you to contact the programs of interest to you. Some of these companies also offer a free hotline service you can call to get an area's current average mortgage rate. To find this service in your area, contact the Board of Realtors in the area in which you are buying a home. Ask them if there is a local survey company, and, if one exists, whom you can contact. An example of such a service, and the first of its kind, is:

> Peeke and Associates, Inc.
> 101 Chestnut Street
> Gaithersburg, MD 20877
> 301-840-5752—general information
> 301-231-3777—mortgage hotline

> The company regularly surveys 120 lenders in the Washington, D.C., metropolitan area, fifty lenders in the southern Florida area, and eighty lenders in the Baltimore area. They publish a weekly *Peeke Report* for each of these areas. The easy-to-read report lists mortgage lenders in alphabetical order and provides data on the lenders' four most popular programs. Current information on rates, points and maximum loan amount is given in a chart allowing for easy comparison. The company also offers the mortgage hotline, listed above, which the public is invited to call to get a recording of the latest average mortgage rate for the D.C. metropolitan area. The Peeke report is available for $20 for the first report and $15 for each subsequent issue ordered.

Rural Housing Properties
Farmers Home Administration (FHA)
U.S. Department of Agriculture
14th Street and Independence Avenue, SW
Washington, DC 20250   202-447-7967
This office maintains a listing of reasonably priced rural single-family properties identified for sale by local FHA offices. The current listing includes 8,800 properties acquired through loan default. Eligible areas are rural, open counties with populations of not more than 10,000 and in areas where credit is scarce. Land properties are also available.

Seminar Library
P O Box 8930
Anaheim, CA 92802   800-545-5456

This private membership organization is for those interested in hearing more than one of the hundred or so real estate investment tapes which are currently on the market. Members have free access to all seminar tapes for approximately the same cost as attending *one* seminar. Membership ranges from $295 to $595.

State and Local Housing Departments

Many state and local governments offer low-interest loans and other financial assistance. An example is the state mortgage purchase program offered by many states. The objective of this program is to assist first-time home buyers in purchasing a home. Mortgage rates are available at a thirty-year fixed-rate below current market rate. The maximum purchase price of a home is established by the state and may vary from county to county. To be eligible, applicants must reside in the state and must meet the annual income requirement. For more information, contact your state Community Development Administration or state and local housing department.

U.S. Department of Agriculture

Farmers Home Administration
14th Street and Constitution Avenue, SW, Room 5503 South
Washington, DC 20250   202-447-4323

The U.S. Department of Agriculture maintains a number of financial aid programs for those who wish to live or invest in homes and real estate in rural areas. Listed below are those programs specifically aimed at the real estate investor. Remember, the Department of Agriculture has additional programs aimed at the individual homeowner which can also be used by investors. For more information on individual homeowner programs contact your local Department of Agriculture office or the office above. Details about each of the programs listed below include: 1) a short interpretation of what the money is given for, 2) the official name of the program, 3) the official number given to the program in the *Catalog of Federal Domestic Assistance*, 4) the type of financial assistance available, and 5) the name and address of the main government office responsible for the program:

■ **Money to Farmers and Ranchers for Rehabilitation Due to Erosion, etc.**—Emergency conservation program (10.054), direct payments. Contact: Conservation and Environmental Protection Division, Agricultural Stabilization and Conservation Service, U.S. Dept. of Agriculture, PO Box 2415, Washington, DC 20013, 202-447-6221.

■ **Money for Landowners with Migratory Waterfowl Nesting, Breeding and Feeding Areas**—Water bank program (10.062), direct payments. Contact: Conservation and Environmental Protection Division, Agricultural Stabilization and Conservation Service, U.S. Dept. of Agriculture, PO Box 2415, Washington, DC 20013, 202-447-6221.

■ **Money to Farmers and Ranchers for Pollution Control and Water Conservation**—Agricultural conservation program (10.063), direct payments. Contact: Conservation and Environmental Protection Division, Agricultural Stablization and Conservation Service, U.S. Dept. of Agriculture, PO Box 2415, Washington, DC 20013, 202-447-6221.

■ **Money for Small Forest Land Owners**—Forestry incentives program (10.064), direct payments. Contact: Conservation and Environmental Protection Division, Agricultural Stabilization and Conservation Service, U.S. Dept. of Agriculture, PO Box 2415, Washington, DC 20013, 202-447-6221.

■ **Money to Landowners to Improve Water Quality**—Rural clean water program (10.068), direct payments. Contact: Conservation and Environmental Protection Division, Agricultural Stabilization and Conservation Service, U.S. Dept. of Agriculture, PO Box 2415, Washington, DC 20013, 202-447-6221.

■ **Grants and Loans for Farmers to Build Housing and Recreation Facilities for Employees**—Farm labor housing loans and grants (10.405), grants and loans. Contact: Multi-Family Housing Processing Division, Farmers Home Administration, U.S. Dept. of Agriculture, Washington, DC 20250, 202-382-1604.

■ **Loans to Small Farmers, Resort Operators, and Teenage Entrepreneurs**—Farm operating loans (10.406), loan guarantees. Contact: Director, Farm Real Estate and Production Division, Farmers Home Administration, U.S. Dept. of Agriculture, Washington, DC 20250, 202-447-4572.

■ **Loans to Small Farmers, Ranchers, Forest Businesses, and Resort Operators to Purchase Real Estate**—Farm ownership loans (10.407), loan guarantees. Contact: Administrator, Farmers Home Administration, U.S. Dept. of Agriculture, Washington, DC 20250, 202-382-1474.

■ **Loans to Investors in Rental Housing in Rural Areas**—Rural rental housing loans (10.415), loan guarantees. Contact: Administrator, Farmers Home Administration, U.S. Dept. of Agriculture, Washington, DC 20250, 202-382-1604.

■ **Free Money to Landowners to Prevent Erosion or Improve Recreation**—Great plains conservation (10.900), direct payments. Contact: Deputy Chief for Programs, Soil Conservation Service, U.S. Dept. of Agriculture, PO Box 2890, Washington, DC 20013, 202-447-4527.

VA Guaranteed Home Loans for Veterans
Veterans Administration
941 North Capitol Street, NE
Washington, DC 20421   202-275-1325

Eligible veterans and service personnel may obtain GI loans from private lenders for a home, manufactured home and/or lot, or certain types of condominiums. VA direct loans are available to eligible veterans with permanent and total service-connected disabilities, but only to supplement a grant to acquire a specially adapted home. Your local VA office can provide the specifics regarding eligibility requirements and will send you the following booklet:

- *VA Guaranteed Home Loans for Veterans* (No. 26-4)—a question-and-answer guide, this will help homebuyers understand what the Veterans Administration can and cannot do for the home purchaser. Free.

VA Status Hotline
Veterans Administration (VA)
941 North Capitol Street, NW   202-275-1325
Washington, DC 20421   Hotline 202-275-0690—DC area only

Each VA regional office operates a "status hotline" announcing the status of properties on the VA Resale List. The hotline is a recorded message played twenty-four hours daily. It is updated each workday between 3:30 and 4:00 P.M. While you do not have to be a veteran to obtain a VA Resale home, you do have to get additional information and purchase the property through a broker.

WHAT TO READ

Commerce Clearing House (CCH)
4025 West Peterson Avenue
Chicago, IL 60646   312-583-8500

A publisher of topical law reports, CCH offers the following publications on buying and selling a home. Discounts are given for bulk purchases.

- *Tax Break for Buying and Selling a Home*—a booklet that explains the factors that you should keep in mind in order to take advantage of the tax benefits available on the sale or purchase of residential property. Cost is $2.
- *Tax Benefits for Homeowners*—provides an easy-to-understand review of tax benefits available to homeowners. Cost is $2.

The Common-Sense Mortgage: How to Cut the Cost of Home Ownership by $100,000 or More
by Peter Miller
Harper & Row
Mail Order Department
2350 Virginia Avenue
Hagerstown, MD 21740   301-824-7300
  A complete overview of the real estate financial system through specific concepts and strategies is given in this book. It provides you with information necessary to acquire the best deal. Cost is $16.45 plus $1 postage and handling.

Consumer Handbook on Adjustable Rate Mortgages
Federal Trade Commission
Office of Consumer/Business Education
6th Street and Pennsylvania Avenue, NW, Room B-3
Washington, DC 20580   202-523-3598
  The fundamentals of ARMs are described in this booklet. It is designed to help consumers understand this complex new product available to home buyers. Free.

How I Turned $1,000 into Five Million in Real Estate—In My Spare Time
by William Nickerson
Simon and Schuster
Customer Service
1230 Avenue of the Americas   212-698-7000
New York, NY 10020   800-223-2348
  Nickerson first published this get-rich-quick book in 1959 under the title: *How I Turned $1,000 into a Million in Real Estate;* in 1969 he revised it as: *How I Turned $1,000 into Three Million in Real Estate.* This third edition, published in 1980, continues to be a best seller and is available at virtually every public library. The book offers detailed advice on managing real estate investments, including: buying your first property, improving your property for a profit, managing rental property, obtaining loans, and using tax laws to your advantage. The book costs $19.95 (hardcover) and can be purchased in bookstores or ordered from the toll-free number above.

Internal Revenue Service (IRS)
Contact your local office, or   800-424-FORM
  A variety of publications of interest to real estate investors, including:
  - *Tax Information on Selling Your Home (#523)*
  - *Rental Property (#527)*
  - *Tax Information for Homeowners (#530)*

■ *Depreciation (#534)*
■ *Tax Information on Condominiums and Cooperative Apartments (#588)*

Landlording
Express, Inc.
PO Box 1639
El Cerrito, CA 94530   415-236-5496
This handy book, now in its fourth edition, is a how-to guide for the independent landlord or landlady. The cost is $17.95 plus $2 postage and handling.

The Mortgage and Real Estate Executives Report
Warren, Gorham, and Lamont, Inc.
210 South Street   617-423-2020—in MA
Boston, MA 02111   800-922-0066
Published twice a month, this eight-page report offers a quick inside look at what industry leaders are doing in real estate investments, mortgage finance, and development. Every issue analyzes trends and provides forecasts of key developments in real estate investments, planning, and mortgage lending procedures. Cost is $125 a year.

Mortgage Basics for Home Buyers
Citicorp
Public Affairs Department
Box 0630
New York, NY 10043   212-559-8609
This booklet will direct you step by step through the process of home financing. It explains most of the new mortgage plans and points out significant differences between plans. Free.

Nothing Down
by Robert Allen
Simon and Schuster
Customer Service
1230 Avenue of the Americas   212-698-7000
New York, NY 10020   800-223-2348
As the title implies, this book focuses on the creative financing aspects of purchasing real estate: how to buy without using any of your own money as a down payment, using such tactics as balloon mortgages and wrap-around mortgages. Also discussed are: selling and trading for maximum gain, legal tax cuts, locating bargain properties, and successful negotiation. The 1984 edition is widely available in public libraries and local bookstores. It may be ordered by calling the publisher's toll-free number. Cost is $17.95 (hardcover).

Real Estate Development Report
Phillips Publishing
711 Montrose Road
Potomac, MD 20854   800-722-9000——phone orders
This eight-page monthly newsletter provides advice on technical and legal matters for those who are not real estate pros and do not have a lot of time to manage their real estate investments. Cost is $95 per year.

Reed Publishing
342 Bryan Drive   617-491-6562
Danville, CA 94526   800-544-1016—phone orders
The following publications are available from the above:
- *John Reed's Real Estate Investor's Monthly*—this eight-page monthly newsletter covers new laws, court decisions, interest rates, vacancy rates, fuel prices, insurance premiums, and other factors that change the rules for investing in real estate. Cost is $98 per year.
- *Aggressive Tax Avoidance for Real Estate Investors*—this 280-page book shows how to make sure you aren't paying one cent more in taxes than the law requires. Cost is $21.95.

Straight Talk—Mortgage Policy
Manufacturers' Bank
100 Renaissance Center
Detroit, MI 48243   313-222-4000
This brochure guides potential home buyers to a better understanding of mortgage financing procedures, as well as basic mortgage loan policies. Free.

PEOPLE TO TALK TO

Warren Lasko
Executive Vice President
Mortgage Bankers Association of America (MBA)
1125 15th Street, NW
Washington, DC 20005
Mr. Lasko is responsible for the overall management of MBA including, research, education, and extensive government liaison activities. He has also been associated with the Government National Mortgage Association, the Federal National Mortgage Association, and the Department of Housing and Urban Development. Mr. Lasko is credited with introducing major innovations into the mortgage-backed securities programs that have been widely instituted in the securitization of mortgages throughout the financial community.

Investing in Yourself: Starting and Running Your Own Business or Nonprofit Organization

See also:
How to Find Information on a Company
Industry Information and Market Studies

From free market studies to loans for teenagers to expert advice, there's plenty of help for the budding—or experienced—entrepreneur.

Several associations exist to meet the special needs of home-based businesses and cottage industries. County Extention Service Offices in over 1,000 locations nationwide offer free help to people wanting to start home-based and other types of enterprises.

There are many places you can turn to for aid from the federal government. The Department of Agriculture offers loans of up to $10,000 to teenagers. The Small Business Administration Answer Desk at 800-368-5855 will direct you to a myriad of free services ranging from seminars to technical advice to getting listed in the PASS database designed to match small businesses with large government contractors needing assistance. Even the IRS offers something for the entrepreneur—a one-day workshop to help you figure out record-keeping and other basics you need to know when tax time rolls around. And at the Department of Commerce you'll find an almost endless list of services. Industry experts can advise you about the field you're planning to compete in; the specialists in the Department's International Trade Administration can tell you all about doing business overseas or who your international competitors are; overseas trade missions can be arranged; you can get temporary office space and translating services while abroad; and the Department's Census Bureau can give you manufacturing reports and all kinds of data helpful to the market researcher. Commerce's free publication *Business Services Directory* will tell you all about what's available. Or you can call Commerce's Roadmap Program for guidance. If you're doing business overseas, you'll want to get in touch with the State Department to get free country background reports. The Overseas Private Investment Corporation, reachable toll-free, can also help you do business abroad.

The most important organizations listed are the state sources. More is going on here than at the federal level because states as a group are experiencing a surplus, while the federal government has one of the largest deficits in history. State governments, realizing that the key to economic growth is in the growth of small businesses, are responsible for most of the new jobs created in our country. This means opportunities for would-be entrepreneurs. Not only can you get grants, loans, and loan guarantees to help start your business, but many states also provide such services as: finding you a friendly banker who will keep you afloat, hooking you up with a free consulting firm that will prepare your business plan, or getting you involved in one of the country's hottest new idea-incubators. Incubator programs will help you find money to start or expand your business. They can provide office space, equipment, and technical expertise and will then watch over you like a mother hen to make sure you make it. So whether you are a typist wanting to start your own word-processing company, a grandmother wanting to start a chocolate factory, or an inventor with an idea for the next Apple computer, your best starting place is likely to be one of the state sources listed below.

AGENCIES, INSTITUTES, AND ORGANIZATIONS

American Entrepreneur Association
2311 Pontius Avenue
Los Angeles, CA 90064   213-479-3987

This association is geared toward both individuals who are in the planning phase of starting a business and those who have actually undertaken an enterprise. It has published more than 200 manuals to assist people in setting up a business. The Association also sponsors a telephone network of business counselors who will provide members with advice about and referrals to literature, organizations, or people. Subscription to the following magazine entitles you to membership privileges.

> ■ *Entrepreneur Magazine*—a monthly publication aimed at those interested in going into business for themselves, each issue contains a detailed article about setting up a specific business, as well as feature stories on successful entrepreneurs. There is coverage of operating techniques, such as "How to Get the Best Advertising," "Designing a Brochure," and "Accumulating Venture Capital." Each January, the magazine reports its "Franchise 500," a summary analysis of the top 500 franchises available. The annual subscription rate is $24.50.

Center for Entrepreneurial Management (CEM)
83 Spring Street
New York, NY 10012   212-925-7304

CEM, a nonprofit educational and membership association for entrepreneurial managers, provides information for small growing businesses. Special in-depth reports are prepared by CEM on specific topics such as venture capital. Among CEM's publications are: -

- *The Entrepreneurial Manager's Newsletter*—a twelve-page monthly source of information for those who advise entrepreneurial managers and professionals. The subscription price is $71 for nonmembers and free to members.
- *How to Prepare and Present a Business Plan*—this 300-page guide by Joseph Mancuso describes writing a business plan that will attract venture capital investors. It includes sample business plans, and costs $20.

Future Homemakers of America (FHA)
1910 Association Drive
Reston, VA 22091   703-476-4900
A nationwide association, with chapters in many high schools, for teens interested in home economics, leadership skills, career planning, and community service, the Future Homemakers of America publishes:

- *Unique Boutiques*—focuses on teen entrepreneurs who share their successful ideas on starting and running a business. Cost is $1.50.
- *Dough Art to Dollars*—a four-page step-by-step guide to making dough art, plus a feature on a teenager who started her own business selling her dough art creations. Cost is $1.
- *Guide to Student Fundraising: 129 Ways to Raise Money*—This eighty-page paperback book, with illustrations and photos, is a helpful handbook for community leaders and teens. It includes sections on: Why Raise Money?; Selecting and Planning a Fundraiser; Promoting the Fundraiser, and other tips. Cost is $9.95.

  Please note: $5 minimum order.

Internal Revenue Service (IRS)
U.S. Department of Treasury
1111 Constitution Avenue, NW
Washington, DC 20274   202-566-4024
Most IRS offices nationwide conduct one-day workshops for taxpayers who own businesses or want to start one. You can learn about all aspects of federal taxes that pertain to business, including Social Security taxes and unemployment. Contact your local IRS office. Two publications and a film particularly helpful to small business owners are described below:

- *Record Keeping for a Small Business (Publication 583)*—this 176-page book covers such subjects as setting up a tax records system, determining net income, tax credits, and business assets. Free.
- *Tax Guide for Small Business (Publication 334)*—this guide explains how to file forms and compute the taxes for a small business. Free.
- *Hey, We're In Business*—this instructional film, prepared by the IRS, stresses the free assistance available to small businesses in areas such as good record keeping, obligations to employees, and expenses and depreciation. This film, and others, are loaned free of charge.

■ ■

Your Own Business and Real Estate Are the Best Ways to Get Rich

Nearly 60 percent of those answering a *Money* magazine poll felt that working hard is the best way to get rich in America today. (Too bad the poll didn't ask for a definition of working hard.) If working hard isn't your cup of tea, the next two choices were investing in real estate and owning your own business.

■ ■

National Alliance of Home-based Businesswomen
PO Box 306
Midland Park, NJ 07432   201-423-1026
    Seeking to stimulate professionalism and economic growth for women (and men) who operate businesses from home, the alliance serves as a forum for the exchange of information and maintains a network of contacts. It also publicizes members' goods and services in its quarterly newsletter, *Alliance*.

National Association for the Cottage Industry (NACI)
PO Box 14460
Chicago, IL 60614   312-472-8116
    Membership in this association consists of people who work at home or have flexible worksites. An example of a flexible worksite is the home use of a computer connected to a main system. The NACI's purposes are to provide information on marketing, promotion, and financing, to promote legislation helpful to home-based workers, and to develop solutions to their unique problems. Two newletters are published by the Association: *Cottage Connection* and *Mind Your Own Business at Home.* Send a self-addressed, stamped envelope to obtain more information.

National Association of Home Based Businesses
PO Box 30220
Baltimore, MD 21270   301-466-8070
    Established to provide support services and professional consulting to home-based business owners, the Association maintains a staff of lawyers, CPAs, marketing experts, and others who can assist the entrepreneur. Services include business profiles and four business expositions a year. The *Home Based Business Directory* for each state serves as a yellow pages for the products and services of the membership. Affiliate membership, for those whose business is

in the preparation stages, is $3 monthly with a $45 one-time-only registration fee; full membership is $4 monthly with a $125 one-time-only registration fee.

The following quarterly is published either as a newsletter or newspaper, depending upon the size of the local chapter:

- *Home Based Business Quarterly*—in addition to news on chapter activities, this publication features advertisements by larger companies that provide the home-based business with services such as computers, secretarial help, incubators, and shared office space. Free to members.

National Federation of Independent Business

600 Maryland Avenue, SW, Suite 700
Washington, DC 20024   202-554-9000

Approximately half a million small-business owners belong to this federation,which represents members' interests before the federal government and keeps them advised of regulatory activities that affect them. The Federation has offices in all fifty states, each offering business owners counseling and referral services. Some of the state offices provide medical insurance programs, and NFIB plans to expand this to other states. There is no set membership fee. Contact the office nearest you or get a referral from the address above. The Federation offers a vast number of publications to assist the small business entrepreneur, including the following:

- *Business Edge*—the Federation's newsletter, published six times annually, informs members of its lobbying efforts and keeps them abreast of the latest legislative developments. Helpful how-to articles are often featured. Free to members.
- *Quarterly Economic Report*—soon to be a monthly, this report is a barometer of small-business development and it forecasts the outlook of the economy as a whole. Economists and researchers consider it very accurate. Free to members.
- *Small Business in America*—this 11-inch-by-34-inch poster includes graphs and illustrative information about small business in America. Free to members.
- *A Century of Entrepreneurs*—another poster, which provides short biographies about six successful twentieth-century entrepreneurs. Free to members.

National Coalition for Science and Technology

2000 P Street, NW, Suite 305
Washington, DC 20036   202-833-2326

This lobbying organization is a nonprofit, nonpartisan association of scientists, engineers, educators, professional societies, universities, R & D intensive companies, and state governments. The objective of the NCST is to generate federal policies and funds needed to support research and development in the sciences. The organization publishes a newsletter, *NCST News*. Individual memberships range from $35 to $1,500 per year; institutional memberships range from $250 to $15,000.

Small Business Development Centers (SBDC) Program
U.S. Small Business Administration
1441 L Street, NW, Room 317
Washington, DC 20416   202-653-6768
There are approximately 300 SBDCs around the country to help new and growing small businesses with management and technical problems. They can help you prepare a business plan, identify venture capital, produce a market study, sell overseas, or get a loan. They are normally operated through colleges and universities and most of the services are free; 50 percent of SBDC financing comes from the Small Business Administration and 50 percent from state and local sources. The easiest way to identify an office near you is to contact your local Small Business Administraiton Office (SBA) or call the SBA Answer Desk at 800-368-5855.

U.S. Department of Agriculture (USDA)
Office of Information, Room 402A
Washington, DC 20250   202-447-8005
The USDA is responsible for approximately twenty-nine money programs which entrepreneurs can use to start or expand a business. Although most programs are for farm or ranch-related operations, some, like the Business and Industrial Loan Program can be used to start almost any kind of business as long as it is in a town of fewer than 50,000 people. They also have a unique program available through the Production Loan Division, which gives youngsters aged between ten and twenty-one up to $10,000 to start their own business.

Loans from this program can be used to support both farm and nonfarm ventures, such as small crop farming, roadside stands, custom work, and lawn mower service businesses. These loans are normally made through youth groups. For information contact the Production Loan Division, Farmers Home Administration, U.S. Department of Agriculture, Washington, DC 20250, 202-447-4572.

USDA staff economists can supply information on a wide variety of agricultural subjects. They are knowledgeable on all aspects of the distribution chain, from producer to end user, and are a good marketing information resource. You can contact them by phone or mail at the above address.

More help, courtesy of the Department of Agriculture, is available through the County Cooperative Extension Services, which operate in 3,165 counties nationwide and in the territories. The Extension Services provide education and information on a myriad of subjects and are especially helpful when you want to establish a home-based business. Assistance is free by phone, by mail, or in person. Check your phone directory under county government or contact

USDA/ES, Room 340A Administration Building, Washington, DC 20250, 202-447-4111.

U.S. Department of Commerce
Office of Business Liaison
Washington, DC 20230   202-377-3176
This department offers myriad services useful to business people. For a detailed listing, contact the above office for their free business service directory. A few of these services are described below.

ROADMAP PROGRAM—this is an excellent place to begin a search for federal assistance to help start a business. In addition to directing you through the government maze, staff can provide information, contacts, reports, and referrals to other sources of help. Contact the program at the address above.

OFFICE OF PRODUCTIVITY, TECHNOLOGY & INNOVATION (OPTI)—OPTI reviews issues of industrial innovation and productivity enhancement in the private sector. It provides a variety of information services to the private sector and to state and local governments. Its Small Business Technology Liaison Division provides information about the innovation process, resources available, and a financial sensitivity model available for purchase. It links small firms, state and local governments, and other organizations involved in innovation, and provides federal policy input on smaller firms and technology. This division also produces the *Guide to Innovation Resources and Planning for the Smaller Business,* which is described separately later in this section.

OPTI's industrial technology partnership program provides information and training on the Research and Development Limited Partnership (RDLP), which is a financing mechanism; prepares feasibility packages to identify high-technology projects suitable for RDLPs; assists in the establishment of cooperative research and development projects; and provides federal policy input on research and development tax policy.

OPTI's Productivity Center answers productivity inquiries with free publications. Its staff can provide you with bibliographies, reading lists, and articles, and refer you to other sources. The telephone number is 202-377-1093.

INDUSTRY ANALYST—the Commerce Department experts themselves are a smorgasbord of marketing research information. The Bureau of Industrial Economics maintains a staff of a hundred analysts who monitor specific industries. They are a terrific resource for research into any industry or product. You can call 202-377-1405 and ask to speak to the expert who specializes in your field, or write to them at the Bureau, Room 4878, Department of Commerce.

CENSUS DATA—the Bureau of the Census also maintains a staff of experts who can tell you what census data is available in their subject areas. They can be contacted by telephone at 301-763-1580 or by writing the Bureau at the

Department of Commerce. Much of the data collected by Census is available in publications and machine-readable format. Contact the Census Data User Services Division by mail or call 301-763-4100.

DATABASES—the Commerce Department maintains several databases which help small businesses. Searches and printouts are available, providing characteristics on 27,000 minority businesses and providing access to one million government research titles from the National technicial Information Service. The fees vary. The telephone number for the minority database is 203-377-2414; for the NTIS database, call 703-487-4640.

LIBRARY REFERENCE SERVICE—the U.S. Department of Commerce Library has a free reference service that will answer quick questions about commerce and business. Services it will perform include consulting standard business reference books for company information and supplying foreign telephone numbers listed in its collection of overseas telephone books. Call or write: Library, Department of Commerce, Washington, D.C. 20230/202-377-2161.

PUBLICATIONS—unless noted otherwise, the following publications are available from the National Technical Information Service, 5258 Port Royal Road, Springfield, Virginia 22161/703-487-4650:

- *Directory of Federal Technology Resources*—this publication describes one hundred federal laboratories, agencies, information centers, and engineering centers willing to share expertise, equipment, and services. The 150-page directory costs $25.
- *Guide to Innovation Resources Planning for the Smaller Business*—more than fifty federal and eighty-five state government offices that assist smaller businesses are identified in this guide, which has two basic sections. The first examines the many steps in the innovation process and the skills and resources needed. The second section identifies a wide range of resources (federal, state, and private) available to assist the smaller business in areas such as financing, information gathering, and management. The capabilities of these resources are summarized, and contact phone numbers and addresses are provided. Each resource has been identified by the stage of the innovation process to which it applies. The eighty-five-page publication costs $13.50.
- *State Technical Assistance Centers and Federal Technical Information Centers Available to U.S. Businesses* (PR-767)—nearly 200 centers across the U.S. which offer direct technical assistance to technology-oriented businesses are listed in this booklet. In many states, these centers also serve as a link to state programs and services providing financial, management, and innovation assistance programs designed to help companies become more competitive. Free.

- *U.S. Industrial Outlook*—published each January, this book provides an overview and prospectus for more than 300 U.S. industries. The book gives the name, telephone number, and address of an expert for nearly every industry in the country. These specialists can tell you about the latest developments in the field and refer you to other experts and literature. The 1,000-page book costs $14 and is available from: Superintendent of Documents, U.S. Government Printing Office, Washington, DC 20402/202-783-3238.

U.S. Department of Housing and Urban Development
See listing under REAL ESTATE.

U.S. Small Business Administration
1441 L Street, NW
Washington, DC 20416   800-368-5855
   With more than a hundred regional/local offices nationwide, the Small Business Administration (SBA) offers assistance to anyone wanting to start a business. Training programs and courses, available through the regional offices, cover financial and legal aspects of starting a business, marketing strategies, and follow-up programs. A few of SBA's services are described below.

   LOANS AND LOAN GUARANTEES—if you don't believe that the SBA is providing loans to small businesses, ask to see their annual report and you will see that last year they provided over 20,000 new and small businesses with financial assistance. The major financial programs include: Loans for Small Business, Physical Disaster Loans, Loans to Small Business Investment Companies, Handicapped Assistance Loans, Small Business Energy Loans, and Veterans Loans.

   OFFICE OF PRIVATE SECTOR INITIATIVES (OPSI)—the Office of Private Sector Initiatives follows state and local activities regarding business incubators. Staff can provide you with information about legislative activities in this area. The office sponsors conferences and educational programs on developing and managing successful incubator facilities. Technical assistance is available to communities and organizations sponsoring small business incubator projects. Through SBA's the Office of Advocacy and Local Affairs you can get current information on state and legislative initiatives to promote small business incubators. Contact SBA at above address or call OPSI at 202-634-9841.

   SCORE AND ACE—the Service Corps of Retired Executives (SCORE) and the Active Corps of Executives (ACE) are two groups of volunteers that offer management counseling to small business owners. A volunteer's expertise is matched to the needs of your business; individual analysis and advice is offered at no charge. Contact the Office of Management Counseling Services, SCORE, or ACE at the above address.

SMALL BUSINESS INSTITUTE PROGRAM—in this SBA program, seniors and graduate students from the nation's leading business schools provide on-site counseling to small business owners and fledgling entrepreneurs at no cost. There are hundreds of locations nationwide. Call the SBA toll-free number for information.

TECHNOLOGY ASSISTANCE PROGRAM—the Small Business Administration's Office of Innovation, Research, and Technology, in cooperation with the University of Connecticut and the University of Southern California, will provide a fast-reaction technology information service for small businesses interested in participating in the Small Business Innovation Research (SBIR) Program. The service provides, within five days, state-of-the-art information useful in preparing SBIR proposals or in guiding SBIR research efforts. The output is a comprehensive bibliography (often with abstracts) derived from a computerized search of a wide variety of databases. The cost of this service to small businesses is $125 an inquiry. SBA provides supplemental funding to offset actual costs which are significantly higher. Documents can also be ordered for an additional fee and can typically be delivered within three weeks. To obtain this service or additional information, contact one of the following university-based centers:

> University of Southern California
> Western Research Applications Center (WESRAC)
> 3716 South Hope Street, #200
> Los Angeles, CA 90007
> 213-743-6132
> The University of Southern California provides service for small firms in the states of Alaska, Arizona, California, Colorado, Hawaii, Idaho, Montana, Nevada, North Dakota, Oregon, South Dakota, Utah, Washington, and Wyoming.

> University of Connecticut
> New England Research Application Center (NERAC)
> Mansfield Professional Park
> Storrs, CT 06268
> 203-486-4586
> For all states not served by WESRAC.

PUBLICATIONS—the SBA's publications include management aids, starting-out series, and small business bibliographies geared to all types of businesses. For a list, call the toll-free number. The following are a few worth writing for:

■ *Business Loans from the SBA*—describes the business loans, eligibility, credit requirements, terms of loans, and collateral. It also outlines how to apply for a loan. Free.

■ *Women's Handbook: How SBA Can Help You Go Into Business*—explains the services offered by SBA to women starting new businesses. It also provides general guidelines for women thinking of going into business on their own. Free.

■ *Can You Make Money With Your Idea or Invention?*—tells you how to identify an idea that has some value and what to do to exploit its fullest potential. Free.

■ *Ideas Into Dollars*—a twenty-four-page booklet, this can act as a companion piece to *Can You Make Money With Your Idea or Invention?* It describes a variety of government and private organizations and programs that can help ensure that a good idea turns into a success. Free.

■ *Incubator Times*—a quarterly newsletter, this will keep you up to date about incubator programs, literature, conferences and more.

■ *Checklist for Going Into Business/Thinking About Going Into Business*—this pamphlet tells you what you will need to know about the many aspects of small business: taxes, pricing, the market, finances, and where to get help. Free.

■ *Starting and Managing* series publications—this series is designed to help the small entrepreneur start a business. *Starting and Managing a Small Business of Your Own* deals with the subject in general terms. Each of the other volumes deals with one type of business in detail. The general booklet is available for $3.50.

■ *Small Business Incubators*—a resource summary prepared in cooperation with the National Council for Urban Economic Development. This eight-page publication includes an overview of what an incubator is and how it functions. It also provides a list of SBA publications relating to incubators as well as relevant publications produced by other organizations. A contact list of people and organizations that supply information is also included. Free.

■ *Starting a Small Business Incubator*—a sixty-page handbook for sponsors and developers. The majority of the text concerns state programs available to businesses in Illinois. The book describes the role and characteristics of an incubator and the steps of development, including where to get help in starting and managing an incubator. Free.

■ *Small Business Bibliographies*—presents detailed, selected information on managing specific businesses or on management functions or subfunctions. The bibliographies instruct the small business owner or manager in such activities as marketing, personnel, new product development, and innovation management.

Women's Economic Development Center
60 East 42nd Street
New York, NY 10165   800-222-2933
    Call the toll-free number above for information, referrals and low-cost
consulting services. Although the Center itself is not a source of funding, it can
refer you to sources that do provide funding. And for a nominal fee ranging
from $5 to $25, you can phone an expert for help with start-up procedures
and problems.

WHAT TO READ

Catalogue of Federal Domestic Assistance Programs
Superintendent of Documents
U.S. Government Printing Office
Washington, DC 20402   202-783-3238
    This publication describes all federally funded domestic assistance pro-
grams. These include seven financial types (e.g. formula grants, project grants,
and direct loans), as well as eight nonfinancial types. The *Catalogue* contains
program descriptions, appendices, and indices, as well as information about
application procedures, eligibility of applicants, and forms required to apply for
assistance. The 1,000-page publication is published annually in May, with a
supplement in December. The latter covers new programs and changes to
programs. Check for it at major public libraries, or at the office of your member
of Congress. The cost is $30.

Coopers & Lybrand
1800 M Street, NW
Washington, DC 20036   202-822-4000
    Coopers & Lybrand, a large accounting firm with offices in major U.S.
cities and abroad, offers a variety of good, free publications. Examples are:
        ■ *Three-Way Budget: A Businessman's Guide to Cash Control,* by James
        F. Lafond, Walter F. Maischoss and High R. Tidby—this 1982 booklet
        describes a basic cash control program for owner-managers, focusing on
        how a budget is used to monitor performance, evaluating the need for
        change and providing data required for seeking bank loans. Also included
        are step-by-step instructions for preparing a budget.
        ■ *Profit Improvement Opportunities for Retailers 1*—these question-
        naires, published in 1980, focus on five key areas that have a direct impact
        on profits—buying and merchandising; receiving, checking and marking
        merchandise; sales promotion and advertising; retail selling activities and
        nonselling activities. Included are checklists for evaluating current systems
        and controlling shortages in inventory.

■ *Profit Improvement Opportunities for Retailers 2*—this 1980 monograph, the second in the set, contains questionnaires for retailers to use in reviewing cash management, insurance, taxes, procedures for purchasing supplies, freight and traffic.

■ *A Guide to Purchase Order Management*—this 1979 brochure by Robert M. Zimmerman offers guidelines on the four major functions of a purchase order system: purchase order processing; receiving, checking, and marking; distribution; and invoice processing.

■ *Retail Accounting and Financial Control*—this unique and comprehensive book by Louis C. Moscarello, Francis C. Grau and Roy C. Chapman (1976) adapts sound accounting theory and practice to the distinctive techniques, procedures, and problems of retailing establishments. Included are many case examples, forms, formulas, and schedules that enhance the book's usefulness as a working manual as well as a guide to policy, planning and operating decisions.

■ *The Entrepreneur's Starter Kit*—this is a two-part compendium (1984) of advice, reminders, and references for the business person managing a growing business. Volume 1, *Performance Workbook,* deals with the three major stages of business development: preparing to launch an enterprise, startup, and growth and maturity. Volume 2, *Facts and Forms,* covers the use of various business forms and federal tax forms, and recommends other Coopers & Lybrand publications of interest to the entrepreneur.

■ *Profit Improvement Opportunities: Checklists for Emerging Businesses*—provided in this Coopers & Lybrand newsletter reprint (1979) are tactics keyed to accelerating cash receipts and delaying cash disbursements; a survey of daily income funds using short-term instruments; profit improvement management techniques and a questionnaire for evaluating your business. (June 1979).

■ *Management in a Period of Uncertainty*—this do-it-yourself questionnaire assesses the effects of combined inflation/recession on small and medium-sized businesses and measuring their ability to cope.

■ *1984 Guide to ERISA Reporting and Disclosure Requirements*—this is a brochure (1984) containing guidelines, in chart form, on ERISA reporting and disclosure requirements for pension, profit-sharing, and welfare plans. Plan sponsors, plan administrators, plan trustees, and attorneys are given guidelines on which forms to file, where to file, who must file, and the due dates.

■ *Business Planning in the Eighties: The New Competitiveness of American Corporations,* Coopers & Lybrand/Yankelovich, Skelly and White, Inc.—this 1983 pamphlet includes an in-depth study of the corporate planning function: what it means to most organizations today, and how it is likely to change in the future.

■ *Collaborative Ventures: A Pragmatic Approach to Business Expansion
in the Eighties,* Coopers & Lybrand/Yankelovich, Skelly and White, Inc.—
this 1984 brochure discusses the results of an in-depth study of collaborative ventures, based on forty-four personal interviews with senior managers
who have had recent first hand experience in forming collaborative ventures.

■ *Profit Improvement Opportunities: Checklists for Emerging Businesses*—a Coopers & Lybrand newsletter reprint (1979), this provides
tactics keyed to accelerating cash receipts and delaying cash disbursements; a survey of daily income funds using short-term instruments; profit
improvement management techniques; and a questionnaire for evaluating
your business.

■ *Choosing or Changing the Business Form*—this 1984 monograph compares the three forms of business organization—regular corporations, S
corporations, and partnerships—and analyzes the advantages and disadvantages of each.

Dun & Bradstreet
99 Church Street
New York, NY 10007   212-285-7841

Dun & Bradstreet has eighty regional offices located throughout the
United States, and offers services geared to wholesalers and manufacturers.
Contact the office in your region for the following brochures:

■ *Pitfalls in Managing a Small Business*—this twenty-two-page booklet
by W. H. Kuehn outlines the major pitfalls encountered in managing
a small business, and suggests ways they can be avoided. Single copies
free.

■ *How to Control Accounts Receivables for Greater Profits*—a concise,
practical discussion with case histories of the function, control, and effective collection of receivables. Single copies are free.

■ *The Failure Record*—this provides a concise but comprehensive analysis
of business failures and their causes. Single copies are free.

■ *Reports & Reference Books*—described are the elements comprising a
Dun & Bradstreet Business Information Report and how to use the reference book in your business for greater profits. Free.

■ *Cost of Doing Business—Corporations*—this delineates the cost of
goods sold, gross margins, and selecting operating ratios for 185 lines of
business, based on a sample of federal income tax returns. Single copies
are free.

■ *Cost of Doing Business—Partnerships & Proprietorships*—includes selected profit and operating expense ratios for 120 lines of business, based
on federal income tax returns. Write to the Communication Department. The above listing is available only for college use. Single copies are
free.

The Enterprise Kit
Chamber of Commerce of the United States
Special Projects Division
1615 H Street, NW
Washington, DC 20062   202-659-6000
  The *Kit* is a complete reference folder containing illustrated catalogs and brochures which describe award-winning motion pictures, videotapes, slide presentations, and booklets available from the U.S. Chamber of Commerce on the subject of free enterprise. Single copies free (quantity shipments can be arranged for teacher workshops and conferences).

Getting Yours
Viking Penguin, Inc.
40 West 23rd Street
New York, NY 10010
  A condensed version of the *Catalogue of Federal Domestic Assistance* described earlier in this section, this book provides a capsule description of funding opportunities available from the federal government. The new edition also contains information on state assistance programs that offer grants, loans, scholarships, and other assistance for many endeavors. Directed toward the general public, it gives examples of people and projects that have received funding as well as advice about how to select programs that would be most receptive to your idea. The book, which is updated periodically, is available from most bookstores for $8.95.

Inc.
Inc. Publishing Corporation
38 Commercial Wharf
Boston, MA 02110   617-227-4700
  Inc. magazine is a monthly publication that provides information about trends, investment companies, capital, and company profiles. Sometimes special features relate to venture capital. Annual subscription to the 150- to 200-page publication is $24.

Success
342 Madison Avenue, 21st floor
New York, NY 10173   212-503-0700
  Published ten times a year, this magazine provides innovative ideas for selling, managing, and entrepreneuring. Annual subscriptions are $14.95.

Franchising

One of the safer ways to start a new business is by purchasing a franchise. Franchises have a significantly lower failure rate than other new enterprises because most franchise arrangements include the buiness experience and expertise normally lacking in new business owners. The following organizations and publications will help you find the right franchise for you.

AGENCIES, INSTITUTES, AND ORGANIZATIONS

Federal Trade Commission
Bureau of Consumer Protection
Division of Enforcement   202-376-2805—John M. Tifford,
Pennsylvania Avenue at 6th Street, NW   Franchise Program Adviser
Washington, DC 20580   202-376-2893—Neil J. Blickman, Esq.

The Federal Trade Commission enforces federal laws pertaining to business franchising. The Bureau of Consumer Protection publishes several free papers and guides designed to aid franchisers and franchisees to comply with federal regulations, including an explanation of the FTC disclosure rule. These publications include:

- *Franchise and Business Opportunities*—a four-page guide to things to consider before buying a franchise.
- *The Franchise Rule: Questions and Answers*—a one-page summary of the disclosure rule and penalties for infractions by the franchiser.
- *Franchise Rule Summary*—a seven-page, detailed technical explanation of the federal disclosure rule, which requires franchisers to furnish a document (with information on twenty topics) to the potential franchisee before a sale. This includes an explanation and description of the Uniform Franchise Offering Circular (UFOC) required in fourteen states.

International Franchise Association
1350 New York Avenue, NW   202-628-8000—Peter Fisher,
Washington, DC 20005   Director of Information Services

Founded in 1960, the International Franchise Association (IFA) has more than 600 franchiser members, including thirty-five overseas. IFA members are accepted into the organization only after meeting stringent requirements regarding number of franchises, length of time in business, and financial stability. The IFA offers about twenty-five educational conferences and seminars yearly, including an annual convention and a legal symposium. There is a program on financing and venture capital which is designed to bring together franchisers and franchisees. Each year the association also sponsors several trade shows, open to the public, so that franchisers may attract potential franchisees. There is a library, but as yet no database, for members. Peter Fisher, Director of Information Services, will answer inquiries from the public and make referrals for speakers, courses, and resources on franchising. The IFA also publishes:

- *Investigate Before Investing*—a thirty-two-page booklet offering tips on evaluating a franchise. Cost is $3.
- *Answers to the 21 Most Commonly Asked Questions About Franchising*—informative pamphlet for newcomers to the field. Cost is $1.
- *How to be a Franchisor*—step-by-step details on how to launch a franchise, including details on legal and operational procedures. Cost is $5.95.
- *Is Franchising for You?*—a self-evaluation guide for potential franchisers. Cost is $3.95.
- *FTC Franchising Rule: The IFA Compliance Kit*—a kit in a three-ring binder, with updates on all advisory opinions issued by FTC, this publication provides an overview of disclosure requirements, together with checklists and comparisons. Cost is $80.
- *U.F.O.C. Guidelines*—instructions for completing the Uniform Franchise Offering Circular, this was prepared by the Midwest Securities Commissioners Association for use by franchisors in meeting state and federal disclosure requirements. Cost is $10.
- *Directory of Membership*—listings of all IFA members. Cost is $3.95.

U.S. Department of Commerce
International Trade Administration
14th Street and Constitution Avenue, NW
Washington, DC 20230   202-377-0342

This office provides comprehensive information of interest to franchisers and franchisees. It has published the following guidebooks, which may be ordered from the U.S. Government Printing Office, Superintendent of Documents, Washington, DC 20402:

- *Franchise Opportunities Handbook*—a bible of franchising information, this 390-page directory includes detailed listings of 1,265 companies, facts about the franchising industry, guidance for investing in a franchise, resource listings of helpful agencies and organizations, and a bibliography. Cost is $13.50; it is available from U.S. Government Printing Office, Superintendent of Documents, Washington, DC 20402, 202-783-3238.
- *Franchising in the Economy—1983-85*—a detailed ninety-three-page survey, with numerous charts and statistics on the international growth of franchising. Includes information on types of franchise companies, minority enterprises, and sales figures for retail and service firms. Cost is $4.50.

EXPERTS

Brian Bond
Business Development Office
U.S. Small Business Administration
1441 L Street, NW
Washington, DC 20005   202-653-6881
    Coordinator of a coalition between the International Franchising Association (IFA) and the Small Business Administration (SBA), Mr. Bond is available to answer questions and provide assistance to regional offices of the SBA. He is currently developing training materials and seminars, as well as a database system for regional/district officess, such as the one now in use in the Chicago area.

Andrew Kostecka
Commodity Industry Specialist
Office of Service Industries
International Trade Administration
U.S. Department of Commerce
14th Street and Constitution Avenue, NW
Washington, DC 20230   202-377-0342
    The federal government's leading expert on franchising, Mr. Kostecka is the compiler of the annual *Franchise Opportunities Handbook*. He can guide potential franchisers to reputable consulting firms and can provide assistance and referrals to resources for franchisees. He is a frequent speaker at franchise seminars, trade and business association conferences, and educational seminars throughout the world.

Patents, Trademarks, and Copyrights

    Protecting your invention, copyrighting your work, and obtaining a patent or trademark are often necessary parts of doing business. Described below are the major sources you can consult when you need information about any of these procedures.

AGENCIES, INSTITUTES, AND ORGANIZATIONS

Disclosure Statement
Commissioner of Patents and Trademarks
Patent and Trademark Office
Department of Commerce
Washington, DC 20231   703-557-3225

You can protect your idea or invention for up to two years by officially recording evidence of the date you conceived your invention. You can do this by filing a "Disclosure Statement," which will be kept in confidence by the Patent and Trademark Office. The cost is $10, and it is a much simpler process than applying for a patent.

Library of Congress
Copyright Office, Room 401
Washington, DC 20540   202-287-6840
The Library of Congress provides information on copyright registration procedures and copyright card catalogs which cover 16 million works that have been registered since 1870. The Copyright Office will research the copyright you need and send you the information by mail. Requests must be in writing and you must specify exactly what it is you need to know. Contact the Copyright Office, Reference & Bibliographic Section, Library of Congress, Washington, DC 20559, 202-387-8700.

Subscriptions to the following Library of Congress catalogs are available from the Superintendent of Documents, Government Printing Office, Washington, DC 20402. Each lists material registered since the last issue was published.
- *Part 1: Nondramatic Literary Works*—this quarterly costs $30 a year.
- *Part 2: Serials and Periodicals*—this semiannual costs $6.50 a year.
- *Part 3: Performing Arts*—this quarterly costs $27 a year.
- *Part 4: Motion Pictures and Filmstrips*—this semiannual costs $7 a year.
- *Part 5: Visual Arts*—this semiannual does not include maps and costs $10 a year.
- *Part 6: Maps*—this semiannual costs $4.75 a year.
- *Part 7: Sound Recordings*—this semiannual costs $14 a year.
- *Part 8: Renewal*—this semiannual costs $8 a year.

Patent and Trademark Office (PTO)
U.S. Department of Commerce
2021 Jefferson Davis Highway   703-557-5168
Crystal Plaza   703-557-2276—patent search
Arlington, VA 22202   703-557-3881—trademark search
United States patent and trademark laws are administered by PTO. The Office examines patent and trademark applications, grants protection for qualified inventions, and registers trademarks. It also collects, assembles, and disseminates the technological information disclosed on patent grants.

The PTO maintains a collection of more than 4 million United States patents issued to date, several million foreign patents, and 1.2 million trademarks, together with supporting documentation. You can visit the office to research a trademark. If that's not possible, PTO will recommend someone you can hire to do the search for you.

Facilitating public access to the more than 25 million United States patents is the job of PTO's Office of Technology Assessment and Forecast (OTAF). It has a master database which covers all United States patents, and searches are available for a fee. OTAF extracts information from its database and makes it available in a variety of formats, including publications, custom patent reports, and statistical reports.

Copies of the specifications and drawings of all patents are available from PTO. Design patents, trademark copies, and plant patents not in color are $1 each; plant patents in color are $8 each. For copies contact Patent and Trademark Office, Department of Commerce, PO Box 9, Washington, DC 20231, 202-377-2540.

Patent Depository Libraries
Patent and Trademark Office
2021 Jefferson Davis Highway
Arlington, VA 22202   800-435-7735
Patent Depository Libraries receive current issues of United States patents and maintain collections of patents issued earlier. The scope of these collections varies from library to library, ranging from patents of only certain years in some libraries to all or most of the patents issued since 1790. All of these libraries offer CASSIS (Classification and Search Support Information System), which provides direct, on-line access to Patent and Trademark Office data. For information about the Patent Depository Library Program and the location of a library near you, call the toll-free number listed above.

Selling to and Licensing from the Government

The federal government buys more computers, broom handles, writing services, and anything else that you can think of than anybody. And, because they are interested in helping small businesses, starting your business with a government contract is one way to get it off the ground without investing a lot of capital. Some government offices will give you money up front to help you get a contract; most federal agencies have special consultants whose sole responsibility is to ensure that new and small businesses get their share of contracts.

Using government licenses is another way to get a business off the ground. The government has thousands of products and technologies it has discovered as a result of federally funded research projects. But the government is not in the position to market and thereby take advantage of its discoveries. As a result, government agencies are always looking for private entrepreneurs who will do the marketing for them.

AGENCIES, INSTITUTES, AND ORGANIZATIONS

General Services Administration (GSA)
18th and F streets, NW
Washington, DC 20405   202-523-1250
    The GSA is the place to start to learn how you as an individual or small business can obtain government contracts. There are seven offices around the country where officials are available to help you identify who in the government buys your product or service, as well as how to get through the necessary contracting paperwork. The names and addresses of the regional offices are listed below along with the territories they cover. Contact the office that covers your area.

WASHINGTON, D.C., AND NEARBY MARYLAND AND VIRGINIA
    GSA Business Service Center
    7th and F streets, NW
    Washington, DC 20407
    202-472-1293

MAINE, VERMONT, NEW HAMPSHIRE, MASSACHUSETTS, CONNECTICUT, RHODE ISLAND
    GSA Business Service Center
    John W. McCormick Post Office and Courthouse
    Boston, MA 02109
    617-223-2868

NEW YORK, NEW JERSEY, PUERTO RICO, VIRGIN ISLANDS
    GSA Business Service Center
    26 Federal Plaza
    New York, NY 10278
    212-264-1234

PENNSYLVANIA, DELAWARE, WEST VIRGINIA, MARYLAND, VIRGINIA
    GSA Business Service Center
    9th and Market streets
    Philadelphia, PA 19107
    215-597-9613

NORTH CAROLINA, SOUTH CAROLINA, GEORGIA, TENNESSEE, KENTUCKY, FLORIDA, ALABAMA, MISSISSIPPI

GSA Business Service Center
75 Spring Street, SW
Atlanta, GA 30303
404-221-5103
404-221-3032

OHIO, INDIANA, ILLINOIS, MICHIGAN, MINNESOTA, WISCONSIN

GSA Business Service Center
230 South Dearborn Street
Chicago, IL 60604
312-353-5383

MISSOURI, IOWA, KANSAS, NEBRASKA

GSA Business Service Center
1500 East Bannister Road
Kansas City, MO 64131
816-926-7203

Office of Energy-Related Inventions
National Bureau of Standards
U.S. Department of Commerce
Building 202, Room 209
Gaithersburg, MD 20899   301-921-3694

Inventors and small businesses can get technical assistance from the National Bureau of Standards. A staff of trained specialists evaluates energy-related inventions and make recommendations to the Department of Energy for inventors to receive grant money.

Procurement Automated Source System (PASS)
U.S. Small Business Administration
1441 L Street, NW, Suite 627
Washington, DC 20416   202-653-6586

Large businesses with government contracts access this system to find qualified small businesses for subcontracting work. Listings are free to new and small businesses, and it provides an excellent source for obtaining work from government prime contractors.

Small Business Innovation Research Program (SBIR)
The SBIR Program stimulates technological innovation, encourages small science- and technology-based firms to participate in government-funded research, and provides incentives for converting research results into commercial

applications. Twelve federal agencies with research and development budgets greater that $100 million are required by law to participate: the departments of Defense, Health and Human Services, Energy, Agriculture, Commerce, Transportation, Interior, and Education; the National Aeronautics and Space Administration; the National Science Foundation; the Nuclear Regulatory Commission; and the Environmental Protection Agency.

Businesses of 500 or fewer employees that are organized for profit are eligible to compete for SBIR funding. They must be in business for profit by the time they receive the award. Nonprofit organizations and foreign-based firms are not eligible to receive awards.

SBIR representatives listed below can answer questions and send you materials about their agency's SBIR plans and funding.

DEPARTMENT OF AGRICULTURE

Ms. A. Holiday Schauer
Office of Grants and Program Systems
Department of Agriculture
1300 Rosslyn Commonwealth Building, Suite 103
Arlington, VA 22209
703-235-3628

DEPARTMENT OF DEFENSE

Mr. Horace Crouch, Director
Small Business and Economic Utilization
Office of Secretary of Defense
Room 2A340 Pentagon
Washington, DC 20301
202-697-9383

DEPARTMENT OF EDUCATION

Dr. Ed Esty
The Brown Building
1900 M Street, NW, Room 722
Washington, DC 20208
202-254-8247

DEPARTMENT OF ENERGY

Mrs. Jerry Washington
SBIR Program
U.S. Department of Energy
Route 270
Gaithersburg, MD 20545
301-353-5867

DEPARTMENT OF HEALTH AND HUMAN SERVICES

Mr. Richard Clinkscales, Director
Office of Small and Disadvantaged Business Utilization
Department of Health and Human Services
200 Independence Avenue, SW, Room 513D
Washington, DC 20201
202-245-7300

DEPARTMENT OF THE INTERIOR

Dr. Thomas Henrie, Chief Scientist
Bureau of Mines
U.S. Department of the Interior
2401 E Street, NW
Washington, DC 20241
202-634-1305

DEPARTMENT OF TRANSPORTATION

Dr. Robert Ravera, Acting Director
Transportation System Center
Department of Transportation
Kendall Square
Cambridge, MA 02142
617-494-2222

ENVIRONMENTAL PROTECTION AGENCY

Mr. Walter Preston
Office of Research Grants and Centers
(RD-675)
Office of Research and Development
Environmental Protection Agency
401 M Street, SW
Washington, DC 20460
202-382-5744

NATIONAL AERONAUTICS AND SPACE ADMINISTRATION

Mr. Carl Schwenk
National Aeronautics and Space Administration
SBIR Office—Code A
600 Independence Avenue, SW
Washington, DC 20546
202-755-2306

NATIONAL SCIENCE FOUNDATION

Mr. Ritchie Coryell
Mr. Roland Tibbetts
SBIR Program Managers
National Science Foundation
1800 G Street, NW
Washington, DC 20550
202-357-7527

NUCLEAR REGULATORY COMMISSION

Mr. Francis Gillespie, Director
Administration and Resource Staff
Office of Nuclear Regulatory Research
Nuclear Regulatory Commission
Washington, DC 20555
301-427-4301

U.S. Department of Agriculture

Acquisition and Assistance
6505 Belcrest Road, Room 528A
Hyattsville, MD 20782   301-436-8402

Government patents resulting from agricultural research discoveries are available for licensing to United States companies and citizens. There is no charge for licensing. For a description of the types of patents available, contact the above address.

WHAT TO READ

Government Inventions for Licensing

National Technical Information Service (NTIS)
Department of Commerce
5385 Port Royal Road
Springfield, VA 22161   703-487-4600

The NTIS newsletter is designed to help the general public identify new products and technology invented by the federal government and available to the public for licensing. Annual subscription cost is $205.

Grants for Scientific and Engineering Research

National Science Foundation (NSF)   202-357-9498—Office of Legislative
1800 G Street, NW   and Public Affairs,
Washington, DC 20550   Public Affairs and Publications Group

This publication contains instructions and applications for submitting a proposal for NSF funding. It goes hand-in-hand with the Foundation's *Guide* to its programs, which is a helpful tool for identifying the various subject areas for which NSF funds research projects. These and other NSF publications are available free of charge from NSF while its supply lasts. After that, publications must be purchased from the Superintendent of Documents, U.S. Government Printing Office, Washington, DC 20402, 202-783-3238.

Selling to the Military
Superintendent of Documents
U.S. Government Printing Office (GPO)
Washington, DC 20402   202-783-3238
This is a guide for people wanting to do business with the Department of Defense and all its military departments. It is a listing of items purchased by defense agencies and locations of military purchasing offices. Updated irregularly, the 138-page publication (stock # 008-000-00345-9) is available for $6 from GPO.

Small Business Guide to Federal R&D Funding Opportunities
Office of Small Business R&D
National Science Foundation
1800 G Street, NW
Washington, DC 20550   202-357-7464
The purpose of the guide is to provide scientifically and technically oriented small businesses with information about opportunities for obtaining federal funding for research and development activities. It contains information about the substantive priorities of federal research and development programs; the criteria that companies must meet in order to do business with the federal government; the procedures used by federal research and development programs to publicize funding opportunities, to solicit ideas from the private sector, and to fund extramural research and development activities; certain of the federal laws, regulations, and policies that affect small business participation in federally funded research and development activities; and points of contact for obtaining additional information about each research and development program. The 136-page publication (stock # 038-000-00522-7) is available for $6 from the Superintendent of Documents, U.S. Government Printing Office, Washington, DC 20402, 202-783-3238.

Selling Overseas

If you have an idea for starting a business that involves selling a product or service overseas, there are dozens of free and low-cost services available to help insure your success. Government programs will not only help you identify markets for your products in foreign countries, they will also line up distributors for you and even lend your customers money so that they can buy your product. Listed below are the major starting points for taking advantage of these opportunities.

AGENCIES, INSTITUTES, AND ORGANIZATIONS

Export/Import Bank
811 Vermont Avenue, NW   800-424-5201
Washington, DC 20571   202-566-8860
    This agency facilitates and aids in the financing of exports of U.S. goods and services. Its programs include: short-term and medium-term credits, small business support, financial guarantees, and insurance.

Overseas Private Investment Corporation (OPIC)
1129 20th Street, NW   800-424-OPIC
Washington, DC 20527   202-653-2800
    OPIC is best known for its insurance of private U.S. foreign investment against the political risks of inconvertibility of currency or loss of investment due to expropriation by the host government, war, revolution, or insurrection. The Corporation encourages investment by small and medium-sized United States companies interested in the growing market potential of developing countries. The Public Affairs Office furnishes kits that include OPIC's annual report, a country listing, and other helpful information on its assistance to private individuals and firms via market studies, seminars, investment missions, and financial assistance. You can call the Small Business Information Hotline above to get more details and request their free newsletter, *TOPICS,* which can inform you of specific investment opportunities.

State Sources
    Many state governments provide assistance to businesses who wish to sell overseas. The amount of assistance varies from state to state and can range from simple market study preparation to complete trade missions. Many states also maintain offices in major trading countries like Germany and Japan.

U.S. Department of Commerce
International Trade Administration
Export Promotion Service
Washington, DC 20230   202-377-4811
    The U.S. Department of Commerce has dozens of programs aimed at helping new and small businesses sell overseas, including;
> ■ *International Trade Administration Country Desk Officers*—for information on marketing and business practices in almost every country in the world, contact the experts at the International Trade Administration. A listing of these specialists is available free of charge. Call 202-

377-3022 or write to the ITA, Department of Commerce, Washington, DC 20230.

■ *New Product Information Service (NPIS)*—if you want to establish a market abroad, you can receive free export promotion services from the New Product information Service (NPIS). NPIS will publicize your product in foreign markets and test their interest. Contact Export Communication Section, Room 1620, at the Department of Commerce address above, or call 202-377-2440.

■ *Trade Missions*—the International Trade Administration sponsors small tours of U.S. businessmen offering a single product. The groups make three or four stops overseas in order to evaluate market potential. These trips are prepared by the staff of the U.S. Department of Commerce and take up to two years of planning. Contact the Office of Export Management Support Services, Export and Foreign Commercial Service, International Trade Administration, Department of Commerce, Room 2806, Washington, DC 20230, 202-377-4908.

■ *Temporary Office Space Abroad*—while traveling abroad, you can obtain temporary office space and assistance at the U.S. Department of Commerce's Export Development offices. Translation services and local market information are also available. A nominal fee is charged. Contact the Office of Event Management, Event Management Division, International Trade Administration, Department of Commerce, Room 2111, Washington, DC 20230, 202-377-2741.

■ *International Market Studies*—a series of reports referred to as international market research, country market survey, global market survey and international marketing information are produced on a one-time basis and are made available at prices ranging from $10 to $280. Custom market studies are available for almost any product for approximately $500. Contact the Foreign Commercial Service, Export Promotion Service, P.O. Box 14207, Washington, DC 20044, 202-377-2434.

■ *Joint Services with State Department*—some services sponsored jointly by the departments of Commerce and State assist with establishing a market abroad. To find out about the following services contact your nearest U.S. Department of Commerce District Office (which is your local contact for all Department of Commerce services): the Trade Opportunities Program (TOP)—which provides specific export sales leads of U.S. products and services; *World Traders Data Report (WTDR)*—which provides detailed financial and commercial information on individual firms abroad upon request from U.S. companies; *Agent Distributor Service (ADS)*—which helps U.S. firms find agents or distributors to represent their firms and market their products abroad; and *Information about Foreign Markets*—for U.S. products and services and U.S.-sponsored exhibitions abroad in which American firms can participate and demonstrate their products to key foreign buyers.

Venture Capital

If you don't have enough of your own money or you can't find state or federal money to start your business, your answer may lie in finding venture capital. These individuals and organizations are willing to invest in new or growing venture for a percentage of equity. The sources will show you how to identify these investors.

AGENCIES, INSTITUTES, AND ORGANIZATIONS

American Association of Minority Enterprise Small Business Investment Companies (AAMESBIC)
915 15th Street, NW, Suite 700
Washington, DC 20005   202-347-8600
This trade association is composed of minority enterprise small business investment companies (MESBICs). The Association only represents investment companies that provide venture capital for minority-owned small businesses, many of which are high-technology oriented, particularly in the field of telecommunications. A convention is sponsored each year, which includes workshops, meetings, and guest speakers. The staff can answer your questions about minority investment companies and, in particular, can inform you about regulations and legislation affecting MESBICs. Several publications are available:

- *AAMESBIC Directory*—a listing of the approximately 150 MESBICS across the country including names, addresses, and telephone numbers. It also describes each company's investment preferences and investment policy. The twenty-page publication costs $3.
- *Perspective*—a monthly newsletter that is geared toward minority small business investors. It contains articles about legislation and regulations affecting MESBICs, including those regarding venture capital investment. The subscription to the two- to six-page newsletter is $36 a year.
- *Small Business Perspective*—a monthly newsletter intended for the general small business investment company. It focuses on legislative issues and regulations, including those that affect venture capital investment. Subscription rate to the two- to four-page newsletter is $25 a year.
- *Journal of Minority Small Businesses Enterprise*—an annual periodical containing five to ten articles about specific areas of interest. Recent issues have focused on small businesses and high technology, obtaining capital, and start-up companies. The journal averages forty pages in length and costs $5.50.

Arthur Young and Company

National Headquarters   212-407-1715—Director of Marketing
277 Park Avenue   800-3HI-TECH—National High-Tech Group
New York, NY 10172   415-393-2731—in CA

Arthur Young's High-Tech Group works with companies through every stage of development, offering professional business services. The Group helps companies develop business plans and determine sources of financing, including venture capital funding. Arthur Young offers many publications and newsletters directed to the interests of high-tech companies, and will send a publications list upon request. These publications can be ordered from High-Tech Center, Arthur Young and Company, 1 Post Road, San Francisco, CA 94104, 800-344-8324, in California 415-393-2731. Some of these publications are:

> ■ *Helping High Technology Companies Grow*—a free sixteen-page booklet that describes Arthur Young's services to high-tech clients. Several other information sources are recommended in it.

> ■ *Research and Development Partnerships: Maximizing the Advantages*—a booklet that offers an overview of the business aspects of research and development partnerships. It reports on the advantages and disadvantages of these partnerships with respect to cost, risk, control, benefits for the investor and the company, and different sources of investment. The twenty-six-page publication is available free.

> ■ *Outline for a New High-Technology Business Plan*—a booklet describing how to develop a business plan for a growing business. It covers topics such as marketing, analysis, research and development, manufacturing, management and ownership, and financial backing. The twelve-page booklet is available free of charge.

Coopers & Lybrand (C&L)

1251 Avenue of the Americas
New York, NY 10020   212-536-2000

C&L provides accounting, tax, and business advisory services to its clients, many of whom are growing businesses and high-potential start-up companies. Helping entrepreneurs obtain venture capital financing is a primary service. C&L can provide you with a free copy of the following publication:

> ■ *Three Keys to Obtaining Venture Capital*—this three-page booklet is designed to provide entrepreneurs with insights into obtaining the venture capital needed to launch or expand a business. A step-by-step guide on how to prepare a business plan is included.

Deloitte Haskins and Sells

1114 Avenue of the Americas
New York, NY 10036   800-842-9526

This international firm of independent CPAs provides business consulting services to various companies. Through some of its individual offices, it sponsors local seminars and workshops on financial strategies for high-tech and other entrepreneurs. Staff at the local offices can assist you with questions about venture capital as well as send you the following complimentary publications:

- *Raising Venture Capital*—a 150-page entrepreneur's guidebook prepared by the firm's High-Technology Industry Group. It contains advice and suggestions for competing successfully for venture capital. It shows how to organize a business, write a business plan, describe the product, convince a prospective investor that you have a market, determine financial expectations, and negotiate a final deal.
- *Strategies for Going Public*—a 109-page guidebook prepared for the firm's High-Technology Industry Group. It provides the information necessary to understand how to go public successfully. An appendix surveys alternatives to going public.
- *Forming R&D Partnerships*—the 109-page guidebook's main text provides general information about the workings of R&D partnerships, as well as explaining how to form one.

National Association of Small Business Investment Companies (NASBIC)
1156 15th Street, NW, Suite 1101
Washington, DC 20005   202-833-8230

This national trade association for the small business investment company industry serves as an information clearinghouse on venture capital. Staff can direct you to venture capital sources, experts, and literature. NASBIC publishes several industry guides and research studies on a regular basis. Of particular interest are:

- *The SBIC Venture Incentive Compensation Survey*—updated approximately every other year,this publication is a tabulation of salaries, bonuses, and fringe benefits paid by companies in the industry. It is broken down by type and size of firm. The price is $25 a copy.
- *SBIC Audit Fee Survey*—updated annually, this publication provides data on audit costs for various sizes and types of SBICs. Total assets of private capital are broken down into four categories, and venture firms are classified into six categories. Price is $50 a copy.
- *Venture Capital: Where to Find It*—published every spring, this twenty-eight-page guide lists more than 350 small business investment companies (SBICs) and minority enterprise SBICs (MESBICs) representing approximately 90 percent of the industry's resources. It gives the name of the manager, address, phone number, investment policy, industry preference, and preferred dollar limits on loans and investments. Known also as the *NASBIC Membership Directory,* it enables members to contact each other. The *Directory* is available for $1.

National Venture Capital Association (NVCA)

1655 North Fort Meyer Drive

Arlington, VA 22203   703-528-4370

This association is open to venture capitalist organizations, financiers, and individuals who are responsible for investing private monies in young companies on a professional basis. The purpose of NVCA is to improve the government's knowledge and understanding of the venture capital process. The staff can answer questions about federal legislation and regulations, as well as provide several pages of statistics on venture capital. Some of their publications include:

> ■ *NVCA Fact Sheet*—gives an overview of the industry from 1969 to the present.
>
> ■ *NVCA Membership Directory*—a free forty-page brochure that describes the association and its activities, including a listing of the membership with addresses, phone numbers, and contacts.

Price Waterhouse

Smaller Business Services

1801 K Street, NW

Washington, DC 20006   202-296-0800

This certified public accounting firm provides auditing, taxation, management consulting, and a variety of other business services to public and private businesses and organizations, as well as to the government. It sponsors seminars that sometimes cover venture capital. Several publications are available, including:

> ■ *Business Review*—a four-page newsletter that is published eight times a year. It deals with management topics, especially those affecting small businesses and entrepreneurs, and often features current statistical information and legislative issues. Available free of charge to companies and entrepreneurs.
>
> ■ *Financing Your Business*—this guide for smaller businesses and entrepreneurs deals with getting funds for a start-up situation. It directs the user to finding sources including venture capital. The sixty-five-page guide costs $5.

U.S. Small Business Administration

Office of Investment

1441 L Street, NW

Washington, DC 20416   202-653-6672—John Werner

This government office licenses, regulates, and funds about 500 small business investment companies (SBICs) nationwide. It is the only federal source of venture capital in the United States. Staff can direct you to your nearest SBIC and provide information about approaching the SBIC. The office can also send you a list of licensed small business investment companies, an information kit designed for people interested in forming an SBIC, and a directory of the 500 SBICs supported by SBA.

Venture Capital Clubs

There are approximately a hundred of these clubs around the country, and their number keeps growing. Although each club operates a little differently, they are basically places where almost any entrepreneur can present his or her idea to a group of potential investors or representatives of investors. At a typical monthly meeting, two entrepreneurs might give ten-to-fifteen-minute presentations on their ideas; two minutes each might be allotted to anyone else who has an idea. It is not uncommon to have at least one project receive funding from such a meeting. The following organizations can help you identify clubs in your area:

> State Small Business Assistance Office
>
> Identified in main section of Investing in Yourself under State Sources, the office for your state should be able to provide you with venture capital club contacts in your area.

> International Venture Capital Institute
> PO Box 1333
> Stamford, CT 06904
> 203-323-3143
>
> The president of this institute, Carroll Greathouse, serves as a speaker and adviser (for a fee) to venture capital clubs around the world, helping them to organize and manage their programs. The Institute publishes a bimonthly directory called the *IVCI Directory of Clubs,* which identifies over ninety venture capital clubs. The cost for a single issue is $7.50; a year's subscription is $35.

> Association of Venture Capital Clubs
> 425 Camino Del Monte Sol
> Santa Fe, NM 87501
> 505-983-3869
>
> This association is the headquarters for approximately forty venture capital clubs. They can help you locate their affiliates in your area or assist you in starting your own club.

Venture Capital Network, Inc.
23 School Street
Concord, NH 03301   603-224-5388

This private nonprofit corporation is organized by the Business and Industry Association of New Hampshire in cooperation with the University System of New Hampshire's Office of Small Business Programs. Its purpose is to introduce entrepreneurs to active, informal, independent investors. It maintains a computerized database of entrepreneurs and investors, and the data are compared regularly to determine if potential matches exist. The staff can answer your questions about smaller-scale equity investments, and can send you information.

Venture Economics, Inc.
PO Box 348
Wellesley Hills, MA 02181   617-347-8600
This company provides information, research, and consulting services for corporations, major institutions, and state and local government agencies on venture capital trends. The firm's database contains information on about 6,000 companies that have received venture capital. The information includes business descriptions, financing resources, and specific investors. The database forms part of the firm's Venture Intelligence Service, which is available by subscription. Venture Economics sponsors approximately twenty-five regional seminars a year on how to raise venture capital. Staff can answer questions as well as refer you to other information sources. Brochures describing the company and the services available, as well as the following publications, can be sent upon request:

- *Venture Capital Journal*—a monthly periodical that cites new issues and trends in venture capital investments. It also provides the Venture Capital 100 Index in each issue, which tracks the market performance of each company. The subscription rate to the fifty-five-page publication is $495.
- *Pratt's Guide to Venture Capital Sources*—an annual directory that lists 500 venture capital firms in the U.S. and Canada. Also included are twenty articles recommending ways to raise venture capital. The 530-page publication is $95.
- *Venture Capital Journal Yearbook*—an annual publication that summarizes the investment activities of the previous year. It includes statistics and data about capital commitments and investment activities in specific industries. The fifty-page publication costs $150.
- *Venture Capital Investments*—an annual review of the industry with overviews of the industry by categories. It also identifies technological trends, identifies newly backed companies, and looks at sources of venture capital. The cost of the 150-page publication is $925 to nonsubscribers of the Venture Intelligence Service.
- *The Venture Capital Industry—Opportunities and Considerations*—an annual study and comprehensive analysis of venture capital for prospective corporations and institutional investors. It has information about the history of the industry, legal considerations, industry performance and trends. The hundred-page publication costs $2,500.

WHAT TO READ

A Businessman's Guide to Capital Raising Under Securities Laws
c/o Packard Press
Tenth Street and Spring Garden
Philadelphia, PA 19123   215-236-2000
   This fifty-five-page nontechnical pamphlet familiarizes the business person with the currently more favorable regulatory environment for raising capital by selling securities. It assists business people in anticipating and understanding the decisions that must be made, and the process to follow in the securities offering. It is updated every year and can be ordered for $10.

How to Raise Capital: Preparing and Presenting the Business Plan
c/o Dow Jones-Irwin
1818 Ridge Road
Homewood, IL 60430   312-798-6000
   This book is a complete guide to writing a proposal that will attract potential investors and lenders. It offers detailed explanations on technical business terminology and concepts. The 250-page publication is available for $24.95.

Venture Capital Handbook
Prentice-Hall, Inc.
200 Old Tappan Road
Old Tappan, NJ 07675   201-592-2000
   The *Handbook* covers the entire relationship between the venture capitalist and the entrepreneur. It explains how to prepare a proposal, what negotiations are like, what the investor is looking for, and what occurs at closing. The 402-page publication costs $35.

Venture Magazine
521 Fifth Avenue
New York, NY 10175   212-682-7373
   This monthly magazine is for entrepreneurs who want to invest, and includes articles about start-up companies. It has information about financing, such as new trends and different ways to finance public offerings, and profiles venture capital firms. Each June the magazine lists the hundred largest venture firms, the Venture Capital 100. Each December a directory of venture capital firms is included. Subscription rate to the 150-page magazine is $18.

ADDITIONAL EXPERTS AND RESOURCES

William E. Wetzel, Jr., Professor of Finance
Whittemore School of Business and Economics
University of New Hampshire
Durham, NH 03824   603-862-2771
     Professor Wetzel's special interest is seed capital financing of entrepreneurial ventures. He is knowledgeable about risk capital from individual investors, and can tell you what circumstances are necessary for an entrepreneur to seek funding from individuals as opposed to a professional venture capital firm. He has had articles published in journals, and has conducted research focusing on individual investors. The resulting 120-page report, *Informal Risk Capital in New England* (PB81-196149), costs $13 and is available from NTIS, 5285 Port Royal Road, Springfield, VA 22161.

Part Four

INVESTING FOR LIFELONG SECURITY

Overall Resources for Retirement and Financial Planning

See also:
Estate Planning
IRAs and Keogh Funds
Pensions and Social Security
Trusts

There was once a man of about seventy who went into the hospital after having a heart attack. When he was about to leave, he kept making references to the fact that his mother was coming to pick him up. Thinking that his illness might have affected his mind, the hospital staff kept him there a little bit longer, until one day, lo and behold, his ninety-year-old mother did show up to bring him home. The point of this story, which the AARP likes to cite, is that people are living much longer today, with average life expectancies in the seventies; it is therefore less surprising that a seventy-year-old has a mother who is still living. Twenty-eight million Americans were sixty-five or older in 1984—12 percent of the population. With this in mind, it is all the more important that we plan well for our retirement; and planning well means planning ahead.

The American Association of Retired Persons (AARP) advises "the earlier the better" for planning how much money you will need for your retirement, how you will spend your time (you can't fish 365 days a year), and where you will live. On the negative side, your income will probably be greatly diminished. But on the bright side, so are your expenses; and if they aren't, figure out how to fill the gap. AARP says, for instance, that you will need 70 percent of your after-tax preretirement earnings for your first year of retirement to maintain the same standard of living. But you can usually comfortably reduce your expenses, and, sell your house or other valuables; furthermore, you can take advantage of your extra time to shop wisely, using senior discounts and other benefits, and you will probably have a social security or retirement check coming in. You might even consider a new career or at least a part-time job to supplement your income. You'll also have to take into consideration emergencies, especially health-related ones that will cost money. Medicare won't necessarily cover all the bills, any more than social security will be enough to live on.

The worst retirement mistake you can make today is not planning at all. Planning ahead can make the difference between a retirement that is fulfilling and enjoyable and one that is poverty-stricken and fraught with problems. Experts recommend you begin retirement planning at least fifteen years before your actual retirement date. This will give you an opportunity to evaluate your benefits and assets, with plenty of time left to develop a retirement strategy.

You may need to consult a financial adviser, lawyer, or other professional. But much of what you'll need to know to help you plan is available through free or inexpensive publications and resources such as trade associations, government agencies, and private businesses. Following are some of those.

AGENCIES, INSTITUTES, AND ORGANIZATIONS

American Association of Retired Persons (AARP)
1909 K Street, NW
Washington, DC 20049   202-872-4700

AARP is the nation's largest organization of older Americans, with a membership of over 17 million. A nonprofit, nonpartisan organization, AARP serves its members through legislative representation, educational and community service programs, and direct membership benefits. Many audiovisual programs, covering a wide range of topics of concern to older persons, are produced by AARP. A free audiovisual catalog may be obtained by writing the Program and Resources Department. Examples of publications available from AARP are:

■ *Looking Ahead: How to Plan Your Successful Retirement*—the ninety-two-page book has answers and information on a variety of important topics such as: reasons for planning retirement, financial security, housing choices, midlife roles, health and fitness, and legal affairs. Cost is $9.95.

■ *Take Charge of Your Money*—a workbook to help you manage your financial resources in retirement. Free.

■ *What to Do with What You've Got*—a practical guide to money management in retirement. The cost of a softcover copy is $7.95.

■ *Modern Maturity Magazine*—published ten times a year, this magazine runs regular articles about money management and aging. The subscription fee is included in the $5 a year association membership dues.

"Pay Your Bills on Time" May Be All There Is to Being a Good Money Manager

If you think there may be a lot of sophistication to being a good money manager, you are not among the majority in the country. When *Money* magazine asked what they think being a good money manager means, eight out of ten said paying your bills on time. A nearly identical number think the key to good money management is nothing more complicated than saving money.

American Council of Life Insurance
1850 K Street, NW
Washington, DC 20006-2284   202-624-2000

This organization, which represents major life insurance companies, will provide information about the insurance aspects of financial planning. A free catalog of the council's publications and audiovisuals about life and health insurance will be sent to you upon request. Resource speakers are available on a limited basis for large groups and their program topics include estate planning, retirement planning, and current public policy issues affecting the life and health-insurance business. A slide/tape program entitled *Plan for Retirement* can be borrowed on a two-week free-loan basis or purchased for $25. The following publication is offered free of charge:

> ■ *Securing Your Retirement Dollars*—this easy-to-read twenty-two-page booklet explains how to plan for retirement. It tells you how to plot a retirement timetable, provides information about investing, and discusses estate planning.

College of Financial Planning
9725 East Hampton Avenue
Denver, CO 80231   303-755-7101

A twenty-four-month program of study in financial planning is offered by this college. Courses on retirement planning and employee benefits are taught as a part of the program. For consumers the college offers the following free publication:

> ■ *Financial Planning Bibliography*—a selected list of books and reference materials on all aspects of financial planning.

International Society of Pre-retirement Planners (ISPP)
2400 South Downing Avenue
Westchester, IL 60153   312-531-9140

ISPP membership is comprised of personnel directors, financial planners and consultants. The society serves as a clearinghouse for current information regarding common methods, techniques, materials, devices, and content used in preretirement counseling and planning programs. ISPP publishes the following publications:

> ■ *Directory of Pre-retirement Consultants*—a listing of members of ISPP. Free.
>
> ■ *Perspective*—a quarterly newsletter that reports on legislative changes that impact upon retirement planning. It is available to members only.
>
> ■ *Retirement Planning*—published quarterly, this journal contains a variety of articles about issues affecting retirement planning. It is available for $20 a year.

National Committee to Preserve Social Security and Medicare
1300 19th Street, NW, Suite 310
Washington, DC 20036   202-822-9459
   The committee is a nonprofit, nonpartisan organization which lobbies for
the continuation of the Social Security Program and Medicare. Speakers are
available on a limited basis to address large groups about policy and political
issues affecting these programs. Numerous free educational publications are
available from the committee. A complete listing of these publications may be
obtained free of charge. The following are of special interest:
   ■ *How to Estimate Your Retirement Income Needs*—explains how to
   determine your retirement income needs. Free.
   ■ *Saving Social Security*—a bimonthly newsletter containing news of proposed legislation that affects the Social Security Program and Medicare.
   This publication is included in the yearly membership fee of $10.

Senate Special Committee on Aging
G-233 Dirksen Senate Office Building
Washington, DC 20510
   This Senate committee reviews legislation concerned with income and
employment issues of the elderly. Staff members will answer questions and
refer you to other sources of information. Speakers are available as staffing
permits. The committee will send you a complete list of its publications on
request. Below are the most frequently requested free ones:
   ■ *Development on Aging*—an annual report which reviews all legislative
   changes affecting the elderly.
   ■ *Aging Reports*—a quarterly report on legislative issues of interest to the
   elderly.
   ■ *Turning Home Equity into Income for Older Americans*—a fact sheet
   describing the steps necessary to turn home equity into income.
   ■ *Guide to Individual Retirement Accounts*—an information paper which
   provides a general introduction to IRAs and discusses the various savings
   and investment vehicles available.
   ■ *Protecting Older Americans Against Overpayment of Income Tax*—a
   fact sheet to help assure that senior citizens claim every legitimate income
   tax deduction, exemption, and tax credit.

State Office on Aging
   Most Offices on Aging offer a referral service to aid the older American
with retirement financial planning. For retirees thinking of moving to another
state, these offices are an excellent source of information about retirement
housing, care facilities, and cost-of-living statistics. Inquire as to the resource
material available. Contact the governor's office in your state capitol to identify
the office which serves your area.

■ ■

HOW TO FIND A FINANCIAL PLANNER

Almost anyone can call themselves an investment adviser—your insurance salesman, stockbroker, etc. However, an investment adviser may or may not be a certified financial planner. Being a certified financial planner means that one has completed training as well as continuing-education courses in financial planning. The two industry organizations which offer such training will also help you in finding a financial planner in your area.

Free directory of financial planners. Ask for copy of "Directory of Registry of Financial Planning Practitioners" from the International Association of Financial Planning, 2 Concourse Parkway, #800, Atlanta, GA 30328, 404-395-1605

Free listing of five planners in your zip code. Contact the Institute of Certified Financial Planners, 10065 East Harvard Avenue, #320, Denver, CO 80231, 303-751-7600

■ ■

United Business Service Company
210 Newbury Street
Boston, MA 02116   617-267-8855
United Business Service is one of the oldest and largest advisory services in the country. It provides a full range of advisory and investment-related information services. Retirement questions from clients are answered on an irregular basis through the newsletter.

> ■ *United Retirement Bulletin*—published monthly, this bulletin is designed to assist people planning for retirement or already retired. It offers general financial planning information and discusses other relevant topics such as health, insurance, retirement living, andtravel. Cost is $21 a year.

WHAT TO READ

And One Day You Retire
Corporate Communications, DA21
Aetna Life & Casualty
151 Farmington Avenue
Hartford, CT 06156   203-273-0123—public relations resources
Several aspects of retirement years are covered in this publication, geared to those aged fifty and over. It will provide information on how to plan for retirement income, insurance, leisure time, and other concerns. The cost is $2 and it is available in single copies only.

- -

QUIZ YOUR FINANCIAL PLANNER
BEFORE YOU TAKE HIS OR HER ADVICE

The National Association of Personal Financial Advisors recommends that you interview at least two potential advisers. Here are eleven useful questions to ask:

Does your financial planning service include:

- A review of my goals
- Advice on
  _____ Cash management and planning
  _____ Tax planning
  _____ Investment review and planning
  _____ Retirement planning
  _____ Estate planning
  _____ Insurance needs:
    _____ Life insurance
    _____ Disability insurance
    _____ Property/casualty insurance
    _____ Other: _____
  _____ Other areas: _____

Do you provide a written analysis of my financial situation and your recommendations?
_____ Yes _____ No

How is your firm compensated for the financial services you provide:
_____ Fees only (flat fee or hourly rate)
_____ Commissions only (from securities, insurance, etc., that I might buy from your firm)
_____ Fees and commissions

If you charge a fee, what is it based on?
_____ An hourly rate of $_____
_____ A percentage based on _____
_____ A flat fee based on _____

Is your firm registered with the Securities and Exchange Commission?
_____ Yes _____ No

If "fee only," is your firm affiliated with a broker/dealer?
_____ Yes _____ No

If "fee and commission" (or if affiliated with a broker/dealer), approximately what percentage of your firm's annual income comes from:
Fees charged to clients _____ %
Commissions earned from clients' purchase of investment products
_____ %
Other (explain) _____ _____ %

If "fee and commission" or "commission only" (or affiliated with a broker/dealer), what percentage of your commission income comes from:
Insurance products _____ %
Annuities _____ %
Mutual funds _____ %
Limited partnerships _____ %
Coins _____ %
Stocks and bonds _____ %
Other (explain) _____ _____ %

Will you furnish me with no-load (no sales charge) product alternatives, if available?
_____ Yes _____ No

Do you or any member of your firm act as a general partner or receive compensation from the general partner or from investments which may be recommended to me?

_____ Yes _____ No

What is the average income in fees from a typical client?

$_____ (annual fee income divided by number of clients served)

What is the average income in commissions from a typical client?

$_____ (annual commission income divided by number of clients served)

■ ■

Are You Planning on Living the Rest of Your Life?
Superintendent of Documents
U.S. Government Printing Office
Washington, DC 20402   202-783-3238
The seventy-two-page guidebook provides information useful in planning your retirement. It is available for $2.25.

Changing Times
The Kiplinger Magazine
1729 H Street NW
Washington, DC 20006   202-887-6400
This monthly magazine publishes articles on preretirement and retirement financial planning as well as updates about how new legislation affects retirement planning. The publication's staff will respond to written inquiries for additional information, and when possible staff will speak before groups to address topics covered in the magazine. Annual subscription fee is $15. Order from: *Changing Times,* The Kiplinger Magazine, Editors Park, MD 20782.

Money
Time and Life Building
Rockefeller Center
New York, NY 10020   212-841-4881
A monthly magazine, *Money* periodically contains articles about retirement planning. The magazine will provide speakers to large organizations as staffing permits. Annual subscription fee is $29.95. Order from *Money,* P.O. Box 14429, Boulder, CO 80322.

Money Guides
PO Box 999
Radio City Station
New York, NY 10019   Written requests only
The publishers of *Money* magazine (described above) produce several guides devoted to timely subjects. Examples of relevant guides include:

■ *Money Guide to Retirement Planning*—contains information about all aspects of retirement planning. It costs $29.95.
■ *Money Guide to IRAs*—contains current information about IRAs. It costs $3.95.

Retirement Letter
47 Chestnut Avenue
Larchmont, NY 10538   914-834-8910

Published monthly, this is a financial and investment newsletter for mature people who are either contemplating retirement or are retired. Four special issues are also published yearly. A unique feature of the newsletter is the personal counseling service it offers its subscribers. Readers can contact the editor for answers to specific questions they may have about retirement finances. By sending a stamped, self-addressed envelope to *Retirement Letter* you can receive free basic information about retirement finances and a sample copy of the newsletter. Newsletter subscription fee is $48 a year.

Retirement Preparation: What Retirement Specialists Need to Know
Lexington Books
125 Spring Street
Lexington, MA 02173   800-428-8071

Edited by Helen Dennis, this book gives the retirement specialist the information he or she needs to develop and conduct preretirement programs and services for middle-aged and older adults. Experienced contributors explain important considerations and specific techniques for financial planning, health promotion, retirement planning for minorities and women, retirement counseling, and the various work schedules that older adults may choose as an alternative to full retirement. An extensive annotated listing of books, audiovisuals, organizations, and informal networks points the retirement specialist to vital resources. This 224-page book is available in softcover for $14.

50 Plus
850 Third Avenue
New York, NY 10022   212-593-2100

Informational booklets as well as a monthly magazine are available from 50 Plus. Examples are:

■ *50 Plus*—this magazine focuses on a wide variety of retirement issues. Annual subscription is $15.
■ *50 Plus Money Plan for Retirement*—this booklet presents all financial options for retirement. It costs $2.15.
■ *Money and Your Retirement*—this booklet is a guide for the small investor who is facing retirement. It costs $2.15.

PEOPLE TO TALK TO

Helen Dennis
Leonard Davis School
Ethel Percy Andrus Gerontology Center
University of Southern California
University Park, MC 0191
Los Angeles, CA 90089-0191
   Helen Dennis is a project director and lecturer at the Andrus Gerontology Center, University of Southern California. Her work focuses on issues of aging, employment, and retirement. She teaches a course on retirement planning and is editor of *Retirement Preparation: What Retirement Specialist Need to Know* (see What to Read in this section). She also directs the first national training program to address age issues in management.

Peter Dickinson
47 Chestnut Avenue
Larchmont, NY 10538   Written inquiries only
   Editor of the *Retirement Newsletter: The Money Newsletter for Mature People,* Mr. Dickinson is an authority on the subject of retirement planning. He has served as a special investigator for the U.S. Senate Committee on Aging. Mr. Dickinson is the author of the best-selling, *The Complete Retirement Planning Book.* This 258-page book covers the five basic areas of retirement planning—finances, health, housing, leisure time, and legal needs. It is available from the above address for $10.95 in softcover and $17.95 in hardcover.

Peter Weaver
5100 Camack Drive
Bethesda, MD 20816   301-320-5101
   Peter Weaver is an authority in the field of personal finance. He is the author of *Strategies for the Second Half of Life,* a book about anticipating and planning for retirement while still middle-aged. Mr. Weaver writes a syndicated column, "Your Retirement Dollar," which is carried by several major American newspapers. He is currently producing for AARP TV news and public affairs pieces on issues of interest to retired people.

Grace Weinstein
c/o Harold Ober Associates
40 East 49th Street
New York, NY 10017   212-759-8600
   Ms. Weinstein is the author of the column "You and Retirement" in the *Elks* magazine, and of several books, including *The Lifetime Book of Money*

Management, Life Plans: Looking Forward to Retirement and *Retire Tomorrow-Plan Today.* She has also written numerous publications on retirement for large organizations, as well as articles in national magazines. Knowledgeable in all aspects of financial management, Ms. Weinstein is a frequent speaker to diverse groups.

ADDITIONAL RESOURCES

Your Employer

Check with your employer to see if he/she offers any preretirement planning services.

Estate Planning

See also:
Overall Resources for Retirement and Financial Planning
IRAs and Keogh Funds
Pensions and Social Security
Trusts

As little as we like to think about it, we must all die sooner or later. And when we do, we want to be sure that our material possessions are disposed of as we would like. In many cases, a simple will does the job, if the deceased person has only a few items that can be simply bequeathed. But when the assets are considerable and in many different forms, it is probably necessary to have a formal estate plan.

Estate planning is usually done by a lawyer, banker, or other professional. However, you can also write your own will or estate plan, as you will see in this section. It consists of reviewing all of your wealth and developing a plan to manage and dispose of it at the best possible tax savings to your heirs. In the process, you may find that you need to change your will, or how your property is owned (jointly, separately, and so on), or the kinds of investments you have. You will be advised on such things as state and federal inheritance-tax laws, how to make your assets more liquid, how to word your will properly, whether or not to have a trust, and whether your insurance is sufficient or too much for your needs. The unpleasant subject of funerals also comes into estate planning. If you don't want your heirs to be caught up in expensive and elaborate funeral arrangements, you might consider alternatives such as crema-tion or memorial services. There are also low-cost funerals available from memorial societies which can conduct respectable funerals without trying to sell your heirs fancy accessories.

Your will, of course, is a key to good estate planning. It is especially important because, without one, your survivors may find that what they had expected to come to them automatically has been distributed differently by the state, which takes over in such cases. You should review your will every so often in case the circumstances of your life have changed; it may be that Cousin Alice, to whom you are no longer speaking, was the prime beneficiary in your original will and so you will want to change accordingly. The federal gift tax and estate laws have also been revised in the past few years, so any will or estate plan you drew up more than five years ago should be looked at again now. Most average estates will no longer be subject to any federal estate taxes. And you can give up to $10,000 a year to relatives, friends, or organizations to reduce your estate without paying taxes.

To help you familiarize yourself with the complicated plans, terminologies, and processes involved in estate planning, the following resources are a good place to begin. By having some knowledge of these things before you seek professional help, you'll be one step ahead of the game.

AGENCIES, INSTITUTES, AND ORGANIZATIONS

American Bar Association (ABA)
Order Fullfillment Department
750 North Lake Shore Drive
Chicago, IL 60611   Written requests only

or

Your state or local ABA
Check your telephone directory.

Referrals to attorneys specializing in estate planning are provided by state and local ABAs. If you hire an attorney and run into a problem, you can report it to the ABA, whose staff will investigate your complaint. Free or inexpensive, informational booklets about the basic steps of estate planning and the role of the attorney in the process are available from the office listed above or at your local ABA. An example is:

■ *Planning for Life and Death*—this twenty-page booklet offers a concise, comprehensive explanation of probate, wills, and estate planning objectives. The first copy is free; the cost for twenty-five copies is $12; there are discounts for fifty copies or more.

Community Colleges
(Check your telephone directory yellow pages under Schools for a listing.)

Most community colleges offer courses in estate planning. Call the schools in your area for a current schedule of classes.

County Extension Office
(Check the county government section of your telephone directory for a listing.)

The first stop for information on estate planning should be your county extension office. Staff will answer your questions and refer you to other sources in your community. Some county extension offices also offer estate planning courses. Free publications, written by estate planning specialists, are also available. For example, the one described below is offered by Virginia County Extension Service Offices:

■ *Our Estate Inventory*—a seventeen-page workbook that outlines the five steps in developing an estate plan. It contains planning forms and takes you through the process of estate planning in an understandable way.

■ ■

Do Women Really Let Men
Make Their Investment Decisions?

No. A study conducted by *Glamour* magazine among women 18 to 65 years of age who were married or living with a man showed that most women *share* investment decisions with men. Fewer than 20 percent of the women responding let a man make most of the investment decisions for them.

■ ■

HALT (Help Abolish Legal Tyranny)
201 Massachusetts Avenue, NE, Suite 319
Washington, DC 20002   202-546-4258

HALT is a national nonpartisan public interest group dedicated to reducing the cost and improving the quality and accessibility of legal services in America. To help citizens represent themselves or with an attorney, HALT publishes educational materials instructing members in the basic principles and procedures of the legal system. HALT also provides a legal services referral network to its members. Following are some of the publications included in the yearly membership fee of $20.:

   ■ *Americans For Legal Reform*—a quarterly newsletter reporting on legal reform news and opinion. Regular features include book reviews and the Legal Advisor column.

   ■ *Estate Planning*—this manual will insure that your heirs receive the greatest possible value from the property you leave them. It will help you manage the things you own—your estate—so that they serve your best interest and those of your heirs.

   ■ *Probate*—this manual makes probate simple enough handle by yourself, while cutting costs and delays, and minimizing fees and taxes.

   ■ *Using a Law Library*—this manual will teach you how to find the answer to most routine legal questions in legal reference books and materials. The appendix is especially useful. It contains: a sample will and trust, specific rules governing property and related estate planning information for the fifty states, tax (inheritance, estate, and credit estate) for each state, and a list of memorial societies in the United States.

Society of Certified Public Accountants
(Check your local or state telephone listings.)

Through its state chapters, this organization offers free information pamphlets on estate planning. It will also provide referral service to CPAs specializing in estate planning. Some of the societies will identify CPAs who will speak to groups on estate planning. Check your telephone directory for the nearest chapter or for a member in your area.

State Tax Departments
(Check the state government section of your telephone directory for a listing.)
Before establishing an estate plan, check with your state tax department for information about current estate tax laws.

Trust Department of Your Bank
The officers in a bank trust department can provide literature on estate planning and help you evaluate your needs. This department can also refer you to the professionals with the expertise to help you establish a viable estate plan.

WHAT TO READ

The CPA as Estate Planner
American Institute of Certified Public Accountants
1211 Avenue of the Americas
New York, NY 10036   212-575-6200
This free four-page pamphlet describes the role of the CPA in the estate planning process.

The Days Ahead
Corporate Communications, DA21
Aetna Life & Casualty
151 Farmington Avenue
Hartford, CT 06156   203-273-0123—public relations resources
For the widowed and others who must help settle an estate, this booklet offers information on what to expect emotionally and financially. You will learn where to go for help and how to plan for the future. Single copies are free.

People Choose Investment Advisers
Seven to One over Stockbrokers
to Help Them Plan Their Savings

Financial planning specialists led the list, beating the second choice, accountants, by nearly two to one.

Estate Planning: A Guide for Advisors and Their Clients
Dow Jones-Irwin Co.
1818 Ridge Road   800-942-8881—in IL
Homewood, IL 60430   800-323-1717
   Among the questions answered in *Estate Planning:* How can you ensure that your assets are distributed among your heirs according to your wishes? How do you make sure the government doesn't become your beneficiary? and How can you—legally—give less to the IRS? This guide, written by D. Larry Crumbley and Edward E. Milam, looks at the whole estate planning process and encourages a wealth-building approach. It provides a step-by-step process for evaluating an estate, investigating the utility of deferrals, gifts, and trusts, assessing tax liabilities, and formulating a realistic estate plan. Cost is $19.95.

Estate Planning Made Easy
Liberty Publishing Company
50 Scott Adam Road
Cockeysville, MD 21030   301-667-6680
   This practical, well-organized handbook explains what everyone should know about estate planning in down-to-earth language. Included are explanations of Living Trusts, Buy-Sell Agreements, legal and administrative costs, probate, and taxes, as well as many other important aspects of personal finance. It is written by Herbert F. Starr. Cost is $10.95.

Income and Estate Tax Planning
Oceana Publications, Inc.
Dobbs Ferry, NY 10522   914-693-5956
   Written by Irwin J. Sloan, this book is No. 50 in the eighty-four-volume Legal Almanac Series. It outlines the author's "Rule of Three," which covers the three areas of a family's financial responsibility: protection, savings, and investment. The following subjects are covered: social security, pension laws, life insurance, savings and investment, federal estate tax forms, wills, and gifts and trusts. The charts in the appendix are of great help in showing how your savings can increase each year at different rates of interest. Check your library for the complete set.

The Next Step
State Farm Insurance Co.
One State Farm Plaza
Bloomington, IL 61701   309-766-2311
   This free booklet is available from State Farm Insurance (ask your local agent for a copy) to make the handling of financial affairs after a death a little easier for the survivors. Explanations are given of the role of the professional in settling the estate, probating the estate, and tax considerations.

Now Is the Time
Overlook Company
910 North Overlook Drive
Alexandria, VA 22305   Written requests only
    This estate planning workbook by Benjamin Katz discusses: funeral plans, finances, records, taxes, wills, probate, and settling the estate. The Appendix includes helpful planning forms. Cost is $4. The book has been tape recorded in cassette form and is available on a free loan from the Washington Volunteer Readers for the Blind, Inc., District of Columbia Regional Library for the Blind and Physically Handicapped, 901 G Street, NW, Washington, DC 20001, 202-727-2142.

Planning With Your Beneficiaries
American Council of Life Insurance
1850 K Street, NW
Washington, DC 20006   202-862-4000
    This booklet discusses wills, trusts, investments, life insurance, and how these tools can help in planning for security. It encourages the policyholder and the beneficiary to plan together to insure future financial security. Free.

What to Do Now?
Life Insurance Management and Research Association
PO Box 208
Hartford, CT 06141   203-677-0033
    This inexpensive booklet describes the steps a widow must take to settle her husband's estate. Cost is $1.

PEOPLE TO TALK TO

D. Larry Crumbley
Texas A&M University
College of Business Administration
Department of Accounting
College Station, TX 77843-4353   Written inquiries only
    Dr. Crumbley is Deborah D. Shelton Taxation Professor at Texas A&M University. He is the author or co-author of fifteen books, including three on estate and gift taxes. His most recent book is *Estate Planning: A Guide for Advisors and Their Clients* with Edward E. Milam (see What to Read section of this chapter for a description of the book).

Stephen R. Leimberg
American College
270 Bryn Mawr Avenue
Bryn Mawr, PA 19010   Written inquiries only

Mr. Leimberg serves as professor of taxation and estate planning at the American College. He is the author of over twenty books on taxes and estate planning. His most recent book on estate planning is *Get Rich/Stay Rich.* A frequent speaker on both technical and inspirational topics for numerous estate planning councils and life insurance company conventions, Mr. Leimberg has also testified before Congress as an expert witness on IRAs.

ADDITIONAL RESOURCES

Your Estate: Planning With Your Beneficiaries
Free-Loan Scheduling Center
Modern Talking Pictures
5000 Park Street North
St. Petersburg, FL 33705   Written inquiries only

This slide/tape presentation gives general guidelines for estate planning, covering such basic topics as wills, life and health insurance, and pensions and other employee benefits; it encourages the use of professional advisers in developing an estate plan. It is designed for use in financial planning programs and workshops and at club and community meetings. The set contains sixty slides, a fifteen-minute cassette tape, and a leader's guide. The set may be purchased for $25, or it can be borrowed free of charged for two weeks.

IRAs and Keogh Funds

See also:
Mutual Funds
Overall Resources for Retirement and Financial Planning

Many government and economic forecasters predict that the nation's social security system eventually will run out of funds. And retired people are now discovering that social security alone cannot support an individual at retirement. Only three years after Congress liberalized Individual Retirement Accounts (IRAs) to include nearly anyone with earned income, 23 million households opened accounts. Today between $210 and $220 billion is invested in IRAs, and a recent Investment Company Institute survey shows that millions more Americans would invest if Congress would expand the spousal IRA, permit additional contributions, or allow limited access to the funds without imposing the 10 percent penalty for withdrawal before the age of fifty-nine and a half.

What exactly is an IRA? It is an arrangement in which you contribute to your own retirement fund, held by a bank or other institution. Your payments are tax-deductible and the taxes on the earnings of the account are deferred. Almost every financial institution is offering some form of IRA. You can find them at banks, savings and loans, investment companies, brokerage houses, insurance companies, and credit unions. Banks and other deposit institutions hold most of the IRA funds, but mutual funds and brokerage firms are dramatically increasing their IRA assets. Keoghs are the most widely used type of retirement plan for the self-employed, but Super IRAs or Simplified Employee Pension (SEP) plans are gaining in popularity. SEPs permit small businesses and people who work for themselves to contribute up to $30,000 a year, depending on profits, to their own IRA accounts and those of their employees. There are other retirement income tax shelters that may be better for you. You will need to decide if an IRA is the best way for you to go.

If you do decide an IRA is right for you, the next big question is where you should have it. A three point difference in interest can be worth tens of thousands of dollars by retirement time. It's essential to shop around. Each financial institution is hawking its own IRA version and the barrage of information can be overwhelming. Don't be misled by ads that make it sound like you will be a millionaire in your old age. You can build a tidy nest egg, but after taxes and inflation, you won't really have money to burn. Compare the features offered by the different places, such as interest rates, annual yield, minimum amounts to open, management fees, and how your funds are insured. Most financial institutions offering IRAs can send you brochures describing the features their version has to offer. And, generally speaking, it's easy to move your IRA from one institution to another, although there may be fees involved.

The Center for the Study of Services has prepared a handbook called *The IRA Book,* which is an intelligible and comprehensive guide to IRA investments. This and other resources described in this chapter can help you learn how to get the most from IRAs and Keoghs, and how they can fit into your retirement planning.

Under the new tax law, beginning with the tax year 1987, IRAs have been restricted to those who are not covered by an employer pension plan, but if you are covered by a pension plan, you can participate in an IRA tax advantage if as an individual you make less than $35,000 or $50,000 as a couple. Congress may be considering new laws in the future. Make sure that you are aware of the latest rules before you make an IRA investment.

AGENCIES, INSTITUTES, AND ORGANIZATIONS

Brokerage Firms

Offering a wide variety of IRA investments and other financial services, brokerage firms can help you set up, evaluate, and manage your IRA. Most offer free publications on the subject. Two examples are given below.

> E. F. Hutton
> One Battery Park Plaza
> New York, NY 10004
> 212-742-5000
> This firm offers:
> - *The IRA Record Keeper: An IRA Calculator*—this will show you how various rates of return can affect the growth of your assets. Free.
> - *Managing Your IRA*—this booklet will help you determine how best to manage your IRA in light of your personal needs, economic outlook and attitude toward risk. Free.

> Merrill Lynch Service Center
> PO Box 2021
> Jersey City, NJ 07303
> 201-547-3800
> 800-MERRILL
> - *How to Save Taxes on Up to $30,000 in Income with Merrill Lynch Basic (Keogh Plus) Retirement Plan*—as the title suggests, this brochure addresses the distinct tax advantages of a Keogh retirement plan. Free.

Commercial Banks, Savings and Loans, and Credit Unions

IRA investment opportunities are offered by each of these financial institutions. All employ an IRA specialist who can answer your questions and send you free information about his/her institution's product. Your local yellow pages will identify relevant institutions in your area.

■ ■

> ### Company Savings Plans More Popular Than Mutual Funds and Real Estate by a Margin of Almost Two to One
>
> But company savings plans trail CDs, money market accounts, and IRAs as savings and investment vehicles held by household financial decision makers who took part in a *Money* magazine survey.

■ ■

Fidelity Distributors Corporation
The Fidelity Building
PO Box 193   800-544-6666
Boston, MA 02101   617-523-1919

Fidelity offers a large variety of investment services and publishes descriptive brochures about each of their products. For information or a copy of the following brochures call the toll-free number above.

- *IRA Owner's Guide*—this guide will answer your questions about IRAs and will show you how one can benefit you. Free.
- *Keogh Booklet*—a twenty-five-page booklet with basic information on setting up Keogh accounts, how they grow, tax implications, and the various different places money may be invested. Free.
- *IRA Booklet*—a twenty-five-page booklet with basic information on IRA accounts for those wanting to find good choices for investment of their IRA money. Free.

Insurance Companies
A lot of information about IRAs is available from life insurance companies. Contact the offices in your community for information and free brochures.

Investment Company Institute (ICI)
1600 M Street, NW
Washington, DC 20036   202-293-7700

ICI is the national association of mutual funds. Its public information staff has made a conscious effort to establish and maintain media relationships not only with professional, technical, and financial media, but with consumer and general interest media as well. The institute has surveyed American's response to IRAs and their possible reactions to additional legislative changes. The staff in the Public Information Office will answer your IRA-related questions and will send you free information on the benefits of such an account. The Institute's membership directory is available free of charge and it gives contact information for 90 percent of the mutual fund industry.

If you need to speak to an expert on IRAs the public information office will refer you to an expert, or they will answer your questions themselves. Contact the office above for a listing of free publications covering IRAs. The following film is available:

> ■ *Future Funds*—this colorful eight-minute film explains the tax advantages of IRAs and how mutual funds can be used. It can be borrowed for up to three days. Free.

Money Concepts
1523 King Street
Alexandria, VA 22314   703-684-1277

This financial planning center is a franchise of International Financial Services, Inc. Money Concepts offers many types of informational seminars, all free to the public. Seminar workshops cover IRAs, Keoghs, mutual funds, annuities, money management, and personal finance. The purpose of these seminars is to help individuals and organizations better understand money management, financial planning, and investments. As a free service, a staff person will analyze your personal financial situation and after three interviews will prepare a written plan with specific investment recommendations. To find out if there is a member company of International Financial Services in your area, contact their headquarters: 1 Golden Bear Plaza, U.S. Highway One, North Palm Beach, FL 33408, 305-627-0700.

Schabacker Investment Management
8943 Shady Grove Court
Gaithersburg, MD 20877   301-840-0301

A publisher of mutual funds investment newsletters, this company also manages accounts over $100,000. As a consulting service to the general public, it offers the following service and publications:

> ■ *Telephone Advice Privilege*—Mr. Schabacker or a portfolio manager will give you personal advice on how to improve your investments. Cost is $200.

Commercial Banks Are Favorite Parking Place for IRAs

They beat out savings institutions by 50 percent, according to a *Money* magazine survey.

■ *No Load Low Load Mutual Fund Directory*—this directory is valuable to those with IRAs. It provides the name, address, and phone number of mutual funds and the minimum deposit required. Free.

■ *Retirement Fund Advisory*—published monthly, six-to eight-page newsletter specifically analyzes Keogh and IRA funds and offers performance guidelines and advice on these funds. Annual subscription fee is $59.

United States League of Savings Institutions (USL)
111 East Wacker Drive
Chicago, IL 60601   312-644-3100

If you have a question about IRAs or Keoghs, the USL suggests that you try to get help from your savings and loan institution. If you are not satisfied with their service, you can call the league and an economist or researcher will help answer your general question or refer you to the proper source. The U.S. League is not engaged in giving legal or accounting advice, but they will refer you to a competent professional. The following publication is available from the public relations department:

■ *IRA/86*—this is a question and answer guide on IRAs. It includes a short section on Keogh retirement plans for the self-employed. Single copies are free.

WHAT TO READ

The ABCs of IRAs
Dell Trade Paperbacks
1 Dag Hammarskjold Plaza
New York, NY 10017   212-605-3000

Written by William J. Grace, Jr., this book answers the 100 most asked questions about IRAs. It includes a short section on transfers. You can find it in most bookstores. Cost is $4.95.

Consumers' Guide to I.R.A.
New York State Banking Department
2 World Trade Center
New York, NY 10047   212-618-6642

This pamphlet will provide you with the information you need to shop around and choose the IRA best suited to your particular needs. Free.

The Dow Jones-Irwin Guide to Using IRA's
Dow Jones-Irwin
1824 Ridge Road   800-323-1717
Homewood, IL 60430   800-942-8881

This guide helps you understand the rules and regulations governing IRAs so that you can avoid costly mistakes. It describes easy-to-follow steps for opening an IRA, managing it through its growth years, and selecting one of the optional means of distribution during retirement years. The 320-page book costs $25.95.

Extraordinary Investments for Ordinary Investors
Putnam Publishing Group
200 Madison Avenue
New York, NY 10016   212-576-8811
Written by Wayne F. Nelson, this book gives advice on how to pick an IRA account. It provides suggestions for obtaining information before investing in mutual funds. Cost is $16.95, plus $1.50 for postage and handling.

How Your IRA Can Make You a Millionaire
Crown Publisher, Inc.
34 Engelhard Avenue
Avenel, NJ 07001   201-382-7600
How to manage your IRA is discussed in this practical guide. It explains how the average wage earner can retire rich. Cost is $3.95 plus $2 postage and handling.

Individual Retirement Plans
Commerce Clearing House
4025 West Peterson Avenue
Chicago, IL 60646   312-583-8500
Rules and penalties of IRAs are discussed in this forty-eight-page booklet. It also discusses annuities and simplified employee pensions among other topics. Cost is $3.

IRA and Keogh: New Opportunities for Retirement Income
Federal Reserve Bank, Philadelphia
Public Information Department
PO Box 66
Philadelphia, PA 19105   215-574-6115
Directed toward the general public, this pamphlet discusses retirement options available under Keogh and IRA plans as expanded by the Economic Recovery Tax Act of 1981. Free.

The IRA Book: The Complete Guide to IRA's and Retirement Planning
The Center for the Study of Services
806 15th Street, NW, Suite 925
Washington, DC 20005   202-347-9612

This book is intended to give you the IRA facts that you won't find in industry brochures. It covers how an IRA can fit into your overall retirement planning, the alternatives to an IRA, and the advantages and disadvantages of various types of investments—from bank accounts to common stocks. Cost is $6.95.

The IRA Handbook: A Complete Guide
New Century Publishers, Inc.
220 Old New Brunswick Road
Piscataway, NJ 08854   201-981-0820
The authors, M. P. Pancheri and D. H. Flynn, both lawyers, discuss, in plain language, the legal ins and outs of an IRA. Rather than a "get rich quick" point of view, the authors discuss building a money base that can be substantially increased once you are familiar with every aspect of an IRA. Cost is $10.95.

Keoghs
Franklin Watts, Inc.
387 Park Avenue, South   800-672-6672
New York, NY 10016   212-686-7070
Written by James E. Cheeks and published in May 1986, this book is a 320-page step-by-step guide to establishing the right Keogh for tax saving and financial independence. It gives case studies, sample IRS forms, and reference tables to help you do it yourself.

You will learn who qualifies, how to make your assets grow, how Keoghs work with IRAs, taxes and estates, and how to get started. Cost is $19.95.

Money Guide to Your IRA
Money
Box 999
Radio City Station
New York, NY 10019   212-586-1212
The editors of *Money* magazine have written this clear, direct, easy-to-use guide to give you the hard information you need to manage and make the most of your IRA. Cost is $3.95.

New York
755 Second Avenue
New York, NY 10017   212-880-0700
Each spring *New York* magazine offers consumers its annual report on investment funds for IRAs. It is highly recommended by *Money* magazine. Each weekly issue contains a financial column on various money matters that consumers may find helpful. Issues may be purchased separately on newsstands. Cost is $1.95.

United of Omaha Life Insurance Company
Mutual of Omaha Plaza
Omaha, NE 68175   402-342-7600
United of Omaha offers the following free booklets to any interested consumer:

- *Questions and Answers on the Individual Retirement Annuity*—this pamphlet discusses who is eligible to establish an IRA.
- *A Comparison of Funding Methods*—a bank or savings and loan IRA is compared to United's Ultrannuity. Free.

100 Highest Yields
Advertising News Service, Inc.
Box 088888   305-627-7717
North Palm Beach, FL 33408   800-327-7717
Published weekly, this newsletter lists high yields on IRAs across the country. It provides the names, addresses, and phone numbers of federally insured institutions and gives you practical information that you can use immediately. Cost is $84 for an annual subscription or $19 for six issues.

PEOPLE TO TALK TO

Michael Pancheri
Director of Personal Planning Services
Phoenix Mutual Life Insurance Co.
1 American Row
Hartford, CT 06115   203-275-5000
Mr. Pancheri, a tax attorney, has been heavily involved in developing IRA programs for banks. He has answered hotline questions on IRA rules for the banking industry and consumers. He is co-author of *The IRA Handbook: A Complete Guide* (see this section).

Richard S. Graber, Vice President
Widdell and Reed
PO 1343
2400 Pershing Road
Kansas City, MO 64141   816-283-4000
Mr. Graber is a Certified Financial Planner and a Certified Pension Consultant with ten years' experience in the retirement plans marketing business. He worked on the first IRA prototype plan and currently writes occasional articles for trade magazines.

Stephen R. Leimberg
American College
270 Bryn Mawr Avenue
Bryn Mawr, PA   Written requests only

Mr. Leimberg serves as professor of taxation and estate planning at the American College. He is the author of over twenty books on taxes and estate planning. A frequent speaker for estate planning councils and life insurance company conventions, Mr. Leimberg has also testified before Congress as an expert witness on IRAs.

Pensions and Social Security

There was once a woman who worked for twenty-odd years for a company that had a pension plan. When she retired she found, to her surprise, that she was entitled to nothing from the plan because her pension benefits were linked to her social security earnings. That is, her pension was reduced because of the amount of social security she was due. This is a true story, cited by the Pension Rights Center in Washington, D.C., to illustrate one of the pitfalls of private pension plans if a consumer does not fully inform him- or herself of all the provisions of his/her particular plan. Many people may not be aware of clauses such as the "integration" clause cited above. Experts advise that you look carefully at any pension plan in order to know, not just what you are entitled to at retirement, but what you get for various contingencies such as early retirement or layoff; and how many years you have to work in order to be qualified to collect your benefits. One of the biggest problems with pensions is that many people change jobs frequently and may lose benefits they could have had by working a few more months or years.

In order to plan your retirement financing you also need to inform yourself as to what method will be used to pay your pension—whether it will be in a lump sum, monthly, quarterly, or what. Under the Employee Retirement Income Security Act (ERISA) of 1974, your employer, is required to provide you with a "summary annual report" of your pension. Since pensions vary from employer to employer you should begin your search for pension information by talking with your employer. After that, you may want to get further information from the sources listed in this chapter.

The first thing you'll want to know about your social security benefits is exactly what they will be when you retire. You can find out by contacting one of the 1,300 offices around the country which serve taxpayers locally, of which there is one or more in every city. The phone numbers are listed in the yellow pages. Ask the office to send you a copy of form #7004—the Request for Statement of Earnings. After you fill this out and send it back, it will be returned to you with your total earnings listed, including a more specific breakdown for the past three or four years. Even if you are not thinking about retiring imminently, the Social Security Administration advises that you check this statement every few years anyway to make sure there are no errors. The government does make mistakes and you'll want to correct errors before you need to draw benefits. The local offices will also answer any questions you may have about your benefits and outline your options to you, although they cannot give you financial planning advice.

Once you know what your social security benefits will be, you can be in a better position to make your retirement plans. But keep in mind, if you have any special problems, that social security also includes disability benefits, survivors' benefits, and Medicare. Again, your local office can tell you more about these items.

Social security and pension plans have become the foundation of a retiree's financial security. Today one out of every six Americans is supported by social security, and 7.3 million Americans receive income from private pension funds.

Even though your social security or pension benefits may be the mainstay of your retirement income, they may not provide all of the funds you will need. That is why it is so important to get as much information as possible about these benefits, and the following sources should help.

AGENCIES, INSTITUTES, AND ORGANIZATIONS

American Federation of Labor and Congress of Industrial Organizations (AFL-CIO)

815 16th Street, NW
Washington, DC 20006   202-637-5000

A federation of autonomous trade unions, the AFL-CIO is an advocate of matters of importance to unions. It serves its union members as a policymaking body and a clearinghouse for information about pensions and other employee benefits. The AFL-CIO offers no service to the individual worker.

Business Roundtable

200 Park Avenue, Suite 2222
New York, NY 10166   212-682-6370

An association for chief executives of major companies, this group studies how public issues affect corporation pension programs. Task forces chaired by chief executives develop position papers on subjects such as changes in the Social Security Program and tax codes. These position papers are available free of charge. The association publishes:

> ■ *Roundtable Report*—a monthly newsletter that summarizes the positions and actions of the association. This newsletter is available free of charge.

Employee Benefit Research Institute (EBRI)

2121 K Street, NW, Suite 860
Washington, DC 20037   202-659-0670

EBRI is a nonprofit, nonpartisan public policy research organization. The Institute provides educational and research materials to employers, employees, retired workers, public officials, members of the press, academics, and the general public. Through its books, policy forums, and monthly subscription service, EBRI provides information about health, welfare and retirement policies. Speakers are available for large groups as staffing permits. Funded by 130 corporate sponsors, the Institute conducts research on all aspects of employee benefits. Publications available from the Institute are:

■ *EBRI Publications*—an index of all periodicals and books published by the Institute. Free.

■ *List of Issue Briefs*—a complete listing of all *EBRI Briefs* published in the last two years. Free.

■ *EBRI Issue Brief*—published monthly, each brief is devoted to expert evaluation of a single employee benefit issue. This publication may be purchased for $10 a single copy. A one-year subscription for *EBRI Issue Brief* and *Employee Benefit Notes* (described below) is available for $100 a year.

■ *Employee Benefit Notes*—a bimonthly publication containing summaries of legislative and regulatory transactions affecting employee benefits. Information on current EBRI research projects is also reported. This publication may be purchased for $10 a single copy. A one-year subscription to *EBRI Issue Brief* (described above) and *Employee Benefit Notes* is available for $100 a year.

ERISA Industry Committee (ERIC)

1726 M Street, NW, Suite 301
Washington, DC 20036   202-833-2800
ERIC is the principal organization representing the views of major U.S. corporations which, in total, sponsor pension and welfare benefit plans for an estimated 10 million U.S. workers. The organization membership is derived principally from the Fortune 500 and includes most major U.S. corporations. It frequently provides representatives to testify before Congress and to appear before organizations, companies, and groups interested in national benefits policy. ERIC also serves as a clearinghouse for information on developments affecting major sponsors of pensions and welfare benefit plans. Occasionally ERIC publishes analyses of legislation and these are available to nonmembers at a small fee. The following publication is published by ERIC:

■ *ERIC Executive Report*—a biweekly newspaper that provides coverage of regulations, court cases, legislation and major events dealing with employee benefits. Free.

General Accounting Office (GAO)

441 G Street, NW
Washington, DC 20548   202-275-6241
GAO prepares reports about retirement and pension issues. Upon your request, staff members will search GAO's Bibliographic Data Base for complete bibliographies of GAO-sponsored reports. Searches and printouts are available free of charge. The following free reports concerning pension plans may be ordered from GAO Documentation Distribution Center, PO Box 6015, Gaithersburg, MD 20760:

■ *Benefit Levels of Nonfederal Retirement Programs*—this report estimates the levels of benefits available from nonfederal retirement programs
using selected studies and databases. The purpose of the report is to assist
Congress in its efforts to design a new retirement program for federal
employees covered by social security.

■ *Features of Nonfederal Retirement Programs*—this report depicts the
prevailing features of nonfederal retirement programs as shown by selected
studies and/or databases. The purpose of the report is to assist Congress
in its efforts to design new retirement programs for federal employees
covered by social security.

House Select Committee on Aging
712 House Office Building, Annex #1
Washington, DC 20515   202-226-3375
This congressional committee of the U.S. House of Representatives takes
an advocacy role for the elderly. It covers legislative matters dealing with
private pensions, health benefits, supplemental security income, social security
and Railroad retirement. Copies of hearings and committee reports are available free of charge upon request. A complete listing of the committee's publications is also available. The committee publishes:

■ *Aging Info*—a frequent newsletter which provides information about
legislative issues affecting the elderly. Free.

Labor-Management Services Administration
Pension and Welfare Benefit Programs
U.S. Department of Labor
200 Constitution Avenue, NW
Washington, DC 20216   202-523-6045
The Employee Retirement Income Security Act (ERISA), which regulates
pension plans and ensures the worker's stake in them, is administered by this
administration. You can obtain information and publications from the main
office cited above or from any of the Administration's field offices listed below.
It produces the following publications and audio/visual shows, all available
free of charge:

■ *What You Should Know About the Pension and Welfare Law*—a sev-
enty-six-page booklet explaining the rights of participants in employee
benefit plans and the responsibilities of plan managers.

■ *Know Your Pension Plan*—this eleven-page booklet explaining various
aspects of pension plans includes checklists for participants to fill in important information about their plans.

■ *You and ERISA*—a twenty-minute slide/sound show designed to help
participants of employee benefit plans understand their basic rights under
the pension reform law. Also available on videotape (available on loan
only).

■ *The SPD and You*—an informative eleven-minute slide/sound show to help plan administrators prepare their summary plan description. Also available on videotape (available on loan only).

■ *What You Should Know About Your Pension Plan*—a twenty-eight-minute videotape of a talk-show program of guests describing their pension problems and experts from the Labor Department advising how problems can be avoided (available on loan only).

LABOR-MANAGEMENT SERVICES ADMINISTRATION AREA OFFICES

Labor-Management Services
Administration
1365 Peachtree Street, NE
Atlanta, GA 30309
404-881-4090

Labor-Management Services
Administration
110 Tremont Street
Boston, MA 02108
617-223-6736

Labor-Management Services
Administration
111 West Huron Street
Buffalo, NY 14202
716-846-4861

Labor-Management Services
Administration
175 West Jackson Boulevard
Chicago, IL 60604
312-353-7264

Labor-Management Services
Administration
555 Griffin Square Building
Dallas, TX 75202
214-767-6831

Labor-Management Services
Administration
1961 Stout Street
Denver, CO 80294
303-837-5061

Labor-Management Services
Administration
231 West Lafayette Street
Detroit, MI 48226
313-226-6200

Labor-Management Services
Administration
300 Ala Moana
Honolulu, HI 96850
808-546-8984

Labor-Management Services
Administration
911 Walnut Street
Kansas City, MO 64106
816-374-5261

Labor-Management Services
Administration
300 North Los Angeles Street
Los Angeles, CA 90012
213-688-4975

Labor-Management Services
Administration
111 Northwest 83rd Street
Miami, FL 33169
305-350-4611

Labor-Management Services
Administration
100 North 6th Street
Minneapolis, MN 55401
612-725-2292

Labor-Management Services
Administration
1808 West End Building
Nashville, TN 37203
615-251-5906

Labor-Management Services
Administration
744 Broad Street
Newark, NJ 07102
201-645-3712

Labor-Management Services
Administration
600 South Street
New Orleans, LA 70130
504-589-6173

Labor-Management Services
Administration
26 Federal Plaza
New York, NY 10007
212-264-1980

Labor-Management Services
Administration
601 Market Street
Philadelphia, PA 19106
215-597-4961

Labor-Management Services
Administration
1000 Liberty Avenue
Pittsburgh, PA 15222
412-644-2925

Labor-Management Services
Administration
210 North 12th Boulevard
St. Louis, MO 63101
314-425-4691

Labor-Management Services
Administration
211 Main Street
San Francisco, CA 94105
415-556-2030

Labor-Management Services
Administration
Carlos Chardon Street
Hato Rey, Puerto Rico 00918
809-753-4441

Labor-Management Services
Administration
909 1st Avenue
Seattle, WA 98174
206-442-5216

Labor-Management Services
Administration
1111 20th Street, NW
Washington, DC 20036
202-254-6510

National Committee to Preserve Social Security and Medicare
1300 19th Street, NW, Suite 310
Washington, DC 20036   202-822-9459
The Committee is a nonprofit, nonpartisan organization that works in an advocacy role to promote the Social Security Program and Medicare. Speakers knowledgeable about the policy and political issues affecting these programs are available on a limited basis for large groups. Numerous free educational publications can be obtained from the Committee. These cover a wide range of topics, for example: social security records, appealing social security decisions, social security benefits for widows and widowers, and Medicare plus

supplemental health insurance. A complete listing of these publications may be obtained free of charge. The following periodical is published by the committee:

- *Saving Social Security*—a bimonthly newsletter containing news of proposed legislation that impacts the Social Security Program and Medicare. This publication is included in the yearly membership fee of $10.

National Council of Senior Citizens
925 15th Street, NW
Washington, DC 20005   202-347-8800
An advocacy organization, the Council's members work for state and federal legislation to benefit the elderly, and they promote senior citizen interests in communities across the U.S. Included in the annual membership fee of $9 is a subscription to its newsletter.

- *Senior Citizen News*—this report is published monthly and states the Council's position on current federal legislation concerning Medicare, social security and the food stamp program.

Policy Center on Aging
Heller Graduate School
Brandeis University
Waltham, MA 02254   617-736-2000
Funded by the Administration on Aging, the Center researches the adequacy of private pensions, health insurance policies, and social security. It makes policy recommendations to federal agencies concerned with topics affecting senior citizens. A free list of the Center's reports is available. It also publishes:

- *Of Current Interest*—a periodic publication for the professional in the aging network. It contains synopses of the Center's research findings. Free.

Older Women's League
1325 G Street, NW
Lower Level B
Washington, DC 20005   202-783-6686
A national advocacy group concerned with issues that affect older women, this group has studied pension and social security. The League often testifies before Congress on these subjects and it has produced several research papers analyzing pensions and social security issues from an older woman's perspective. These papers and the following publications are available to the public:

- *Owl Observer*—published once a month, this tabloid provides information about how older women's issues are affected by federal and state legislation. The subscription fee is included in the League's annual membership dues of $5.

■ *Resource Publication List*—a listing of publications available from the league. Free.

Pension Benefit Guaranty Corporation (PBGC)
2020 K Street, NW
Washington, DC 20006   202-254-4827
PBGC monitors pension benefit plans of companies that have gone bankrupt and, if necessary, assumes custody of these plans. Speakers are available as staffing permits to address all aspects of private-sector pension benefit plans. The following publication is available:
> ■ *Your Guaranteed Pension*—a thirteen-page booklet that answers the questions most frequently asked by pension plan participants about the Pension Benefit Guaranty Corporation and its termination insurance program for single employer pension plans.

Pensions Rights Center
1701 K Street, NW, Suite 305
Washington, DC 20006   202-296-3778
The center is a nonprofit public interest group whose basic goal is to protect pension rights for workers, retirees, and their families. It functions as a clearinghouse for information about pensions. Technical and educational assistance is provided for professionals and individuals having pension problems and questions. The Pension Rights Center will provide experts to speak on panels or at workshops. Numerous publications are available. A free publications list may be requested. Please include a self-addressed stamped envelope.

Railroad Retirement Board
844 Rush Street
Chicago, IL 60611   312-751-4930
A government agency, the Board administers retirement-survivor and unemployment-sickness benefit programs federally mandated for the nation's railroad workers and their families. It maintains one hundred field offices across the country. For the address of the field office nearest you check your telephone directory under "U.S. Government," or consult your local post office. Brochures providing information on benefits are available from the field offices. Individuals conducting research on government benefits can obtain information from the Board's headquarters in Chicago.

Social Security Administration
Department of Health and Human Services
6401 Security Boulevard   301-594-2520 or your local office
Baltimore, MD 21235   listed in your telephone directory

This government agency administers the Social Security Program. Upon request, its field offices provide speakers for preretirement seminars. The agenda for these seminars includes an explanation of the Social Security Program, the requirements for eligibility, documents necessary for the first visit to a field office and what to expect in benefits. A complete list of information pamphlets and films is available from any of the 1,320 Social Security field offices across the country. Your local office can send you a computerized printout of your quarterly earnings and contribution to Social Security. You should check this periodically to see you've been credited for your payments. To get a copy request *Form 7004 Statement of Earnings.* The agency publishes:

> ■ *Social Security Bulletin*—a monthly publication that lists the latest changes in the Social Security Program as well as statistical data and surveys relating to the program. This publication is directed toward the professional and is available by subscription from the Government Printing Office for $23 a year. Order from: Superintendent of Documents, Government Printing Office, Washington, DC 20404, 202-783-3238.
>
> ■ *Estimating Your Social Security Retirement Check*—a guide for estimating retirement benefits using the "indexing" method, this also explains how to figure benefits for the worker's dependents. This fourteen-page publication is available free of charge.
>
> ■ *Thinking about Retiring*—this twelve-page leaflet, in a question-and-answer format, provides information about retirement and social security. Free.

Social Security Subcommittee
House Committee on Ways and Means
1102 Longworth House Office Building
Washington, DC 20515   202-225-9263

This U.S. Congressional subcommittee is responsible for introducing legislation, in the House of Representatives, regarding Social Security. A schedule of hearings and copies of testimony are available free of charge.

U.S. Office of Personnel Management
Compensation Group
Bureau of Retirement
900 E Street, NW
Washington, DC 20415   202-632-7700

While the Office of Personnel Management administers the civil service retirement system, the responsibility for carrying out the federal retirement program is delegated to the individual government agencies. The Civil Service Retirement Information Office serves the retired federal worker. The retired worker may call to receive information on changes in the program or problems of current interest. Retirement technicians are also available to handle individual problems.

Veterans Administration (VA)

810 Vermont Avenue, NW   202-389-2073 or toll-free number
Washington, DC 20420   listed in your telephone book

Federal benefits for veterans and their dependents are administered by this government agency. For information regarding benefits call the toll-free number listed in the government section of your telephone directory under "U.S. Government." The Veterans Administration publishes several publications that describe available benefits and list all Veterans Administration regional offices. Examples are:

■ *A Survey of Veterans Administration Benefits*—a pamphlet which briefly describes current benefits. It is available free of charge from any Veterans Administration regional office.

■ *Federal Benefits for Veterans and Dependents*—a seventy-two-page pamphlet which describes the wide range of benefits available to veterans and their dependents. This publication is available for $2.50 from the Superintendent of Documents, Government Printing Office, Washington, DC 20402, 202-783-3238.

Women's Equity Action League (WEAL)

1250 I Street, NW, Suite 305
Washington, DC 20005   202-898-1588

WEAL is a national, nonprofit membership organization specializing in women's economic issues. It conducts research and education projects, supports litigation, and lobbies. Staff members are available to speak to large groups about issues of concern to women. The league produces numerous publications that address social security issues of concern to women. Publications available from WEAL are:

■ *WEAL Washington Report*—a bimonthly periodical that focuses on issues of concern to women including: current legislation, Supreme Court rulings, executive branch actions. Nonmember subscription rate is $35 a year.

■ *WEAL Informed*—a legislative alert mailed first class five or six times a year. Nonmember subscription rate is $20.

■ *WEAL Facts*—a list of all available WEAL publications. This list is free of charge.

■ *Single Fact Sheets*—information sheets on social security issues of concern to women. The following titles may be obtained by mailing $3 and a self-addressed stamped envelope to WEAL.

Social Security Is a Women's Issue
Social Security and Minority Women
Social Security Amendments of 1983: Impact of Financing Provisions on Women
Women's Provisions in the Social Security Amendments of 1983
Earnings Sharing Under Social Security

WHAT TO READ

Complete Tax Guide to U.S. Civil Service Retirement Benefits (Publication 721)

Internal Revenue Service
Public Affairs Division
Department of Treasury
1111 Constitution Avenue, NW, Room 2315
Washington, DC 20224   Written inquiries only

Publication 721 explains how the federal income tax, estate tax, and gift tax rules apply to benefits that federal retired employees receive under the Civil Service Retirement Act.

Consumer Information Center

General Services Administration
Washington, DC 20405   Written requests only

The center searches out the best new federal consumer booklets about pensions, social security, and Medicare. To order the following free publications write to the Consumer Information Center (T), ATTN: S. James, PO Box 100, Pueblo, Colorado 81002.

- *A Woman's Guide to Social Security* (514N)—what women should know about benefits on retirement, disability, widowhood, or divorce.
- *Your Social Security* (515N)—all about social security and Medicare benefits, including who gets them and how to apply.

Pension Facts (509)

American Council of Life Insurance
1850 K Street, NW
Washington, DC 20006-2284   202-862-4124

An information resource for those involved with pensions, this annual publication outlines major pension and retirement programs in the United States, presents statistical data about these plans and traces their development. It includes a glossary and annotated bibliography. The sixty-one-page booklet is available free of charge.

Social Security Bibliography (SB-165)
Superintendent of Documents
Government Printing Office (GPO)
Washington, DC 20402   202-783-3238
    All social security publications available from GPO are described in this subject bibliography. Free.

PEOPLE TO TALK TO

Dr. James H. Schulz
Policy Center on Aging
Heller Graduate School
Brandeis University
Waltham, MA 02254
    Dr. Schulz is Director of the Policy Center on Aging at Brandeis University. He is the author of over sixty books, reports, and articles in the general area of income distribution, pensions, and the economics of aging. He is especially well known for his computer simulation projections of the future economic status of the retired population. Dr. Schulz has testified before various congressional committees, the President's Commission on Pension Policy, and the National Commission on Social Security. He served on the Senate Special Committee on Aging's Task Force on the Economics of Aging. He has also lectured throughout the United States and in many foreign countries. His most recent book is entitled *The Economics of Aging.*

Trusts

See also:
Estate Planning

Trust arrangements are set up by banks or attorneys—and often both—to hold money for a specific purpose, usually in case the trustor (owner of the money) dies. Some are used to provide educational funds or charitable contributions with tax benefits for the person giving the money. Examples of the more popular trusts are:

- A revocable trust which can be changed at any time by the owner
- An irrevocable trust which cannot be altered unless the beneficiary agrees
- A living trust between two living people
- A testamentary trust which is set up after the death of the person giving the money
- A bypass trust whereby money or assets are put in trust for beneficiaries with any income generated going to the trustor as long as he/she is alive
- A Clifford Trust (or short-term trust), for ten years and a day, with income from it going to the beneficiary—often for educational expenses. After ten years, the principal goes back to the trustor. These trusts have decreased in popularity because under the new tax law trusts started after March 2, 1986, do not receive the same tax advantage as one started before this date.

According to experts, the most common mistake made when setting up a trust is that the creator doesn't give clear instructions to those involved. Often conflicting information is given to the beneficiary, the bank, and the attorney. Unfortunately everyone then has a different understanding of the trust.

To avoid this situation experts suggest you first sit down with the beneficiary and make sure he/she understands what you want done with the money or other assets. Next, you and your beneficiary should visit the attorney and the bank trust officer to outline your needs. Then, if a trust is written for the record, be sure everyone reads and understands it before it is signed. Two of the most common problems that arise on someone's death are that the beneficiary often wants more money or wants it sooner than the bank will release it. The bank bases its decision on its interpretation of the trust—so again be certain all parties understand what the trust entails.

What should your first step be if you are interested in learning about or setting up a trust? Call the trust officer of your bank. They don't charge fees for advice and they can often refer you to experienced attorneys if necessary. Some trusts don't require attorneys to set them up; others do.

Most revocable trusts do not derive tax benefits for the trustor. Ask an attorney or tax accountant for advice on this. In some states banks, attorneys, and accountants can be trustees, but banks usually handle them.

This chapter identifies resources to help you learn what you need to know about setting up a trust. The American Bankers Association (ABA) is an excellent resource with many publications to help you. The ABA will also refer you to its members for help.

If you want to bypass professionals and learn on your own, contact NOLO Press, which offers books and other publications. It is a self-help, legal-oriented publisher. Communication Channels, Inc., is another publisher offering directories of trust organizations and magazines to help you understand trusts.

AGENCIES, INSTITUTES, AND ORGANIZATIONS

American Bankers Association (ABA)
1120 Connecticut Avenue, NW
Washington, DC 20036   202-467-4101

A professional association of bankers, ABA is concerned with exchanging information and meeting the needs of the public. It maintains a comprehensive library on banking, finance, management and law. Extensive specialized research and information services are available for members and to the public. Reference staff in ABA's Trust Department is available to answer consumer questions about trusts and will make referrals. These are all described in ABA's catalogue of publications, available free of charge. Some of the trust publications are:

■ *The Trust Business*—a comprehensive overview is given in this 300-page book. Contents include the role of the trust department in a commercial bank and a description of the services provided by the trust department to individuals and institutions. Cost is $30.

■ *Trust Letter*—published monthly, this newsletter is produced and written under the direction of the ABA Trust Division and its Government Relations Staff. It is recognized as the trust industry's leading newsletter for timely, reliable, and accurate information on national legislation and regulations. Cost is $45 a year.

■ *Trust Management Update*—published ten times a year, this compendium of articles written by industry leaders, includes: notices of national and regional conferences; workshops and schools; and information on new products and services. Cost is $37.50 a year.

Communication Channels, Inc.
6255 Barfield Road
Atlanta, GA 30328   404-256-9800

A diversified magazine publishing company, Communication Channels offers a *Directory of Trust Institutions* and also a monthly magazine, *Trusts and Estates.* You are invited to submit questions on estate planning and administration, including developments in these fields under recent and proposed legislation. Answers to selected questions will appear in the magazine.

- *Trusts and Estates*—published monthly, this magazine serves the field of estate planning administration and also serves the related areas of investments, laws, taxes, life insurance, property appraisal and liquidation. It offers a free question-and-answer service to its readers. Subscribers receive a free copy of the *1986 Directory of Trust Institutions.* Cost is $49 a year.
- *1986 Directory of Trust Institutions*—a master guide, this directory lists more than 5,000 banks with trust departments and their key trust, pension, and other estate planning professionals. The names, addresses, and phone numbers and the trust volume dollar of trust assets of each bank. It is free to subscribers to *Trusts and Estates.* Cost is $29.50.

WHAT TO READ

A Guide to Wills and Trusts
The Circular
Bank of America
Department 3120
PO Box 37120
San Francisco, CA 94137   415-622-3208
This consumer information report explains, in easy-to-understand language, how to set up a trust. Order #AD-266. Cost is $1.

Plan Your Estate: Wills, Probate Avoidance, Trusts and Taxes
NOLO Press
950 Parket Street
Berkeley, CA 94710   415-549-1976
Authored by Denis Clifford, this book tells you how to plan your estate and set up a living trust. Cost is $15.95.

US Fiduciary Income Tax Return, Form 1041
Internal Revenue Service (IRS)
Available from all local IRS offices, this publication is used to report the income of an estate or trust. It gives general information on trusts, such as who must file and what to file. It also provides definitions and descriptions of all the various types of trusts. Free.

PEOPLE TO TALK TO

Roy M. Adams
Schiff Hardin and Waite
7200 Sears Tower
Chicago, IL 60606   312-875-1000
    A partner in the Chicago law firm of Schiff Hardin and Waite, Mr. Adams answers consumer questions about estate planning through a question-and-answer service provided by *Trusts and Estates* magazine (see in this section). He also writes articles for the magazine. A professor at Northwestern University School of Law in Chicago, Mr. Adams teaches courses on estate planning.

Life Insurance

For the investor, the tax-reform typhoon has not blown down every shelter on the beach. While IRAs and mutual funds appear to be losing their investment momentum, single premium life (SPL) insurance policies are drawing more and more attention as a tax-free haven within which the investor can weather the storm.

SPL is an insurance policy which not only allows an individual to take advantage of the security of the death benefit, but unlike the case with term insurance, the individual can use the money tax-free and normally interest-free in his or her lifetime. This is how it works. A one-time premium of $5,000 or more (there is usually no limit) is paid up front. That $5,000 accrues interest at a competitive rate. As that interest grows, the policyholder not only receives tax-free distributions but can also borrow against the accrued interest tax-free and interest-free, usually without having to pay any fee for the loan. Among the advantages of investing in an SPL are: building a substantial nest egg for retirement, funding college education, making charitable endowments and purchasing real estate.

Before considering SPL as a tax shelter, one expert advises consumers to first consider their personal financial situation, taking into account the following: personal cash flow, need for insurance, risk profile, liquidity needs, and their tax situation. If you decide to invest in SPL, experts agree that you should shop carefully and deal only with companies that have top ratings. The American Council of Life Insurance provides the A. M. Best Co. rating for each insurance company; this rating indicates a company's financial strength. Consumers are encouraged to call their toll-free number (800-423-8000) for rating information, or to obtain other general life insurance information.

The following organizations and publications will offer you guidance on how to take advantage of this unique tax shelter with the security of a paid-up life insurance policy.

AGENCIES, INSTITUTES, AND ORGANIZATIONS

American Council of Life Insurance
1850 K Street, NW   202-862-4124
Washington, DC 20006   800-423-8000
Representing the life insurance business in legislative and regulatory areas at the federal, state, and local levels of government, the American Council of Life Insurance serves the public as a central source of information about life insurance. It provides information about the purpose and uses of life insurance, maintains research facilities to record performance of the business, and mea-

sures attitudes of the public on issues relevant to the insurance business. Consumers may call the toll-free number above and receive a rating for a particular insurance company, compiled by the A. M. Best Co. These ratings indicate the financial strength of a particular company. Consumers are encouraged to call and ask general questions about the different types of life insurance polices available. The following publications are available at no charge:

■ *A Consumers' Guide to Life Insurance*—this twenty-one-page booklet will help you make informed decisions about purchasing life insurance. It describes the major types of coverage and tells you how you can use it to protect your family. It describes all basic types of insurance, including the important feature of "cash value" and how to borrow money from a policy.

■ *File Insurance Fact Book*—published in alternating years, this book provides an overview of the year's developments in the life insurance business through text, tables and charts. It makes available annual data on the performance of the life insurance business.

National Insurance Consumer Organization (NICO)

121 North Payne Street
Alexandria, VA 22314   703-549-8050

A nonprofit public interest group with a national membership, NICO offers advice to help consumers purchase life insurance. It provides how-to information, including a newletter, booklets, manuals, and special reports to help consumers cut their insurance costs. NICO offers a personalized computer comparison of the rate of return on investments of a whole life policy versus other investment options. The staff is available to answer general questions and provide referrals. The following publications are available:

■ *Buyers Guide to Insurance*—this thirteen-page booklet includes a section on how to purchase life insurance. It provides guidelines to help consumers evaluate costs of different policies. Free.

■ *Taking the Bite Out of Life Insurance*—guidelines are given in this fifty-four-page book on the maximum prices you should pay for life insurance policies. It tells you which companies are best, discusses universal life, and provides the pros and cons on whether to trade in an old policy for a new one. Cost is $7.25. Free to members.

Rate of Return Service (ROR)

James H. Hunt
National Insurance Consumer Organization (NICO)
8 Tahanto Street
Concord, NH 03301   602-224-2805

For whole life, universal life, variable life, or any mix of death protection and cash value insurance, NICO will calculate RORs by the "Linton Yield" method, usually for five, ten, fifteen, and twenty years. This service seeks to estimate a policy's internal investment return. You are sent a computer printout showing the annual renewable term (ART) rates used, average annual ROR for five, ten, and fifteen years, "marginal" RORs for years 6-10, 11-15 and 16-20, and taxable gains on surrender after five, ten, fifteen, and twenty years. For fast service, send your proposal(s) with a self-addressed, stamped, business envelope to the address above. Cost is $25 and $20 for each extra policy sent at the same time.

Shearson Lehman Brothers
Investment Planning and Management Group
400 Perimeter Center Terrace, NE
Suite 290   404-399-7413
Atlanta, GA 30346   800-241-6900
    For consumers interested in a single premium insurance policy of $25,000 or more, analysts will answer any questions on taxed or tax-free investments Use their toll-free telephone number listed above.

Tax Planning Seminars
PO Box 812
Riverton, NJ 08077   609-772-1502
    Frank Miller, president of tax planning seminars and also a financial consultant, gives seminars on single premium and whole life insurance to producing agents, brokers, and the public upon request. He will answer consumer questions about the sixty policies described in the publication listed below:
    ■ *Marketing Single Premium Whole Life II*—updated for the New Tax Reform Law, this nontechnical booklet provides an easy-to-understand comparison of sixty policies sold as of January 1987. Cost is $16.95.

WHAT TO READ

Brennan Reports
Brennan Reports Inc.
Valley Forge Office Colony
PO Box 882   215-783-0647
Valley Forge, PA 19482   800-523-7289
    Published monthly, this newsletter analyzes sophisticated tax-advantaged investments such as single premium variable life insurance and other investment strategies. It will tell you in plain English what's good or bad in the investment marketplace, and how you can use the new tax law to your benefit. Cost is $184 per year.

Forecasts and Strategies
Phillips Publishing Inc.
7811 Montrose Road
Potomac, MD 20845   301-349-2100

Published monthly, this investment newsletter provides information on how to invest your money tax-free. It analyzes new products, including single premium life insurance. Back issues specifically about investing in life insurance are available. Cost is $95 per year.

The Insider's Guide to Single Premium Life
David T. Phillips & Co.
3200 North Dobson Road
Building C   602-897-6088
Chandler, AZ 85224   800-223-9610

A comprehensive yet concise exploration of single premium life insurance (SPL), this report and audio cassette package was prepared as a result of thousands of requests from investors for an authoritative, easy-to-understand explanation of SPL as an investment opportunity. Written after the Tax Reform Act, it introduces some of the creative ways in which SPL is being used to meet certain financial goals by providing tax-free retirement income. Cost is $39.95 for a three-cassette package and $69.95 for a six-cassette package.

The Insurance Forum
Insurance Forum Inc.
PO Box 245
Ellettsville, IN

A four-page monthly periodical, the *Insurance Forum* reports on issues facing the insurance industry. The following back issues are available: Observations on Single-Premium Life Insurance" (2/87); "How Not to Promote Cash-Value Life Insurance" (2/85), and "Credit Life Reinsurance and Antirebating Laws" (3/86). Cost is $30 a year or $2 for a single back copy.

Life Insurance: A Consumer's Handbook
Indiana University Press
10th and Morton streets
Bloomington, IN 47405

Author Joseph M. Belth, Professor of Insurance in the School of Business at Indiana University, shows in clear and simple language how a consumer can save money by shopping carefully for life insurance. Topics include: "How to measure life insurance needs" and "Choosing the appropriate type of life insurance as an investment." Cost is $12.50 prepaid.

■ ■

> ## Saving for a Rainy Day?
>
> Thirty-seven percent of American households keep less than $3,000 in savings and investments. A study conducted in July 1986 by *Money* magazine showed the median amount of savings and investment in a household was $7,000—including savings accounts, money market funds, CDs, stocks, bonds, and mutual funds, but not including real estate. Of the 37 percent, 10 percent kept no savings or investments at all. Only 7 percent had $100,000 or more.

■ ■

Tax Reform Act of 1986 "TRA Analysis"
Coopers & Lybrand
Tax Department
1251 Avenue of the Americas
New York, NY 10020　　　　　　　　　　　　　　　202-536-2000

This brochure by the professional tax consulting service describes in simple language the most significant provisions addressing life insurance in the tax law. It explains the new law for policyholders and for life insurance companies. Free.

PEOPLE TO TALK TO

David Phillips
David T. Phillips & Co.
3200 North Dobson Road
Building C　　　　　　　　　　　　　　　　　　　602-897-6088
Chandler, AZ 85224　　　　　　　　　　　　　　　800-223-9610

Mr. Phillips is one of the nation's leading experts on single premium life insurance. He has written articles for a number of prestigious financial publications and has been a featured speaker at financial conferences around the world. Mr. Phillips is co-author of *The Insider's Guide to Single Premium Life*. He will answer questions from consumers at the toll-free number listed above.

James H. Hunt
Director
National Insurance Consumer Organization (NICO)
8 Tahanto Street
Concord, NH 03301   602-224-2805
     Mr. Hunt is a former Vermont insurance commissioner and a NICO director with thirty years of life insurance experience. He provides the Rate of Return Service described above. For members of NICO, he will answer questions and provide guidance on insurance investments. For nonmembers, Mr. Hunt will act as a consultant for a fee.

Appendix One

Guidance for the
Next Generation of Investors

Kids and Money

See also:
Games

With interests ranging from fast food to video games to designer jeans, kids today are exercising their buying power. And sooner rather than later they will be exercising their investing power. Listed below are a number of sources to help children begin to understand the basics of money and investing.

AGENCIES, INSTITUTES, AND ORGANIZATIONS

The Academy for Economic Education
Figgie International, Inc.
1000 Virginia Center Parkway
Richmond, VA 23295   804-264-5851
    The Academy offers:
        ■ *Ump's Fwat: An Annual Report for Young People*—a unique annual report just for kids, this humorous, full-color twenty-three-page booklet tells the story of how a business begins. Instead of numbers or percentages, the report refers to such terms as "flinks," "fwats," and "fwappers." Ump, a caveman, discovers that his fwat (baseball bat) is in great demand, so he invests some flinks (money) to start producing them and hires three friends. Before long, his company is turning a profit and paying a dividend of twenty cents. Economic principles are taught in an entertaining style sure to delight youngsters from fourth to eighth grade. Up to five copies are free; over five copies cost fifty cents each, a Teacher's Kit, containing thirty copies of *Ump's Fwat* and a teacher's guide is $100.
        ■ *Economic Baseball Game*—a game suitable for ages six and up. Players participate in three market exchange sessions of buying and selling base-balls. The game materials are keyed as to what price to pay and what price to sell. Bartering occurs between buyers and sellers. The players experience how supply and demand is used to determine market price and how fluctuation in supply and demand affects price. An instructor's guide is included. Cost is $5.

Comic Books
Federal Reserve Bank of New York
Publications Section
33 Liberty Street
New York, NY 10045   212-791-5000

If your child is hooked on comic books, you may want to send off for these free educational comic books:

- *The Story of Money*—describes how coin, paper, and checkbook money have evolved over the ages.
- *The Story of Banks*—shows how banks act as financial "supermarkets" in our society and link borrowers and savers.
- *The Story of Checks and Electronic Payments*—describes how checks are used and processed.
- *The Story of Inflation*—explains how inflation is a serious economic problem, difficult to cure.
- *The Story of Consumer Credit*—describes the impact of consumer credit on our lives.

Dow Jones & Company, Inc.

The Educational Service Bureau
PO Box 300
Princeton, NJ 08540   609-452-2000

If you are a student or a professor, you may be able to take advantage of this company's program, which offers discounts on *Wall Street Jounal* subscriptions. Groups of seven or more students are eligible; have your professor call the Educational Service Bureau to arrange it. Your professor will get a complimentary subscription. Dow Jones also offers the following free publication you may want to ask for.

- *How to Read Stock Market Quotations*—a stock selected from the journal's NYSE Composite Transaction list and the Over-the-Counter list are used to illustrate this guide to the figures and symbols found in most daily newspaper market listings. One copy is free; educators may order up to fifty copies.

New York Stock Exchange

11 Wall Street, 18th Floor
New York, NY 10005   212-623-2089

The New York Stock Exchange publishes two helpful guides for teachers who wish to introduce youngsters in their junior or senior high school classes to the world of Wall Street:

- *Taking Stock in the Future*—this teaching portfolio is free to classroom teachers. It is geared for grades 7-12. It would be appropriate for junior high social studies classes or high school business, economics, finance, consumer education, or math classes. There is a teaching guide to seven units, activity sheet masters, transparencies, and an evaluation form.
- *You and the Investment World*—a companion piece to the above-mentioned *Taking Stock in the Future,* this thirty-two page supplementary workbook/activity book contains six chapters. There are projects in applied economics and personal investment for students working individually

or in groups. Graphs, charts, and illustrations are included. It costs $5 for a single copy or $75 for twenty-five copies.

Securities Industry Association   212-608-1500—Shari Sala,
120 Broadway   Economic Education Coordinator
New York, NY 10271   212-685-5499

The Securities Industry Association, through its Committee on Economic Education, sponsors a unique nationwide program, known as the *Stock Market Game,* a computer-based simulation designed primarily for high school and college students in a classroom setting. It involves students in costs and benefits in economic decision-making, explains the sources and uses of capital, and helps students gain a practical knowledge of the stock market.

In connection with an appropriate course, students form teams to compete against each other in ten-week sessions during the fall and spring of each year. Each team invests a hypothetical $100,000 in common stocks on the New York and American Stock Exchanges. Transactions are then processed at various centers throughout the country and teams are issued weekly portfolios, which include: current holdings, brokerage fees, margin interest, and rankings which list how teams fared in the competition that week. At the end of the competition, award ceremonies are held to recognize winners, which are those teams that have increased their portfolios by the largest amount.

More than 200,000 students in thirty-nine states have participated in the *Stock Market Game,* and by 1988 more than a million students will have participated. The success of this program is due largely to the support given by interested volunteer members of the Securities Industry Association—experienced stockbrokers with some of the best-known brokerage firms in the country. If you'd like to know more about how the *Stock Market Game* can be part of the curriculum at a high school or college in your area, write or call the Securities Industry Association, in care of the Joint Council on Economic Education, at the above address.

Teachers (elementary through high school) will especially like the free, twenty-eight-page booklet *Aspects of Economic Education in the Classroom: An Inventory of Educational Materials and Findings,* also available from the Securities Industry Association, Foundation for Economic Education. It contains descriptions of more than 300 books and audiovisual materials (filmstrips, slide shows, etc.) suitable for classroom lessons on a variety of economics-related topics (earning money, consumer awareness, credit, free enterprise system, history of money, taxes, banking, family budgeting, and more). Grade level, price, and ordering information are included. Be sure your school library sends for a copy of this!

Games

See also:
Kids and Money

If you've ever played *Monopoly,* you probably know the thrill of wheeling and dealing in big money, even if it *is* only make-believe. Investment games can also give you that same wheeling and dealing feeling as well as teaching you about some of the basic investing fundamentals, which can eventually be put into practice. Whether your interests are in stocks and bonds, real estate investments, or foreign currency, you'll find everything from board games to computer simulation games listed here. Although most are for adults, some will delight both you and your kids.

GAMES

Avalon Hill Game Company
4517 Harford Road
Baltimore, MD 21214   301-254-5300

Avalon Hill, which has grown from a garage-operated business in the 1950s to a multimillion-dollar game design and publishing company today, produces several money-related and business strategy games, including:

■ *Acquire*—a two-hour game for two to six players, that plunges you into the glamorous world of hotels. Players start hotel chains and expand them while buying stock in active chains, even those begun by other players. Players with the most stock in a chain control that chain and then try to make a profit by arranging mergers. The winner is the person with the most money at the end of the game after all profits and stockholder bonuses have been given out. Cost for a board game is approximately $20, and a computer game, suitable for Atari 400/800, Apple II, TRS-80 Models I/III, and PET CBM 2001, is approximately $25.

■ *Stock Market*—actually two separate games, with playing time of about one hour each, for up to six players. Each player starts with some money and some shares of stock. In Game I, players decide what they will buy and sell, placing their orders at the Trading Post. A Trend Card is then drawn and market prices change accordingly. The winner is the player with the greatest net worth at the end of the game. Game II adds rules for preferred stock, convertible bonds, warrants, and stock splits. Special rules are provided for solitaire play. Cost is $15.

■ *Stocks and Bonds*—here's your chance to be a Wall Street genius in this one-hour game featuring both "bear" (declining) and "bull" (advancing) markets. Players choose a general strategy and then invest in stocks that fit their strategy. You can play it safe or gamble (or do a little of both). The winner is the one with the most money earned after completing all transactions. Cost for a board game is approximately $15 and a computer game, suitable for TRS-80, PET, Atari 400/800, Apple II, and IBM PC, is approximately $25.

■ *Business Strategy*—find out how it feels to be the president of a major corporation in this two-hour game for two to four players. *Business Strategy* is actually four games in one: the Family Game, the Basic Business Game, the Classroom Game, and the Corporate Game. Each of these games adds more rules or situations to the basic strategy. Each player begins with two factories, some raw materials, some finished products, and some money. A player bids for more raw materials, but because there are never enough to go around, only the highest bidders are able to stay in the game. In the course of making finished products and selling them, players are challenged by unexpected problems such as workers' strikes or consumer boycotts. You must be shrewd, logical, and opportunistic to win. A gameboard, business climate cards, pack of money, tokens, and rulebook are included. Cost is approximately $14.

■ *Foreign Exchange*—this two-hour game simulates the international currency situation. It is rather complex and is recommended for economics students or those with more than a casual interest in world money matters. International companies realize gains and losses when changing currency rates alter the value of their income in foreign countries. Players can buy and manage multinational companies in cities throughout the world. The game has three levels of difficulty and is designed for two to four players. Cost for a board game is approximately $16 and a computer game for TRS-80 Models I/III is approximately $25.

■ *Gold*—an international investment game for the whole family, this game is for two to eight players and takes about one hour. Each player starts by selecting multi million dollar holdings (the portfolio) in U.S. and foreign investments, choosing from U.S. stocks and bonds, Japanese yen, German deutschmark bonds, British sterling gilts, Swiss franc deposits, and, of course, gold. Investments may prove safe or risky, and players learn strategy to win high earnings. Cost is approximately $19.

Match Wits with the Harvard MBA's: The $100,000 Inheritance
by Tom Fischgrund
Fawcett/Columbine
201 East 50th Street
New York, NY 10022   212-572-2382

"Most of us dream of having a lot of money some day," says Tom Fischgrund, a Harvard Business School graduate, "but the truth is that most of us wouldn't really know the best way to handle *real* money." *Match Wits with the Harvard MBA's,* an investment strategy game book, pits players head-to-head with three Harvard MBAs who are financial experts. Players decide, along with the pros, how to invest $100,000. It's a painless lesson in how to make, or lose, millions. Beating the experts takes skill, and players learn the fundamentals of investment strategies, such as CDs, risk return tradeoffs, and risks of investing in new companies, futures, and options. *Monopoly* players and other financial hobbyists will enjoy this 320-page challenge. Cost is $6.95.

Securities Industry Association
See listing under KIDS AND MONEY.

Stock Market Specialist
American Stock Exchange
Publications Services Division
86 Trinity Place
New York, NY 10006   212-306-1390
For future financial wizards (ages sixteen and up) and those interested in sharpening their investment skills, *Stock Market Specialist* offers the players the chance to be AMEX specialists, responsible for maintaining fair and orderly markets in their books while they strive to increase their net worth. This board game, for up to four players, simulates activity on the trading floor. Cost is $19.95, plus $3.95 shipping and handling.

COMPUTER GAMES

The following companies produce computer games to challenge stock market enthusiasts and investment hobbyists. These are sophisticated simulation games for players with some technical knowledge.

Blue Chip Software
6744 Eton Avenue
Canoga Park, CA 91303   818-346-0730
Several computer software games, compatible with IBM, Apple, and Commodore computers, are offered by Blue Chip Software:

- *Millionaire*—a stock market venture in which players receive $10,000 to trade fifteen blue chip stocks, including IBM and General Motors. Players can trade call and put options and borrow up to 80 percent of their net worth. Each session starts in the fourteenth week of a ninety-one-week trading period. The player reviews graphs and headlines about each stock and industry and as in real life, players are charged brokerage commissions. Taxes are computed at a 30 percent rate on profits, and tax credits and losses are figured. At the end of the ninety-one-week session, holdings are converted to cash and a new session starts. Cost is $59.95.
- *Baron*—a real estate game in which players buy and sell residential, commercial, and underdeveloped properties. General pricing trends and

news are supplied and closing costs, taxes, and cash flow are figured in. Players can borrow against their holdings and can buy or sell second mortgages. Cost is $59.95.

■ *Tycoon*—a commodities game in which players start with $10,000 and can trade only wheat, soybeans, cattle, and pork bellies. As you make money, you can trade up to fifteen commodities. You become a "tycoon" when you reach one million dollars. Cost is $59.95.

■ *Squire*—perhaps the most complex of Blue Chip's computer games, *Squire* challenges your investment skills and strategy in the bond market, rare collectibles, real estate, money market funds, and other areas. The game starts in the fourteenth month of a 240-month simulation period. At the end of the twenty-year period, you should have increased your nest egg sizably. You study newspaper headlines and financial trend graphs in order to make your decisions on where and how much to invest. Cost is $69.95.

Beat the Street

MEA Software Associates
PO Box 2385, Department A
Littleton, CO 80161   303-796-7100

This stock market game, created by a veteran of the New York Stock Exchange, allows the player to pick a stock or have the computer pick a stock at random from the 175 Big Board listings. The screen duplicates actual price movements. When familiar technical patterns appear, buy and sell signals are flashed. The successful player will be able to distinguish true signals from false ones. Each simulation takes about fifteen minutes. There are additional disks covering about 700 companies, including those on the NASDAQ and the American Stock Exchange. *Beat the Street* is compatible with Apple II computers. Cost is $49.95.

Comex

The Commodity Exchange of New York
4 World Trade Center
New York, NY 10048   212-938-2900

According to one reporter, this game resembles a graduate course in options and futures trading. More than one Wall Street brokerage firm uses *Comex* to train new brokers. It is complex and tricky and will try the patience of even the most skillful player. Starting with $25,000, you make fifty moves within one hundred days to boom or bust. The game runs on IBM and IBM-compatible computers. Cost is $69.95.

Speculator
OCO Software
PO Box 1067
Belvedere, CA 94920   800-446-3400
    This is an animated simulation game in which you place an order and a broker appears, or a runner heads for the trading pits to fill an order. Players can trade in twenty-two commodities, including foreign currencies, T-bills, metals, and agriculture. This game works with actual market data from 1984. There are simulated tickers and flashing news headlines. Lots of flash and excitement. Runs on IBM computers. Cost is $69.95.

Appendix Two

The Down Side

Arbitration and Mediation

Should you have a dispute or disagreement with a securities firm, you can resolve it by impartial arbitration at one of the organizations described in this section. These organizations generally handle two kinds of disputes: (1) those between a customer and a brokerage firm and (2) intra-industry disputes. Examples in the first category include the following: (1) you think you've been the victim of some type of fraudulent activity, such as churning (excessive trading in an account for the purchase of generating commissions); or (2) you think your stockbroker has misrepresented a stock he convinced you to invest in. The second category covers disputes between firms.

AGENCIES, INSTITUTES, AND ORGANIZATIONS

Securities Arbitration Organizations

You can file a suit at whatever stock exchange or organization your brokerage firm is a member, regardless of where the security in question is traded. Arbitration is conducted in accordance with a uniform code established by the Securities Industry Conference on Arbitration. To obtain further information, contact the Director of Arbitration at any of the organizations listed below. He or she will send you information pamphlets and forms along with a set of instructions for filling them out. (Note: MSRB and NASD are described in this section; for information about the exchanges listed below see Stock Exchanges.)

Director of Arbitration
American Stock Exchange, Inc.
86 Trinity Place
New York, NY 10006
212-306-1000

Director of Arbitration
Boston Stock Exchange, Inc.
1 Boston Place
Boston, MA 02108
617-723-9500

Director of Arbitration
Chicago Board Options
  Exchange, Inc.
LaSalle at Van Buren
Chicago, IL 60605
312-786-5600

Director of Arbitration
Cincinnati Stock Exchange, Inc.
205 Dixie Terminal Building
Cincinnati, OH 45202
513-621-1410

Director of Arbitration
Midwest Stock Exchange, Inc.
120 South LaSalle Street
Chicago, IL 60603
312-368-2222
(This exchange is involved only in settling disputes between its members.)

Director of Arbitration
Municipal Securities Rulemaking
  Board (MSRB)
1150 Connecticut Avenue, NW,
  Suite 507
Washington, DC 20036
202-223-9347

Director of Arbitration
National Association of
  Securities Dealers,
  Inc. (NASD)
2 World Trade Center,
98th Floor
New York, NY 10048
212-839-6251

Director of Arbitration
New York Stock Exchange, Inc.
11 Wall Street
New York, NY 10005
212-656-3000

Director of Arbitration
Pacific Stock Exchange, Inc.
618 South Spring Street
Los Angeles, CA 90014
213-614-8400

Director of Arbitration
Philadelphia Stock Exchange, Inc.
1900 Market Street
Philadelphia, PA 19103
215-496-5000

Municipal Securities Rulemaking Board (MSRB)
1818 N Street, NW, Suite 800
Washington, DC 20036-2491   202-223-9347

MSRB is authorized to develop and interpret rules governing securities firms and banks involved in underwriting, trading, and selling municipal securities, i.e., tax exempt bonds and notes. The Board, composed of members of the municipal securities industry and the general public, is a self-regulatory body which sets standards for the industry. It has adopted rules in a number of areas, including the arbitration of disputes involving municipal securities transactions. Staff members can answer your questions. Publications include:

- *Arbitration Information and Rules*—a thirty-three-page booklet containing reprints of MSRB's arbitration rules as well as *Arbitration Procedures* and *How to Proceed with the Arbitration of a Small Claim* (these two titles are described under Publications in this section). The booklet also has a glossary of terms and a list of securities sponsoring organizations. Free.
- *Instructions for Beginning an Arbitration*—this eighteen-page booklet sets out the step-by-step method for beginning an arbitration and is arranged so that you need only to read the pages pertaining to your case. It is written for public customers as well as dealers and associated persons. Free.

National Association of Securities Dealers, Inc. (NASD)
(District No. 12 Office)
1 World Trade Center, 98th Floor
New York, NY 10048   212-839-6251

A nonprofit association, NASD is the self-regulatory organization for the over-the-counter securities market. More than 5,700 broker-dealer firms— virtually all firms which do a securities business with the public—belong to the NASD and agree to abide by its rules as a condition of membership. The association offers an arbitration service, through its fourteen district offices, which enables you to sue to recover money. Each office also offers a complaint service through which you can register complaints against a stock broker or firm. *Arbitration Procedures* (described in this section under What to Read) is available free of charge from each of the following NASD district offices:

NASD DISTRICT OFFICES

District No. 1
1 Union Square, Suite 1911
Seattle, WA 98101
206-624-0790
Bradford M. Patterson, Director

District No. 2
425 California Street, Room 1400
San Francisco, CA 94101
415-781-3434
Theodore F. Schmidt, Director

District No. 2S
727 West Seventh Street
Los Angeles, CA 90017
213-627-2122
Kye Hellmers, Director

District No. 3
1401 17th Street, Suite 700
Denver, CO 80202
303-298-7234
Frank J. Birgfeld, Director

District No. 4
911 Main Street, Suite 2230
Kansas City, MO 64105
816-421-5700
Jack Rosenfield, Director

District No. 5
1004 Richards Building
New Orleans, LA 70112
504-522-6527
Edward J. Newton, Director

District No. 6
1999 Bryan Street, 14th Floor
Dallas, TX 75201
214-969-7050
Peter M. Walker, Director

District No. 7
250 Piedmont Avenue, NE
Atlanta, GA 30308
404-648-9191
Bennett Whipple, Director

District No. 8
3 First National Plaza, Suite 1680
Chicago, IL 60602
312-236-7222
E. Craig Dearborn, Director

District No. 9
1940 East 6th Street, 5th Floor
Cleveland, OH 44114
216-694-4545
George W. Mann, Jr., Director

District No. 10
1735 K Street, NW
Washington, DC 20006
202-728-8400
Thomas P. Forde, Director

District No. 13
50 Milk Street
Boston, MA 02109
617-482-0466
William S. Clendenin, Director

District No. 11
1818 Market Street, 12th Floor
Philadelphia, PA 19103
215-665-1180
John P. Nocella, Director

Securities Industry Conference on Arbitration (SICA)
c/o Arbitration Director
New York Stock Exchange, Inc.
11 Wall Street
New York, NY 10005   212-656-2772
    This group consists of members of each of the stock exchanges, the
National Association of Securities Dealers, and the Municipal Securities Rule-

---

STOCKHOLDERS HAVE A BETTER THAN EVEN CHANCE OF WINNING ARBITRATION CASES AGAINST STOCKBROKERS

Year	Total cases received	Rulings found in favor of public
1980	830	50%
1981	1,042	49%
1982	1,340	53%
1983	1,731	53%
1984	2,449	50%
1985	2,796	55%
1986	2,838	52%

Requirements for bringing a dispute to arbitration:
- Customers can bring almost any dispute against a broker-dealer to arbitration.
- The dispute must be fewer than six years old and under $500,000 in value.
- Choosing arbitration means that you give up your right to pursue your problem through the courts.

Source: Securities Industry Conference on Arbitration.

making Board, as well as four representatives from the public and one representative from the Securities Industry Association. It drafts the arbitration, rules used by all agencies administering securities arbitration and monitors securities arbitration to determine if any changes in rules or procedures need to be made. Publications include *How to Proceed with the Arbitration of a Small Claim* and *Arbitration Procedures,* both of which are described under Publications in this section.

WHAT TO READ

Arbitration Procedures
National Association of Securities Dealers, Inc.
2 World Trade Center, 98th Floor
New York, NY 10048   212-839-6251
    This booklet is designed to assist you or your attorney by explaining arbitration procedures and answering some of your questions. It is not an interpretation of the rules, nor is it designed as a substitute for the rules. Topics covered include a definition of arbitration, how arbitration is begun, preparing for a hearing, and more. A schedule of fees, glossary of terms and list of organizations offering impartial arbitration are also included. This booklet is available free of charge from NASD's district offices, SICA, and most of the other securities arbitration organizations described in this section.

How to Proceed with the Arbitration of a Small Claim
U.S. Securities and Exchange Commission
Publications
450 5th Street, NW
Washington, DC 20549   202-272-7460
    This booklet, prepared by SICA, describes the procedures you must follow if you go to an impartial arbitrator to resolve a dispute, of $5,000 or less, with your securities firm. Although the pamphlet is not designed to give legal advice, it explains the arbitration procedures to accommodate claimants who choose to represent themselves as well as those who choose to be represented by counsel. The pamphlet includes a reprint of small claims rules, as well as a glossary of terms and a list of securities industry organizations with arbitration facilities. The twelve-page publication is available free of charge. (Note: This publication is also available from NASD district offices, SICA, MSRB, and other securities arbitration organizations.)

Index

ABOUT THE AUTHOR

Matthew Lesko's highly successful business, Information USA, Inc., is a service that advises businesses on how to get the information they need. He lectures to consumer and professional groups on information-gathering techniques and has written feature articles for the *Washington Post, Industry Week, Inc.* magazine, *Boardroom Reports,* and other publications.